American Horror Film

American Horror Film

THE GENRE AT THE TURN OF THE MILLENNIUM

EDITED BY
STEFFEN HANTKE

UNIVERSITY PRESS OF MISSISSIPPI / JACKSON

www.upress.state.ms.us

The University Press of Mississippi is a member of the
Association of American University Presses.

Copyright © 2010 by University Press of Mississippi
All rights reserved
Manufactured in the United States of America

First printing 2010
∞
Library of Congress Cataloging-in-Publication Data

American horror film : the genre at the turn of the millen-
nium / edited by Steffen Hantke.
    p. cm.
  Includes bibliographical references and index.
   ISBN 978-1-60473-453-9 (cloth : alk. paper) — ISBN
978-1-60473-454-6 (ebook) 1.   Horror films—United
States—History and criticism. I. Hantke, Steffen, 1962–
   PN1995.9.H6A385 2010
   791.43'617—dc22   2009047222

British Library Cataloging-in-Publication Data available

CONTENTS

Part Three

LOOK BACK IN HORROR
Managing the Canon of American Horror Film

INTRODUCTION

They Don't Make 'Em Like They Used To
On the Rhetoric of Crisis and the Current State of American Horror Cinema

—Steffen Hantke

A DECADE OF AMERICAN HORROR FILM: THE PESSIMIST'S VIEW

Even though the horror genre has been fed by tributaries from many national literary traditions—from German Romanticism to French surrealism and South American magical realism—and even though horror cinema has prospered and developed its unique forms of expression in many film industries around the globe, it is in the United States and in the American film industry that horror, for as long as cinema itself has existed, has been a staple genre, a consistently profitable endeavor, an audience favorite, and a richly diverse form of artistic expression for writers and directors. More than any other film industry around the world, Hollywood—aided by intrepid and independently minded filmmakers around and beyond its margins—has created horror films that have come to define the genre. Its cinematic reinventions of characters from outside its own national culture—think of Dracula, courtesy of Bela Lugosi, or Frankenstein's creature, brought to you by Boris Karloff—have supplanted their respective originals in the collective pool of pop-culture images. Up to the present day, horror film directors from around the world tend to end up—sooner or later in their careers, and either by choice or by economic necessity—on the American shores. For fans and critics of horror film, America looms large, a touchstone of the genre at its finest.

Ask fans, however, and they will tell you that American horror film in the last decade—from roughly the mid-1990s, through the turn of the century, and far into the first decade of the new millennium—has fallen into a slump. While horror film is doing just fine elsewhere, American horror film is in crisis. Not that no more horror films are being made; on the contrary, as far as popularity and profitability go, the American horror film seems near the top of its game as Hollywood lavishes a steady stream of horror films upon its audience. With the exception of a few high-profile films of blockbuster proportion—one might think of the Will Smith vehicle *I am Legend* in 2007 or the films in the *Resident Evil, Underworld,* and *Blade* franchises—most of these films operate at mid-level budgets. They tend to perform below the top-fifty grossing films of each year but are reliably recouping their moderate production costs in foreign markets and through ancillary release via cable and DVD sales and rentals.¹ These films never fail to find an audience, but most of them just aren't any good—or so popular opinion has it. Apparently, even those who go to see them are not heading out to the Cineplex every weekend with high expectations. There is a sense of fatigue or outright dissatisfaction with Hollywood horror these days. Who is doing the complaining? And what exactly are the complaints? Do they have any substance? And even if they don't, what do they mean?

From a pessimist's point of view, the last ten years have seen American horror film at its worst. As one subgeneric cycle followed another with ever-increasing rapidity, the genre on the whole was in decline. When exactly this slump began is a matter of opinion. The Wikipedia entry on horror film, which, while noting recent developments in the genre past 2005, pinpoints the "start of the 2000s" as the moment that "saw the horror genre going into a slump as movies dealing with the supernatural had mild but not memorable success" (en.wikipedia.org/wiki/Horror_film).² The critic David Church reaches back even further, opening his survey of American horror film since *The Silence of the Lambs* with this statement: "As the 1980s came to a close, the American horror film seemed locked into an endless loop of formulaic repetition," sounding a note of skepticism that would reverberate for many fans into the 1990s with its predominant subgenre of horror, the so-called neo-slasher (Offscreen.com 2006). Successful with mainstream audiences but received with apprehension by fans and critics, Wes Craven's *Scream*, released in 1996, was—depending on who you asked—either the best or the worst thing to happen to American horror film. According to the critical voices, *Scream's* recycling of "classic" precursors transformed the more politically attuned horror film of the previous generation into self-indulgent postmodern play. Calling it "more of a parody than a complicated critique of banal horror formulas," Church blames the film for inspiring a host of "slick, teen-oriented horror films (many featuring young TV stars) with far less imagination and self-reflexive awareness" and serving "as an unlikely conduit for the recycling of those formulas for a new generation during the late-1990s and beyond" (Offscreen.com 2006). Even the popularity of horror film in the wake of *Scream* turned out to be a mixed blessing. "On the web," Mark Jancovich points out, "one can find a wealth of fan materials that discuss the film, and while some are clearly positive, others are more guarded and even outright hostile. The guarded responses [. . .] are also clearly troubled by the film's commercial success" (Jancovich, "A Real Shocker" 475).

If guardedness and outright hostility weren't bad enough, fans were even less thrilled with what came after the neo-slasher. The abandonment of original scripts began with a mindless series of remakes, starting with Joel Silver's and Robert Zemeckis's production company Dark Castle and its remakes of gimmicky William Castle films from the 1950s and 1960s, most of which had never been remade because nobody had ever thought them good enough to deserve a remake. Then came the indiscriminate plunder of Asian horror films—a practice that, as it confirmed the vitality, creativity, relevance, and intensity of horror film in other countries, made the lack of these qualities strikingly obvious in American cinema. The cycle started with remakes of Japanese horror (J-horror) films and then diversified moderately with remakes of films from such countries as South Korea, Hong Kong, and Thailand.

The motivation for this practice seems, at first glance, to derive from the assumption that, as Terence Rafferty put it in a review of the Hollywood remake of Danny and Oxide Pang's *The Eye*, "horror is by its nature a good deal friendlier to cross-cultural transplantation than most movie genres, because fear is universal in a way that, say, a sense of humor is not: what we dread is far less socially determined than what we laugh at" (*New York Times*, January 27, 2008). Having given Hollywood the benefit of the doubt, Rafferty then goes on, however, to eviscerate most of the remade Asian horror films: "'The Eye' and 'One Missed Call' aren't the worst of the J-horror remakes," he writes, "that distinction would go to Jim Sonzero's witless 'Pulse' (2006), which treats its source, Kiyoshi Kurosawa's great 2001 horror poem 'Kairo,' as if it were a dirty limerick." In the final instance, Rafferty concludes that remakes seem to thrive especially when coupled with horror film because of what he calls "the traditional shamelessness of the horror genre."

On the occasion of the release of the Hollywood remakes of, respectively, the Pang Brothers' *The Eye* and Takeshi Miike's *One Missed Call*, another reviewer—Joe Queenan, writing for the *Manchester Guardian*—reiterates the complaints Rafferty and other reviewers have voiced about the cycle of J-horror remakes. Though Queenan concedes to Gore Verbinsky's *The Ring* the status of having been "the only American reworking of an Asian horror film that even vaguely approaches the quality of the original" (*Guardian*, February 22, 2008), he has nothing positive to say about the rest of the Asian horror film remakes. "*Dark Water*, starring Jennifer Connelly, is a dud," he complains, "as is *Pulse*, while the two American remakes of *Ju-on: The Grudge* are no more than passable."[3] Where Rafferty sees the horror film as a genre amenable to "cross-cultural transplantation," Queenan, after laying some of the blame for the failure of these films on individual directors, comes to the conclusion that, in fact, the opposite is true:

> the Japanese and Chinese and Korean directors who make these movies not only know what they are doing but truly enjoy working in the genre, while the American directors assigned to do the remakes are lazybones, pouters or clods who are merely phoning in work-for-hire [. . .] certain elements of

Asian horror—water, hair, the trauma of secondary school, ghosts, and most especially creepy little girls—do not resonate in the west in quite the same way they do in the east [...]. It may well be that western directors are trying to shoehorn Asian films into a culture that cannot fully accommodate them [...]. Perhaps this is why remakes of Asian horror movies tend to be mildly profitable enterprises that few adults talk about—serious critics hate them—while in Japan, horror movies seem to be taken seriously [...]. Since remakes of Asian horror movies are not terribly expensive to produce, and since there are dozens of these pictures waiting to be repackaged, we can expect to see many more films in this genre. (*Guardian*, February 22, 2008)

While Rafferty and Queenan disagree about the question of how easily, or whether at all, horror films translate from one culture to another, both agree on the artistic failure of the vast majority of American remakes of Asian horror films. The crucial point here is not the origin of the source material, it is the fact of the remake itself. To them, remakes demonstrate the triumph of economic over artistic considerations, signaling the creative bankruptcy of a national film industry or a cinematic genre operating within this film industry.

While more J-horror and Asian horror films were—and still are—in the pipeline, Hollywood lowered its sights yet again and began moving from foreign to domestic remakes. This secondary cycle of remakes, which began to take shape roughly four to five years after the cycle of Asian remakes had arrived in theaters, now took on horror films from the so-called neo-horror phase of American cinema, a period around the late 1960s and early 1970s that boasted "classics" of the American horror films by directors like John Carpenter, Tobe Hooper, or George Romero. Consequently, recent years have seen new versions of Bob Clark's *Black Christmas*, John Carpenter's *Halloween* and *Assault on Precinct 13*, Wes Craven's *The Hills Have Eyes*, Robert Harmon's *The Hitcher*, and Fred Walton's *When a Stranger Calls*. The reception of some of these films has varied. While the Craven remake can at least boast directorial hopeful Alexandre Aja, who had been freshly imported from his native France after scoring a major international hit with *Haute Tension* in 2003, the remake of the Walton film is nothing but a pointless exercise in style—and not a very successful one at that. James Berardinelli's review is typical of the film's general reception; he blames "second-rate director Simon West" for the utter wretchedness of the remake, calling him a director "who understands a lot about cheap shocks and nothing about suspense, and who hasn't met a horror movie cliché he eschews" and the film itself "as emasculated and lifeless as any recent 'scary' movie" (Review of *When a Stranger Calls*).

At the current moment, nothing seems safe from the greedy hands of studio executives out for a quick remake. George Romero was targeted with a remake of

Night of the Living Dead (Zach Snyder, 2004), Carpenter by Rob Zombie with a remake of *Halloween* (2007), and Hitchcock became fair game too: after Gus Van Sant's *Psycho* (1998), a remake of *The Birds*, helmed by Martin Campbell, is in the works (expected release date 2009). *Variety* also reports that a series of remakes of 1930s Universal horror films is currently being planned, starting with films on Dracula and the Wolf Man, each helmed by a respectable director.[4] At what must be considered the bottom of the slump, even remakes of remakes are possible now. The recent announcement of a new version of "John Carpenter's *The Thing*" in the *Guardian*, for example, reads like this:

> Hollywood is remaking John Carpenter's 1982 horror film *The Thing*, the latest in a line of updated versions of the director's oeuvre. The 1982 version starred Kurt Russell as a member of an Antarctic research base that comes under attack by a deeply unpleasant alien. Other Carpenter remakes include *The Fog* and *Assault on Precinct 13*, while Rob Zombie is preparing his no doubt unique take on *Halloween*. ("In Brief")

What is striking about this announcement is not so much the omission of any reference to John W. Campbell's original story, but to Christian Nyby's *The Thing from Another World* (1951), which suggests that, with the obliteration of all historical memory among viewers and makers of horror film, we also see the vanishing of the boundary between original and remake, which, in turn, signals the abandoning of originality as a standard of critical evaluation. One wonders how long it will take, after this latest remake has been released, that someone will begin thinking about remaking the remake of John Carpenter's remake of *The Thing from Another World*. And after that . . . if the money's right . . . remaking *that one* . . . and after that . . . the sky's the limit!

Not surprising, the response from fans is overwhelmingly negative. A cursory cruise through some horror-related Web sites produces pages with titles such as "The Ten Worst Horror Remakes of All-Time" (FilmSchoolRejects), "I spit on your horror movie remakes, sequels: A horror fan laments the current state of one of his favorite genres" (msnbc.com), and "Something Must Be Done about Horror Movie Remakes" (Jake Hjelmtveit).[5] The horror film Web site Bloody-Disgusting.com hosted a discussion among its readers in the late fall of 2005 in which the basic question—"Do you think horror movies are done for?"—itself is indicative of the mood among fans.[6] The horror film director Larry Fessenden sees this slump not in the future but as already in progress: "Recently, horror movies have fetishized serial killers and clinically gruesome effects, as we become possessed by the arbitrariness of violence and our ability to recreate it in the movies. This is a slump" (Glass Eye Pictures). In an article on the state of horror film in the *Onion*, Scott

Tobias writes: "It seems to me that the genre has hit a crisis point creatively. J-horror is dying off, Hollywood is running out of '70s and '80s horror staples to remake, and surely at some point, the *Saw* and *Final Destination* franchises will lose their novelty" ("Crosstalk").

While directors like Fessenden himself linger in the economic margins of the genre, mainstream Hollywood settled on the promotion of a small number of younger directors as the next generation of great horror auteurs. With three films under his belt at the end of 2007, Rob Zombie is offered up as an exemplary new voice—an attempt that falls short since his first two films (*House of 1000 Corpses*, *The Devil's Rejects*) are deeply mired in 1970s "hillbilly horror" and his third and most recent film is a remake of a canonical horror film, John Carpenter's *Halloween*. Similarly, Alexandre Aja has made a name for himself with a mainstream remake of Wes Craven's *The Hills Have Eyes*, and is slated for two other remakes: *Silent Night, Deadly Night* and *Piranha* (imdb.com/name/nm0014960/). This leaves Hollywood hopeful Eli Roth, whose next project is not based on an original screenplay but is an adaptation of Stephen King's novel *Cell* (imdb.com/title/tt0775440/), and whose reputation so far rests on only one original film and its sequel. Even though the original *Hostel* stirred up considerable controversy, and could even pride itself on having initiated the cycle of "torture porn" films, its sequel already proved to be commercially disappointing.[7] If this is the field of contenders to replace 1970s neo-horror directors, then not only does the present look bleak, the future looks dubious, too.

"UTTERLY WRETCHED": THE ACADEMIC DISCUSSION

Academic studies of American horror film published between 2002 and 2006 chime in with such dirges when they reach the present moment. Reynold Humphries, writing in 2002, concludes his discussion in *The American Horror Film* with a section aptly titled "Where Do We Go From Here?" It begins with this statement: "The state of things is not conducive to optimism, let alone enthusiasm" (189). Though Humphries finds a few rare exceptions to the general malaise (he praises Craven's *Scream* and the films of M. Night Shyamalan), he also concludes that "several swallows do not make a summer," adding, somewhat despondently: "It is patent that we shall see no more films of the caliber of *The Texas Chainsaw Massacre*, which represents for the present writer everything that a horror movie can and should be. I shall therefore conclude by repeating my question: where do we go from here?" (195).

Kendall Phillips, writing four years after Humphries, concludes his book *Projected Fears* (2006) on a similarly somber note when he states: "the American horror film has fallen back into one of its periods of slumber" (195). Immediately, he zeroes in on the plague of remakes, citing Silver's and Zemeckis's Dark Castle films as cautionary examples, calling them "predictable" and "utterly wretched" (195). Though the George W. Bush years, with their "general sense of hysteria, fear, and paranoia" (196) would, in theory, provide fertile breeding ground for the horror film, Phillips speculates, "horror films may have been muzzled for a time" (196). Given the constraints on commercial filmmaking in the mainstream, politically sensitive topics may be . . . well, just *too sensitive* even (or especially?) for horror films to tackle. Nonetheless, Phillips ends on a slightly more positive note than Humphries, casting a vote of confidence for the genre's "remarkable capacity to transform itself and reconnect, no matter how irrelevant it may seem, to the cultural currents of the day" (197).[8]

Unlike Phillips's and Humphries's straightforward disdain for the current horror film, Peter Hutchings strikes a slightly less judgmental note in his discussion of recent trends in horror in the concluding section of *The Horror Film*, published in 2004 and entitled "The View from Here and Now." Hutchings lists Hollywood's exploitation of Japanese films, as well as recent trends in European horror cinema, as phenomena whose true significance in the development of the genre will require historical distance to emerge clearly (216–17). "Our retrospective views of horror history," Hutchings cautions his readers, "have often tidied up the genre in their attempts to categorise and make sense of it, stressing the importance of some generic types and marginalizing or ignoring others" (217). In accordance with his ability, throughout the entire book, to integrate distinctions into his arguments finer than those in Humphries and Phillips, Hutchings defers judgment. "I have no idea what the future of the horror genre might be," he concludes, "but I look forward to it with keen interest" (217).

Despite such expressions of optimism, there is a sense that, as much as Hutchings may strive for level-headed objectivity, not everything is right with the horror film today. When Hutchings states his belief in "the changeability and unpredictability" of the genre (216)—a vote of confidence echoing Phillips's belief in the genre's "remarkable capacity to transform itself"—one wonders why such a vote of confidence is necessary at all. If the genre were at the top of its game, it would hardly require such hearty endorsement. Similarly, Hutchings closes with an appreciative look not at recent American productions, but at British, German, and French horror films, suggesting that this is where potentially significant trends in horror film are taking place. As a rhetorical gesture, the omission of American films from those closing remarks speaks volumes.

A similar slight by omission can also be found in those recent books on the horror film that do not follow a strict chronology and thus do not necessarily find themselves confronted with teleological problems in discussing the genre's development.

Joseph Maddrey's *Nightmares in Red, White and Blue*, published in 2004, imports such teleological arguments by positing legitimate end points in the development of American horror film. The book's last chapter, detailing the final stage in horror film history, is devoted to Wes Craven's *Scream* films.[9] Also, in the second section of the book, in which each chapter presents one notable horror auteur, the final chapter is given to Craven. After Craven, so Maddrey insinuates, nothing much of significance happens. Obviously, for a book published eight years after the release of *Scream*, making this particular director the pinnacle of horror film is a deliberate and significant choice. Since *Nightmares in Red, White and Blue* is one of the more popular (if not populist) treatments of the horror film, straddling the fence between academic and general audiences, Maddrey's obvious sympathies for Craven's *Scream* are not all that surprising. After all, the controversy about the film seemed to be a purely academic matter; mainstream audiences, by and large, liked the film, and only hardcore fans of horror appeared "clearly troubled by the film's commercial success" (Jancovich, "A Real Shocker" 475).

Mark Jancovich, editor of *Horror: The Film Reader*, also feels compelled to wrestle with *Scream* and its position at the end of horror film history. Writing in 2002, he cannot yet account for what is to come when he states that, "as the cycle of post-*Scream* films seems to be coming to an end, it is difficult to say where the genre will go next" (7). Though this section of his introduction, entitled "A Brief History of the Horror Film," ends on a somber note similar to that in Humphries and Phillips, the following section, "Re-examining the History of Horror," also recognizes that periods "rewrite the past and so create their own heritage" (8). Jancovich acknowledges that all narrative histories depend on a sense of proper ending that endows them with "a sense of perfect fulfillment" (9), and thus with a set of criteria that allow critics to make comparable value judgments. This idea of the essential constructedness of all genre histories, which is also present in Hutchings's excellent discussion, suggests that the key issue here is not so much the consensus about the current crisis in horror film that seems to reign among all critics mentioned before. Instead, it raises the question how critics lacking such meta-awareness position themselves toward this trope, and thus how it affects the writing of horror film history.

THE RHETORIC OF CRISIS RECONSIDERED: ACADEMIC ANXIETIES

Jancovich's comments illustrate the problems that all writers of film histories face when they are dealing with a genre that, at the time of writing, is still a vital element in the cultural landscape. Who knows what twists and turns, ups and downs, this genre is going to go through in the future? Though academics are not in the business of predicting the future, most historiographic writing, especially when it approaches the present, requires a sense of direction for its narrative to take shape. Without such teleological underpinnings, it is difficult to show similarities and differences, trace patterns of influence, and demonstrate developments in the interplay between texts and their variable contexts. One critic might tell the story of American horror cinema as the story of the slow and steady decline of the genre; another, as the story of its ascent from modest, inauspicious beginnings to prominence; yet another critic might tell it as the story of the birth, death, and rebirth of the genre. Just as the question of beginnings, of proper origins, is a crucial one for the construction of such narratives, so is the problem of endings. History does not end, but historiographic narratives require closure; the demands of form and format exceed those of empirical objectivity. It is for this reason, as much as for their professed personal reasons, that the critics cited above express such optimism on the genre's future. Such a statement serves as a rhetorical ritual that grants their narratives closure, even if the logic of the argument makes such closure impossible. The ritual, common to all historical narratives that end in the present, acknowledges the fact that nobody knows what is going to happen in the future, and by acknowledging it, neutralizes its effects. It gives historians the opportunity to legitimize their interest in their topic, or their enthusiasm for it, or their confidence that it will remain a vital form of expression relevant to the culture at large.

Hence, I would like to take Hutchings's point about the essential constructedness of all historiographic writing as my point of departure, moving on from a description of the crisis—or rather: the alleged crisis—of American horror film in the last ten years to its analysis. Let's take the complaints about sequels. While, on the one hand, it is easy to see how the sequel, especially when it becomes the dominant expression of a cinematic genre, signals this genre's creative exhaustion—the triumph of the box office over the auteur's chair—film historians, as much as they dislike sequels, will be forced to concede that sequels are the bread and butter of horror film. If the examples of *Friday the 13th*, *Halloween*, or *Nightmare on Elm Street* will demonstrate the ubiquity of sequels but, simultaneously, underwrite the argument about creative exhaustion, then perhaps reaching further back into the past is necessary to make the point that sequels are not irreconcilable with creativity. A canonical horror film from the studio era like James Whale's *Bride of Frankenstein* demonstrates that a sequel—in this case to Whale's own *Frankenstein*, which is generally considered the lesser film—can sometimes be more inspired than its original. In fact, critics have acknowledged that Universal Studios based its formative influence on American horror film, starting in the 1930s, on the franchising of monsters and the creation of sequels as parts of these franchises—a fact that has not hampered their acceptance into the canon of American horror cinema. More recent examples of respected sequels are those of the *Alien* franchise, helmed by respectable mainstream directors like James Cameron or David Fincher. Pointing to past examples of what one might call successful sequels does not exonerate all sequels from the suspicion of creative attenuation, but it does cast doubt upon equating the concept of the sequel with creative bankruptcy.

Similarly, the argument that considers remakes—both of foreign and of domestic films—symptomatic of the crisis of contemporary American horror film fails to hold up when seen in the context of past practice. I have already mentioned John Carpenter's 1982 remake of *The Thing*, considered both a commercial and critical success. Richard Matheson's *I am Legend* had been adapted to the screen twice before it was turned into a Will Smith vehicle in 2007. *Invasion of the Body Snatchers* went through three incarnations before Oliver Hirschbiegel, freshly imported to Hollywood after helming the German blockbuster *Der Untergang*, had the opportunity for a new adaptation in 2007.[10] No matter whether these examples prove a particular susceptibility of the horror genre for the remake or not, Hollywood could never resist the temptation to go with projects that came with the preapproval of prior commercial success. It is simply good business to capitalize on a general awareness of material that does not have to be created from scratch in costly advertising campaigns, minimizing the risk of commercial failure and translating this element of predictability into easy marketability.

Similarly, Hollywood has always entertained complex yet lively relationships with other national film industries. One example of this readiness to import what's been true and tested elsewhere is the readiness with which foreign talent has always been welcomed to America. Just as without the European refugees during the 1930s and 1940s there would have been no film noir, American horror cinema profited from such émigrés as Karl Freund or Val Lewton. Consequently, there is nothing new in Hollywood's importing of directors like Alexandre Aja from France, Guillermo del Toro from Mexico, Oliver Hirschbiegel from Germany, or Hideo Nakata from Japan in order to capitalize on their talent, experience, and credentials.

Once we see all of these complaints—about sequels, remakes, and foreign imports—in the larger historical context, what begins to emerge is one possible, albeit broad, response to the complaint that American horror film is in a crisis, which goes like this: things have always been this way. What appears as a sorry state of creative attenuation is, in fact, nothing more than a local manifestation of industrial practices that are a tried-and-true element of Hollywood filmmaking. Those who tend to see the symptoms of the crisis of American horror film today—or perhaps even its causes—within these practices suffer from historic myopia and must, therefore, be wrong.

Unfortunately, this line of reasoning is unlikely to put an end to the complaints about the sorry state of American horror film because it brackets—regardless of production and marketing practices—the question of quality. However historically consistent the conditions of production for horror film have been, it is equally true that there have always been good and bad, successful and unsuccessful, popular and unpopular horror films—present films included. To insist that there is no current crisis because "things have always been this way" would be to insist that there have never been bad horror films at all. The anecdotal evidence may be convincing, but the argumentative logic is flawed.[11]

If the question seems impossible to answer whether there actually is or isn't a crisis in contemporary American horror film, then it makes more sense to ask how the trope of crisis functions within the discourse on horror. That is, regardless of whether any individual fan, reviewer, or critic is right or wrong, we can try to determine, by looking at the larger patterns within the public debate, which ideologies are served or rebuked through the rhetoric of crisis.

A useful starting-point for such deliberations might be to examine the term "crisis" and its connotations. Besides suggesting a crucial sense of urgency, the word "crisis" refers to a period of instability or danger that, eventually, will reveal itself as a turning point, a moment of decisive change, within a larger narrative. It suggests upheaval, a separation of the past from the future, of the wheat from the chaff. And yet, as strongly as the term emphasizes the traumatic nature of the experience, all of its uses carry the connotation that the current moment, fraught with disappointment or uncertainty as it might be, is merely an episode in a larger story—the word "slump," used by many of the fans and reviewers I have cited earlier, also reflects this sense of brighter days ahead. So do the assurances by academic critics like Kendall Phillips or Reynold Humphries who close their historical overviews with a sense of guarded optimism about the ability of horror to bounce back, repair itself, and return to the spotlight as a vital and relevant cinematic genre.

The last time that this was true for American horror film, if the majority of the critics is to be believed who lament the current decline of the genre, was the 1970s when "neo-horror" stepped onto the scene. David Church's perceptive remark that "American horror's renaissance in the 1970s remains a largely romanticized period now" explains precisely the critical move that accompanies so many of the negative accounts of contemporary American horror film. In his preface to Jay McRoy's anthology *Japanese Horror Cinema*, for example, Christopher Sharrett complains that "distinguished works," by which he means the films of Romero, Hooper, and Craven, "have been replaced by hi-tech rollercoaster rides," and that "important horror films of the past [. . .] have been subjected to indulgent, insulting remakes that strip away the original work's radical or contentious ideas" (xi).[12] Other critics equally assess the horror film by "the many radical challenges" it has "made to dominant culture" (Sharrett xi): one might think of Reynold Humphries's wistful assessment of one of the key films of that period: "It is patent that we shall see no more films of the caliber of *The Texas Chainsaw Massacre*, which represents for the present writer everything that a horror movie can and should be" (*The American Horror Film* 195).[13]

Sharrett's and Humphries's high opinion of 1970s neo-horror, which reflects an attitude common among the academic authors I have cited before, validates a period in the horror genre for the same qualities that incurred its condemnation in its own time: its willingness to transgress more radically social boundaries than any of its predecessors, as well as for its refusal to incur cultural capital; Romero's *Night of the Living Dead*, for example, is symptomatic for this attitude, both because of its legendary effect on its original audience, documented famously by Roger Ebert's review of the film, and because of its notoriously minimal budget.[14] Within academic criticism, 1970s neo-horror has already been safely integrated into postwar American cultural history. It is when measured against this criteria of its canonization—transgressiveness coupled with the mystique of rebellion and political subversiveness—that contemporary horror films, with their mainstream credentials, fall short.

It is important to be historically precise in the discussion of this canonization. David Church's insight was not that the current rhetoric of crisis about contemporary American horror film has *triggered* the canonization of 1970s neo-horror, but that, in fact, it "*remains* a largely romanticized period" (Offscreen.com, my emphasis). In other words, 1970s neo-horror had already been canonized before the mid-1990s, so that the current rhetoric of crisis most likely constitutes a reiteration, a confirmation, and, most important, an instrumentalization of this canonization. Church's use of the term "romanticized" suggests a more complex and involved stage of development than that of discovery and initial recognition.

If one were to look for signs of this initial stage, it would be best to look for signs of anxiety on the part of the authors—an anxiety concomitant with neo-horror's noncanonical status. Symptoms of this anxiety can be found in what I would consider the foundational text of scholarly engagement with neo-horror—Carol Clover's *Men, Women and Chainsaws*, published in 1992. Clover proceeds against the suspicion that the sheer popularity of the low-budget slasher film would make it less of a worthwhile object of study. The problem of academic legitimacy is also exacerbated by the fact that she has chosen the least-respectable horror subgenre at the time. In the introduction, Clover describes encounters with people who, as she puts it, "'come out' to [her] about their secret appetite for exploitation horror" (7), an embarrassing position from which she can distance herself only by insisting upon her own scholarly status setting her apart.[15]

To some degree, Clover's anxiety is triggered by the lack of academic legitimacy that clings to all popular culture, among which horror film in general would have to take its place. But since James Twitchell had already noted in 1985 that horror was becoming a legitimate subject of academic study because "the canon of literature is being expanded" (9), the broader concern about legitimacy is outweighed by a more specific one: that neo-horror, at the time Clover is writing, is still lacking the legitimacy that "classic" horror had already attained. While, after decades of serious academic work on the horror film by scholars of high caliber, someone revisiting the "classics" of the genre would hardly have reason any longer to feel like a pariah among his peers, someone studying *The Texas Chainsaw Massacre* would. This, I think, is a process that repeats itself periodically. As generations of scholarship dovetail more or less smoothly with successive moves toward canonization, the old anxieties return and are put to rest. Applied to the rhetoric of the current crisis of American horror film, this means that the anxiety that attaches itself to the most recent period of production is a symptom of the convergence of two factors: the negotiation of legitimacy in the context of institutionalized professional structures on the one hand, and the perpetual misalignment between film production and academic criticism on the other.

One way in which scholars respond to this anxiety is by reorienting themselves toward spaces of safety; that is, toward the canon. Kendall Phillips, for example, works his way through twentieth-century American horror cinema in *Projected Fears* by devoting each of his nine chapters to a film he considers essential to the genre. The canonical lineup contains no surprises—from *Night of the Living Dead*, *Halloween*, and *The Exorcist* to *The Silence of the Lambs* and *Scream*, Phillips is content with rounding up the usual suspects. Each film is introduced by a plot summary—a gesture that seems redundant if the film were, in fact, as well known as the author suggests, but still makes perfect sense as a rhetorical move that reinforces, by way of ritualized repetition, the idea that tribute must be paid to canonical texts. The summary is followed by a discussion of cultural contexts, key themes, and motifs, as well as by a brief consideration of the film's legacy. Given the fact that Phillips's book is published in 2005, it is significant that, having started with Browning's *Dracula* (1931), it ends with M. Night Shyamalan's *The Sixth Sense* (1999), ignoring, or perhaps even dismissing, six years of more recent production.

Humphries and Maddrey follow the same pattern, working their way from the early period of American horror cinema, through the Universal films and Val Lewton's RKO films in the 1930s and 1940s, toward the cold war, and ultimately to the late 1960s, when "classic" horror film gives way to "neo-horror." Phillips, Reynolds, and Maddrey retrace the same essential trajectory. With varying degrees of subtlety, they shift their critical emphasis only slightly, ultimately confirming the basic narrative of American horror film as it was already laid down in earlier histories of the horror film—I am specifically thinking of Carlos Clarens's *An Illustrated History of the Horror Film* (1967), to be followed, in the mid-1980s, by James Twitchell's *Dreadful Pleasures* (1985).[16]

While these studies confirm canonical assumptions about American horror cinema, Mark Jancovich's *Horror* and Peter Hutchings's *The Horror Film* address canonicity itself. Hutchings's book embeds the analysis of individual films in a broader discussion of the questions that academic criticism has been asking about these films. As it gathers ideas around themes like, for example, audience behavior, gender issues, and representations of otherness, the book constantly raises the question of why anyone would be interested in these films. It asks not just what it is that *should be* appreciated in a horror film—the question that stands at the forefront of Phillips's *Projected Fears* and Maddrey's *Nightmares in Red, White and Blue*. It also describes what it is that consecutive generations of critics *have appreciated* about a horror film. Both approaches confirm the canonicity of the films discussed—the former by reaffirming the value of the films themselves, the latter by entrenching critical judgments that have come to gather canonical legitimacy themselves.

In his role as editor, Jancovich is in the privileged position to further particularly the canonicity of horror film scholarship. Many of his selections have been frequently anthologized: Robin Wood's "The American Nightmare: Horror in the 70s," Linda Williams's "When the Woman Looks," Carol Clover's "Her Body, Himself: Gender in the Slasher Film," Barbara Creed's "Horror and the Monstrous-Feminine: An Imaginary Abjection."[17] The frequency with which these critics and their work are cited illustrates which critical paradigms currently dominate the discussion of horror film, just as their inclusion in Jancovich's anthology reinforces this dominant position.[18]

This commercial rationale of academic publishing tends to underwrite such canonization as well. While academic publishing is not strictly subject to the same business rationale as commercial publishing in the mainstream, making a profit is as much a concern here as anywhere else. As university presses act in accordance with this economic rationale, they are more likely to solicit or greenlight books that promise revenues not just from the small, specialized audiences of experts working in the same field, but from a broader audience within the same professional field that gathers around this small community of experts. In the absence of a strong current trend in scholarship, to which academic publishers could hitch their wagon, and the absence of a high-profile celebrity author, the most reasonable choice is publishing books that have the potential of being used as textbooks for college classrooms. Academic studies of horror film with a narrow, historically or thematically specific focus are the least likely candidates for such classroom use. Broadly conceived introductions to the genre, though not specifically written as textbooks, are best suited to such use, and thus promise the best returns on one's investment.

FAN DISCOURSE: CULTURAL CAPITAL AND GENERATIONAL CHANGE

Since the reasons that academics have to subscribe to this rhetoric of crisis are intricately connected to the social pressures of their professional environment, these reasons may interact with the realm of reviewers and fans, but they are unlikely to be valid outside of the specific professional niche. What fans and general audiences have to say about American horror film today contributes to the broader discussion but is not restrained by the social and professional pressures under which academics speak and act. In order to understand their predominantly negative responses to recent American horror film production, let me return briefly to a source I quoted earlier—Mark Jancovich pointing out about Wes Craven's *Scream*: "The guarded responses [by fans] are also clearly troubled by the film's commercial success" ("A Real Shocker" 475).

To the degree that horror film fans consider themselves members of a distinct subculture, they adhere to the rules and conventions that define what Sarah Thornton, in reference to the French sociologist Pierre Bourdieu, has called "subcultural capital." Subcultural capital strives to delineate the boundaries of subcultures as they set themselves aside from—or diametrically against—mainstream culture; it defines membership in the subcultural community as conferring "status on its owner in the eyes of the relevant beholder" (Thornton 11), which is likely to be another member of the same subculture but could also be a (real or perceived) member of the mainstream. Just as subcultures require a well-calibrated degree of secrecy, by which they affect mechanisms that balance exclusion and self-perpetuation, subcultural capital, as Thornton reminds us, is essentially "embodied in the form of 'being in the know'" (11).

Subcultural capital is threatened by, and thus must be defended against, the continuing and perhaps even rising popularity of American horror film. More important, however, it must defend itself against production and distribution strategies that, by virtue of their very success, have begun to expand the audience demographics for the horror film genre to include large audiences without a pronounced genre preference with the result that no clearly discernible segment of the market remains the sole property of hardcore fans. Predominant among strategies of demographic expansion are the popularization of the PG-rated horror films, which have dovetailed with the box office hits of so-called quiet horror films like M. Night Shyamalan's *The Sixth Sense* (1999) or Alejandro Amenabar's *The Others* (2001); the crossover of horror film into fantasy and action-adventure, especially at the budgetary level of the summer blockbuster, ranging from the *Blade, Resident Evil,* and *Underworld* to the *Mummy* franchises; and the casting of hot young actors and actresses for which *Scream*—featuring Courtney Cox, erstwhile from *Friends*, and Neve Campbell, wildly popular at the time from *Party of Five*—provided the commercial blueprint.[19] To the degree that the American film industry is marketing horror films as products not for a niche market, limited by the highly restrictive ratings that come with extreme violence and graphic gore, but for the broadest possible audience, those who consider themselves fans of horror film will have to patrol the boundaries of their territory more aggressively than ever before.

One such form of boundary patrolling and ensuring that one is "in the know" is the reorientation of interest and consumption from local to foreign productions. The initial phase of J-horror's rising popularity in the United States, for example, was largely driven by a search, on the part of hardcore fans, for more exotic and extreme forms of horror film: the name of British DVD and video distributor Tartan's imprint for these imports into the English-speaking market—Asia Extreme— is emblematic of this agenda. Since much of the distribution of these foreign films within the American market did not include theatrical release, Motion Picture Association of America (MPAA) ratings could, for the most part, be circumnavigated, linking the appeal of the exotic with the expanded range of transgressive contents.

Another response to the "mainstreaming" of recent American horror films is the horror fans' turning away from contemporary productions and returning to canonical horror films and directors, a trend repeating itself, albeit for slightly different reasons, among academics. What goes along with this move into more obscure, less easily accessible niche markets is, of course, the maligning of the mainstream taste: as one is invested with, the other is divested of cultural capital. The release, for example, of George Romero's long-delayed and highly anticipated *Land of the Dead* in 2005 prompted responses from fans that were not all unanimously positive but consistently deployed terminology in the service of canonical validation both for the film and its maker. Among the User Comments on the *IMDb* Web site, for example, is this review that is representative in its double move of praising the film by distancing it from the present horror film production: "George Romero returns to the genre he had perfected with his 'dead' trilogy," the author writes. "The film, while not perfect, is still a [sic] achievement in bringing a once dead genre back to life. And who better to do it than the master himself, George A. Romero."

Obviously, none of these strategies by which horror film fans create, affirm, and secure subcultural capital are entirely without their problems and ironies. For example, fans who express their admiration for John Carpenter's *Halloween* on the basis of the film's minuscule budget, as opposed to the slickness and high production values of many forgettable contemporary horror films, tend to ignore the fact that the film raked in profits on an unprecedented scale for such a small film for Carpenter and his sponsors, initiating a cycle of horror films defined—like all commercial filmmaking, even if it occurs on a small budget—by the desire to cash in on the formula. Similarly, mainstream attempts at co-opting subcultural capital are omnipresent, from the "grassroots" marketing campaigns for films like *The Blair Witch Project*, to the courting of "classic" neo-horror audiences with such television programs as the Showtime cable series *Masters of Horror*, designed and supervised by Mick Garris, himself a horror film director with, ironically enough, very little subcultural *cache* among hardcore fans. Ultimately, it is difficult, in some cases perhaps even impossible, to draw clear demarcations between the commercial mainstream and the auteurist margin, as both segments appear less in juxtaposition than in constant dialectic negotiation with each other.

The relative merit of such subcultural responses to the mainstreaming of American horror film notwithstanding, the overwhelming and combined effect they produce within the public debate is the maligning of current American horror film production. To indulge in the rhetoric of crisis legitimizes the retreat from the commercial mainstream of the most vocal of all segments of the horror film audience—a fact that explains the curious split between the apparently universal dismay about the quality of recent American horror films on the one hand, and their consistent, reliable commercial success on the other hand. In the final instance, the rhetoric of crisis tells us more about the audiences than about the films they have been watching.

CONCLUSION

While horror film in general has entered the cultural mainstream as an object of consumption and academia as an object of serious scholarly study, both segments of the interpretive community—academics on the one hand, fans on the other—contextualize their response within the same rhetoric of crisis.[20] While mass audiences tend to vote with their feet, fans and academics articulate their position explicitly in all the places where public opinion is generated, from journals and magazines to Web sites and fanzines—from *PMLA* and *Fangoria* to Bloody-Disgusting.com and the User Comments section of *IMDb*. The alignment of the predominant rhetoric that permeates these two most articulate sections of the horror film audience amplifies the sense that, indeed, American horror film today is in a state of crisis. If those most knowledgeable about horror film agree, then it must be true.

As both demographics seemingly validate each other, their shared position acquires a degree of legitimacy that turns it into the framework within which all successive critical statement on the same topic are formulated or perceived. In other words, it develops a gravitational force that pulls in everything else around it. Those, for example, who find merit in a particular film or director will be likely to see their discovery as an exception from the general malaise rather than a confirmation that, in fact, American horror film today is as vital as ever. Hence, even an opinion that contradicts the rhetoric of crisis is ultimately reabsorbed by it and turned into yet another confirmation of its basic assumptions. As a result, critical discourse is blunted: finer distinctions between films and filmmakers grow blurry and aesthetic standards are applied without much sense of their origin or appropriateness. In the final instance, the discursive framework constructed around the rhetoric of crisis leads to a distorted perspective—a distortion that needs to be corrected before the object of study can be seen clearly again. To contribute to this correction in the general discourse on contemporary American horror film, to see it clearly without the distortion caused by the rhetoric of crisis—this is the goal of this anthology.

ABOUT THIS BOOK

Much of the general overview I have tried to provide about contemporary American horror film in the course of my argument is perhaps overly simplified and schematic—less egregiously so perhaps in my general argument, but most certainly in the individual examples marshaled in its support. Any attempt to survey such a wide and internally diversified field is prone to this risk of oversimplification. But to the same degree that any single argument, short of a book-length study, must remain sketchy and superficial, a collection of essays can succeed in encompassing the variety and complexity of American horror film production within a period as long as ten years. Hence, most of the aspects of my argument in the preceding pages are reflected in the essays collected in this anthology.

Each essay takes as its point of departure one of the aspects of the larger discussion I have tried to unfold in the previous pages. All essays, explicitly or implicitly, acknowledge the rhetoric of crisis that surrounds current American horror film. Instead of accommodating its dictate, however, the authors position themselves within it as strategic interventions—to engage with or refute individual aspects of its general argument; to recognize and describe larger trends within American horror film; and to assess their significance critically. Some of these writers, in pursuing their larger critical goal, also examine individual films and directors whose work falls outside of the parameters set by the rhetoric of crisis, having either been unfairly dismissed or underestimated. All work contained in the anthology, though recognizing the rhetoric of crisis, starts from the assumption that American horror films released roughly within the last decade are neither better nor worse than their predecessors. Hence, the goal of the anthology as a whole is to resist the pull that emanates from the rhetoric of crisis, the tendency to equalize differences, to pass overly generalized value judgments, and thus to miss what is genuinely unique about individual films as well as about the total horror film production in the United States during the last decade.

Rick Kleffel, in an interview with writer Chuck Palahniuk, has suggested, perhaps somewhat facetiously, that horror has always flourished in American culture whenever a Republican is in the White House.[21] Hence, the shadow of the George W. Bush administration—the legitimization of its policies by the events of 9/11, as well as its fostering of a state of perpetual domestic crisis and foreign war—falls over many of the essays collected here. To some degree, then, the collection as a whole is taking inventory of the American horror film at a time of great political turmoil. Though the change of administrations with the 2008 presidential elections cannot be simply assumed to mark a radical turning point, it still provides a good opportunity to pause, look back, and take stock of recent years. In exactly this spirit of distinguishing meticulously between historical breaks and continuities, a number of essays included here either transcend the specific historic background by paying attention to the internal continuities of the genre or to the applications and transformations of transnational auteurism; other contributions relativize what might otherwise occupy center stage by looking at the two terms of the Bush administration within the context of a more insidious and far-reaching framework of economically and socially determined identity politics, which goes back, at the very least, as far as the Bill Clinton years. As each author included in the collection frames and re-frames these issues, American horror film appears in ever-increasing depth and complexity.

The first of the book's three sections, entitled "Bloody America: Critical Reassessments of the Trans/-national and of Graphic Violence," devotes itself to the task of drawing up a cognitive map of American horror film at the present moment by posing specific challenges to two widely held beliefs about American horror film: that it constitutes a purely, or at least primarily, national discourse that should only be read in relation to U.S. politics and culture; and that it has been characterized by a steady increase in graphic violence, much of it self-indulgent and gratuitous and thus dissociated from any directly political function. Based on the recognition that the rhetoric of crisis is grounded, among others, in these two presuppositions, two of the four essays lay, respectively, the foundation for a critical reassessment, while the two other essays, respectively, apply the foundational challenge to a specific director (and the unique shape of his style) and to a specific film (and to the body of films assembled, both synchronically and diachronically, around its basic conceit). Christina Klein's essay, with which the book opens, takes on the first of these beliefs—the idea that American horror films must, first and foremost, be seen in the context of American culture, politics, and history; or, in other words, that horror films *made in* the United States must fundamentally be *about* the United States. Upon closer inspection, however, this just isn't so. To the same degree that the U.S. film industry has already been integrated into global networks of financing, production, and distribution, something which we still, somewhat unthinkingly, like to call American cinema has become a questionable critical presupposition. "American horror film," therefore, deserves a skeptical set of quotation marks. Klein's essay suggests a number of basic variants of the new Hollywood, which, in all of its aspects, operates within a transnational arena. The essay tilts the debate about cinematic genres from simple notions of national identity toward more complex considerations of globalized networks of cultural production. Based on Klein's work, Tony Perrello sets out to trace the transnational career of Alexandre Aja, one of the hot young horror directors who has migrated from his native country to the U.S film industry. Within the larger framework of transnationality, Perrello focuses specifically on the characteristic features of Aja's style and his thematic preoccupations, which have survived the transition from France to the United States. What emerges from the analysis is a reconsideration of the classic auteur's creative autonomy within the context of what Klein describes as genre cinema's ability to transcend national and cultural boundaries. The essay by Blair Davis and Kial Natale takes on the second tacit assumption about contemporary horror film, challenging the validity of the widely held belief that American horror films, since the 1970s and 1980s, have grown consistently more violent and visually explicit. Approaching their daunting subject with the tools of quantitative statistical analysis, the two authors survey a vast number of American horror films with a critical eye on violence. Apart from mapping out larger trends, their argument also suggests, through the self-conscious choice of categories of evaluation, how the aesthetics of American horror film has shaped itself around crucial representational issues. Just as Klein's work prepares the ground for Perrello's analysis, so Davis's and Natale's work sets the stage for Reynold Humphries's examination of graphic violence in director William Malone's *FearDotCom*. Against Malone's less-than-stellar reputation as a horror auteur, and against this particular film's virtually unanimous critical dismissal by fans and reviewers alike, Humphries traces in detail the film's uneasy position between two modes of the fantastic, as well as its unfortunate release in advance of a commercially far more successful horror film cycle—that of so-called torture porn—which would have created more favorable conditions of reception. Reading the film self-consciously at the end of the Bush years, and thus in the context of Abu Ghraib, CIA renditions, and the debate on American torture, Humphries gives the film and its director credit not only for being oddly prescient of the political issues that were to define America's role in the new century, but also for articulating these issues more provocatively than many of their more highly appraised successors.

The second section of the book, entitled "The Usual Suspects: Trends and Transformations in the Subgenres of American Horror Film," devotes itself to the cast of characters we all know so well from many horror films. Each one of these iconic figures has gathered a substantial subgenre of American horror film around itself: the teenager (both as a character and as a member of the audience), the ghost, the slasher, and the serial killer. Maneuvering through a number of representative films, the two authors of the first essay in this section, Pamela Craig and Martin Fradley, carefully delineate the political and ideological issues surrounding teenage protagonists. Pointing to many films' self-conscious and often politically astute articulation of social class, gender, and race, their essay exonerates—wherever such exoneration is called for or overdue—the American teen horror film from its critical dismissal as adolescent escapism or shameless pandering to the youth demographic. Andrew Patrick Nelson's essay stays close to the teenager—as hero/ine, victim, and audience member—by examining the figure of the slasher through the lens of recent remakes. Instead of reiterating the tired assertion that remakes *per se* are a sign of a genre's creative exhaustion—a staple trope in the rhetoric of crisis— Nelson starts with a comparison between John Carpenter's *Halloween* and its recent remake by Rob Zombie, and then expands this comparison into a demonstration of the larger transformative mechanisms by which American filmmaking has been appropriating earlier texts to new social and political circumstances. Honing in on one unique variant of the mad slasher in American horror films, Philip L. Simpson's essay provides a cogent critical overview of the serial killer film, especially in the light of the subgenre's intense cultural significance during the 1980s and 1990s and its subsequent descent into relative insignificance after 9/11. While pondering the larger questions of why and how horror film archetypes drift in and out of the culture's focus of attention, Simpson also demonstrates how the serial killer film, though often pronounced dead, has instead managed to spread throughout a field of cultural production much larger than that of a strictly defined and narrowly circumscribed cinematic genre. In fact, Simpson argues, the serial killer has even made a comeback with recent high-profile productions directed by auteurist filmmakers such as Spike Lee (*Summer of Sam*) and David Fincher (*Zodiac*). While it is graphic body horror to which both the slasher and the serial killer film are dedicated, James Kendrick's discussion of the spiritual horror film turns toward the quieter, less visually assaultive branch of the genre. Like the essays preceding it, however, it also acknowledges the fluctuations in popularity that come with genre cycles—fluctuations that are often mistaken for the waxing and waning in the relevance of a horror film subgenre. Taking as its point of departure the phenomenal box office success of *The Sixth Sense* and the cycle of American ghost stories it initiated, Kendrick's argument not only reaches back to the historical traditions which feed into contemporary ghost stories; it also speculates about the resonance that these films with their spectral theme have for contemporary viewers, and how they are positioned within a larger cultural landscape that often favors more overtly violent forms of body horror.

With its third section, "Look Back in Horror: Managing the Canon of American Horror Film," the book returns yet again to the rhetoric of crisis by reading contemporary American horror film against its own past. All three essays collected in this section deal with the instrumentalization of this past—as a source of canonical legitimacy for the genre at large, as well as a repository of aesthetic and political positions. In his analysis of the careers of David Cronenberg and George A.

Romero, Craig Bernardini charts the evolution of two notable horror film auteurs, from their origins in what the rhetoric of crisis has construed for many as the golden days of 1970s neo-horror, all the way toward the present moment. Whether this present moment does, indeed, constitute a low point of American horror cinema or not, is also a question that resurfaces in Ben Kooyman's analysis of two other canonical American horror auteurs—Stuart Gordon and John Landis. In its detailed analysis of identity politics in the context of the Showtime television series *Masters of Horror*, Kooyman also broadens a discussion that otherwise would remain purely focused upon the world of cinema to include contextual media. To the same degree that Bernardini and Kooyman recognize the processes of canonization and their strategic use within contemporary American horror film, Jay McRoy reads the aesthetic instrumentalization of canonicity in Robert Rodriguez' and Quentin Tarantino's *Grindhouse*. Like his fellow critics' analysis, McRoy's reading focuses on the internal contradictions, the ruptures, rifts, and inconsistencies that run through these uses of the past, real or imagined—not simply to dismiss these efforts as disingenuous or inauthentic but to assess them within the larger context of a culture in which notions of authenticity have long since become problematic.

Since, in this very introductory essay, I have drawn time and again on an essay entitled "Return of the Return of the Repressed: Notes on the American Horror Film (1991–2006)," which is easily the most comprehensive, well-informed, and cogent summary statement on the current state of affairs of American horror film published so far, it is fitting that this book concludes with a closing statement by its author, David Church. His essay takes as its point of departure personal reflections on having been a fan *and* a scholar of horror film, in turn troubled and delighted by his chosen genre. Church rounds out the deconstruction of the rhetoric of crisis I have begun in this introduction by adding to the discussion the consideration of the demographics, which plays a crucial role in the reception and the discursive response to American horror film. As Church outlines the difficulties in narrativizing the history and development of a genre as rich and varied as this one, he also reiterates, in the context of one specific film and specific historical events of the last ten-odd years, the continued cultural significance of horror film as a form of cultural expression. Though the age of an author hardly matters anywhere else in this anthology, I consider it fitting that the final statement in the book belongs to a young critic at the start of his academic career. In more ways than one, Church's afterword opens the discussion to a future that's not always going to be smooth and easy but promises never to be dull either—of American horror film as much as of its critical discussion within the academic community.

NOTES

I would like to express my gratitude to the Research Department of Sogang University, which, by providing a Special Research Grant in 2008, made the completion of this book, as well as the writing of this introduction, possible. Integrated into this essay are ideas initially developed in an essay entitled "Academic Film Criticism, the Rhetoric of Crisis, and the Current State of American Horror Cinema: Thoughts on Canonicity and Academic Anxiety," published in *College Literature* 34.4 (Fall 2007). These ideas have also been presented at the conference "New Nightmares: Issues in Contemporary Horror Cinema" at Manchester Metropolitan University in the spring of 2008. I would like to express my gratitude to the staff at *College Literature*, as well as the organizers of the conference, for their support of this project. This also goes for all contributors to this book—for their hard work, patience, and dedication, as well as for Leila Salisbury, for her exceptional kindness. More broadly, my thanks go to friends and colleagues whose contributions have been less direct yet none the less significant: David Willingham and Elizabeth Frasier, Donald Bellomy and Jae Roe, Jay McRoy, and Rudolphus Teeuwen. I also want to thank my family for their unwavering support, and, last in this list but first on my mind, Aryong: thank you for enduring more cinematic chills with me than any fan of romantic comedies should reasonably be expected to.

1. For more detailed information, see, for example, the top 100 list of "2007 Domestic Grosses" at the *Box Office Mojo* Web site: http://www. boxofficemojo.com/ yearly/ chart/?yr=2007&p=.htm.

2. The slump is defined primarily in economic terms as the entry continues: "Even the re-release of a restored version of *The Exorcist* in September of 2000 didn't quite cause a stir. Also, near-defunct franchises such as *Freddy Vs. Jason* somehow made it into theatres" (en. wikipedia.org/wiki/Horror_film).

3. Just to illustrate how much these assessments reflect personal taste, let me add Rafferty's take on the same film: "The best, I'd say, is Walter Salles's 'Dark Water' (2005), whose 2002 Japanese original was, like 'Ringu,' adapted from a story by Koji Suzuki and directed by Mr. Nakata. It's much simpler than the elaborate 'Ring' saga: just a straightforward haunted-house tale set in a decrepit apartment building, where a mother and her little daughter suffer the supernatural consequences of previous tenants' sins" (Rafferty, *New York Times*, January 27, 2008).

4. For further information, see Diane Garrett, "Proyas to direct Universal's 'Dracula,'" *Variety*, July 10, 2007. http://www.variety.com/ article/VR1117968320.html?categoryid=13&cs=1.

5. See http://www.filmschoolrejects.com/opinions/the-ten-worst-horror-remakes-of-all-time.php, http://www.msnbc.msn.com/id/9805698/, and http://media.www. msureporter.com/ media/storage/paper937/news/ 2006/05/02/Varietycommentary/Something.Must.Be.Done .About.Horror.Movie.Remakes-2021768.shtml.

6. For the full discussion of this question, access http://bloody-disgusting.com/forums/ archive/index.php/t-3839.html.

7. Roth is primarily associated with the horror film cycle David Edelstein has famously referred to as "torture porn." Given the recent success of such films as Matt Reeves's *Cloverfield* (2008) and Frank Darabont's *The Mist* (2008), one might surmise that the "torture porn" cycle has already played itself out. For detailed information on "torture porn," see David Edelstein's article, "Now Playing at Your Local Multiplex: Torture Porn," *New York Magazine*, January 26, 2006. http://nymag.com/movies /features/15622/.

8. David Church also takes this position when he concludes his survey of recent American horror film with this statement: "Though it is a consistent moneymaker, the horror film's creative pulse seems to rise and fall periodically from one decade to the next, and it appears to be in a trough at the moment" (Offscreen.com).

9. This is in spite of the fact that the final chapter of the book's historical overview of the horror film genre is devoted to recent vampire films—a somewhat shoddy glitch in the book's structuring.

10. The term "remake" might have to be modified in these two cases, since both remakes can claim fidelity to the original novel, by Richard Matheson or Jack Finney, respectively, rather than having to stand up in a direct comparison with another film.

11. Similarly, we can rule out two other options that evolve from this insistence on the historical continuity of production and marketing conditions: that American horror films today really *are* all bad, and, conversely, that American horror films today are actually *better* than their predecessors. The gross overgeneralization involved in each assertion aside, I have found no evidence that any critic actually takes one or the other extreme position. In the final instance, Sturgeon's Law seems to apply to American horror cinema as much as to the field of science fiction about which Theodore Sturgeon had originally made his famous pronouncement (that is, that 90 percent of everything is crap).

12. I have discussed elsewhere horror film's subversive potential and the specific significance, as well as the specific attraction that it, therefore, holds for academics—an attraction that reverberates through both Reynolds's and, even more so, Sharrett's words. See Steffen Hantke, "Shudder as We Think: Reflections on Horror and/or Criticism," *Paradoxa: Studies in World Literary Genres* 17 (Fall 2002): 1–9.

13. Perhaps this anxiety has also become superimposed upon some of the millenarian rumblings that happened to take place roughly in the middle of the ten years that comprise the time period under investigation. Mark Edmundson's popular and, at the time of its publication, much-quoted book *Nightmare on Main Street: Angels, Sadomasochism, and the Culture of Gothic* (Cambridge, Mass.: Harvard University Press, 1997), is rife with references to millennial *angst*. Edmundson cites, for example, the "rise of the recovered memory movement" during the 1990s (36), "John Wayne Bobbitt and his wife Lorena" (14), the "Nancy Kerrigan–Tonya Harding episode" (15), and the O. J. Simpson trial (9–12) as examples of what he considers the Gothic side of American culture. To this, Edmundson posits a counterforce that he calls "the culture of facile transcendence," best exemplified by "the angel craze," "power ads," and other "formulas for easy self-remaking that now flourish in the American marketplace" (xv). Taken together, these two factors made, according to Edmundson, "the last decade of the century (and millennium)" a "time of anxiety" and "dread about the future" (3). Later critics, such as Kendall Phillips, see the effect of 9/11 and, more important, its instrumentalization throughout the Bush years, as the cause for the "general sense of hysteria, fear, and paranoia" (196) which provides, simultaneously and somewhat paradoxically, fertile breeding ground for the horror film as well as the conditions for the curtailing by means of deliberate censorship and public opinion ("horror films may have been muzzled for a time"). Kendall R. Phillips, *Projected Fears: Horror Films and American Culture* (Westport, Conn.: Praeger, 2005), 196.

14. Ebert's review, originally published January 5, 1967, in the *Chicago Sun Times*, can be found at rogerebert.com. http://rogerebert. suntimes.com/apps/pbcs.dll/article?AID=/19670105/REVIEWS/.

15. To some degree, this is not an anxiety about the horror genre but about the popular. In *Projected Fears*, Kendall Phillips openly admits to this anxiety. "While it is certainly true that the

study of popular culture has gained great ground in academic circles over the last few decades," he writes, "there is still a strong strain of contempt for those cultural artifacts and icons that attain wide levels of popularity" (1).

16. Twitchell lists a series of earlier books on horror film, most of them from the 1970s—a list worthwhile considering as evidence for neo-horror's effect on the standing of the genre (9). However, in contrast to Twitchell's own book, published by Oxford University Press, most of the books on Twitchell's list are published by more mainstream publishers, suggesting a progression from a fan audience to an audience that increasingly was composed of academics and scholars.

17. Wood's importance is indisputable: his work is referenced in every single book I mentioned, often quite extensively as well. Creed and Clover, already anthologized in Ken Gelder's *The Horror Reader* (New York: Routledge, 2000), are referenced in both Phillips and Hutchings; Humphries references Clover, but not Creed.

18. Stephen Prince's anthology *The Horror Film*, published by Rutgers University Press in 2004, deserves notable mention as the only introductory reader, published roughly within the same time frame as the ones discussed above, that assembles a refreshingly idiosyncratic group of texts. For a more detailed discussion of this reader, see my review of the book in *Paradoxa: Studies in World Literary Genres* 20 (Fall 2006): 312–15.

19. Examples among more recent films would have to include the careers of such actresses as Naomi Watts or Sarah Michelle Gellar in the wake of seven seasons of *Buffy the Vampire Slayer* on the WB network.

20. David Church considers this split in the audience, "between film-savvy purists and a more inexperienced youth audience" not just as a manifestation of the split between different segments of the audience—between margin and mainstream—but also as the manifestation of a "generation gap": "Meanwhile, a generation gap between film-savvy purists and a more inexperienced youth audience widens—but the recent films of directors like Romero and Roth remind us of the progressive potential that is still very possible beneath so much gore and exploitative mayhem in popular films consumed by people on all sides of the divide" (David Church, Offline.com).

21. According to Kleffel, the Nixon administration gave rise to the horror boom surrounding *The Exorcist* in the 1970s; the Reagan years oversaw the phenomenal boom of horror fiction that brought us Stephen King, Peter Straub, and Anne Rice; and George W. Bush can take credit for new genre-defying horror writers like Palahniuk himself (interestingly enough, the literary horror boom came to an end when a Democrat, Bill Clinton, was in the White House: further study of Kleffel's theory is advised). For the full interview, see Rick Kleffel, "Chuck Palahniuk," *The Agony Column*, September 7, 2003. http://trashotron.com/agony/indexes/audio_interview_index.htm.

WORKS CITED

"2007 Domestic Grosses." *Box Office Mojo*.http://www.boxofficemojo.com/yearly/chart/?yr=2007&p=.htm (accessed March 3, 2008).

Berardinelli, James. Review of *When a Stranger Calls*. http://www.reelviews.net/movies/w/when_stranger.html (accessed March 3, 2008).

Bloody-Disgusting. "Do you think horror movies are done for?" bloody-disgusting.com/forums/archive/ index.php/t-3839.html (accessed December 10, 2006).

Church, David. "Return of the Return of the Repressed: Notes on the American Horror Film (1991–2006)." *Offscreen.com* 10.10 (November 25, 2006). http://www. offscreen.com/biblio/ phile/essays/return_of_the_repressed/ (accessed March 1, 2008).

Clover, Carol. *Men, Women, and Chainsaws: Gender in the Modern Horror Film.* Princeton, N.J.: Princeton University Press, 1992.

Ebert, Roger. Review of *Night of the Living Dead. Chicago Sun Times*, January 5, 1967. http:// rogerebert.suntimes.com/apps/pbcs.dll/article?AID=/19670105/REVIEWS/701050301/1023 (accessed March 5, 2008).

Edmundson, Mark. *Nightmare on Main Street: Angels, Sadomasochism, and the Culture of Gothic.* Cambridge, Mass.: Harvard University Press, 1997.

Fessenden, Larry. Glass Eye Pictures. www.glasseyepix.com/html/vamp.html (accessed December 10, 2006).

Gelder, Ken, ed. *The Horror Reader.* London: Routledge, 2000.

"Horror." Wikipedia. en.wikipedia.org/wiki/Horror_film (accessed December 10, 2006).

Humphries, Reynold. *The American Horror Film: An Introduction.* Edinburgh: Edinburgh University Press, 2002.

Hutchings, Peter. *The Horror Film.* Harrow: Pearson/Longman, 2004.

"In Brief: Jolie Bodyguards Arrested in Mumbai." *Guardian Unlimited Film*, November 18, 2006. http://film.guardian.co.uk/news/story/0,,1950607,00.html (accessed November 17, 2009).

Jancovich, Mark, ed. *Horror: The Film Reader.* London: Routledge, 2002.

———. "'A Real Shocker': Authenticity, Genre and the Struggle for Distinction." *The Film Cultures Reader.* Ed. Graeme Turner. London: Routledge, 2002. 469–81.

Kleffel, Rick. "Chuck Palahniuk." *The Agony Column.* Posted September 7, 2003. http:// trashotron.com/agony/indexes/audio_interview_index. htm (accessed June 1, 2008).

"Land of the Dead—User Comments." *IMDb.* http://www.imdb.com/title/tt0418819/ (accessed November 18, 2006).

Maddrey, Joseph. *Nightmares in Red, White and Blue: The Evolution of the American Horror Film.* Jefferson, N.C.: McFarland, 2004.

Phillips, Kendall R. *Projected Fears: Horror Films and American Culture.* Westport, Conn.: Praeger, 2005.

Queenan, Joe. "Bring on the creepy girls." *Guardian*, February 22, 2008. http://film.guardian .co.uk/features/featurepages/0,,2258634,00.htm.

Rafferty, Terence. "Screams in Asia Echo in Hollywood." *New York Times*, January 27, 2008. http://www.nytimes.com/2008/01/27/movies/27raff.html?ex=1202187600&en=77584d657c 6bc915&ei=5070&emc=eta1.

Sharrett, Christopher. "Preface: Japanese Horror Cinema." *Japanese Horror Cinema.* Ed. Jay McRoy. Edinburgh: Edinburgh University Press, 2005. xi–xv.

Thornton, Sarah. *Club Cultures: Music, Media and Subcultural Capital.* Hanover, Conn.: Wesleyan University Press, 1996.

Tobias, Scott, and Noel Murray. "Crosstalk: The State of Horror Cinema." *Onion*, October 25, 2006. www.avclub.com/content/node/54480/2.

Part One

BLOODY AMERICA

Critical Reassessments
of the Trans/-national
and of Graphic Violence

THE *AMERICAN* HORROR FILM?

Globalization and Transnational
U.S.-Asian Genres

—Christina Klein

Scholars and fans alike tend to think about film genres as products of national film industries and as expressions of national culture. We talk about the American musical, the Hollywood Western, the Japanese samurai film, or the Chinese martial arts film. Yet as film industries around the world undergo the processes of economic globalization, they are gradually becoming less national and more transnational in everything from the workers they hire to the audiences they cater to. Commercial genres are among the best places to observe this process of transnationalization taking place, as bodies of visual and narrative conventions once strongly identified with one or perhaps two national film industries are appropriated, revised, and remade across the globe. In recent years the once unambiguously "American" horror film has been challenged—in the marketplace and in fans' affections—by films that have been profoundly shaped by Hollywood, both directly and indirectly, but that cannot be classified as American in any simple way. Like other genres that are undergoing a similar process, the horror film is becoming—and is being recognized—as a transnational genre. Today, scholars of genre are increasingly extending the geographic scope of their analyses and focusing attention on the transnational inflections within American martial arts films, German and Thai Westerns, Korean monster movies, crime and war films, and Hong Kong gangster and action films.[1] To truly understand the changes that are taking place in the horror film today, therefore, we have to extend our critical vision beyond the films themselves. We must pay attention to the changes taking place in film industries around the world and recognize how the transnationalization of the genre is a function of the larger transnationalization of the industries that produce these films.

The very nature of genre films—their structural balance of repetition and variation, rigidity and flexibility, familiarity and innovation—makes them ideal candidates for this process of transnationalization. Because of their formulaic construction and

3

their derivation from other films, they do not demand from viewers a deep familiarity with a foreign culture or cinematic tradition, but rather a more easily acquired mastery of a recurring set of conventions. Modular in construction, genre films also localize well. Their "Lego pieces"—as Jeanine Basinger calls the recurring bits of story, setting, and character out of which genre films are composed—are often ideologically neutral, capable of expressing a range of meanings depending on how they are arranged and how they resonate with the world outside the film. Once absorbed into a new film culture, these Lego pieces can be combined by local filmmakers in fresh ways to carry locally specific meanings.

Hollywood today is a global film industry headquartered in Los Angeles, not an American one. Hollywood, of course, has operated globally since the 1910s. But its global reach expanded dramatically in the 1980s, as the forces of economic globalization—including the opening up of formerly socialist economies, the worldwide reduction in trade barriers, the diffusion of digital technologies—combined to create a globally integrated capitalist economy. Suddenly, the Hollywood studios—now the prime content providers for global media conglomerates—were scooping up the lion's share of viewers and box office earnings in most countries around the world. Today, Hollywood's working parameters—its financing, its stories, its workers, its production and post-production locations, its markets, its profits—are increasingly global in scope. And Americans are a shrinking sector of its audience: in 2007, the twenty-three highest-grossing Hollywood films earned $4 billion in the United States—and $6 billion overseas (Hollinger).

Filmmakers around the world, unprepared for the onslaught of Hollywood films that accompanied the economic transformations of globalization, were stunned by declines in their industries' box office revenues and the subsequent drops in film production rates. But many of them didn't stay stunned and they didn't accept the domination of their markets by Hollywood as a given of the new economic order. Instead, they began searching for ways they could globalize their own industries and move beyond the limits of the nation in their thinking about production, markets, and financing. They also began to reconsider the terms of their relationship with Hollywood, and many filmmakers came to embrace the idea of both collaborating with Hollywood and competing more vigorously against it. Hollywood's global expansion and other industries' responses to it constitute the material terrain on which the transnationalization of the horror film (and other genres as well) has taken place.

In what follows I want to explore four different ways in which we can see the transnational dimensions of the contemporary horror film, paying particular attention to relations between Hollywood and its counterpart industries in Asia.[2] This is not an exhaustive catalog of all the ways in which the horror film is becoming transnational. But it is a broad enough overview to suggest the scope of the changes that are taking place, and to show how the national and cultural identity of any given horror film is something to be interrogated rather than assumed.

REMAKES

Hollywood remakes of Asian films are perhaps the best-known example of the transnationalization of the horror film. Roy Lee, the so-called remake king whom *Variety* identifies as "the man who brought Asia's horror film culture to America," has been the engine driving this trend (Frater). He has brokered the sale of rights to remake numerous Asian films to American producers, earning himself and his company, Vertigo Entertainment, producer credits in the process (Friend). Lee began the process with J-horror films in the early 2000s, with remakes of *Ringu* (1998) (remade as *The Ring* in 2002), *Ju-on* (2003) (remade as *The Grudge* in 2004), and *Dark Water* (2002) (remade with the same title in 2005). He has since expanded into other parts of Asia. He brokered the remake of *The Eye* (2002) from Hong Kong (remade under the same title in 2008), *Sigaw* (2004) from the Philippines (remade as *The Echo*, 2008), and *A Tale of Two Sisters* (2003) (remade as *The Uninvited*, 2009) and *Jungdok* (2002) (remade as *Possession*, 2009), both from South Korea. Lee has turned his attention toward Europe as well, arranging the remake of Spanish film *[Rec]* (2007) (new title: *Quarantined*, 2008).

Remakes are one of the primary reasons that global Hollywood inspires such loathing among admirers of Asian cinema. They tend to see these films as proof that studio executives think only in terms of "product" ready to fill their global pipelines aided by an ever-increasing number of media platforms. American fans of Asian and horror cinema often condemn these remakes for homogenizing the distinctive creative visions of Asian directors (Hendrix) and as the product of a racism so entrenched in Hollywood that producers feel they have no choice but to replace Asian faces with white ones (Larsen).

While there is truth in these criticisms, they do not tell the whole story. Remakes are part of the larger process of the globalization of Hollywood's labor pools. Instead of limiting themselves to workers in Los Angeles or even the whole United States, producers of Hollywood movies today regularly combine American workers with above- and below-the-line workers drawn from film industries around the world. In buying the remake rights to a film, Hollywood studios are buying the labor of the original film's screenwriters. This is one way for Hollywood to save time and money. And while "cost cutting" and "Hollywood" don't often appear in the same sentence these days, saving money does have its attractions in an industry where the average cost of shooting and releasing a film now hovers around $100 million. It is generally cheaper and faster to buy the rights to an already-polished script than it is to commission American screenwriters to draft a script from scratch and endlessly rewrite it. In buying the remakes rights, Hollywood is also buying a script that has been test-marketed: if a genre script attracted audiences in Hong Kong, or Japan, or Korea, chances are that it will do the same in the United States. And while racism is certainly alive and well in Hollywood, Americans are not the only ones playing the remake game: Asian filmmakers have joined in, too. *The Ring Virus* (1999), for example, is a Korean remake of the Japanese *Ringu*, complete with Korean actors, dialogue, and setting. This suggests that the desire for cultural specificity and familiar actors also play important roles in the remake process.

Remakes of Asian horror films can serve the interests of Asian filmmakers as well as those of producers in Hollywood. Not only do remake rights provide a new revenue stream for the original film's producers, the remakes themselves are serving as vehicles through which Asian directors and actors find entrée into Hollywood. In other words, remakes allow Hollywood to draw on a transnational labor pool of actors and directors as well as writers. Takashi Shimizu, the Japanese director of the original *Ju-On* films, went on to direct the Hollywood remake *The Grudge* (2004) as well as the Hollywood-originated second installment in the series, *The Grudge 2* (2006). Similarly, Hideo Nakata, the Japanese director of the original *Ringu* films, directed *The Ring 2* (2005). In a further step into Hollywood's mainstream, Nakata and his producing partner Taka Ichise have signed on to make 20th Century Fox's *Inhuman*, an original film that is not part of a Japanese-originated franchise.[3] For Nakato and Ichise, the English-language remakes served as stepping-stones to their new roles as producer and director of original Hollywood films (Hazelton). Similarly Hong Kong directors Oxide and Danny Pang, who directed the original *The Eye*, made their Hollywood debut with an original horror film, *The Messengers* (2007) (Yi).

From one perspective, this transnationalization of labor pools can be seen as an aggressive, or even imperialist, act by Hollywood. The studios are poaching the best talent from other film industries, which have invested their own limited resources in developing the skills of these high-end workers, and in the process are weakening the ability of these industries to compete with global Hollywood in their own domestic markets. From a different perspective, however, the transnationalization of labor pools gives non-American directors and producers access to much larger resources and markets than their home industries can provide. Working on Hollywood movies can also serve as an education in new production processes, technologies, and management strategies, the lessons of which these workers often carry back to their home industries. Today, the move into Hollywood is often more of a temporary sojourn than a permanent emigration, with the back-and-forth movement between industries furthering the transnational dimension of contemporary cinema.

Remakes severely problematize familiar notions of cinematic style and cultural identity. When Hollywood remakes a Korean horror film, how much of a distinctly Korean cultural or aesthetic sensibility adheres to the new version? When Japanese directors make films in Hollywood, how much of a distinctly Japanese style do they bring to their American scripts and actors? DreamWorks' remake of the Korean *Tale of Two Sisters* is clearly a Hollywood horror film, but is it an *American* horror film?

LOCAL LANGUAGE CO-PRODUCTIONS

A somewhat less visible category of transnational horror film is the Hollywood "local language" co-production. Beginning about ten years ago, studio executives started to notice that audiences in many parts of the world were showing a renewed interest in locally made films. This interest has been steadily increasing, to the point that in 2006 local films took in over 50 percent of the box office earnings in China, Korea, and Japan—markets that once belonged to Hollywood. Viewers, it turned out, like to see their own stories and hear their own languages up on the screen, even as they also enjoy the English-language blockbusters churned out by Hollywood. In response to this renewed competition, the studios began to set up specialty divisions and enter into partnerships with overseas film companies to make "local" films. Today, virtually all Hollywood studios have overseas operations and are making films in Spanish, Russian, Hindi, Portuguese, Mandarin, Cantonese, German, Arabic, French, and other languages—films that are tailored to the tastes and cultures of local markets. The studio typically takes charge of distribution in the local market and will plug the film into its global distribution network if executives in Los Angeles believe that it has broad export potential (Dawtrey). The studios have also stepped up their acquisitions of local films that they had no hand in producing, distributing these films in their own domestic markets and sometimes in select export markets as well. The Hollywood studios have thus found ways to invest in and profit from resurgent film industries around the world.

Horror films have been among the more successful local-language studio productions. In Japan, Warner Bros. had one of the first local-language successes with the *Death Note* films, a manga-derived franchise about a supernatural notebook that kills anyone whose name is written in it. Warner Bros. co-produced *Death Note* (2006) and *Death Note: The Last Name* (2006) with Nippon Network Television Corporation (NTV) and took charge of distributing the films in Japan, where together they earned a very respectable $65 million (Gray). The *Death Note* films make visible one of the paradoxes of contemporary world cinema: as local film industries strive to reclaim their own domestic markets from Hollywood, one of the most successful strategies for doing so is to enter into a partnership with Hollywood. In 2006, the year that both *Death Note* films performed so well at the Japanese box office, the Japanese film industry reclaimed a majority share of its own domestic market from Hollywood for the first time in twenty-one years (Schilling).

Local-language productions muddy the distinction between Hollywood films and local films. Hollywood has become such an integral player in overseas film industries at the level of production, distribution, and exhibition that the idea of competition between national industries is coming to seem quaintly outmoded. Hollywood studios earn money when their English-language blockbuster films do well in Japan; they are also starting to earn money when local Japanese films perform well in theaters, both at home and abroad. While the content of a local–language film may have wholly local origins, one must ask if the participation of a Hollywood studio shapes its expressive form, particularly its narrative form, given Hollywood's adherence to a relatively strict body of conventions regarding characterization, clarity, and structure. The *Death Note* films are clearly Japanese films, based on Japanese source material and using Japanese actors and director; and yet, given Warner Brothers' involvement in their production, are they also *American* horror films?

REGIONALIZATION

One transnational alternative for local filmmakers who do not want to collaborate with a Hollywood studio (or who do not have that option) is the regional co-production. The Hong Kong-based Applause Pictures is a prime example of how some film companies outside the United States are pushing to regionalize their industries as one way to navigate the rapidly changing landscape of filmmaking. Founded by the Hong Kong producer and director Peter Chan in 2000 amid the slow-motion collapse of the Hong Kong industry, Applause Pictures makes commercial films that draw on the human and material resources of multiple industries, which, taken together, are greater than any one Asian industry can provide. In doing so the company seeks to improve the quality of its films and boost their earning power by attracting viewers in multiple markets, each of whom is drawn by the participation of familiar actors, directors, and other name talent. For Chan, the goal of regionalization is to compete with Hollywood on a more equal footing by creating a larger "domestic" market for Asian films. "In Hong Kong," says Chan,

> the market is only 6 million, which is too small to support even independent films. But if we add the population of Korea, which has 40 million; Thailand, which has 60 million; Japan, which has 150 million; Taiwan, which has 20 million; and Singapore, which has 3 million—the total population is around

300 million, which is even bigger than the U.S. domestic market. Hollywood films are successful because they have a strong domestic market, and they can produce a large volume of films. If Asian films have a larger domestic market, we can do exactly the same thing. (Po)

By making films that relate to Asia as a single regional market rather than a collection of small national markets, Chan hopes that he and other Asian filmmakers can establish an economic foundation for their industries equivalent to that enjoyed by Hollywood.

Applause Pictures produces films from across the genre map, including musicals (*Perhaps Love* [2001]), war films (*The Warlords* [2007]), dramas (*Jan Dara* [2001]), and, of course, horror. *Three Extremes* (2004) is one example of its transnational approach to the genre. It is an omnibus film composed of three shorts, each one directed by a popular and respected director from a different Asian country: Fruit Chan of Hong Kong ("Dumplings"), Park Chan-wook of South Korea ("Cut"), and Takashi Miike of Japan ("Box"). Because each segment also employs the language and actors from the director's home country, the film automatically appeals to a three-country market. The film aims, however, to extend that regional market into the future: by exposing viewers in one country to the talents and styles of two other film industries, it hopes to increase the willingness of viewers to watch more films from those countries in the future. Applause Pictures' model of regionalization is becoming more common as individual Asian film industries become stronger and the idea of successfully competing with Hollywood in their own markets becomes less far-fetched. This process of regionalization is bringing together film industries that have historically had very few ties. The horror film *Muoi* (2007), for example, about a Korean writer looking for new material in Vietnam, is the first co-production between these two countries (Paquet, January 4, 2007).

These pan-Asian films are not "American" in terms of their content, production, financing, or distribution; there is no direct studio involvement at any level. But their very pan-Asianness is shaped by Hollywood, insofar as it is a calculated response to Hollywood's overwhelming presence in Asia and part of a careful strategy for competing with Hollywood. Is it possible to think of these horror films, with their multiethnic Asian casts and multiple languages, as somehow, peripherally *American*?

TAKING AIM AT THE U.S. MARKET

One final form of transnational cinema is the film wholly made by one industry and aimed at a specific export market by using the language, actors, and locations of that market. As film markets mature—that is, approach the saturation point in terms of number of theaters and attendance rates and thus experience slower rates of growth—they turn to export markets as the arena for economic expansion. The United States is the prime example of a mature film market, and Hollywood today regularly aims its films at a mass global market: think of all those spectacle-heavy and star-laden franchise films that perform well in almost every market in the world.

But Hollywood also makes films that cater to specific national markets, such as Clint Eastwood's *Letters from Iwo Jima* (2006). This is a Japanese-language film produced by Warner Bros. without any international partners. It features Japanese stars, is based on Japanese sources, and tells the story of a major World War II battle from the Japanese point of view. Why would a studio make such a film? There are a number of reasons, including Eastwood's desire to make a companion piece to *Flags of Our Fathers*, which narrated the same events from an American perspective, and thus to capture the experience of a battle in greater complexity. And perhaps the film expresses Americans' unease with the war in Iraq and the growing sense of being caught up in a war that is not as morally black and white as we initially believed. Still, market consideration undoubtedly played a role in the decision to make the film, as well: Japan is Hollywood's single-biggest export market. *Letters from Iwo Jima* was aimed directly at Japanese viewers and it hit its mark: the film earned over 60 percent of its total earnings in Japan, more than three times as much as it earned in the United States.

As other film markets around the world mature they, too, are looking to foreign markets to increase their revenues. For these relatively small industries, finding export markets can be the key to maintaining a solid stake in their own domestic markets. Growing revenues are necessary to raise film production budgets to levels beyond what their domestic market alone can support, and these big budgets are required to make films with high-enough production values that they can compete against imported Hollywood blockbusters at home.

South Korea is one industry that, facing market maturation at home, is starting to make films aimed at specific foreign markets, most remarkably the United States. The Korean turn toward export markets began with the Korea Wave in the early 2000s, when Korean films and TV serials made for the domestic market began finding substantial audiences in other Asian countries, such as Japan, China, and Vietnam (as well as in more far-flung markets like Egypt). As the production values of Korean films began earning praise around the world, including in the United States, and as the popularity of these culturally Korean films showed signs of waning in Japan, their single largest export market, Korean film companies began to consider the radical idea of making films explicitly for the U.S. market, which is notoriously closed to foreign-language films (Yang). Instead of making films with

Korean actors, dialogue, and settings that would enter the market visibly marked as foreign films, Korean companies decided to start financing and producing English-language films with American actors and settings that would be culturally similar to the local product. Shim Hyung-rae's *Dragon Wars* (2007) (released as *D-War* in the United States) was one of the earliest instances of this strategy. A big-budget film about a dragon that wreaks havoc on Los Angeles—and thus a horror film in the broadest sense of the term—this English-language film starring Jason Behr and Amanda Brooks was shot primarily in California, although a Korean company produced the high-quality special effects. Like *Letters from Iwo Jima*, the film hit its target audience: in addition to topping Korea's annual box office chart, it earned over $10 million in the United States, which is the highest return for any Korean movie released in the United States.

Other Korean media companies are pursuing an alternative approach to cracking the U.S. market by financing the production of low-budget English-language and American-set genre films directed by Korean Americans. Eschewing *D-War's* strategy of aiming at a mainstream American market (the film was released on over two thousand screens), these companies are seeking to enter the United States via the ethnic niche market. CJ Entertainment, the largest entertainment company in Korea, produced *West 32nd Street* (2007), an ethnic gangster film set in Manhattan's Korean-American business district and directed by Michael Kang (*The Motel* [2005]) and starring John Cho (*Harold and Kumar Go to White Castle* [2004]). Another big Korean media company, iHQ, is producing *American Zombie* (2007), a horror mockumentary directed by Grace Lee (*The Grace Lee Project* [2005]) about a community of un-dead living in Los Angeles (Harvey; Paquet, February 13, 2007).

How should we categorize the national and cultural identity of these films? Are they Korean? American? Korean American? These films raise the possibility of cultural identity being determined by consumption rather than production. Are these Korean-financed and -produced films really *American* films because they are aimed at American audiences? And finally, what is it about the horror film that makes it so open to transnationalization?

Some genres, of course, transnationalize better than others. Films whose meanings depend heavily on dialogue or culturally specific social codes, such as the romantic or situation comedy, tend to be less mobile. In contrast, films that produce pleasure primarily through visual spectacle and simple, archetypal storytelling have a better chance of crossing national boundaries. It is no surprise, then, that physical comedy (think Charlie Chaplin), Westerns (think Sergio Leone), and the various forms of action films—including martial arts, crime, gangster, adventure, spy narratives—have undergone the most extensive transnationalization. The conventions and the appeal of the horror film, however, are somewhat different from these other transnational genres. While certain subgenres, such as the monster film, emphasize visual spectacle, the horror genre as a whole is perhaps defined less by what it puts on screen than by the visceral feelings it produces in the viewer: suspense, dread, anxiety, fear, revulsion, surprise, shock. While the cinematic means that produce these responses vary widely, from Hollywood's bloody slashers to Japan's ethereal ghosts, the emotions themselves are foundationally human and thus common across cultures. Crucially, these emotions are best stimulated through nonverbal cinematic means. In addition, the genre's transnationalization may also be facilitated by the fact that it was an international genre from the outset. Before cross-border exchanges became quite commonplace, many industries around the world had developed their own distinct traditions of horror cinema based on their unique aesthetic traditions (Germany), spiritual beliefs (Indonesia), historical experiences (Japan), or political anxieties (the United States). Horror's transnational turn was perhaps facilitated as much by globalization's drive toward heterogenization as well as toward homogenization: the desire among filmmakers and audiences to discover new means of stimulating those familiar emotions. Foreign horror films offered a tantalizing mix of the familiar and the new.

As a result, the national and cultural identity of many contemporary horror films is increasingly open to question. Not even the criteria by which such an identity might be determined are clear. What is it that makes a film American or Korean or Japanese or Vietnamese? Is it the financing? The production company? The director? The stars? The language? The visual and narrative styles? The themes? The markets? Even if we could pinpoint the sources of a film's identity, can we really disentangle these threads from one another? This question of cultural identity extends, of course, beyond the realm of genre films and into questions about audiences and national culture more generally, all of which are becoming less culturally coherent. In an era when we are all eating one another's food, listening to one another's music, attending one another's universities, and watching one another's antics on You Tube, to what extent can any of us be said to possess a distinct, singular, and neatly bounded national cultural identity? The horror film is thus one instance of globalization's more general drive toward an inescapable cultural hybridity.

NOTES

1. See, for example, scholarly work by Meaghan Morris, Siu Leung Ki, and Stephan Chan Ching-kiu, eds., *Hong Kong Connections: Transnational Imagination in Action Cinema* (Durham, N.C.: Duke University Press, 2005); Gina Marchetti and Tan See Kam, eds., *Hong Kong Film, Hollywood, and the New Global Cinema* (New York: Routledge, 2007); David Desser, "Global Noir: Genre Film in the Age of Transnationalism," *Film Genre Reader III*, ed. Barry Keith Grant (Austin: University of Texas Press, 2003), 516–36; Wimal Dissanayake, ed., *Melodrama and Asian Cinema* (Cambridge: Cambridge University Press, 1993); Tassilo Schneider, "Finding a New *Heimat* in the Wild West: Karl May and the German Western of the 1960s," *Back in the Saddle*

Again: New Essays on the Western, ed. Edward Buscombe and Roberta E. Pearson (London: BFI, 1998), 141–59; Christina Klein, "Why American Studies Needs to Think about Korean Cinema, or, Transnational Genres in the Films of Bong Joon-ho," *American Quarterly* 60.4 (2008): 871–98; and David Scott Diffrient, "*Han'gul* Heroism: Cinematic Spectable and the Postwar Cultural Politics of *Red Muffler*," South Korean Golden Age Melodrama: Gender, Genre, and National Cinema, ed. Kathleen McHugh and Nancy Abelmann (Detroit: Wayne State University Press, 2005), 151–83.

2. I focus on Asian industries both because they are the subject of my current research and because they have been among the most creative in their responses to globalization's pressures.

3. The material is based, however, on a true Japanese crime.

WORKS CITED

Dawtrey, Adam. "Hollywood Expands its Global Grip." *Variety*, October 19, 2007. http://www .variety.com/article/VR1117974381.html?categoryid=13&cs=1.

Desser, David. "Global Noir: Genre Film in the Age of Transnationalism." *Film Genre Reader III.* Ed. Barry Keith Grant. Austin: University of Texas Press, 2003. 516–36.

Diffrient, David Scott. "*Han'gul* Heroism: Cinematic Spectacle and the Postwar Cultural Politics of *Red Muffler.*" *South Korean Golden Age Melodrama: Gender, Genre, and National Cinema.* Eds. Kathleen McHugh and Nancy Abelmann. Detroit: Wayne State University Press, 2005. 151–83.

Dissanayake, Wimal, ed. *Melodrama and Asian Cinema.* Cambridge: Cambridge University Press, 1993.

Frater, Patrick. "Hollywood's Remake King Roy Lee Takes Bigger Bite." *Variety Asia*, January 2, 2007. http://www.varietyasiaonline.com/content/view/553/53/.

Friend, Tad. "Remake Man." *New Yorker*, June 2, 2003. http://www.newyorker.com/ archive/2003/06/02/030602fa_fact?currentPage=1.

Gray, Jason. "*Death Note 2* Passes $40 million at Japanese box office." *Screen Daily*, January 23, 2007. http://www.screendaily.com/ScreenDailyArticle.aspx?intStoryID=30410&strSearch=d eath%20note&strCallingPage=ScreenDailySearchNews.aspx.

Harvey, Dennis. "American Zombie." *Variety*, March 23, 2007. http://www.variety.com/review/ VE1117933177.html?categoryid=31&cs=1.

Hazelton, John. "J-Horror Hit Makers Join Forces for US project." *Screen International*, June 3, 2007. http://www.screendaily.com/ScreenDailyArticle.aspx?intStoryID=32980&strSearch= j-horror%20hit&strCallingPage=ScreenDailySearchNews.aspx.

Hendrix, Grady. Kaiju Shakedown blog. http://www.varietyasiaonline. com/component/ option,com_myblog/Itemid,10021/limit,10/limitstart,10/.

Hollinger, Hy. "23 U.S. films top $100 mil o'seas." *Hollywood Reporter*, January 18, 2008. http://www.hollywoodreporter.com/hr/content_display/international/news/ e3i5852afde016b3624567f116c20120c62.

Klein, Christina. "Why American Studies Needs to Think about Korean Cinema, or, Transnational Genres in the Films of Bong Joon-ho." *American Quarterly* 60.4 (2008): 871–98.

Kuipers, Richard. "Muoi: The Legend of a Portrait." *Variety*, October 10, 2007. http://www .variety.com/review/VE1117935055.html?categoryid=31&cs=1.

Larsen, Erika. "The American Remake: A New Form of Cultural Imperialism." http://www .zmag.org/content/showarticle.cfm?ItemID=8079.

Marchetti, Gina, and Tan See Kam, eds. *Hong Kong Film, Hollywood, and the New Global Cinema*. New York: Routledge, 2007.

Morris, Meaghan, Siu Leung Ki, and Stephan Chan Ching-kiu, eds. *Hong Kong Connections: Transnational Imagination in Action Cinema*. Durham, N.C.: Duke University Press, 2005.

Paquet, Darcy. "Muoi' Marks First." *Variety*, January 4, 2007. http://www.variety.com/article/VR1117956671.html?categoryid=13&cs=1.

———. "iHQ sets Eye on Global Ambition." *Variety Asia*, February 13, 2007 http://www.varietyasiaonline.com/content/view/764/53/.

———. "Korea Develops Game Plan to Raise Wave Again." *Variety Asia*, September 3, 2007. http://www.varietyasiaonline.com/content/view/2002/53/.

Po, Jin Long. "The Pan-Asian Co-Production Sphere: Interview with Director Peter Chan." *Harvard Asia Quarterly* 6.3 (Summer 2002). http://www.asiaquarterly.com/content/view/123/3/.

Schilling, Mark. "Japanese Auds Turn Against Hollywood." *Variety*, January 11, 2007. http://www.varietyasiaonline.com/content/view/594/53/.

Schneider, Tassilo. "Finding a New *Heimat* in the Wild West: Karl May and the German Western of the 1960s." *Back in the Saddle Again: New Essays on the Western*. Eds. Edward Buscombe and Roberta E. Pearson. London: BFI, 1998. 141–59.

Yi, Ch'ang-ho. "Hollywood Adapts Korean Horror Story." *KOFIC Newsletter*, June 4, 2007. http://www.koreanfilm.or.kr/KOFIC/Channel?task=kofic.user.eng.b_filmnews.command.NewsView1Cmd&searchPage=1&Gesipan_SCD=1&Gesimul_SNO=679.

Yang, Sung-jin. "Korean Movie Industry at a Crossroads." *Korea Herald*, March 7, 2007. http://www.hancinema.net/korean-movie-news_8876.php.

A PARISIAN IN HOLLYWOOD

Ocular Horror in the Films of Alexandre Aja

—Tony Perrello

Through the postwar period of the twentieth century, French cinema maintained a viable film industry complete with indigenous popular genres and stars and a high-profile auteurist tradition. In all these aspects, it successfully maintained a sense of national identity. However, that identity is increasingly in flux due not only to internal ideological struggles, the weight of repressed history, and pressure from the increasingly multicultural French population and French culture, but also to global influences (like Hollywood) and transnational developments in the film industry. As Elizabeth Ezra and Terry Rowden point out, national sovereignty no longer wields the regulatory power it did in the last century, and this fact is changing the nature, purpose, and reception of films being made, exported, and consumed in the global marketplace: "The impossibility of assigning a fixed national identity to much cinema reflects the dissolution of any stable connection between a film's place of production and/or setting and the nationality of its markers and performers" (1). Shifting borders and geopolitical climates were marked by the fall of the Berlin wall, the establishment, consolidation, and expansion of the European Union, while digital media and other technologies that allow films to be reproduced and delivered immediately and on a wide scale flourished. In response to these trends, cinematic nationalism has perhaps coalesced—more than ever before—around the figure of the *auteur*, who was both the epitome and standard-bearer of his nation's identity as it was perceived by the world. Jean Renoir, François Truffaut, and Jean-Luc Godard produced narratives identified as essentially or typically French.

However, in an increasingly interconnected and interdependent world, certain "hybridizing tendencies" (Ezra and Rowden's phrase) have reduced or effaced national insularity in film, and though the "transnational" may transcend the "national," it remains indebted to it. Hybridity problematizes the concept of foreign film, but the global has also impacted American film and its own often imperialistic identity. If the "performance of Americanness is increasingly becoming a 'universal' or 'universalizing' characteristic in world cinema" (Ezra and Rowden 2), American cinema is also increasingly flavored by non-American matter and actors. A glance at the major categories of the 2007 Academy Awards reveals a globalizing impulse even in mainstream American cinema: Daniel Day-Lewis (British), Best Actor; Marion Cotillard (French), Best Actress; Javier Bardem (Spanish), Best Supporting Actor; Tilda Swinton (Scottish), Best Supporting Actress; *Ratatouille* (set in Paris, co-directed by Jan Pinkeva), Best Animated Feature Film.

In an effort to conquer world markets, several French directors have traded on their success at home, revisited popular genres, and won acclaim in Hollywood. Young Alexandre Aja is one such success story. His career provides an example of how globalization in the film industry allows foreign directors to succeed in the "national" arena (Aja's earliest efforts are French language films starring French actors, settings, stylistic conventions, and roots), and then conquer the "global" world. He did this by pursuing a popular genre not as readily available to him in his native France, adopting transnational textual strategies, and "naturalizing" himself as an American filmmaker. As part of the "splat pack," a new generation of filmmakers who do not shy away from gratuitous gore and disturbing images, Aja also provides the supreme example of the cross-cultural nature of contemporary horror, which seems to have entered the global marketplace as an exotic newcomer with hopes of making it its permanent home.

INTRODUCTION: AJA AND THE EYE

Aja received international attention in 2003 with his award-winning film *High Tension*. Hybrid in its use of language, freely mixing French and English dialogue and featuring French, Italian, and English pop songs, *High Tension* would seem to owe something to an emerging cinematic genre dubbed "torture porn" by a reproachful mainstream media (the term is usually applied to films such as *Saw* and *Hostel* in which the primary emphasis seems to be on watching the graphic suffering of others). In contrast to the grittiness of its American counterparts, however, *High Tension* has an arresting beauty, featuring stylish camera work, poignant montage, and haunting musical arrangements along with the mandatory bloodletting. The film, which features a plucky (and deadly) antiheroine, was influenced stylistically by the giallo film, but certainly owes something to the French film movement of the 1980s known as Cinéma du look, with its slick, glossy style, elevation of image over substance, and focus on young, alienated characters recalling the marginalized youth of Francois Mitterand's France (notable examples of Cinéma du look include *Diva* [1981] and *Nikita* [1990]).

High Tension caught the eye of Wes Craven, who dubbed Aja "a director's director" and worked with him on the remake of his 1977 film, *The Hills Have*

Eyes. Craven praised Aja's ability to build suspense, his visual style, his energy and pace, and his use of sound (Craven). This was a significant moment in the story of transnational horror, as the established master of the American brand of horror passed the torch to his young counterpart. Aja brings his European influences to the genre, employing a variety of catchy styles of world music in counterpoint to the images he creates, building suspense by drawing upon horror codes and conventions established by Alfred Hitchcock and his followers, and turning the screen into a richly colored bloody canvas. He also satisfies gore-hounds with an unflinching portrayal of brutality, something resisted in Europe, as Aja explains in an interview:

> in Europe there is no horror movie. It's very hard to make a slasher or gory movie. There is no audience for that. I think the main difference between Europe and the U.S. is that there is a kind of freedom. We don't have this Puritanism problem. We don't have this stupid, silly problem with nudity. On the other hand we have this problem with violence. It's very hard to get very far. A movie like *The House on the Left* [*sic*] would be very hard to do in Europe. Like *High Tension* was. It was not very easy to do and find money to make the movie because it was so violent. We don't have a nudity problem, the only problem we have is too much violence. To give you an example, *The Devil's Rejects*, which I saw before I was leaving for L.A. It's a great movie. It's an amazing movie but it'd be very hard to do in Europe. Because it's very violent and traumatic but sometimes you are on the side of the killers and that'd be something they'd have a problem with. (Aja)

Aja seems to have found a home in America, or at least a workplace. Like many directors currently working in the field of transnational horror, he has recently completed a remake. He has directed the remake of a Korean horror film, *Into the Mirror* (*Geoul sokeuro*, 2003), called *Mirrors*, starring the popular American actor Kiefer Sutherland. He is also capitalizing on an American techno-trend in a remake of the 1978 horror-comedy, *Piranha*, slated for release in 2009 as *Piranha 3-D*.

Aja enjoys box office success and freedom in Hollywood despite clashes with the MPAA board, as in the case of *High Tension*. One reason for his appeal and something that sets him apart from the rest of the splat pack is his sense of composition and style. He is certainly aware of the mannerisms of the filmmakers that preceded him, but his work is not merely derivative. His films are hybrid in several senses, making him a synecdoche for the globalization of cinema, stylistically as well as in the marketplace. Examples of his idiosyncratic style are his use of point-of-view editing and the camera eye to build a peculiar sense of suspense and intensity. His handling of the camera eye follows a unique visual rhetoric, and his appropriation of the ocular effects encoded in horror films has something of the quality of a fingerprint.

Aja's films emphasize several aspects of the gaze. After all, *Over the Rainbow* (1997)—one of Aja's earliest works—begins with a voyeur stalking and killing a woman observing herself in a mirror. *The Hills Have Eyes* (2006) provokes goose-flesh precisely because the mutant family is always watching its "normal" counter-part; the film ends, in fact, with an extreme long shot from the rocky landscape of the New Mexico hills, evidence that "they are still watching." *Mirrors* (2008) enacts the inescapability and violence inherent in the reflected gaze. The plot of *High Tension* turns on a voyeuristic moment involving a shower scene designed in clear allusion to Hitchcock, another director obsessed with the implications of the voyeuristic camera. Time and again, Aja uses the eye as a rich site of (sometimes conflicting) meanings. Perhaps his genius lies in the fact that no one theoretical paradigm contains these meanings: he uses the eye metacinematically; he knowledgeably alludes to iconic scenes, not all of them from horror film history (like Luis Buñuel's slit-open eye in *Un Chien Andalou*); he rewrites the philosophy of the gaze, demoting the eye in the hierarchy of senses and thus following the theoretical lead of critic and philosopher Georges Bataille; he links the eye to rape; and he celebrates the eye as an insurgent force against the repressive symbolic order. The range of deployments of this single trope in Aja creates a mirroring effect described by Noël Carroll: viewers feel vulnerable, shudder, and experience visceral revulsion at what they see. They shrink and contract, like the characters whose fear they witness, to avoid contact with unclean creatures in the mind's eye, and they experience paralysis in conjunction with an urge to flee. This mirroring effect is a key feature of the horror film for Carroll; the monsters, the images, the body parts, and the victims all make horror films frightening, but it is the eyes of Aja's viewers watching eyes watching horror that make his films monstrous and uncanny (Carroll, *Philosophy* 17–18).

A salient characteristic of Aja's films, the ocular may be key to his international success. The eye is an archetype in cinema, and especially in horror films the world over. Note, for example, *The Eye* (2008), a remake of the Asian film *Gin gwai* (2002); Bigas Luna's *Anguish* (Spain, 1987); Michael Powell's *Peeping Tom* (U.K., 1960). Central texts in world literature—*Oedipus Rex, King Lear*, "The Tell-Tale Heart"—fixate upon the eye as a site where the dramas of guilt, terror, and castration anxiety are enacted. It's no mistake that the medium of film has seized upon its power. Long ago, before the slashers of the 1980s lumbered across the movie screens of America, S. S. Prawer noted the prominence of the eye in horror cinema and the various roles it plays: "Within the face it is of course the eye which leads most directly to where we live—and the human eye has, indeed, played an especially important part in the terror film" (75). He speculates about the ambiguous nature of the cinematic eye, which may reveal in frightening close-ups an unbalanced and distorted mind, or may mirror a sad or terrified soul, or possibly evoke squeamishness and revulsion in the viewer by virtue of its vulnerability and texture. In the final chapter of *Men, Women, and Chainsaws,* "The Eye of Horror," Carol Clover offers an exhaustive list of horror films that feature eyes in their titles or images of eyes on their box covers, posters, and promotional materials, claiming, "Horror privileges eyes because, more crucially than any other kind of cinema, it is about eyes" (167). She then qualifies, "More particularly, it is about eyes watching horror" (167). Clover's metacinematic turn helps explain the final cause of horror, its effect on the viewer: horror is not, strictly speaking, induced by the thing itself (monster, mutilated body, etc.); rather, horror takes effect when a viewer watches a viewer watching horror. Clover implies that our horror depends on our identification with some aspect of what we see and on a vulnerability we share with either the eye of the victim or of the killer. But there is perhaps a suggestion that the informed viewer is embedded in the language and gestures of the horror film and can, therefore, articulate a certain understanding of the genre.

Hitchcock's *Psycho* (1960), the cinematic urtext of slasher films, exerts an anxiety of influence over all directors who follow. The forty-five minutes leading-up to the shower had centered on Marion Crane's ill-fated plot to embezzle money and join her lover, and her murder less than halfway through the film must have shocked and alienated viewers. The ocular horror of the sequence is arguably what makes it iconic. The flow of eye-like images begins with a view down into the circular motion of a flushing toilet, moves to a low-angle shot of an eye-like shower head, the screaming O of Marion's mouth during her stabbing, back to the shower head, and then to water circling the drain in the bathtub, which dissolves into the lifeless, staring eye of the victim, the focal point of a slow zoom out.

The hybrid film *Anguish* (aka *Angustia*) explores as fully as possible the metacinematic notion of ocular horror. The initial plotline features John Pressman (Michael Lerner), an orderly in an optometrist's office and a caretaker for a collection of eyeballs in jars at a teaching hospital. John is driven by his mother (Zelda Rubenstein), who controls him psychically and drives him to murder people and cut out their eyes. At one point, Aja has his camera pull back out of the screen to focus on a sickened, terrified, and fascinated audience watching John's drama, a film called *The Mommy.* Soon, a seemingly hypnotized psychotic (Angel Jove) who has seen *The Mommy* one too many times begins murdering people in the theater. His actions are mirrored on the screen. Plots dovetail. As one of the survivors of the ordeal in the theater lies in a hospital bed, John from *The Mommy* enters her room in search of more eyeballs: "Like the doctor said, it's all in your imagination. I really don't exist." The closing credits roll on a screen within the film as a theatrical audience clears out.

Anguish is indebted to *Psycho* on many levels, but it remains an important horror film in its own right because it reifies horror film's assault on vision and places viewers in a *mise en abyme* of visual identification and terror. Wes Craven famously offers a self-reflexive horror film in *Scream* (1996), which features a horror fan/victim who quickly realizes that the film she is preparing to watch is one in which she, herself, must perform. The opening sequence in which Casey (Drew Barrymore) is menaced and eventually butchered by a crank phone caller demonstrates the centrality of the eyes to horror. Casey flirts with the caller as she makes popcorn and prepares to watch a horror movie. After the caller reveals that he is watching her every move and threatens to "gut [her] like a fish," she gazes through the peephole of her door, and the viewer gets, as Casey does, a distorted view of an empty porch. When she asks, desperately, "What do you want?" she gets the horrifying answer: "To see what your insides look like." Soon, she will see what her boyfriend's insides look like as he sits, eviscerated, on the back porch because she missed a "game show" question about *Friday the 13th*. Craven subverts viewers' expectations in this film, as Hitchcock did before him, by having the bankable actress playing Casey, a seeming prototype for "the final girl" of the slasher genre, killed within the first ten minutes. Like Patty (Talia Paul), John's "final victim" in *Anguish*, Casey prepares to watch a horror movie but is unable to grasp the fact that she is in one. Horror comes upon the heroine when she realizes that she, the watcher, is now the watched; the emphasis on watching, an impulse of cinematic horror, has certainly left its mark on this opening sequence.

THE VOYEURISTIC CAMERA EYE

Aja, born in 1978, is a student of American horror, especially of Craven's work, and so is fluent in the language of the genre. He understands the centrality of the eye to horror and his deployment of the eye and the gaze has been central to his art from his very first effort, a ten-minute film entitled *Over the Rainbow*. Despite its brief running time, *Over the Rainbow* is filled with techniques and interests that Aja will explore in his later, full-length films. *Over the Rainbow* is filmed entirely in black and white with a handheld camera and steadicam. It is experimental and self-reflexive, satirizing *film noir* with its sordid city atmosphere, shady characters, night-for-night shooting, and twisted plots dealing with misdirected passion and violent crime. Aja also satirizes *cinema vérité* through the film's visual style and faux investigative journalistic technique. Comic and grotesque, its dominant features involve a self-conscious, roving camera eye and point-of-view editing. It is unmistakably a French film: French is the only language used, it is set in France, and it features French music and conventional French character types. The film is available only as a streaming video, allowing it to reach a world market without corporate commercial distribution.

In *Over the Rainbow*, Aja's editing skill, particularly his use of point-of-view editing, establishes the horror of the cinematic look. At times, Aja's point/glance shot shows a well-defined watcher and an ensuing reaction shot offers a cause-and-effect explanation for the events filmed. At other times, though, the looker is off-screen or the point/glance shot cut altogether, creating what Catherine Zimmer calls "a *cinematic* organ of vision" (36). This sinister voyeurism described by Zimmer lies at the heart of the horror effect for Aja. For example, the opening sequence of *Over the Rainbow*, which traces the unsteady vision of a roving gaze from out of the darkness and into the light of a canal toward an unsuspecting woman later identified as "Madame Nero," dispenses with the point/glance shot altogether.[1] Ghostly, ethereal music creates a mysterious aura, and the distorted sounds of the woman's humming as the eye approaches create an effect of distance, as in a dream or a memory. The eye is positioned before the mirror, but we still see no subject, only the woman's shock at being watched, and we hear her terrified scream as she turns her cucumber-masked face toward her assailant.[2] Continuity editing here gives way to sudden montage as the woman's scream merges with the escaping steam of the pressure cooker and the ethereal music yields to the contrapuntal sound of French comic music. The identity of the stalker with whom viewers are forced into identification remains a mystery. Zimmer complains that "the distinction between the camera's vision and the human eye is often elided" in cinematic discussions of voyeurism, and sets out to demonstrate that, since *Peeping Tom*, the camera eye might be thought of as "embodied within its own phenomenological specificity and its own particularly embodied form of voyeurism" (35–36). The result of the look of this unknown watcher with whom we watch is the sensation of horror—made possible, in part, by technology developed initially from small, hand-held cameras. This category of shots that obscures the identity of the source becomes a source of paranoia and dread in *The Hills Have Eyes*.

THE METACINEMATIC CAMERA EYE

Perhaps Aja was all the more attracted to this remake of the classic Wes Craven film because, as the title indicates, viewers must submit relentlessly to watching watchers watch victims. The variety of shots Aja uses destabilizes point of view from beginning to end. The film begins with an extreme long shot of a barren desert in New Mexico in a region long ago devastated by nuclear testing. The camera moves downward until it settles upon a babbling brook, which had partially reflected the sky and sands surrounding it. It follows a fish that is netted by a person in a HAZMAT suit. Suddenly there is a cut to a belated establishing shot—someone is watching the workers from a distance. A match cut to a medium shot seems to indicate that the watcher has moved closer. Then, viewers adopt the point of view of the worker, seeing through his mask. The point/object is a hand-held Geiger counter picking up large amounts of nuclear radiation. The worker scans the terrain, when a distraught and tattered man crashes into him, crying for help. The point/ glance of the worker moves to the point/object view of the bloody interloper, who then backs away as a look of horror comes over his face, which is now the point/ glance shot that picks up a new point/object—the worker. The point of a pick axe strikes through the back of the HAZMAT helmet and emerges through the visor. Pluto (Michael Bailey Smith) has impaled the government worker through the chest, and repeatedly dashes the body against a rock; he quickly dispatches his companion and hauls them off, chained to the back of a pick-up truck.

An establishing shot of a lonely gas station follows the opening credits. The camera eye moves along with a hapless gas station attendant (Tom Bower), circling behind him. He clutches a rifle and looks about, nervously calling out, "Ruby?" The camera eye trails along a dilapidated fence, which still supports a sign reading "No Trespassing: United States Government Department of Energy," finally lighting upon the gas station attendant in a high angle shot. He will continue to be stalked by an unseen presence until the horn of a car calls him away to the gas pumps— the Carter family has arrived, American flag waving from the antenna of their station wagon. Filmmakers like Dario Argento and Brian De Palma established these point-of-view shot arrangements and the fluid, stalking camera as conventions in the horror genre, and Aja makes expert use of these mannerisms.

The Carter family will be subjected constantly to the eyes of their cannibalistic counterparts, and the stalking begins at the gas station as Ruby (Laura Ortiz), a young mutant girl, follows them around the grounds of the station. The Carters fall under constant surveillance. After a blowout due to machinations by Lizard (Robert Joy) and Goggle (Ezra Buzzington), the family gathers to pray before the men separate and go for help. A medium shot suddenly establishes the family gathering in a circle as the young sister Brenda (Emile de Ravin) ironically remarks, "Ugh. Thank God no one's watching." The camera moves further out and the field of vision is now framed by the shape of a pair of binoculars. Guttural sounds are heard.

The following scene begins with the older sister, Lynn (Vinessa Shaw), breast feeding her infant and talking with her mother. A jump cut to a long shot objectifies the group of women and their voices become distant. Obviously, they are being "scoped-out" by the mutants. Later, when the mutants invade the trailer and rape and kill two of the Carter women, Aja inserts a chilling detail: as Lizard holds Lynn's baby at gunpoint, he undoes her shirt and puts his face to her breast, as if nursing. Was Lizard the watcher in the earlier scene? At film's end, with the mutant family seemingly dispatched, the Carter survivors engage in a group hug. Viewers watch, but step-frame montage thrusts the viewpoint back to a long shot, then to an extreme long shot. *They* are still watching. And that pronoun must remain ambiguous, because viewers are never quite sure who is watching along with them. The vision of the camera eye in *The Hills Have Eyes* creates horror largely through the positioning of the camera, the use of variable shots and editing techniques, and the technological scopophilia of the camera eye. The sum of these techniques, however, goes beyond the objectified image on the screen and becomes internalized and individualized in the audience. With *The Hills Have Eyes*, Aja has entered mainstream Hollywood on the strength of his previous work in Europe. His eclectic style, which could not find full expression in his homeland, has found affirmation in this remake of a "canonical" American horror film.

THE EYE AS INSURGENT FORCE

In his introduction to horror film, Rick Worland seeks the origins and definition of the "splatter film," a subgenre concerned with outlandishly grotesque bodily destruction, dismemberment, and spurting blood. He cites *Phantasm* (1977) as an early paradigm for the splatter film: "In a mortuary concealing the entrance to the netherworld, a flying metallic ball sprouts blades to grind out the victim's eyes, blood spraying. The result was a literal "splatter" (107). The demonic ball in *Phantasm* actually latches onto the temples of victims and drills between the eyes, but the blood certainly does spray. Aja splatters blood freely in his films, and his images are as disturbing as those of any director working today (note, for example, *High Tension*, in which the killer cuts the hands off of Alex's mother [Oana Pellea] and we see an isolated shot of blood spraying against a white wall in an arterial spray scene recalling Miike's *Ichi the Killer* [2001]). Aja's first full-length film, *Furia* (1999), while not as brutal and bloody as his later work, participates in the tradition of ocular horror; it is specifically about eyes, the rape of vision, and the limits of visuality.

From the repeated images of eyes, whether distanced by various lenses (still photos, mirrors, screens, holes, slits, windows, open doorways), or represented by circular objects (sun, moon, circular fans, radio knobs), to the heightened visual language that defines the struggle to maintain artistic vision, *Furia* is emphatically about the implications of looking, being looked at, and the physicality of the eye itself. The film is in the mode of what Tom Conley calls a *lecture de regard*; that is, a meditation on what it means to observe the film in accordance with the way it stares back, leaving us "blinded and seduced by its images" (198). *Furia* takes place in a barren, futuristic dystopia where the government brutally suppresses any sort of artistic expression, particularly the art and practice of drawing. Amid this infertile wasteland, the story of intrigue and forbidden love between two artists takes place. Théo (Stanislas Merhar) and Elia (Marion Cotillard) communicate by way of complex and beautiful chalk drawings rendered on city walls at night. In the morning, authorities work to efface the lovers' visual messages. The eye itself becomes an insurgent force against this oppressive authority, and is, therefore, subject to severe discipline and punishment.[3]

Furia begins with a voice-over describing the struggle and the resistance. A candle stub burns in the foreground; whiskey fills a glass behind it. "Living here means living nowhere," a voice-over informs us. "The harsh desert wind deadens your senses. Maybe out of boredom, or to live before the bomb within us blows, I go out to draw. Not to protest the situation, the curfew, or the ban on posters and writing. Chalking the walls lets me breathe. It's not just political slogans. If a child drew a horse or a dog, they'd erase that, too. Maybe they'll catch me one day but I'll have lived!" At this point, Théo, the hero/artist, breaks from an alleyway, and the camera cuts to a bright full moon in the sky—that and the sun will be recurring images in the film. The voice-over continues as Théo finds a faded image on a wall—it is a face, the face of Elia, his interlocutor, which the authorities could only partially erase. He produces a piece of chalk and begins working feverishly on the eyes. The camera focuses on the wall and the face as a circular white light burns in the upper right-hand portion of the screen. Then, there is a cut to a single, closed eye which opens slowly to reveal an eye with an inky black iris. The camera pans to the other eye. It is blue. In the iris, the film's title, *Furia*, appears. The camera cuts to a landscape as the film begins. The ensuing action involves Théo riding his motorcycle back to a barren city in the desert. The camera scans a wall with a single, dark aperture, then cuts to drab walls full of rows of windows. It slowly descends into Théo's room, where a circular fan turns. One ocular effect bleeds into another: a ringing phone is lowered through a circular hole in the ceiling; a circular ceiling fan (the iris?) is framed by that hole. The camera picks up the circular, eye-like knobs on a radio that transmits fuzzy sounds of gibberish. The camera lingers over Théo staring at himself in the mirror.

Furia's opening moments offer a paradigm for the film as a whole. The drab *mise-en-scène* and homogeneity of the buildings bear witness to the stark nihilism of a world without art. But the dominance of eyes and eye-like, circular objects is most striking. In these seductive images resides the fascination of the film. Aja, a child of the 1980s, certainly learned from the films of that era, and uses these techniques with surprising subtlety. For instance, the ceiling fans in this scene and throughout the film create chilling associations in the fans of eighties horror films: "After the credits, the first thing we see is the vortex of a ventilation fan—an image that, for some reason, became a standard symbol for menace in horror films of the '80s (Tobe Hooper's *The Funhouse* and Alan Parker's *Angel Heart* are but two examples)" (Cumbrow 125). Though Robert Cumbrow is discussing John Carpenter's *Christine* (1983) in this passage, the effect is the same in *Furia*. Circular fans recur time and again in the film, and represent only one of the ocular objects that fill the screen in *Furia*.

Elia's distinct eyes—one black, one blue—usher the viewer into the world of *Furia*, and her face in the opening credits provides a strong visual allusion to a most iconic moment in film. In *Un Chien Andalou*, the incipit ("Once upon a time . . .") is followed by a man (Luis Buñuel himself) sharpening a razor. He steps out onto the balcony and looks at the moon. There is a dissolve to a close-up of a young woman's face. A hand opens her left eye with thumb and index finger. There is a shot of the sky, as clouds bisect the moon; then, there is an extreme close-up of the razor slicing the eye lengthwise. The prelude to this ocular rape and castration opens *Furia*. Elia's eye is not slit by a razor, but by the film's title.

By its reference to the canonical film, Aja taps into the rich reservoir of critical discussion that has been lavished upon Buñuel's work. Jean Vigo, praising *Un Chien Andalou* in its "confrontation between the subconscious and the rational," says of this scene: "Our cowardice, which leads us to accept so many of the horrors that we, as a species, commit, is dearly put to the test when we flinch from the screen image of a woman's eye sliced in half by a razor. Is it more dreadful than the spectacle of a cloud veiling a full moon?" (Buñuel 75). David Cook suggests that the film itself was "as much about the collapse of European culture between the wars as a subterranean voyage through the recesses of the unconscious mind" (310). In an essay entitled "Eye," Georges Bataille lingers over that image, which for him produces contradictory responses of fascination and horror. The eye itself is seductive, but to such an extreme that it is "at the boundary of horror" (17). He calls attention, through italics, to the eye as a *cannibal delicacy* (that can devour, as in the Grandville painting "First Dream," but causes in the viewer such anxiety that we can never bite into it) and the *eye of conscience.* So gripping is the power of the punishing gaze that Buñuel, after filming the slit-open eye, is said to have been sick for a week. But submission to ocular violence, for Bataille, can be liberating. Through enucleation, Bataille tears down the hierarchy of the senses, atop of which rests the eye.[4]

Vision is a force that oppressive authority seeks to control, but Stephen King reminds us of the squeamishness and vulnerability embodied by the eye itself: "We all understand that eyes are the most vulnerable of our sensory organs, the most vulnerable of our facial accessories, and they are (ick!) soft. Maybe that's the worst . . ." (qtd. in Clover 166). Buñuel's film may be a nascent moment of transgression in film. The slit-open eye marks a boundary rarely crossed but always threatened in horror film. Worland is willing to believe that Tobe Hooper was thinking about Buñuel's opening montage in his own *Texas Chainsaw Massacre* (1974):

Hooper conveys Sally's terror with closer and closer views of her screaming face, moving in with a macro lens to depict her eyelashes, pupil, and finally

just huge close ups of capillaries laced in the eyeball. Although I suggested
this sequence alludes to *Un Chien Andalou*, there is no threat to Sally's eyes,
per se; rather the extreme close-ups of the eye capture her complete physical
vulnerability and terror. (Worland 223)

In *Furia*, Aja regards the eye with a creative dexterity that contains multiple
meanings. Often objects of fear and revulsion, eye- and egg-shaped objects also suggest sexuality, fertility, and the feminine. At every instance the film reflects on vision
(literal and artistic), eros, vulnerability, castration, desire, and cinema itself. What
Conley writes about *Un Chien Andalou* is equally true of *Furia*: "*Un Chien Andalou*
is a cavalcade of loosely connected shots but also a very tightly woven story about a
concomitant rape and seduction of the viewer's vision" (197).

THE EYE AND RAPE

As punishment for her artistic vision, Elia not only has her eye "raped"
(like Théo, she tears out her eye because it had been penetrated by the authorities, who discharged a chip into the soft tissue of her eyeball), but she must suffer
a literal rape by Théo's brother, Laurence (Wadeck Stanczak). Rape—as a forced
bodily intrusion, in its etymological sense of seizure and abduction, and as a trope
for a range of seductive violence—is never too far from Aja's cinematic imagination. Sarah Projansky claims that "rape is one of contemporary US popular culture's
compulsory citations . . . embedded in all of its complex media forms, entrenched
in the landscape of visual imagery." She concludes, "the pervasiveness of representations of rape naturalizes rape's place in our everyday world, not only as real physical
events but also as part of our fantasies, fears, desires and consumptive practices.
Representations of rape form a complex of cultural discourses central to the very
structure of stories people tell about themselves and others" (3). Rape is a story told
time and again in cinema, and the rape-revenge film develops alongside the slasher
film in the 1970s and 1980s, appearing in the guises of several genres: *Clockwork
Orange* (1971), *Straw Dogs* (1971), *Deliverance* (1972), *Frenzy* (1972), *Lipstick* (1976),
and *Sudden Impact* (1983) provide examples. In cinema, rape is a palimpsest written
over by sexual and visceral images presented through montage, sound, and *mise-
en-scène*. It explores the tensions between rival factions, and films dramatize the
resulting transgression and retribution that play out in culture in different ways
and to differing degrees. The fault lines or axes routinely explored, as Clover has
shown, are usually male-female or country-city. Rape is invariably tied to the visual;
Clover states bluntly that in horror movies "a hard look and a hard penis (chain saw,
knife, power drill) amount to one and the same thing" (182), referring to the eye's

penetrating and destructive power. As Alex (Malcom McDowell), the young, futuristic gangster of Stanley Kubrick's *Clockwork Orange*, says to the beaten, gagged, and
leering husband of his soon-to-be rape victim, "Viddy well, my little brother. Viddy
well." Spectators—those who "viddy"—are forced into identification with victims,
rapists, and avengers by virtue not only of the story but by the camera that directs
their gaze.

Rape in cinema would seem to be the logical end of a system designed to please
the gaze of men and that shows a fascination with the female form. Laura Mulvey
famously theorized the phenomenon in her seminal essay on the topic, "Visual Pleasure and Narrative Cinema" (1975, rpt. 1999), the basic thrust of which bears direct
relevance to Aja's work as a filmmaker. Mulvey argues that Hollywood is skilled in
the manipulation of its audience's visual pleasure. Enjoining the forces of feminism
and psychoanalysis to her treatment of film, Mulvey observes that scopophilia is
centered on the human form. Like the phallus in language, the cinema has always
reflected the concerns of the patriarchy; men therefore are characterized as active
agents, while women become passive objects of the male gaze. Women are cinematic display objects, but they endanger the male viewer because they remind him,
through their lack of a penis, of his own castration anxiety, the vagina taking on the
status of bloody wound. Women are forever bearers, not makers, of meaning. How
does Hollywood continue to produce visual pleasure in the face of the threat of
castration anxiety? Well, it has become adept at encoding defense mechanisms into
film—namely fetishism, which allows the male to deny the feminine lack of a penis
by substituting some object in its place, in this case cinematic image; voyeurism is
another coping strategy that Hollywood employs to protect its male viewers and
sustain their visual pleasure, as "the extreme contrast between the darkness in the
auditorium (which also isolates the spectators from one another) and the brilliance
of the shifting patterns of light and shade on the screen helps to promote the illusion of voyeuristic separation" (61).[5]

Because rape is present in every one of Aja's films, he certainly participates
in this Hollywood-sexual coding. He has become increasingly adept at seducing
viewers with both visual and auditory cues and using the constant threat of rape
and bodily violation to build tension. Seductive images move across barren terrain
and dark interior spaces in Aja's films, proffering the "carrot" of transgression and
forming forbidding landscapes that seethe with tension. These are in evidence from
the lovelorn custodian in *Over the Rainbow*, who pulls the apologetic young woman
into his drab apartment to her horror and demise, to the killer in *High Tension* who
fellates himself with a severed head in his rusty truck on the roadside, to the rape in
a trailer stuck out in the deserts of New Mexico in *The Hills Have Eyes* (and here,
certainly Aja learned from Wes Craven, who just about invented the rape-revenge
subgenre of horror with *The Last House on the Left* [1972] and revisited it in his own

The Hills Have Eyes). While many of Aja's killers are literal rapists, all of them are classic slashers, having a fetish for sharp, penetrating weapons that are essentially extensions of their bodies—knives, awls, axes, wooden clubs wrapped with a cluster of barbed wire, bandsaws, and so forth. But maybe the greatest horror of all is that viewers (mostly young men) are entrenched in a system of visual codes and signs that make rape natural and ineluctable.

THE GAZE AND THE SYMBOLIC ORDER

The naturalization of rape blunts what ought to be a sharp and terrible recognition of the oppression that a culture of inequalities must repress. Horror films nonetheless represent the forces on either side of the socioeconomic divide as they play out the drama of objectification, violation, and retribution; these forces are usually male-female or country-city. Perhaps the most original aspect of Aja's breakout film, *High Tension*, is that it explores a different rift in our culture of rape—heterosexual and homosexual. Through his gay, lovelorn, insane butcher of a heroine, Marie, he is able to explore prominent themes of 1970s and 1980s horror (the dysfunction of the nuclear family, the return of the repressed, and so on) but does so in a new way. Marie's gaze is arrested by Alex (Maïwenn Le Besco) and she is driven to remove all obstacles to her buried psychosexual fantasies.

The murderous lesbian is of course not Aja's innovation, but he adopts the motif for the slasher genre. In her book *Insane Passions*, in fact, Christine Coffman notes: "At the turn of the millennium, the figure of the psychotic queer woman has made a spectacular return in Western cinema" (191). Among the popular films dealing with this topic—from *Basic Instinct* (1992) to *Single White Female* (1992)—she mentions *High Tension*, released in the United States in 2005. Coffman also mentions several lesser-known films, including cinematic representations and documentary accounts of the Aileen Wuornos story and representations of the Papin sisters (*Sister My Sister* [1994] and *Murderous Maids* [2000]), their brutal assault on their employers in 1933, and Jacques Lacan's discussion of the affair. The relevance to Aja's film is so striking that some discussion of the event and the debate surrounding it is in order.

Christine and Lea Papin were sisters, alleged incestuous lesbians, and domestic servants in the household of Mr. and Mrs. Lancelin and their daughter, Genevieve, who owned a house in provincial Le Mans, about 125 miles southwest of Paris. The sisters worked for Mr. Lancelin, a lawyer, for six years. By all accounts the Lancelins were harsh and austere, demanding a strict regimen of cleanliness. Images of white gloves tracing sills for dust and messages delivered on trays as the usual form of communication dominate. The sisters shared an upstairs room, their *chambre de bonne.* On February 2, 1933, Genevieve and Mrs. Lancelin returned home in a rush, late for a dinner date. A blown fuse caused the lights to go out in the house. Sternly reproached, the sisters reacted with an outburst of violence: they ripped out their employers' eyes with their bare hands; Mrs. Lancelin was brained by a pitcher and, retrieving a knife and hammer from the kitchen, the sisters proceeded to rip and mutilate the legs, thighs, and buttocks of the women, drenching their genitals in blood. When the corpses were discovered several hours later, the police burst into the maids' room to find them washed and cleaned, sitting up in bed and embracing each other. The bloody hammer at the bedside led to their arrest.

Jean Genet was inspired by the Papin murders, initiating the theatrical production of *The Maids* in 1948. His imaginative representation of the affair was violent and subversive. Through Claire and Solange, Genet explores the love/hate relationship those in servitude feel for those who hold their figurative chains. Human identity becomes a shifting succession of masks, gender roles, and moral values. In a 1933 issue of *Le Minotaure*, Lacan argues that the sisters' crime was rooted in their purported homosexual bond. Drawing on Freud's ideas about paranoia and repressed homosexual feelings, Lacan argues that the sisters slew their employers in a fit of paranoid psychotic homophobic projection. The Papin sisters were thus portrayed as brutal and dangerous outsiders to the French bourgeois norms and, Coffman argues, "the incestuous lesbian desire of which the Papin sisters were suspected was also a subterranean current within the bourgeois family" (33–34).

The same perceived threat to the nuclear family drives *High Tension*, and the crisis that unleashes the killer turns on the gaze. Marie and Alex, the two principal characters, are female college students on their way to visit Alex's family, who live in a remote farmhouse. Their relaxing visit is interrupted by a sadist who systematically and brutally slaughters the family from the top of the hierarchy on down. Marie and Alex survive, but Alex is captured, bound, and gagged by the killer, who is by turns pursued by and pursuer of Marie. However, all is not as it seems.

The "high tension" of the title refers to the tension caused by love, in this case, same-sex desire. But the audience does not know that, immediately. The first big hint: Marie goes out for a cigarette and catches sight of Alex showering. She lingers over the vision; then there is a cut to an empty swing. Marie goes upstairs to masturbate while listening to "Runaway Girl" by U-Roy, with the lyrics, "Just another girl, that's what you are." As she orgasms, the rusty van pulls up to the house, containing the serial killer, who will turn out to be the manifestation of Marie's repressed homoerotic desire.

High Tension, like Lacan's narrative of the Papin affair, pits same-sex desire against the traditional patriarchal structure. Lesbianism becomes a "paranoid crime," taking the form of a male serial killer. Marie—the lesbian outsider—destroys the nuclear family and abducts ("rapes") the daughter. The father, as head of the family, has his head removed. The mother has her vocal chords cut and her hands carved off with a small knife (while Marie is situated simultaneously as the immanent killer and the transcendent spectator, beholding the mutilation through the slats of a closet door). The little boy, a "cowboy," is shot. The monster does not die: at the film's end, when Alex is brought in to identify the overtly insane Marie, who is concealed behind one-way glass, Marie senses her presence and turns toward her with open arms. The danger to the nuclear family persists. Like *The Stepfather* (1987), an outstanding 1980s slasher film which offered a critique of patriarchy rather than reinforcing a puritanical ethic, *High Tension* questions family structures and male-centered heterosexual institutions that engender violence. A viable reading of *High Tension* is of course that it is rather conservative in its portrayal of a monstrous, homicidal, deviant destroyer of families. However, both films confront the limiting strictures of family and the whole monolith of a culture that limits people on the basis of biological and sexual difference and tries to force them into predetermined roles.

From the film's outset, Aja establishes tension between the entrenched world of the traditional family, with its drab, nondescript parent figures in their dark and claustrophobic home, and the free and happy world of female bonding. As Alex and Marie journey to the isolated family farmhouse, the sun shines down on them as they joke and sing along to a bouncy Italian pop song, "Sara Perche Ti Amo"—"It will be because I love you"—a proleptic moment in the film. Before they arrive, a killer waits in a rusty truck, fellating himself with a severed head, which he then tosses out the window. At the family farm, Marie is introduced to the symbolic order, and the reception is cold. The dog barks at her. The father quickly retires. Marie learns that Alex is suffering because she likes a man who is already in a relationship. Later, as Marie sits on a swing, smoking, she glances up to see Alex showering. When the camera swings back to Marie, the swing is empty, and the camera lingers over a convergence of feminine images: a full white moon gleaming and reflecting off a pond. Terrible slaughter will ensue after this subtle turning point.

Lacan famously finds the origin of the individual subject in the mirror stage of a child's development. The emergent "self" is always formed in reference to some "other," whether that other is the child's own reflection in a mirror or any other being perceived and identified with. Rather than helping in the formation of a stable and healthy ego, that other is invariably viewed as a rival or a threat to the self, meaning that the subject is always formed out of aggression and alienation. Seeing and looking, "the gaze," then, is perhaps the spring of hostility in life as we begin to make our way in the world.

High Tension points to the importance of Freud's pre-Oedipal stage, a time of plentitude and bonding between mother and daughter, a union that is repressed and, though buried in Marie, longs to reemerge. The swing she sits in as she "scopes out" Alex is her cradle, and she rocks placidly beneath a full moon, observing the object of her desire. In this, Lacan's Imaginary Order, the child is so attuned to the mother that it does not even distinguish between the two bodies. The female child, entering the symbolic order at age five, brings with her the burden of lack—lack of the Name of the Father, his language, his phallus. This difficult transition from the imaginary to the symbolic order begins with the mirror stage when separation from the mother is first perceived. Marie is caught in a struggle to find union and pleasure. She seems to deny her very sexuality; her hair is short, her features masculine. She wears no make-up and dresses in neutral colors (a gray t-shirt and faded blue jeans) and in clothes that conceal her hour-glass shape. She does not look soft. All of this is in contrast to Alex, the *objet a*, who is soft, has flowing hair, and wears make-up and bright colors.

Alex is Marie's tie into the real, the connection lost when Marie was separated from her mother and forced to adopt the Name of the Father. The *objet petit a*, or object small a, is that elusive, missing object that will, in the subject's mind, satisfy the drive for plentitude and wholeness, "*a*" being the first letter of the French word for "other" (*autre*). In the Lacanian scheme, the *objet a* transforms, through metonymy, into the object of desire that in turn motivates the split subject to quest for that initial unity it can never again achieve. The subject, from the moment it employs the gaze, becomes, in Lacan's words, "punctiform," and begins to fall away. At the moment when the rusty van pulls up to the farmhouse, Marie's identity is, in effect, "sucked out of her," as the camera rapidly zooms out from her anxious figure standing in tableaux.

The serial killer is obviously the double, the doppelgänger, of Marie. His scene of masturbation with the severed head parallels Marie's masturbatory experience in the guestroom. The discarded head resembles Alex. But Marie seeks reunion with the mother, and when she finally receives, at circular-saw point, a forced profession of love from Alex, her pleasure is nongenital, the fulfillment of a pre-Oedipal desire for union with the mother. She kisses Alex gently and stares lovingly at her bloody face from out of her own bloody and mutilated countenance. Even after Alex drives a crowbar through her shoulder, Marie continues to gaze at her lovingly, repeating over and over, "We'll never be apart again . . . ." Like the reflection of the moon in the pond, Marie's gaze into Alex's face reestablishes the union of the mirror and casts her back to a time before hierarchies and before the father. The male killer is not seen again.

Marie, at this moment in the film, has returned to the first source of pleasure. In the final scene, Marie sits in her holding cell behind (one-way) glass, dressed in white swaddling clothes, smiling vacantly and lolling her head like a newborn. Like a (fearful) mother, Alex—who has obviously been brought in to identify the killer— whispers, "She can't see us, right?" But the instincts within Marie are too strong, and she turns to look lovingly at Alex and stretch out her twining arms in a gesture that says "hold me." Marie's desperation to return to this pre-Oedipal stage of bliss and plenty is also seen in Aja's meaningful choice of song throughout the film. For instance, as the final scene described above progresses, a song by Muse, "Born Again," begins to play, with its haunting melody and lyrics, "Destroy the spineless / Show me it's real / Wasting our last chance / To come away / Just break the silence / 'cause I'm drifting away, / Away from you." Earlier, when Alex is kidnapped and the killer is admiring the image of her face as he drives (other women's faces are affixed to his "rearview"), Gray Félix's "Á Toutes Les Filles" plays on the radio. The title translates, "To all the little girls," and the song addresses "all the little girls I used to know in Kindergarten," paying homage to little girls who stay little, contrasting the figure of the shy little girl to the fully grown, sexual woman. The song expresses the same *ubi sunt* feel of François Villon's "The Ballad of the Dead Ladies." Marie has repressed the imaginary order and wants only to return to that pleasurable ecstasy. The eye, both a mirror and a lens, is the only means of redress and return.

CLOSING THOUGHTS

Aja began making films in a French culture that, like many developed nations confronted by a new world of globalism and multiculturalism, questioned its national identity. In the hopes of reinforcing the center, subversive art forms were marginalized. Martine Beugnet writes of a "cinema of abjection" in the 1990s, in which filmmakers sought, above all, transgression:

> Some directors concentrate on Taboo subjects (violent crimes, rape, incest), and draw on the conventions of genres such as gore and pornography, that have been marginalized by both mainstream and art cinema. Often, the body as flesh is the raw material of the filmmaking; assaulted, mutilated, violated, it becomes a war zone, symbolic of the attack that is supposedly performed by the same token on social, cultural, and cinematic conventions. (295–96)

The cinema of abjection, then, focuses on those elements of a society that are filthy, aberrant, and must be cast out. They are monstrous, created by a system that loathes them and wants to eliminate them. Aja finds a fascination with these beings. They are terrible, repulsive; nonetheless, viewers are forced into identification with them. Instead of working at the margins of French culture, though, Aja has been imported by Hollywood, where he is free to produce hybridized films which might loosely be called slasher films, but really draw upon a myriad of styles, genres, and influences. His work serves as an example of the cross-cultural, transnational nature of horror film, which may be the future of the genre in America.

NOTES

1. The significance of this victim's name is an early sign of Aja's status as *cinéaste*. The story of Nero's mother as told by Saint Peter was recorded by Jacobus de Voragine in *The Golden Legend*. Nero, obsessed by a desire to see the womb he had once inhabited, had his mother killed and cut open. Nero's perverse desire to gaze upon his mother's viscera is not unlike that of a modern-day slasher. Jacobus de Voragine, *The Golden Legend: Readings on the Saints*, vol. 1, trans. William Granger Ryan (Princeton, N.J.: Princeton University Press, 1993), 347.

2. This grotesque, farcical scene uncannily seems to reproduce the experience of birth, or rather, the trauma that comes with the birth of visibility itself.

3. There are many reasons why Aja may have turned to Julio Cortázar's short story "Graffiti" as inspiration for *Furia*. The short story seems to have been inspired by the so-called Dirty War, which took place in Argentina between 1976 and 1983, during the first years of Aja's life. Amid the state-sponsored torture and murder of possibly as many as 30,000 people, Cortázar chronicles the relationship between two artists who can only communicate by drawing pictures on walls at night, only to have the drawings washed away in the day by the authorities of a repressive regime.

4. Bataille's fullest treatment of eye-rape and degradation is his first novel, *Story of the Eye*, an early edition of which appeared in 1928.

5. Mulvey's essay has been widely studied, taught, appropriated by fellow critics adopting a feminist-psychoanalytic reading of films, and finally, successfully attacked and deflated. Notably, Carroll in 1990 offered an alternative involving the use of paradigm scenarios toward an "image of women in film model" ("Image of Women" 358). Psychoanalysis may well be used inappropriately as a lens through which to read viewers' reception and response to a cinematic image, but psychoanalytic theories of language and development—especially those of Jacques Lacan—can help decipher the dynamics of the eye-function in that terrible love story, *High Tension*.

WORKS CITED

Aja, Alexandre. Interview with Mike Sampson. *JoBlo.com*, June 2005. http://www.joblo.com/ arrow/index.php?id=1486 (accessed October 23, 2008).

Bataille, Georges. *Story of the Eye*. Trans. Joachim Neugroschel. San Francisco: City Lights Books, 1987.

———. *Visions of Excess: Selected Writings, 1927–1939*. Ed. and trans. Alan Stoekl. Theory and History of Literature 14. Minneapolis: University of Minnesota Press, 1985.

Beugnet, Martin. "French Cinema of the Margins." *European Cinema*. Ed. Elizabeth Ezra. Oxford: Oxford University Press, 2004. 283–98.

Buñuel, Luis. *Classic Film Scripts: L'Age d'Or and Un Chien Andalou*. Trans. Marianne Alexandre. New York: Simon and Schuster, 1963.

Carroll, Noël. *The Philosophy of Horror*. New York: Routledge, 1990.

———. "The Image of Women in Film: A Defense of a Paradigm." *Journal of Aesthetics and Art Criticism* 48.4 (Fall 1990): 349–60.

Clover, Carol J. *Men, Women, and Chainsaws: Gender in the Modern Horror Film*. Princeton, N.J.: Princeton University Press, 1992.

Coffman, Christine. *Insane Passions: Lesbianism and Psychosis in Literature and Film*. Middletown, Conn.: Wesleyan University Press, 2006.

Conley, Tom. "*Un chien andalou.*" *Film Analysis: A Norton Reader.* Eds. Jeffrey Geiger and R. L. Rutsky. New York: W. W. Norton & Company, 2005. 196–215.

Cook, David. *A History of Narrative Film.* 4th ed. New York: W. W. Norton & Company, 2004.

Craven, Wes. Interview with Daniel Robert Epstein. *Really Scary,* June 2006. http://www .reallyscary.com/interview_wecraven.asp (accessed November 25, 2007).

Cumbrow, Robert C. *Order in the Universe: The Films of John Carpenter.* Metuchen, N.J.: Scarecrow Press, 1990.

Ezra, Elizabeth, and Terry Rowden, eds. *Transnational Cinema: The Film Reader.* In Focus. New York: Routledge, 2006.

Lacan, Jacques. *Écrits, A Selection.* Trans. Alan Sheridan. New York: W. W. Norton & Company, 1977.

———. "Motives of Paranoid Crime: The Crime of the Papin Sisters." *Critical Texts* 5.3 (1988): 7–11.

———. "The Split Between the Eye and the Gaze." *The Four Fundamental Concepts of Psychoanalysis.* Ed. Jacques-Alain Miller. Trans. Alan Sheridan. New York: W. W. Norton & Company, 1978. 67–78.

Mulvey, Laura. "Visual Pleasure and Narrative Cinema." *Feminist Film Theory: A Reader.* Ed. Sue Thornham. New York: New York University Press, 1999. 58–69.

Prawer, S. S. *Caligari's Children: The Film as Tale of Terror.* Oxford: Oxford University Press, 1980.

Projansky, Sarah. *Watching Rape: Film and Television in Postfeminist Culture.* New York: New York University Press, 2001.

Scream. Dir. Wes Craven. Perf. Drew Barrymore, David Arquette, Courteney Cox, and Neve Campbell. Dimension, 1996.

Ward Jouve, Nicole. *Female Genesis: Creativity, Self and Gender.* New York: St. Martin's Press, 1998.

Worland, Rick. *The Horror Film: An Introduction.* Oxford: Blackwell, 2007.

Zimmer, Catherine. "The Camera's Eye: *Peeping Tom* and Technological Perversion." *Horror Film: Creating and Marketing Fear.* Ed. Steffen Hantke. Jackson: University Press of Mississippi, 2004. 35–51.

"THE POUND OF FLESH WHICH I DEMAND"

American Horror Cinema, Gore,
and the Box Office, 1998–2007

—Blair Davis and Kial Natale

> The pound of flesh, which I demand of him,
> Is dearly bought; 'tis mine and I will have it.
> **—WILLIAM SHAKESPEARE,** The Merchant of Venice

"IT'S FUN TO BE SCARED"—HORROR AND HABITUATION

In 1981, renowned American film critic Roger Ebert decried the state of horror cinema at the time in his reviews of two sequels released that year, *Friday the 13th Part II* and *Halloween II*. In reviewing the former, he describes the film's opening sequence in which a young woman "wakes up, undresses, is stalked by the camera, hears a noise in the kitchen." Ebert continues: "She tiptoes into the kitchen. Through the open window, a cat springs into the room. The audience screamed loudly and happily: It's fun to be scared. Then an unidentified man sunk an ice pick into the girl's brain, and for me, the fun stopped. The audience, however, carried on. It is a tradition to be loud during these movies, I guess."

At the end of the review, which he notes can be substituted for any *Friday the 13th* film of one's choice, Ebert surmises that teenagers in earlier decades would not have been able to understand "a world view in which the primary function of teenagers is to be hacked to death" (142–43). In his review of *Halloween II*, Ebert quotes John McCarty's book *Splatter Films* and the notion that, in splatter movies, "mutilation is indeed the message—many times the only one." *Halloween II*, says Ebert, "fits this description precisely. It is not a horror film but a geek show" (158). By "geek show'" Ebert presumably means that such horror films place an emphasis on exploitive, carnival-like violence, similar to that of the sideshow carnival in which the geek's act consists of biting the heads off of live chickens. Such an act is by most accounts both gruesome and senseless, yet apparently not without its maca-bre charms as demonstrated by its historic role in carnival history. So too then, by Ebert's comparison, are an increasing amount of horror films: gruesome, senseless, but undeniably popular.

The question then becomes: just how gruesome are these films? More specifi-cally, if American horror films were in fact exceedingly gruesome in the early 1980s, how much gore is present in the average horror film some twenty-five years later, when images of torture and mutilation have seemingly become even more preva-lent? Has there indeed been an increase in the sheer amount of gore seen on screen in recent years thanks to the popularity of such films as *Saw* (2004), *Hostel* (2005), and their sequels? This essay is one attempt at answering some of these questions, by studying a recent ten-year period of American horror cinema, from 1998 to 2007, in order to quantify specific trends in the level of how much screen time gore occu-pies in recent horror films.

The larger question behind these inquiries is whether there has been an evolu-tion of gore in the horror genre throughout film history. Certainly, to most people, modern horror films seem gorier than those of decades past—but just how accurate are these perceptions? Do horror films devote more of their total running time to shots and scenes depicting gore with each passing year? If such a trend is not seen year by year, is it revealed decade to decade? In addition to the resurgence of previ-ously dormant subgenres such as zombie films (not regularly seen since the mid/ late 1980s, but revived in large part due to the success of 2002's *Resident Evil* and 2004's *Dawn of the Dead* remake), the current decade has also seen the creation of new subgenres (such as the "torture-porn" film, a moniker tentatively given by critics and many fans to such films as *Saw*, *Hostel*, and the like, and the rise of the "horror-remake" in which older films are updated with modern special effects). Gory mov-ies have increasingly become a target of criticism in recent years, with many critics decrying the progressively violent imagery of the horror genre. The *Christian Sci-ence Monitor* reported, for example, how the formerly "subtle" nature of horror film advertising has since "given way to gory trailers, billboards, and magazine campaigns" (Goodale). The Motion Picture Association of America suspended the rating pro-cess for the film *Captivity* (2007) until its poster campaign, which showed various images of its star being tortured, was suspended. The MPAA also demanded that the poster for *The Hills Have Eyes 2* (2007) be changed because it depicted a hand reaching out from a body bag; the hand was later removed. *Hostel Part Two* (2007) was also criticized for its posters—one shows a nude woman from the neck down holding a severed head (presumably her own), while the other is simply a close-up of a slab of meat—despite the fact that they were actually approved by the MPAA.

Film critics have also become vocal about their dislike of what they see as a new breed of gory horror films in recent years. One critic states: "we've entered a new realm of horror to push through the numbness. Witness the recent rise of truly gory movies such as *Saw, Hostel,* and the remake of *The Hills Have Eyes:* The filmmakers spend more time concocting gruesome visual effects and testing good taste than they do telling an actual story" (Monk). Ebert has himself also been critical of modern horror films, never more vehemently than in his review of the remake of *The Texas Chainsaw Massacre* (2003) which he calls "contemptible" as well as "[v]ile, ugly and brutal. There is not a shred of reason to see it."

> There is no worthy or defensible purpose in sight here: The filmmakers want to cause disgust and hopelessness in the audience. Ugly emotions are easier to evoke and often more commercial than those that contribute to the ongoing lives of the beholders. This movie, strewn with blood, bones, rats, fetishes and severed limbs, photographed in murky darkness, scored with screams, wants to be a test: Can you sit through it? There were times when I intensely wanted to walk out of the theater and into the fresh air and look at the sky and buy an apple and sigh for our civilization, but I stuck it out. (Ebert, "Review")

As he did with *Halloween II* decades earlier, Ebert calls *The Texas Chainsaw Massacre* a "geek show" (the former received two stars from the critic, however, while *Chainsaw* received no stars). Yet if both films are carnival-like in their exploitive approach toward gore, how then has this process changed over time? Certainly there are obvious differences in the amount of violence and gore when comparing horror films of various decades: 1930s horror films arguably appear less gory than those of the 1950s, while the latter typically seems less gory than those of the 1970s, which themselves often appear to have less gore than those of more recent years.[1] This process is reflected in a Halloween episode of *The Simpsons*, with Bart complaining that Lisa's reading of Edgar Allen Poe's "The Raven" wasn't scary. Lisa surmises, "Well, it was written in 1845. Maybe people were easier to scare back then," to which Bart replies, "Oh, yeah—like when you look at *Friday the 13th*, Part 1; it's pretty tame by today's standards" (Richmond and Coffman 37). Has there indeed been a steady process of desensitization over time among horror film viewers, therefore necessitating a constant raising-of-the-bar in terms of how much graphic violence is required in order to scare audiences?

If such a process does in fact occur, Dolf Zillmann and Rhonda Gibson understand it as a form of socialization that takes place among the horror film's primarily young male audience. In "Evolution of the Horror Genre," they describe the horror film as

> a significant forum for the gender specific socialization of fear and its mastery in modern times, a last vestige of the ancient rites of passage. It is a most

popular forum that provides boys with the opportunity to develop, through habituation of the excitory response associated with fear and distress [. . .] mastery of any disturbance from terrifying events. (Zillman and Gibson 25–26)

Similarly, R. H. W. Dillard sees the horror film as allowing viewers to confront and master their fear of death. In so doing, he says, horror films hold up a mirror to death, "the distorting mirror of a deserted funhouse which frightens us out of fear" (Dillard 37). Such desensitization as acquired through a process of "habituation" would therefore entail a progressive approach toward fear-inducing stimuli—such as a persistent increase in gore. It is this process which this essay seeks to explore.

WHAT IS HORROR?: SOME THEORETICAL CONSIDERATIONS

To reach any focused conclusion about the patterns and trends of modern horror cinema, the selection of texts within the genre becomes paramount. In order to discuss our chosen list of horror films, it is therefore necessary first to define the horror genre itself. Regardless of whether or not readers may agree or disagree with our inclusion of any given film as being a "horror film," it is doubtless that the films we have selected each have horrific aspects that connect them to the ensuing definitions of the genre and, therefore, qualify them for inclusion in this study. Peter Hutchings states that when devising lists of horror films, the inclusion of films which some may find questionable is "unavoidable" because "there can be no fixed once-and-for-all list of horror films" (Hutchings 9). Writing on the subject of film genre and classification, Janet Staiger describes how "Hollywood films have never been 'pure'—that is, easily arranged into categories. All that has been pure has been sincere attempts to find order among variety" (Staiger 185).

Such attempts at categorization, Staiger reminds us, often prove to be problematic for many scholars. Stephen Prince notes, "While Horror's popular appeal has proven especially durable, it is not a distinctive factor that sets horror apart" (2). A popular definition, although almost too encompassing alone to prove functional for this study, is that the horror film has the intent to horrify. This is of course an obvious tautology, but it is a useful one nonetheless. Comedies are made with the intent to inspire laughter. Pornographic films intend to arouse sexual desire. Horror films are created with the intent to unsettle the audience and inspire fear—to scare us and to horrify us, ideally instilling an enduring sense of dread and fright that lasts beyond the duration of the film.

Indeed, many modern critics see a growing distinction between these two ideas—the scary and the horrific—comparing films that are deemed to be truly scary with those that merely evoke disgust at increasing levels of gore and blood-shed. Regardless, films that fall under the generic classification of "horror film" share a central concern with the subject of death. Dillard describes horror films as a forum for exploring "the dark truths of sin and death," and our acceptance of the inevitability of death (36). Similarly, Ron Tamborini and James Weaver see horror films as providing "rituals [through which] we confront and learn to deal with our fear of death and our thoughts of what might lie beyond" (12).

Neighboring genres often transverse into the horror film's death-oriented subject matter and fear-based intent: the action film can utilize the threat of omnipresent death and hidden danger, revealing the enemy through a jump-cut, a common device of horror films. Likewise, the thriller aims to create a wild anticipation that is very similar to an important demarcation of horror: sustaining an intangible sense of dread from the disruption of natural law. This common narrative element, however, still lacks clarity when distinguishing the horror film from the serial murderer thriller. Horror, as an umbrella genre of pessimism and mortifying suspense, generally has two common methods for unsettling the audience: that of a tainted or deadly atmosphere (the thriller) and that of the graphic presentation of violence or death.

In literary terms, Devendra P. Varma notes this distinction in approach as being the divide between horror and terror in narrative: "Terror creates an intangible atmosphere of spiritual and psychic dread [. . .] Horror resorts to a cruder presentation of the macabre" (qtd. in Cavallaro 3). Varma further labels this dichotomy as the difference "between the smell of death and stumbling against a corpse" (2). This demarcation of the grotesque (including but not limited to visible gore, often related to shock) and atmosphere (critically acclaimed as building suspense) reveals a theoretical divide in the genre, although both approaches are often combined in a single sequence—one that might create an atmosphere of omnipresent danger and end with a gruesome murder or discovery. The horror film, in the sense of this definition, becomes a consistent, graphic examination of the macabre, characterized by an irreversible destruction of the protagonist's physical or mental well-being through a series of encounters with bloodshed and/or terror.

Jonathan Crane, in regard to films stemming from *Psycho's* "violent" lineage, defines the on-screen gore proliferated through horror as being the "singular hallmark of the genre" (153). While this simplification of his argument may seam naïve, the fact that certain horror films are celebrated for their notable absence of graphic violence (such as *The Others*, 2001) reveals the entrenched prevalence of gore in the horror genre overall. During the gruesome "shock" and macabre spectacle of on-screen gore, the narrative is likewise momentarily dissolved: "Corporeal ground zero is reached once the body has been eviscerated by a gutting that also includes the simultaneous stripping of narrative conventions to the bone" (Crane 162). Through this theoretical framework, horror then becomes a genre focused on the suspension of narrative in favor of horrifying the audience, achieved through the deconstruction of natural/comprehensible law by a supernatural or incomprehensible force.

DEFINING GORE: THE MEAT OF THE STUDY

Fundamental to the study of gore is the bodily context of horror films, which has served as a central concern for many of the genre's scholars. Anna Powell's *Deleuze and Horror*, for example, analyzes the theories of philosopher Gilles Deleuze in relation to the horror genre, particularly his idea of the "body-without-organs." Defined as "the 'true' condition of the human body if freed" from the limitations of its physical confines, Powell cites the film *Hellraiser* (1987) as a "graphically literal" example of the body-without-organs, whereby a character has organs that can "stick themselves back together" (211). Given the blood-soaked imagery conjured by this example, it can certainly be described as "gory" by most accounts. Gore then, as defined by this study, includes the explicitly visible, filmic representation of bloodshed or its direct result: the on-screen defacement or mutilation of—and/or penetration of objects into—a body, as well as the exposure of blood, sinew, organs and/or viscera resulting from such actions. Gore is therefore intrinsically defined by its bodily context: from the decayed flesh of a corpse to the residual blood splatter caused by a zombie bite or knife wound, gore involves a process whereby the human body is in some way wounded (typically by an exterior force or object) and its natural corporeal state altered (be it through blood loss, flesh distortion, physical transformation, and so forth).

In studying cinematic gore, we aim in our investigation to shed an empirical light on the quantity and type of gore present in the modern American horror film. Our intent is to document whether there has been a marked change in terms of how much screen time is devoted to gore—whether viewers are becoming increasingly exposed to gore for longer periods of time in modern American horror cinema. Our focus does *not* examine gore from a qualitative perspective, whereby one might seek to document whether the gore in horror films is becoming more disturbing or frightening to modern viewers via an analysis of the theoretical connections among gore, fright, and disgust and how they apply to audience reactions. To deem something as scary or frightening is ultimately a subjective process that becomes dependent upon such factors as the viewer's psychological profile and their current level of desensitization to images of gore (typically born out of how many horror films they have already seen, but perhaps also related to whether their job exposes them to human carnage, et cetera). Furthermore, individual viewers will undoubtedly react differently to various scenes of gore depending upon the content and context— gunshot wounds might not make someone flinch, but stabbings instill a frightful squeamishness; one may not be fazed by human disembowelment, but may be shocked by the same action committed against an animal, and so forth. Such an approach to studying gore would certainly prove to be a rewarding one, but one that is outside of the scope our current research given that it entails an entirely different methodology than our current empirical focus. Mikita Brottman's *Offensive Films: Toward an Anthropology of Cinema Vomitif* would likely serve as a key text in such a qualitative study of how modern audiences respond to different types of gore.[2]

Our current study argues, then, that gore is something that can be quantified in order to track its prevalence in horror films. Indeed, to a certain extent, any potential study on the qualitative effects of gore on audiences cannot proceed if one does not know *what kinds* of gore are present in horror films, and *in what durations.* In order to study gore levels from an empirical perspective, a certain amount of categorization via a content analysis methodology was required in order to quantify this gore in an exact manner.[3] To begin, a distinction was immediately recognized between gore caused by violent acts as they are happening, and gore caused by violence that has already occurred. As such, the divide between a violent/gruesome act performed on-camera (a stabbing or an autopsy, for example) and the gore resulting from unseen, prior violence to a body (a dead body or a crime scene) is distinguished by the separate notions of "active" and "passive" gore, respectively. An on-screen decapitation, for example, is categorized as active gore, while the common successive shot of the severed head is categorized as passive gore—the aftermath of a bodily mutilation not being presently performed.

Our application of a content analysis methodology took the form of logging the quantities (measured in seconds) and varieties of gore while watching DVD copies of selected films. Our research sample consisted of one hundred American horror films, spanning the time from 1998 to 2007.[4] All such films that had a theatrical release during this period were considered, with their inclusion in the genre being determined according to the aforementioned theoretical definitions. Given the cyclical popularity of specific film genres, it was often difficult to find ten American films in a given year that belonged solely to the horror genre. In such cases, cross-genre films in which horror played a prominent role were included, such as the action/horror film *Anacondas: Hunt for the Blood Orchid* (2004), science-fiction/horror films such as *The Faculty* (1998) and *Hollow Man* (2000), and supernatural-themed films such as *The Gift* (2000) and *Godsend* (2004). Ten films from each year of this ten-year period were then selected using a random-number generator, with each film being screened and its gore quantified.[5]

The latter process occurred through the use of what we designated as our "gore logs": spreadsheets that allowed each instance of gore to be encoded according to more than twenty different categories, which were separated into sections for both active and passive gore.[6] The active gore section included categories for such specific acts as disembowelment, decapitation, dismemberment, burning or melting flesh, eyeball penetration or removal, the disfiguration or removal of skin, blood-splatter/spray/flow, gun-shot wounds, skull breach or brain exposure, cannibalism (explicitly showing human viscera), pus extrusion, as well as visible bone extrusion (e.g., due to breakage, skin decay). Additionally, flesh penetration was quantified in three ways: surface flesh penetration (a scratch or graze producing blood), deep flesh penetration (e.g., by way of a knife, saw, teeth), and full flesh penetration (with the object visibly extruding the exit wound, such as a spear or sword). Passive gore included such categories as severed limbs or heads, the exposure of organs and/or viscera, skin decay or disfiguration, bloody wounds, dried or caked blood, and residual blood splatter or smears on a character or on the ground, walls, and so forth. When coding any of these particular instances for each film, the length of total screen time for each instance of gore was logged in seconds according to the DVD's time code.[7]

In short, these gore logs allowed for the documentation of what specific kind of gore was present, at what point in the film, and for how long it appears. After this process of quantification, we were able to arrive at the total number of seconds of gore present in each of the one hundred films (as well as separate figures for the amount of active and passive gore each film contains). This allowed us to calculate the average number of seconds of gore in the ten films selected in a given year, for the purposes of determining any variations in the average amount of gore over a ten-year period of American horror cinema.

ONE GORE, TWO GORE, RED GORE, BLUE GORE

By far the goriest horror film of 1998 to 2007 was *House of 1000 Corpses* (2003), directed by Rob Zombie. It contains 1,098.5 seconds of gore, or 18.3 minutes total. This amount was a full five minutes more than the film with the second-highest gore total, *Saw 3* (2006), which contains 780.5 seconds. Together, these two offer a snapshot of the survey results in brief: 2003, the year in which *House of 1000 Corpses* was released, stands as the goriest year on average in American horror cinema, with an average of 382.55 seconds of total gore per film. The year 2001 was the second-goriest year for American horror cinema in the last ten years, with an average of 297.85 seconds. Hence, there is indeed an overall rise in the level of gore in comparing 1998–2000 levels with those of 2001 and 2003, with the latter year demonstrating an approximate 44.9 percent increase over 1998.

There has been a marked decrease, however, in the amount of gore in 2004 to 2007 as compared with earlier in the decade (see appendix 1). Despite the steady popularity of the torture-porn subgenre as represented by the constant success of the *Saw* franchise, the average amount of gore actually began to decrease in 2004 and would not ever come close to the amount of gore seen in 2001, let alone 2003's record gore total. In fact, a steady decline from the 2003 total occurred over the next two years, as demonstrated by the chart below detailing the yearly average gore totals:

Year	Average Active Gore Per Film	Average Passive Gore Per Film	Average Total Gore Per Film
1998	44.45 seconds	166.5 seconds	210.95 seconds
1999	41.65 seconds	83.65 seconds	125.3 seconds
2000	66.65 seconds	126.8 seconds	193.45 seconds
2001	72.65 seconds	225.2 seconds	297.85 seconds
2002	43.8 seconds	136.9 seconds	180.7 seconds
2003	63.75 seconds	318.8 seconds	382.55 seconds
2004	37.25 seconds	198.8 seconds	236.05 seconds
2005	52.25 seconds	150.8 seconds	203.05 seconds
2006	60.95 seconds	215.3 seconds	276.25 seconds
2007	40.95 seconds	210.8 seconds	251.75 seconds

In 2004, the gore level fell by approximately 38.4 percent, and then additionally drops approximately 13 percent in 2005. From 2005 to 2006 there is an approximately 36 percent rise in the amount of gore. Despite this rise, however, the average amount of gore still remains well below 2003's level, which is still approximately 27.8 percent higher than the 2006 level of gore. The 2006 level is itself only approximately 23.7 percent higher than 1998 levels, but is also approximately 7.2 percent lower than the 2001 level.

Furthermore, there is an inverse relationship between gore levels and domestic box office performance between 1998 and 2004 (see appendix 2). As the average amount of gore in a given year increases, horror films earn less money on average at the box office than the year before. Conversely, as the average amount of gore decreases, box office averages rise. Year to year, this relationship is as follows:

Year Range	Gore Increase(+)/Decrease(-)	Box-Office Increase(+)/Decrease(-)
1998–1999	-40.6%	2.13
1999–2000	0.406	-31.6%
2000–2001	0.54	-21.8%
2001–2002	-39.3	0.315
2002–2003	1.116	-36%
2003–2004	-38.3%	0.33

Leaving aside for the moment questions of box office gross, which will be discussed shortly, an analysis of these changes in the level of gore is first in order. While post-2003 totals have not approached that year's average gore amount (or even that of 2001), the average amount of gore in films between 2004 and 2007 is still generally higher than that of 1998 to 2000. We use the word "generally" in order to stress that more recent horror films are not always gorier than older ones—1998 saw a slightly higher average gore total than 2005, for example (210.95 seconds in 1998, 203.05 seconds in 2005). On average, however, the period between 1998 and 2000 saw a combined average of 176.56 seconds of gore per year, while 2004 to 2007 saw a combined average of 241.77 seconds. The latter total is still significantly lower than that of 2001 to 2003, which saw a combined average of 287.03 seconds of gore per year.

On the whole, therefore, there has in fact been an increase in the average amount of gore when comparing pre-2001 levels to those of later years. What then accounts for this rise? Have characters such as Michael Meyers, Jason Voorhees, and their peers been mutilating an ever-larger number of teenagers than in years past? Have horror film audiences been subject to more decapitations, disembowelments, and dismemberments in recent years? Surprisingly, the answer is no. The overall rise in gore from pre-2001 levels is *not* attributable to an increase in the amount of active gore seen on-screen. Instead, it is passive gore that has increased since 2001, which means that audiences have been treated to more of the aftermath of violent acts than would have previously been shown on-screen. Active gore totals peaked between 2000 and 2001, as the former year saw an average 66.65 seconds of active gore, while the latter saw an average of 72.65 seconds. Subsequent years would never again equal 2001's active gore total, despite the phenomenal increase in total gore seen in 2003 with such films as *The Texas Chainsaw Massacre, Freddy Vs. Jason, House of the Dead, Wrong Turn* and *House of 1000 Corpses*.

This pattern correlates with the fact that passive gore totals were lowest between 1999 and 2000, with the former averaging 83.65 seconds of passive gore and the latter averaging 126.8 seconds. Passive gore levels would peak in 2003, with an average of 318.8 seconds, but in subsequent years the amount of passive gore would never again be as low as it was in 2000. Hence, despite the proliferation of the torture-porn subgenre, the resurgence of zombie films, and the return of such series as *The Texas Chainsaw Massacre* and *The Hills Have Eyes*, we find that the average number of active on-screen acts of gory violence has not increased since 2001. Instead, it is images of passive gore—imagery stemming from the consequence of acts of violence that have already occurred—that have generally increased in the last ten years of American horror films.

One example of this trend comes in comparing two films: *Bride of Chucky* (1998) and *The Devil's Rejects* (2005). In each film, a victim's body explodes into pieces when hit by a semitruck, the unfortunate result of standing in the middle of a highway. The amount of active gore in each instance of the truck hitting the victim is comparable, with both films depicting this action in a single second. In each case, the death is largely unforeseen by both victim and audience, with the brevity of the action presumably serving to increase its shocking effect. Where the two films differ, however, is in the amount of passive gore shown in each when depicting the aftermath of this death. *Bride of Chucky* contains only a two-second shot of the resultant blood on the truck's front grill, with the dismembered body parts not shown. *The Devil's Rejects* contains far more passive gore in its depiction of a similar scenario, spending a total of thirty-two seconds to show the various severed limbs, organs, and pools of blood that line the highway after the collision. While both *Bride of Chucky* and *The Devil's Rejects* use each death in order to scare audiences with its shocking suddenness, the latter film also apparently seeks to invoke a prolonged sense of disgust and repulsion in the viewer by way of its extended display of the victim's strewn body parts.

Such a comparison can also be made using different films from the same years, *I Still Know What You Did Last Summer* (1998) and *Saw II* (2005). Each of these films features a series of murders that occur throughout the film, with the victims' bloody corpses regularly displayed to the audience. The extent to which these corpses are shown, however, follows the same pattern concerning passive gore as seen when comparing *Bride of Chucky* and *The Devil's Rejects*. *I Still Know What You Did Last Summer* contains a total of 19.5 seconds in which such corpses are seen, while *Saw II* contains 102 seconds. The former typically features a one- or two-second shot of the dead body before cutting away to a new scene, while the latter typically features extended shots as long as eight seconds in which the dead body essentially becomes a part of the set (or a prop therein, at least) around which the other characters interact. As such, each of the two 1998 horror films use passive gore as a means of punctuating a given scene before moving on to a new one, while the 2005 films use passive gore as a compositional element of the scene, framing the scene's action around the gore itself. This pattern is therefore a major contributor to the increase in passive gore since 2001, which explains the overall rise in the average amount of total gore when comparing pre-2001 films with their successors.

GORE VERSUS BOX OFFICE

With these patterns of gore established, questions of their connection to box office performance become vital. Do extremely gory horror films make more money or less money than less gory ones? Is there necessarily a relationship between the amount of gore and a film's box office gross? The top twenty-five highest-grossing

American horror films between 1998 and 2007 are: 1. *The Sixth Sense* (672.8 million worldwide); 2. *Signs* (408.24); 3. *Hannibal* (351.6); 4. *What Lies Beneath* (291.35); 5. *The Village* (256.69); 6. *The Ring* (249.3); 7. *The Blair Witch Project* (248.6); 8. *Sleepy Hollow* (248.6); 9. *The Others* (208.94); 10. *Hollow Man* (190.2); 11. *The Grudge* (187.27); 12. *The Haunting* (177); 13. *Saw 3* (164.86); 14. *Scream 3* (161.79); 15. *The Ring 2* (161.43); 16. *Saw 2* (147.7); 17. *1408* (130.79); 18. *The Omen* (119.49); 19. *Freddy Vs. Jason* (114.88); 20. *Final Destination 3* (113.17); 21. *The Amityville Horror* (108.03); 22. *The Texas Chainsaw Massacre* (107.07); 23. *Saw* (103.09); 24. *Resident Evil* (102.4); 25. *Dawn of the Dead* (102.33).

Four of the top-ten films in this list have gore totals of thirty-seven seconds or less (*The Blair Witch Project*, 37 seconds; *The Others*, 0; *The Sixth Sense*, 35.5; *Signs*, 8—the latter two films having the first- and second-highest box office totals in the above list). Together these four films have an average of 20.1 seconds of gore. Furthermore, nine of the top twenty-five films have gore totals of 62 seconds or less (*The Blair Witch Project*; *The Others*; *The Sixth Sense*; *Signs*; *The Ring*, 62 seconds; *1408*, 62; *The Grudge*, 59; *Final Destination 3*, 52; *The Ring 2*, 25.5). Together these nine films have an average of 37.9 seconds of gore. We might assume from these numbers that horror films tend to make the most money when they contain approximately a minute of gore or less. However, also included in this list of the twenty-five highest-grossing horror films are eight of the twenty-five goriest films: *Saw 3*, 780.5 seconds; *Dawn of the Dead*, 676; *Saw*, 591; *The Texas Chainsaw Massacre*, 579.5; *Freddy Vs. Jason*, 572; *Hollow Man*, 559; *Resident Evil*, 476.5; *Hannibal*, 405. Together these films earned an average of $154.55 million worldwide. Yet this amount is easily eclipsed by that earned by the aforementioned nine films, which together earned an average of $260.49 million worldwide.

Not only do less-gory horror films actually make more money than gory ones, it is the *least*-gory horror films that are often the most successful. This pattern is frequently seen on a year-by-year basis when examining box office performance. In 1999, *The Sixth Sense* and *The Blair Witch Project* have the two lowest gore totals of the year but have the two highest box office totals. In 2001, *The Others* has the lowest gore total (i.e., no gore at all), but is the second-highest grosser of the year. In 2002, *Signs* and *The Ring* have the two lowest gore totals but have the two highest box office totals. In 2003, *House of 1000 Corpses* and *House of the Dead* have the first- and second-highest gore totals, respectively, but are the third- and second-lowest grossing American horror films of the year among those studied. 2005 saw *The Ring 2* with the year's second-lowest gore total but the second-highest box office gross. In 2006, *When a Stranger Calls*, *Final Destination 3*, and *The Omen* have the first-, third-, and fourth-lowest gore totals, respectively, but are the fourth-, third-, and second-highest grossing films of the year. The second-lowest gore total for 2007 belonged to *1408*, but the film is the highest-grossing horror film of the year. Aspiring horror producers would therefore do well to note that there is often more money to be made in horror films that contain relatively low amounts of gore. While "hardcore" horror fans devoted to the genre and its numerous franchises and subgenres may revel in seeing the graphically rendered mutilation of pounds of flesh on screen, there are in fact larger sections of mainstream cinema-going audiences ("softcore" horror fans?) that also like the occasional scary movie, so long as there isn't too much gore shown for too long.

GORE AND SUBGENRE

If certain types of horror films are more successful than others, this leads us to the inevitable question as to which specific subgenres are more successful, and how gory each of these subgenres is compared to others. Are zombie films gorier than those in which deranged hillbillies slaughter unsuspecting travelers? Do slasher films generally make more money than ghost films, and is one type of film gorier than the other?

It must be stated up front that there is a significant market among American audiences for most horror films. In fact, it is extremely rare for a horror film to lose money. Of the one hundred films examined in this study, budget information proved available for ninety-five. Seventy-one of these ninety-five films, or 74.7 percent, made a profit from their domestic box office earnings. An additional twelve films were ultimately profitable when factoring in their international box office earnings. Hence eighty-three of ninety-five films, or 87.3 percent, made a profit from their theatrical release. Furthermore, two of the remaining twelve films that failed to make a profit at the box office came within two million dollars short of their budget, and can therefore be reasonably assured of ultimately making a profit once their post-theatrical sales and rentals (DVD, cable, and network television, and the like) are factored in. Horror films are therefore an extremely reliable genre for investors, another factor in their enduring theatrical presence.

Horror film audiences also appear to be relatively loyal consumers, given that many subgenres earn a remarkably similar average amount at the box office. For example, zombie films such as *Resident Evil* (2002), *House of the Dead* (2003), *Dawn of the Dead* (2004), and *Land of the Dead* (2005) earned an average of $32.51 million in North America. This total is nearly identical with the $32.52 million domestic average earned by what we term the "Killer/Mutant Hillbilly" subgenre, represented by such films as *Wrong Turn* (2003), *The Texas Chainsaw Massacre* (2003), *The Hills Have Eyes* (2006), and their sequels in which a psychotic (and often inbred) individual or family murders passersby in a rural or remote setting. The two subgenres also share a comparable amount of gore, with the hillbilly films averaging 544.2

seconds of gore to the zombie films' 549.5 seconds. The fact that their box office performance and gore totals are nearly identical would indicate that the audiences for both of these subgenres are perhaps one and the same, with certain filmgoers habitually frequenting each of the two types of horror films.

In addition to these two subgenres, three others also earn between thirty and thirty-five million dollars on average in their North American theatrical release. Films that featured some form of extra-sensory perception (ESP) such as *The Gift* (2000) and the *Final Destination* series averaged $30.2 million at the box office. Slasher films—including *I Still Know What You Did Last Summer* (1998), *Scream 3* (2000), *Halloween Resurrection* (2002), *Cry Wolf* (2005) and *Black Christmas* (2006)—earned an average of $33.32 million. Religious-themed horror films, such as *Stigmata* (1999), *Exorcist: The Beginning* (2004), and *The Omen* (2006), earned an average of $35.51 million. While the fact that all five of these subgenres had earning averages within approximately $5 million of one another may suggest that there is a large degree of overlap for audiences of each of these various kinds of horror films, it is perhaps more accurate to hypothesize that there is a stable but not extraordinary market for each of these varieties of horror film. While many individual films may even debut in the number-one position in their first weekend of release, few within these five subgenres ever attained blockbuster status, nor were they financial failures.

Those that do in fact regularly attain this blockbuster status, often earning more than $100 million domestically, are period horror films. Including such films as *Sleepy Hollow* (1999), *From Hell* (2001), and *The Village* (2004), period horror was on average the most profitable subgenre with an $82.26 million average among North American audiences. All were major studio Hollywood films with well-known directors or actors (Tim Burton, Johnny Depp, M. Night Shyamalan). Combined with the fact that these films had only the eighth-highest gore total, the popularity of the period horror subgenre indicates a desire for horror films among the general public, so long as they feature recognizable talent and are not overly gory.

Decidedly gorier is the torture-porn film, a relatively new subgenre (using this pseudo-pornographic moniker, at least). Despite the popularity of the *Saw* franchise, torture-porn films were only the fifth-highest domestic grossing subgenre (with a $57.46 million average), due largely to the poor performance of *Hostel Part Two* (2007). Hence, despite its seeming prevalence, the popularity of torture-porn is ultimately eclipsed by such long-standing subgenres as the ghost film, haunted house film, and period horror. This may indicate that torture-porn is only a current fad, a cycle in horror films similar to the postmodern teen slasher films of the late 1990s; that is, *Scream* (1996) and its sequels and imitations. Given the cyclical nature of genre and subgenre popularity, it is perhaps inevitable that torture-porn films will soon become less frequent. Furthermore, given the fact that horror films have regularly utilized ghosts, haunted houses, and period settings since the early decades of cinema, it is certain that these subgenres will continue to enjoy long-term popularity in the years ahead, despite any cyclical downturns that may emerge.

Another such current cycle is that of the Asian horror remake, which includes *The Ring* (2002), *The Grudge* (2004), and their sequels, and *Dark Water* (2005). The subgenre ranks second in domestic box office performance with an average of approximately $76 million, and also has the lowest average gore total. The relative absence of extensive gore in these films can be seen as a major contributing factor to their enormous popularity among mass audiences, many members of which prefer to see horror films that largely scare them through the threat/suggestion of violence rather than through more explicit means. All of these remakes feature ghosts or a supernatural presence as their means of inspiring fear in audiences, further testament to the enduring popularity of such tropes in the horror genre.

This is not to say, however, that all horror films with minimal amounts of gore will be financially successful. The subgenre with the second-lowest average gore total was that of the "Creature-Feature": films featuring killer animals, insects, reptiles, and the like, some of which may be mutated or enlarged. The subgenre gained prominence in the 1950s with the release of such films as *Them!* (1954), *Tarantula* (1955), *The Killer Shrews* (1959), and *The Giant Gila Monster* (1959), among others. Despite this legacy, creature-features were the lowest-grossing subgenre of the last ten years, with such films as *Bats* (1999), *Lake Placid* (1999), *Willard* (2003), and *Anacondas: Hunt for the Blood Orchid* (2004) earning an average of $22.3 million in the North American market. Typically lacking a supernatural context, creature-features may be too grounded in reality for modern audiences used to seeing the likes of *When Animals Attack* on television. Certainly the enduring popularity of such characters as Freddy Kruger, Jason Voorhees, Michael Meyers, and Leatherface signals that audiences love to root for/against a villain that is, or was, previously human. As such, it would seem that some horror subgenres are not as financially successful as others. Perhaps it is better stated, however, given the cyclical nature of the horror genre as a whole, that there are some subgenres that are still waiting to be reinvented for modern audiences.

CONCLUSION: ALL'S FAIR IN BLOOD AND GORE

When considering the phenomenon of gore in horror films, we must remember that this is not the only genre or medium in which gore is prevalent. Action and crime films among others regularly portray murder and death, as do television programs in such genres. Any discussion of gore must, therefore, ultimately consider its role within popular culture as a whole. Is a corpse shown in a television police drama less gruesome than one shown in a horror film? Is one less morally objectionable than the other?

Television viewers might be surprised to learn that they are often exposed to more gore overall in a single program than in many horror films. A 2007 episode of *CSI* ("A La Cart") in which the discovery of a severed head is investigated contains 139.5 seconds of gore, including a decapitation, numerous shots of the bloody head and torso, as well as skull breach during both an autopsy and a stabbing. The episode actually has a higher amount of gore than forty-four of the one hundred horror films in this study, including *The Ring, The Grudge,* and their sequels; *The Amityville Horror; Bride of Chucky; Halloween Resurrection; I Still Know What You Did Last Summer; The Omen;* and all three *Final Destination* films. If the episode's length and gore total are doubled so as to approximate the running time of a feature film, it becomes gorier than sixty-seven of the one hundred films, including *Saw 2, Wrong Turn, House on Haunted Hill, Ghost Ship, Seed of Chucky, Jeepers Creepers, Stigmata,* and *Halloween H20*—as well as placing it in a tie with the zombie film *Land of the Dead.*

Furthermore, the film *300* (2007), depicting the Battle of Thermopylae in 480 B.C., contains 498 seconds of gore, a total that is surpassed by only fourteen horror films in this study. This total includes a full 270 seconds of active gore, an amount that is itself higher than that of all one hundred horror films (narrowly beating *Freddy Vs. Jason* by one second). This active gore total is accounted for by way of *300*'s multiple sequences featuring stabbings, sword and spear wounds, and their resultant blood splatter. The fact that it is largely Spartan soldiers committing this violence rather than a mutant, monster, or murderer perhaps lessens the impact of this gore upon audiences, causing them to believe that the film is not as gory as most horror films.

By far the goriest American film of the last ten years, however, is one that was not included in our sample of one hundred films. In fact, the film has no connection to the horror genre either in whole or in part: Mel Gibson's *The Passion of the Christ* (2004). A depiction of Jesus Christ's death, the film contains numerous extended sequences of whippings, beatings, and crucifixion, among other acts of violence. Christ appears covered in blood for the film's majority, and there are frequent shots of blood splatter and stains. The film contains 134.5 seconds of active gore, a total that is surpassed by only six of the one hundred horror films. It is in the area of passive gore where Gibson's film exceeds all others in this study, with a total of 1,612.5 seconds. Combined, *The Passion of the Christ* contains 1,747 seconds of gore, or approximately 29.1 minutes. To contextualize this number, recall that this study's goriest horror film, *House of 1000 Corpses,* contains 1,098.5 seconds, or a full 10.8 minutes less gore. The second-goriest horror film, *Saw 3,* contains 16.1 minutes less gore than Gibson's film.

Given such quantities, gore must be understood as a relative concept when examining its prevalence. The question of context becomes paramount: when used to inspire fear or disgust in a horror film, images of gore often inspire different reactions than when equivalently gory images are used for alternative purposes in different genres. If gore is, therefore, not limited to horror films alone, it must be understood that the process of desensitization and habituation to gore is a larger cultural process that is subject to a number of factors and influences outside of simple horror film spectatorship alone.

Finally, as we have previously suggested, while this study has measured changes in the quantity of gore in American horror cinema over time, the issue of quality must also be considered. Just as genres change and evolve over time, so too do film technologies. While many recent horror films may appear more violent to the casual viewer despite the fact that gore levels peaked in 2003, those instances of gore that audiences are exposed to might appear more realistic because of advancements in special-effects technology. As these effects improve, the mutilation of the human body appears increasingly more real looking to many viewers, which may increase their emotional or physiological reaction to such gory imagery (factors around which future qualitative studies of audience reactions to gore might be based). This heightened reaction may cause viewers to assume that recent horror films are indeed far gorier than those of years past, despite the fact that the average amount of screen time devoted to gore is not necessarily higher. Such "realism" is of course extremely relative, given the perpetual evolution in special-effects technologies. Gory images that currently seem real to viewers will inevitably lose their impact over time as the process of desensitization continues. Further study is therefore recommended not only to track further changes in the quantity of gore in horror films, but to examine those changes that occur in the quality of gore as well.

APPENDIX 1: AVERAGE GORE TOTALS

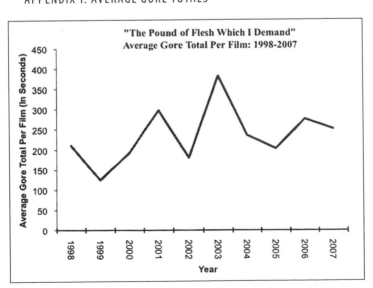

APPENDIX 2: BOX OFFICE PERFORMANCE

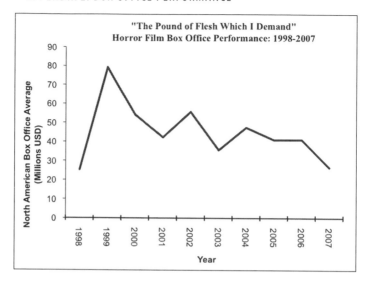

APPENDIX 3: LIST OF ONE HUNDRED RANDOMLY
SELECTED AMERICAN HORROR FILMS, 1998–2007

1998
1. *Bride of Chucky*
2. *The Faculty*
3. *Halloween: H20*
4. *I Still Know What You Did Last Summer*
5. *John Carpenter's Vampires*
6. *The Last Broadcast*
7. *The Night Flier*
8. *Phantoms*
9. *Psycho*
10. *Urban Legends*

1999
1. *Bats*
2. *The Blair Witch Project*
3. *The Haunting*
4. *House on Haunted Hill*
5. *In Dreams*
6. *Lake Placid*
7. *The Sixth Sense*
8. *Sleepy Hollow*
9. *Stigmata*
10. *Stir of Echoes*

2000

1. *Book of Shadows: Blair Witch 2*
2. *The Cell*
3. *Dracula 2000*
4. *Final Destination*
5. *The Gift*
6. *Hollow Man*
7. *Lost Souls*
8. *Scream 3*
9. *Urban Legends: Final Cut*
10. *What Lies Beneath*

2001

1. *13 Ghosts*
2. *Bones*
3. *The Forsaken*
4. *From Hell*
5. *Hannibal*
6. *Jason X*
7. *Jeepers Creepers*
8. *The Others*
9. *Soul Survivors*
10. *Valentine*

2002

1. *Cabin Fever*
2. *Darkness*
3. *FearDotCom*
4. *Frailty*
5. *Ghost Ship*
6. *Halloween: Resurrection*
7. *Queen of the Damned*
8. *Resident Evil*
9. *The Ring*
10. *Signs*

2003

1. *Darkness Falls*
2. *Dreamcatcher*
3. *Final Destination 2*
4. *Freddy Vs. Jason*
5. *House of 1000 Corpses*
6. *House of the Dead*
7. *The Texas Chainsaw Massacre*
8. *Willard*
9. *Wrong Turn*
10. *Jeepers Creepers 2*

2004

1. *Anacondas: The Hunt for the Blood Orchid*
2. *Dawn of the Dead*
3. *Exorcist: The Beginning*
4. *Godsend*
5. *Malevolence*
6. *The Grudge*
7. *Open Water*
8. *Saw*
9. *Seed of Chucky*
10. *The Village*

2005

1. *The Amityville Horror*
2. *Cry Wolf*
3. *Dark Water*
4. *The Devil's Rejects*
5. *The Fog*
6. *Hostel*
7. *House of Wax*
8. *Land of the Dead*
9. *The Ring 2*
10. *Saw 2*

2006

1. *Black Christmas*
2. *Final Destination 3*
3. *The Grudge 2*
4. *The Hills Have Eyes*
5. *The Omen*
6. *Saw 3*
7. *See No Evil*
8. *Stay Alive*
9. *Texas Chainsaw Massacre: The Beginning*
10. *When a Stranger Calls*

2007

1. *1408*
2. *Blood and Chocolate*
3. *Bug*
4. *Dead Silence*
5. *Halloween*
6. *The Hills Have Eyes 2*
7. *The Hitcher*
8. *Hostel Part Two*
9. *The Messengers*
10. *Vacancy*

APPENDIX 4: TOP 25 GORIEST FILMS, 1998–2007

1. *House of 1000 Corpses*, 1098.5 seconds total gore
2. *Saw 3*, 780.5
3. *House of the Dead*, 766.5
4. *Dawn of the Dead*, 676
5. *John Carpenter's Vampires*, 641.5
6. *Thirteen Ghosts*, 627.5
7. *The Hills Have Eyes 2*, 613
8. *Saw*, 591
9. *The Night Flier*, 589
10. *The Texas Chainsaw Massacre: The Beginning*, 583.5
11. *The Texas Chainsaw Massacre*, 579.5
12. *Freddy Vs. Jason*, 572
13. *Hollow Man*, 559
14. *Hostel*, 554.5
15. *Jason X*, 515.5
16. *Resident Evil*, 476.5
17. *The Hills Have Eyes*, 434
18. *Fear Dot Com*, 429.5
19. *Bones*, 408
20. *Hannibal*, 405
21. *The Forsaken*, 358.5
22. *Halloween*, 344.5
23. *Hostel Part Two*, 335.5
24. *Cabin Fever*, 333.5
25. *The Devil's Rejects*, 326

APPENDIX 5: TOP 25 LEAST GORY FILMS, 1998–2007

1. *The Others*, 0 seconds of total gore
2. *When a Stranger Calls*, 4.5
3. *Signs*, 8
4. *Dark Water*, 16
5. *The Grudge 2*, 19.5
6. *Anacondas: Hunt for the Blood Orchid*, 21
7. *The Ring 2*
8. *Godsend*, 30.5
9. *The Sixth Sense*, 35.5
10. *The Blair Witch Project*, 37
11. *Lake Placid*, 42.5
12. *Lost Souls*, 44
13. *Vacancy*, 47.5
14. *Frailty*, 51
15. *Final Destination 3*, 52

NOTES

1. Such conclusions are based on the authors' combined experiences both teaching and learning in university film studies courses in which the horror genre is studied. Students typically recount such conclusions when asked to consider the differences in gore among horror films of various eras. One such example of how horror films of previous decades become viewed as less scary is in how their characters become marketed toward children. Just as Dracula and Frankenstein have by now became cartoon caricatures (such as with Count Chocula and Frankenberry cereals, to name just one example) so too have more recent characters become targeted toward younger audiences. A newspaper article featuring a Halloween costume guide for parents wanting to make their children's outfits includes a section on "How to be a Freddy Krueger." It includes such tips as "Attach plastic knives, or other mock 'tools of torture' to your fingers" (Hyslop).

2. A qualitative approach to gore might also consider Mary Douglas's *Purity and Danger: An Analysis of Concept of Pollution and Taboo* (New York: Routledge, 2002), in which the author discusses notions of fear and disgust in response to impurity and uncleanness. Philip Brophy's essay "Horrorality: The Textuality of Contemporary Horror Films" (*The Horror Reader*, ed. Ken Gelder [New York: Routledge, 2000]) would also prove useful given his focus on the role of the body in horror cinema.

3. "The method of content analysis is based on counting the frequency of certain visual elements in a clearly defined sample of images, and then analysing [sic] those frequencies ... Ensuring that the images you use are representative does not necessarily entail examining every single relevant image, however" (Rose, 61–62).

4. Many DVDs used in this study were labeled as being "extended" or "un-rated," thereby including scenes of gore not featured in the film's theatrical release. These new versions are becoming increasingly typical of how horror films are released and marketed on DVD. Since it was not possible to view celluloid prints of all one hundred films while doing this study (for reasons of both financial cost and the necessity of frequent pausing and rewinding while documenting patterns of gore), such un-rated editions were the only way to screen copies of these films. While using such data taken from films that are slightly different from their theatrical versions in order to correlate it with their theatrical box office performance becomes somewhat problematic, we see the value of the patterns obtained from such a comparison as outweighing this minor methodological inconsistency—particularly since the alternative would mean having to forego such a study altogether.

5. See http://www.randomizer.org/.

6. The logs also allowed for the option of write-in categories for documenting the occurrence of particular types of gore not accounted for in existing categories. Some write-in categories include the presence of a dead body covered in some amount of blood, stitching up a bloody wound, being crushed to death (with bloody results), blood drawn by leeches, spitting or vomiting blood, crying blood, extreme/unnatural stretching of skin, tooth removal, and scalping, among others.

7. Half-seconds were also permitted if a particular shot/instance of gore ended between two full seconds on the DVD's time code.

WORKS CITED

"A La Cart." *CSI*, Season 8, Episode 2, October 4, 2007.

Cavallaro, Dani. *The Gothic Vision*. New York: Continuum, 2002.

Crane, Jonathan. "Scraping Bottom: Splatter and the Herschel Gordon Lewis Oeuvre."

Dillard, R. H. W. "The Pageantry of Death." *Focus on the Horror Film*. Eds. Roy Huss and T. J. Ross. Englewood Cliffs, N.J.: Prentice-Hall, 1972.

Ebert, Roger. *Roger Ebert's Movie Home Companion*. Kansas City: Andrews, McMeel & Parker, 1985.

"Review: The Texas Chainsaw Massacre." October 17, 2003. http://rogerebert.suntimes.com/apps/pbcs.dll/article?AID=/20031017/REVIEWS/310170308/1023.

Goodale, Gloria. "Blood and Gore Find a New Venue: Movie Posters." *Christian Science Monitor*, April 13, 2007. http://www.csmonitor.com/ 2007/0413/p11s04-almo.html.

Hutchings, Peter. *The Horror Film*. Harlow: Pearson, 2004.

Hyslop, Lucy. "Ghoulish Fun With Spooky Makeup and Fake Blood." *Vancouver Sun*, October 10, 2007, B3.

Monk, Katherine. "Top 10 Horror-Film Classics." *Vancouver Sun*, October 16, 2007, H5.

Powell, Anna. *Deleuze and Horror*. Edinburgh: Edinburgh University Press, 2005.

Prince, Stephen. *The Horror Film*. New Brunswick, N.J.: Rutgers University Press, 2004.

Richmond, Ray, and Antonia Coffman, eds. *The Simpsons: A Complete Guide to Our Favorite Family*. New York: HarperCollins, 1997.

Rose, Gillian. *Visual Methodologies: An Introduction to the Interpretation of Visual Materials*. 2nd ed. London: Sage, 2007.

Staiger, Janet. "Hybrid or Inbred: The Purity Hypothesis and Hollywood Genre History." *Film Genre Reader III*. Ed. Barry Keith Grant. Austin: University of Texas Press, 2003.

Tamborini, Ron, and James B. Weaver III. "Frightening Entertainment: A Historical Perspective of Fictional Horror." *Horror Films: Current Research on Audience Preferences and Reactions*. Mahwah, N.J.: Lawrence Erlbaum Associates, 1996.

Zillman, Dolf, and Rhonda Gibson. "Evolution of the Horror Genre." *Horror Films: Current Research on Audience Preferences and Reactions*. Eds. James B. Weaver III and Ron Tamborini. Mahwah, N.J.: Lawrence Erlbaum Associates, 1996.

A (POST)MODERN HOUSE OF PAIN

FearDotCom and the Prehistory of the Post-9/11 Torture Film

—Reynold Humphries

The title of *FearDotCom* refers to a Web site that allows subscribers to access a world where they can watch acts of torture being carried out on helpless victims. Is it make-believe or genuine snuff? Subscribers are challenged by the site's hostess, a sultry blonde, to play a game. The challenge consists of answering questions so as to reveal their most intimate fears. In every case subscribers die forty-eight hours later, victims of precisely that which they feared the most: being drowned, or killed in a car accident, or, in a memorable sequence, being submerged by a tide of cockroaches. The only way those investigating the deaths can put an end to them is to enter the site themselves, which exposes them to the same fate as the victims whose deaths they are trying to elucidate.

I have found it most instructive to visit the IMDb Web site to read and study reactions to the film, directed by William Malone from a script by Josephine Coyle in 2002. One anonymous user of the site suggested that the film be re-titled *Stupid-DotCom*. He or she went on: "The idea of a virus invading the mind threw [*sic*] an optic nerve, and attacking the electromagnetic impulses in the mind is scary, and I hope will never become a reality." Fear is soon dissipated, however, and the spectator accuses the movie of becoming "too unbelievable." One could argue that the film, as summarized by this anonymous viewer-turned-critic, is already "unbelievable." The use of the formula "too unbelievable" indicates that the spectator is willing to suspend disbelief as long as the film manages to engage his or her attention as a work of science fiction or a horror film turning on the supernatural. However, the way *FearDotCom* evolves leads the spectator to lose patience and to refuse to go along with what happens next.

I consider these comments worth quoting as they participate in a general refusal to engage with *FearDotCom*. In order to grasp what specific forms this rejection takes we need to consider other comments on the film. They are almost unanimously negative and damning. For Louis B. Hobson the film has "the feel of a sick music video." He calls it "a grim, ugly exercise," adding: "Logging on to feardot-com won't give you the nightmares you seek, but it might just put you to sleep out of boredom" (Jam!Movies). Michael Rechtshaffen of the *Hollywood Reporter* writes: "Managing to be nonsensical, shamelessly derivative, leeringly exploitative and fundamentally boring all at the same time, *FearDotCom* is the latest in a wave of gro-tesquely inept horror pictures that are giving the genre a horrific name." No other "grotesquely inept horror pictures" are mentioned. Mark Kermode of the *Guardian* accuses the film of cribbing ideas from great horror movies of the last twenty years, such as David Cronenberg's *Videodrome*. Max Messier, writing on the site www. Filmcritic.com, tells his readers that it is a film to "avoid at all costs." Bill Gordon of *Horror Fan Zine* dismisses the film and recommends *Videodrome* and *Se7en* instead. Other films championed by critics the better to excoriate *FearDotCom* are *Polter-geist*, *8mm*, and *The Ring* (the original Japanese film; the Gore Verbinsky remake had not yet appeared). The name of Cronenberg in particular is used repeatedly as a stick with which to beat the wretched Malone.[1]

The vocabulary some reviewers use to denounce *FearDotCom* is all the more interesting for being strongly loaded. Mick LaSalle of the *San Francisco Chronicle* describes as "unpleasant" the way the Doctor—the character in the film who owns and operates the notorious Web site—whispers into one of his victims' ear as he tortures her. Ann Hornaday of the *Washington Post* calls the film "depraved" and accuses Malone of seeming "as titillated as his villain by the sadistic perversions he orchestrates on-screen." The two epithets used by Rechtshaffen are revealing as well: "shamelessly derivative" and "leeringly exploitative." I assume the second for-mula is an accusation that writer and director are pandering to spectatorial voyeur-ism (which is thus taken for granted), whereas "derivative" means that Malone and his scriptwriter have ripped off other horror movies. However, Karina Montgomery considers the Doctor "genuinely scary," arguing that the tortures carried out by him are "more disturbing than any moment in *The Silence of the Lambs*." Now we're get-ting somewhere.

"Unpleasant" and "disturbing" are certainly not synonyms, but I wonder if LaSalle and Montgomery are not saying the same thing, while appearing to react in radically different ways. "Unpleasant" would then designate and incriminate an aspect of the film that the subject prefers to keep at a "safe" distance; that is, to repress. In other words, having recourse to the word "unpleasant" is presented as a criticism of the film, whereas, in reality, it is the critic's own subjectivity that is revealed to be at stake. As in all cases of repression, the object evoking the repression is at the origin of unconscious libidinal stirrings that the subject cannot accept. In the case of the film and its critic, the film is denounced for addressing or stimulat-ing an unconscious desire that the critic would have preferred to remain hidden: a socially forbidden desire has come too close to the surface. Just as the subject wakes from a nightmare in a cold sweat when such a desire is about to obtain realization in the dream, so one critic calls "unpleasant" what another is sufficiently alert to call "disturbing."

Most of all, however, critics are nonplussed by the film's seemingly supernatural element. Subscribers to the fictional feardotcom site are taken over by a force—or a *virus*, as can happen to any computer if not protected—which sends them to their various grisly deaths. The supernatural dimension can be interpreted as a forlorn attempt by writer and director to explain away, as if by magic, something they have not been able to work out or think through themselves within the technological framework the film adapts through its use of the computer. If this is the case, then the film's detractors are right to be so dismissive. However, this supernatural element can also be considered as a metaphor, not for a computer virus, but for the computer *as virus*, a sort of drug that ends up dominating the user until he or she can no longer properly distinguish between the real and the virtual. It is as if the computer were alive, a sort of modern monster sucking in the user, as the television does Max Renn, the protagonist of Cronenberg's *Videodrome*. The unsettling dimension of this confusion—what the user thought was virtual turns out to be real—can trigger feelings of displeasure which are, precisely, disturbing or can be attributed to the existence of the supernatural. What then takes place is an imaginary projection onto a bizarre world outside of the spectator/critic, which prevents the subject from recognizing his or her unconscious role in these feelings.

This perplexity on the part of critics, most commonly expressed through hostility at best and violent rejection at worst, does demand that we reflect a little. Critics are certainly justified in taking the film at its face value as a comment on, or tirade against, the omnipotent computer as fetish, replacing all other means of communication. However, this can prompt another question: are we forced to take this, or any other film, at its face value? It is not a question of transforming any element X into another element Y, which then conveniently becomes a symbol of some latent notion that the critic teases out of the text. Rather, it is a matter of asking why a writer and a director should go to such trouble and resort to horror, with or without a supernatural dimension, to tackle the theme of the computer. Clearly the notion of "virus" lends itself perfectly—but perhaps too easily—to an approach that must perforce turn its back on realism in favor of fantasy, the supernatural, and horror, and especially in favor of scenes of a particularly nasty and grisly nature.

My contention will be that another interpretation is also possible, one that is intimately linked to the theme of torturer and victim, to the place imposed on the spectator in both senses of the word: the real person who goes to see a movie called *FearDotCom*, and the fictitious person belonging to the film's diegetic world who subscribes to the feardotcom site and hence becomes a willing spectator of someone else's agony and death. It is not a question of replacing one interpretation with another or of placing interpretations side by side and inviting readers to take their pick, but of suggesting that the computer is standing in for something else and that the game that gives the film its title has impliciations going far beyond the simple matter of fear. Before tackling these issues, however, we need to outline the filmic intertext that *FearDotCom* creates.

For those conversant in the genre of horror film and its history, the reference to torture and snuff movies most readily evokes both Cronenberg's *Videodrome* and Joel Schumacher's *8mm*. However, I quite fail to see why critics would denounce a film for including within its narrative and *mise-en-scène* references to other movies; it all depends surely on the use made of this intertextual space. At the same time I can only express astonishment over the absence of critical comment on certain films referred to by the makers of *FearDotCom* in quite explicit ways. The first victim, for example, is called Polidori (Udo Kier) and a graffiti on a wall, which we see just before he dies, reads "Dr. Gogol." Readers will remember that John Polidori was part of that select literary gathering that resulted in Mary Shelley creating the character destined to become the most famous "mad scientist" in classic horror cinema: Victor Frankenstein. Besides the nod to the Russian writer of the absurd and macabre who goes by the same name, Gogol is the name of the mad surgeon in Karl Freund's *Mad Love* (1935). We shall see that these references go beyond simple cinephilia; in no way are they merely "derivative." The intertextual dimension also applies to the young woman who is drowned and who is presumably based on one of the victims in that celebrated *giallo*, Mario Bava's *Sei Donne per l'Assassino* (aka *Blood and Black Lace*, 1964).[2] More complex is the figure of a little girl with a ball who haunts the Doctor (Stephen Rea) in *FearDotCom*. While demonic children are a staple of horror films in general, nobody seems to have bothered to ponder specifically over the little girl's ball, perhaps because critics had given up in despair or exasperation over seemingly more important issues, like, for example, the use of the supernatural. Nonetheless, two references come to mind: the little girl in Fritz Lang's *M* (1931), whose bouncing ball becomes the metonymy for her murder off-screen; and the ghost of the little girl haunting an entire village in another Bava thriller, *Operazione Paura* (1966). In this latter film, anyone whom the little girl pursues and fixes with her unblinking gaze is killed or commits suicide later; it is a ghost story, not a *giallo* or a serial-killer movie. The parallel is striking, too striking to be a simple coincidence. But what about Lang's film, in which the little girl is not a demonic presence but, quite on the contrary, the victim of a serial killer? We must remember that the little girl in the Bava was a victim first, prior to returning as a ghost to exact her revenge. In both cases, then, the bouncing ball becomes, as it were, the signifier of a situation in which a victim becomes the executioner. The reverse symmetry brings us back to *FearDotCom*: at the end of the film, it is the Doctor/executioner who becomes the victim.

My argument will be that none of this is mere chance; that both the choice of intertextual references and the torturer/victim dialectic are overdetermined and find their source and their explanation in a number of extra-textual factors inscribed into the film's narrative in the form of metonyms or metaphors. In other words, consciously or not, *FearDotCom* evokes films whose characters and situations bear a striking resemblance to its own and, furthermore, their significance can be brought to light only by grasping the social and economic situations in which the films were made. If we claim, following the intertextual clues, that the Doctor is a throwback to the mad doctors and scientists of the 1930s, what are we, in fact, saying? Is he perhaps the heir to their experiments, some of which were well intentioned (Frankenstein, Jekyll), while others were not (e.g., Dr. Mirakle in *Murders in the Rue Morgue* [1931], Dr. Moreau in *Island of Lost Souls* [1932] and Dr. Vollin in *The Raven* [1935])?

All three examples I have just mentioned confirm this impression of nefarious intent. Moreau carrying out his experiments in vivisection on live animals in his "House of Pain" and Vollin's Poe-inspired torture chamber are early precursors of the Doctor's torture chamber in *FearDotCom*. The remarkable opening sequence of *Mad Love* shows Gogol achieving an orgasm while watching a young woman being tortured in a theater inspired by the Grand Guignol.[3] *Mad Love* presents torture as a *spectacle*, not as a reality, but Gogol becomes increasingly deranged to the point of adopting the position of a real-life torturer in order to obtain the woman who obsesses him. This has obvious ties with *FearDotCom*, which highlights the notion of the virtual image in a context where what is *shown* turns out to be only too hideously *real*.[4]

As already stated, when *FearDotCom* was released critics drew attention to a variety of films they claim the film ripped off or reworked distinctly less well. Of these the most obvious is Hideo Nakata's *The Ring*, the only difference being the computer game replacing the haunted tape. To the same end, *One Missed Call* (Takashi Miike, 2003) exploits that omnipresent technological and cultural artifact, the cellphone. It seems to me, however, that the modern Japanese horror film accepts the supernatural as part of its narrative and thematic logic. It is possible, then, to accuse *FearDotCom* of having its cake and eating it, too: the film's makers are unable to decide whether the supernatural is to be taken literally or not. However, I am less interested in bringing grist to the mill of those who subscribe to this thesis than in showing what I believe *FearDotCom* actually does, thanks to (or despite) its ambiguities.

Let us return to the notion of the computer as virus. The site accessed is presented to the user of the computer, and to us, the film's spectators, as a game. As the subscriber to the site gets more and more caught up in the game, he or she loses all sense of time. Such is the fascination with the sordid violence on the screen: is it real or merely simulated?[25] Then, insidiously, the game takes over until the subscriber can no longer tell the difference between reality and virtuality, between his or her status as game player and the effect of identifying with the events and images on the computer screen. It is at this point that the supposedly supernatural dimension comes into play: one player in the film becomes so totally absorbed by the site that she forgets the world around her, only to find that this world has been modified to the point where her fears become reality and annihilate her. Instead of temporarily losing contact with the real world, while indulging in sado-masochistic fantasies, another player is immersed in a new world where fantasy becomes so real that he becomes the victim of the car accident he had anticipated in utter dread all along. Even worse, this is an accident in which the car takes on a life of its own and seemingly stages the accident that kills the character.

Whatever the intentions of Malone and Coyle were, I am struck by the way *FearDotCom* condenses both the self-referentiality of modernism and the postmodern conceit that, in this image-saturated world of game playing, it has become impossible to decide where the truth lies, or even whether images can any longer represent the truth. There is a certain reactionary pessimism at work here, a sort of retreat from any ethical or political engagement with society or history, that dovetails with two concepts endorsed by Fredric Jameson, the former defining modernism, the second offering a reflection on experiencing sex or violence in a form of eternal present that corresponds strikingly to the world of certain recent horror films. The "great modernists," in Jameson's words, "were all profoundly utopian in the sense of being committed to the fateful premonition of momentous impending transformations of the Self or the World: what I would call essentially proto-political experiences" (Jameson 1998, 131).

This utopian strain, a major concern of Jameson's in his analyses of contemporary alienation both social and psychological, has clearly been repressed in certain manifestations of postmodernism. Jameson continues:

> [what] can descriptively (and non-morally) be called sex-and-violence porn
> does offer something of a grim caricature of current aesthetic notions of an
> absolute present in time. For these films offer, in a powerful reduction to
> the sheer present [*sic*] of sex or violence, intensities which can be read as a
> compensation for the weakening of any sense of narrative time: the older
> plots, which still developed and flexed the spectator's local memory, have
> seemingly been replaced by an endless string of narrative pretexts in which
> only the experiences available in the sheer viewing present can be entertained.
> (128–29)

I am not primarily concerned with what films exactly Jameson may have had in mind.[6] What interests me instead is how the second quote—I shall return to the first quote later—could be a comment on a series of recent films, all made since *FearDotCom*, in which the questions of sex, violence, torture, murder, and time are of crucial importance: *Saw* (James Wan, 2004), *Hostel* and *Hostel II* (both Eli Roth, 2005 and 2007, respectively), and *Captivity* (Roland Joffé, 2007). To this list can be added films that have not given rise to the same degree of controversy: *Wolf Creek* (Greg McLean, 2005), *The Girl Next Door* (Gregory Wilson, 2007), *Untraceable* (Gregory Hoblit, 2007), and *P2* (Franck Khalfoun, 2007).[7] It is certainly neither a coincidence that the jailers/torturers in all these films behave like the Doctor in Malone's film, nor that the confined spaces in which the victims find themselves are not only so many prisons but can be taken as real-life manifestations of the virtual prison symbolized by the computer site and, simultaneously, of the actual prison where the Doctor tortures his victims. With the benefit of hindsight we can place *FearDotCom* as the first in a new cinematic cycle in which torture becomes the expression of the subject's freedom to do whatever he wishes, and in which the films' spectators are addressed directly in regard to their position in this set-up. Given the popularity of these films, as much as the consistency of their key themes, it is surely worth asking the simple question (just how simple is another matter): why all these films about torture at the present time? Are these films merely "titillating" the audience, to adopt a term used by one critic already quoted to denounce Malone's own effort?

I would like to offer an answer to that nonrhetorical question, although certain elements of my interpretation obviously apply to the better-known—and decidedly more controversial—films on the list.[8] First, however, two tasks await us. The first is to sketch in briefly the points of convergence and divergence between *FearDotCom* and some of the more important films I have mentioned above. Inasmuch as Malone's film plays on the virtual/real dialectic, it has obviously far more in common with *Videodrome* that with any of the other films, which are quite unambiguous about the fact that the victims are not just virtually but *really* being tortured to death. The question of quality interests me less than that of politics. I have discussed the political and ideological aspects of *Videodrome* elsewhere (Humphries 2002, 182–83, 187–88), but we can evoke usefully here the parallels between this film and *FearDotCom*. They are to be found both in their raising of the question of totalitarianism and in the representation of the ideology underpinning big business, explicit in Cronenberg, only implied in Malone.

Before exploring and taking further these observations, however, our second task will be to turn the clock back again to the 1930s and reconsider the genealogy of the mad doctor or scientist in the light of recent films about torture and its gratuitous, or perhaps even not-so-gratuitous, enjoyment.[9] Whereas Dr. Gogol in *Mad*

Love gets his sexual kicks from fictional representations of torture, the Doctor in *FearDotCom* needs the real thing. We can express this another way: just as Gogol is a simple *spectator* of the torture of the other, the Doctor inflicts real torture on real victims and the subscribers are, therefore, spectators to murders which they experience vicariously. What was a fiction within a fiction in *Mad Love* has become reality within a fiction in *FearDotCom*.

One way to understand the film is to consider the Doctor as a signifier of something else—something that both harks back to the activities of mad doctors in classic horror films and evokes films as different as *Operazione Paura*, *M*, *Peeping Tom*, and *My Little Eye*.[10] Whether we consider the laboratories of Frankenstein, Dr. Rukh (*The Invisible Ray*, 1936) and Dr. Blair (*The Devil Commands*, 1941), the remote homes of Murder Legendre (*White Zombie*, 1932), Hjalmar Poelzig (*The Black Cat*, 1934) and Dr. Vollin (*The Raven*, 1935) or the islands of Count Zaroff (*The Most Dangerous Game*, 1932) and Dr. Moreau (*Island of Lost Souls*, 1932), we find that the films have in common factors going beyond the simple need of the scientist to hide from prying eyes. The mad scientist refuses all restraint; an extreme individualist, he allows nobody to stand in the way of his obsessive search for the knowledge that will bring him power and recognition. Moreover, his rejection of society stems from his belief in his inherent intellectual superiority, his special rights, and a sense of impatience with society's mediocrity and orthodoxy (Humphries 2006, x, xv). In addition, Moreau's island does not even figure on the charts, and in both *King Kong* and *Son of Kong* the presence of dinosaurs suggests self-contained spaces cut off from time and evolution, another form of the eternal present outlined in Fredric Jameson's remark quoted above.

Money plays a significant role in 1930s horror, most notably through its conspicuous absence. The mad scientist apparently has unlimited funds at his disposal, dispensing him from having to earn his living like the rest of humanity.[11] The films thus foreground class and economics by disavowing them: wealth goes without saying, as if money grew on trees. This, of course, is the basis of capitalist ideology within which a massive presence—that of labor—is transformed into an absence, which then enables the capitalist to place in a realm as hermetically sealed as Vollin's dungeon in *The Raven*, the torture chambers in *FearDotCom*, and the various entries into this new cinematic cycle listed above, the means by which money, profit, and wealth come into existence.[12] What is new in films made since the beginning of the new millenium is not simply the extreme visual horror placed before us, faced with which we may prefer to look away (like the Nicolas Cage character at one point in *8mm*). No, it is surely the self-reflexive dimension that is insisted on, which takes us back to a film that provoked decades ago an outrage verging on hysteria on the part of the guardians of the temple of morality: *Peeping Tom* (Michael Powell, 1960). For what this exceptional film did was to represent the forbidden: the desire to see murder on the screen, a desire rendered explicit by placing the spectator in the position of the highly sympathetic main character who just happens to be a serial killer, a desire too explicit for comfort. Far from encouraging the spectator to *become* a torturer, *FearDotCom* and the other films mentioned here are forcing him or her to ask what it might be like to *be* a torturer, which is hardly the same thing.

As Freud has taught us, desire is unconcious. If I ask myself what it would be like to mutilate another person or cut slices off a live victim's leg (*Hostel II*), I am giving conscious voice to a hypothesis. But hypotheses do not exist in the unconscious: they are represented *as if they had happened*, as if a desire had been realized. Whenever the wish is unacceptable to the subject, who cannot consciously entertain this dimension of desire—especially if the desire is socially proscribed—this representation of it being carried out turns a dream into a nightmare from which the subject awakes trembling. Films such as *Hostel* offer us a *waking* nightmare. Critics react with outrage to these films because, somewhere within their most intimate selves, they have asked this question and been given an answer by the film as if they really had desired something so utterly monstrous (or "depraved"). What is so horrifying about torture—or simply callous mistreatment—in, for example, Guantanamo or the sealed-off secret prisons that receive those abducted by the CIA is the fact that a supposedly average person is at the origin of it.[13] The great discovery of Powell and screenwriter Lewis Marks in *Peeping Tom* was to block all imaginary escape routes the spectator might take by assimilating the desire to go to the cinema and to watch monstrous events to a desire to wonder what it would be like to perpetrate these events: the film's spectators were being indicted and they didn't like it.[14]

It is in this context that Malone and his screenwriter have found, perhaps unwittingly, a metaphor for murder, not in the form of the feardotcom site's direct address to the subscribers, but in exactly the supernatural element so stridently decried by critics. This supernatural element is not to be taken literally but as a conceit destined to prevent both the film's characters (literally, on the level of the plot) and its spectators (figuratively, because we ourselves are not in any actual danger) from wriggling out of a situation in which we are all accomplices to the hideous degradation of a human being.[15]

Nonetheless, the subscribers (subjects of the enounced) and the spectators (subjects of the enunciation) do have one thing in common. They unconsciously seek to obtain knowledge of that which must, by its very nature, remain beyond knowledge: death itself. The characters who die let us off the hook, so to speak, but insufficiently so, in the light of the denunciations and rejection of *FearDotCom*. In other words, the film is too close to the bone: the desire to obtain knowledge about the forbidden via the appalling suffering of the other has entered the subject's pre-conscious and triggered off a totally unacceptable and intolerable pleasure, duly transformed into *un*pleasure through the pressure exerted by the stern superego.

We are in the realm of Lacanian *jouissance*, that desire to go beyond the pleasure principle to achieve the most rapid and unimpeded satisfaction of a drive, which nonetheless risks reaching the point where pleasure turns into its opposite. The problem with *jouissance* is that it cannot be turned on and off like a tap: what is the point where the "beyond" becomes intolerable, inasmuch as we are dealing with an unconscious phenomenon?

The Doctor, a cynical casuist, has found the answer: torture someone for long enough and he will beg for mercy in the form of death. This suits our mad doctor—and, by extension, any torturer, fictional or historical—down to the ground: "you asked for death, so I am no longer your murderer," he tells one victim. Surely, then, the fact that those who get locked into the game die forty-eight hours later is a grim and dire warning on the part of *FearDotCom*: by participating in murder by proxy, the subscribers condemn themselves as if they were being executed for a real murder. That, I would argue, is the "deep meaning" of the supernatural element: by switching its ontological register, the film moves its most unsettling aspect from the diegetic surface into the subtext. Superficially, it appears to let us off the hook, but beneath the surface, it continues to elaborate upon a hypothesis that, for the viewer, remains entirely within the unconscious. The supernatural in the film is an imaginary escape route; this may even be true for the film's makers, unable or unwilling to face up to the implications of the diegetic world they have created: "If only we could put such horrors down to a supernatural force, like the Devil."

More than that, however, is at stake: it is as if all subscribers, by inscribing their subjectivity into that of the game, have become not only the torturer *but the victim too*. The film is asking the subcribers: "How would *you* like to be a victim?" Having first been a torturer by proxy, they fall victim to the site and are killed forty-eight hours later. This is at least part of the function of the intertextual space created by films like Lang's *M*, Powell's *Peeping Tom*, Bava's *Operazione Paura*, and Marc Evans's *My Little Eye* (2001). The serial killer in Lang's film is also a victim of a force he cannot grasp, an unconscious desire that drives him to kill: a death drive that he exteriorizes and imposes upon the little girl. A particularly hateful and vindictive society finds thus a sacrificial victim in the child murderer, not to assuage a vague desire for revenge, but to be able to repress into the unconscious the forces of death (the memory of the Great War, the economics of the Depression, the imminence of Nazism). Mark Lewis, the protagonist of *Peeping Tom*, is a murderer; he is also a victim, of the experiments of his own father, who just happened to be a mad scientist. In Bava's remarkable movie the little girl dies as a result of the indifference of the villagers and returns to exact her revenge. But this revenge, presented as supernatural, has an ideological dimension: the desire of her deranged mother to punish a patriarchal society for its treatment of women. The mother's guilt cannot be understood without this dimension—it is socially and sexually determined. What all these films make abundantly clear is that desire can never be assuaged, except in death. Hence, when the subject is under the control of the death drive, he or she seeks the death of the other but must continue indefinitely once the other has paid the supreme price. The serial killer obtains momentary satisfaction by snuffing out the existence of the victim, turned into an object/body to exploit. Desire, however, cannot cease with that death, for without desire the subject no longer exists and death occurs. Hence the need to repeat the (imaginary sensation of) satisfaction indefinitely, by way of an ever-increasing number of victims. This is the death drive to which the serial killer is unconsciously submitted and to which he submits his unfortunate victims. Poor Mark Lewis believes he can attain the serenity of plenitude by filming his own death, which is what he has unconsciously desired all along, but he has forgotten that he will not be there to watch that particular film.

As the most recent example, and thus the film most attuned to *FearDotCom*, *My Little Eye* deserves a closer look in this context. The film tells the story of a small group of youngsters of both sexes in their early twenties who agree to participate in an experiment: spend six months in an isolated house and win a million dollars. But there is a snag: should anyone venture outside at any moment for any reason, everyone loses their share in the prize. The entire house is under video surveillance; there is no privacy anywhere, including in bedrooms, bathrooms, and even the toilets. Shortly before the six months are up, one member of the group is found dead. Eventually, we learn that the whole experiment is a perverse game conceived by businessmen for their pleasure: they can assuage their desire to see young people indulging in various sexual activities.

For our purposes here the film's interest lies in the role played by the businessmen, crucial elements in the plot that prefigure what is to occur in later, and far more commercially successful, films like *Hostel* and *Hostel II*. In *My Little Eye*, these figures remain invisible. Unlike the torturers in the *Hostel* films, whose individual motives are hastily sketched in, they come to stand in for that egregious formula of "the invisible hand of the market," by which neoliberal ideologues fetishize the market as a person and implicitly reify human social relations by turning people into objects to be manipulated. This notion of reification also happens to be present in *FearDotCom* via a car that seems to have a life, or a mind, of its own as it transports its unsuspecting driver, as if by an "invisible hand," to his death. Both *My Little Eye* and *FearDotCom* are thus incriminating implicitly labor/capital relations as a form of exploitation that can result in the deaths of one party: those who are being manipulated. The action of the businessmen can also be assimilated to *jouissance*. They do not need this sinister game in order to exist but it brings them a surplus: knowing they wield power (of life and death) over the other.

Clearly there is also a sadistic component in the behavior and mentality of the businessmen, a recurring component that becomes far more extreme and sinister after *FearDotCom*, especially with the cycle inaugurated by *Saw*. Sadism now takes the form of torture, and it is interesting to note that the comparatively moderate *My Little Eye* (if one can speak of moderation in these instances) was made before 9/11, whereas all the other films come after.[16] Since 9/11, torture has become a fashionable topic, giving new relevance to the complex problem of sadism. While masochists enjoy the pleasure of pain in their own bodies, sadists force their victims to endure it (Evans 168). However, in the light of Lacan's theory of desire, we cannot stop there. Desire is located in the Other, which does not mean that the subject identifies with the desire of another subject, but that this desire is part of an intersubjectivity determined by the Symbolic Order, by social and ideological factors. Hence, the torturer/sadist is unconsciously carrying out the desire of the Other, an empty place social subjects fill with the ideologies dominant at a particular moment. Writing shortly after 9/11 in *Newsweek* (November 5, 2001), the journalist Jonathan Alter suggested that "we need to keep an open mind about certain measures to fight terrorism, like court-sanctioned psychological interrogation. And we'll have to think about transferring some suspects to our less squeamish allies" (qtd. in Zizek 2002, 102).

If *Hostel II* can be seen as a more or less direct attack on Bush and ultraliberalism, then *FearDotCom* must be considered a "proto-political" movie (I refer the reader to the first Fredric Jameson quote above).[17] Not by coincidence, the Doctor quotes Stalin: "One death is a tragedy, a million deaths a statistic." A reference to the renowned serial killer Joseph Stalin would seem somehow out of place in such a movie, were it not for a remark that follows immediately. To a new victim the Doctor says: "Your death will give meaning to all those sad little lives out there." In Stalin's mouth, this would mean that an innocent victim of a purge has denounced himself as an enemy of the people and that his death will encourage them to see in Stalin the guardian of the Revolution. Ultimately, the Doctor is addressing, via the suffering of the victim, the subscribers to the site. Thanks to misrecognizing their symbolic position in this network of terror, they will find "meaning" in lives under the sway of alienation, commodity fetishism, and reification.[18] They live lives during which subjectivity is in the capable hands of the ideological and financial Other, a subjectivity kneaded like so much dough. Applying the film's pre-9/11 agenda to the peculiarities of the post-9/11 world, we can easily see Malone and Coyle sending out a warning to the film's spectators, real or potential, who are blithely paying dearly for submitting to the desires of the Doctor's real-life political counterparts—those who now justify torture in the name of giving us "security," the keyword in the new repressive mantra that is supposedly giving meaning to our "sad little lives."

Thus, in 2008, ABC News revealed that those at the highest level of the state—Ashcroft, Cheney, Rice, and Rumsfeld—had met in 2002 and 2003 to review the interrogation of alleged Al Quaeda members held by the CIA, with a view to using "enhanced interrogation techniques" (a term that must be equated with torture).[19] Like *Newsweek* journalist Jonathan Alter, both Ashcroft and Rumsfeld had stated in the wake of the terrorist attack on the World Trade Center that the government should not be constrained legally, given that the United States was at war (Zizek 2002, 107). I would suggest that we find here a real-life instance of the lack of restraint that I evoked concerning the behavior of the mad scientist in classic horror films. In which case, *FearDotCom* and the other films on torture I have listed can be seen as prefiguring America's imminent future by repeating Hollywood's distant past. Given that those films of the distant past were acutely aware of the horrors unleashed by fascism since the 1920s—*The Most Dangerous Game* (Ernest B. Schoedsack and Irving Pichel, 1932), for example, explicitly refers to Mussolini in the way Count Zaroff is dressed (Humphries 2006, 204–7)—the current cinematic cycle appears equally attuned to the political climate of its time.

With an eye less on Hollywood horror films and more on the documentary *Standard Operating Procedure*, Slavoj Zizek comes to this eye-opening realization about Abu Ghraib:

> Abu Ghraib was not simply a case of American arrogance towards a Third World people: in being submitted to humiliating tortures, the Iraqi prisoners were effectively *initiated into American culture*. They were given a taste of its obscene underside, which forms the necessary supplement to the public values of personal dignity, democracy, and freedom. (Zizek 2008, 176)

This brilliant insight has its fictional equivalent, albeit one based on real events, in that remarkable and profoundly disturbing film *The Girl Next Door* referred to earlier. The film tells the story of a sick, mentally unbalanced woman imprisoning an adolescent girl and encouraging her sons and neighborhood children to inflict first humiliation, then physical tortures on her, before actually killing her herself. Rather than being a monstrous outsider, an aberration from the norm, the woman in question functions as the signifier of the cultural and ideological climate of the 1950s. An average and vulgar middle-class woman, well aware that her views on the female body and sexuality were socially dominant, she was simply initiating both the victim and her adolescent abusers into the true meaning of such domination, much like lynchings in the Deep South initiated white women and children into the ways of ensuring white supremacy. The adolescents in *The Girl Next Door*, like the soldiers in *Standard Operating Procedure*, considered their acts as normal, approved of by someone in authority, present in the former film, absent in the latter (although, interestingly, Rumsfeld had just paid a visit to the prison).

Normalization via repetition is a theme that also runs through the cycle of torture-porn films. Whereas the representation of the businessmen in *Hostel II* indicates that Roth has used the horror genre to make a political comment on real horrors being committed in the name of the American electorate, the seemingly endless follow-up entries in the *Saw* franchise illustrate perfectly Marx's insight that those who refuse to learn the lessons of the past are condemned to repeat it. *FearDotCom* occupies an uneasy position between the two, revealing as it does an "unconscious knowledge." We can define this as knowledge that cannot find explicit expression and which, therefore, is also condemned to be expressed via a blurring of the virtual and the real. The incoherent aspects of the film betray less a refusal to think on the aesthetic mode than an inability to draw the necessary political conclusions.[20]

NOTES

My thanks to Steffen Hantke for his helpful comments on an earlier version of this essay.

1. Given the violent and hysterical attacks launched on Cronenberg at various points in his long and controversial career (in particular against *Shivers* in 1975 and *Crash* in 1996), I find it both amusing and revealing that the once-reviled Canadian is now used as a yardstick by which to judge and cast into outer darkness more recent practitioners of the horror genre. An analysis of this phenomenon, however, is beyond the scope of this essay. I leave readers to meditate upon the fact that what was vile and inexcusable years ago is now palatable, especially if it can be summoned up to denounce a new moral pariah.

2. The celebrated shot of the drowned woman in the bath, dead eyes staring up at us, is quoted in Dario Argento's *Sleepless* (2000), a recent entry into the *giallo* category.

3. Moreau calls his surgery the "House of Pain" to instil fear in the "manimals" who are the results of his experiments. I use the formula in the title of this essay, not only because it corresponds to the Doctor's torture chamber, but because of the striking recurrence of such a place/space in the contemporary American horror film.

4. See Reynold Humphries, *The Hollywood Horror Film, 1931–1941. Madness in a Social Landscape* (Lanham, Md.: Scarecrow Press, 2006), for more details on these films.

5. This was the question both the characters involved in the plots of *Videodrome* and *8mm* and the spectators involved in watching the films asked themselves.

6. He has written elsewhere about *Videodrome* in terms that make a fundamental distinction between Cronenberg's movie and the snuff movies we are shown, whereas most of *FearDotCom*'s detractors tend to assimilate Malone's film as a whole to the images of torture and Malone to the Doctor. See Fredric Jameson, *The Geopolitical Aesthetic: Cinema and Space in the World System* (London: BFI, 1995), 22–32.

7. I leave aside the subsequent entries in the *Saw* franchise, which, unlike *Hostel II*, add nothing to the original that had the distinction of being, well, original. The recent Franco-Canadian production *Martyrs* (Pascal Laugier, 2007) eschews any sexual dimension in favor of the representation of a neo-Nazi religious sect that subjects its victims to cruel martyrdom in the hope that, at the moment of their final agony, they will offer insight into the beyond as witnesses to God.

8. If the films directed by Roth are more controversial, it is because they are far more explicitly films of their time than Malone's, as we shall see in due course. It is not irrelevant

to remind readers that Malone's previous feature, *House on Haunted Hill*, turned on enforced incarceration, torture, and murder.

9. The volumes of both Skal and Tudor deal with the mad doctor/scientist as a cultural or sociological phenomenon, whereas I have chosen to foreground class, economics, and history via a psychoanalytic reading of the films of the period.

10. I have discussed elsewhere the narrative and symbolic function of space and place in the horror films of the 1930s; see Reynold Humphries, *The Hollywood Horror Film, 1931–1941: Madness in a Social Landscape* (Lanham, Md.: Scarecrow Press, 2006), 241–52.

11. A film that stands apart here is Georges Franju's *Les Yeux Sans Visage* (*Eyes Without a Face*, 1959). If the experiments of Dr. Genessier are carried out away from prying eyes, he has both a public and private practice as a doctor and gives public lectures about science and medicine. The film thus not only shows how he makes his money but highlights the class aspects of the situation: his audiences are mostly wealthy inhabitants of the 16th arrondissement in Paris, his victims students looking for cheap accommodation.

12. One of the merits of *Hostel II* is to foreground quite unambiguously the role of money from beginning to end: money gives you power (of life and death) over the other. This is the thesis of an extraordinary recent Franco-Rumanian film *13 Tzameti* (Gela Babluani, 2005) where members of an East European mafia gamble vast sums on a game of Russian roulette (the former Communist bloc having discovered the joys of global capitalism) where proletarians from the East are united in death, in the forlorn hope of being the last survivor and therefore becoming rich.

13. In *Captivity* the heroine is subjected to blinding lights and deafening sounds, favorite devices of torture used against those arrested in the name of the "war on terror." The sadistic acts of deliberate humiliation inflicted on prisoners at Abu Ghraib by American soldiers (see *Standard Operating Procedure*, Errol Morris, 2007) are, however, devoid of any fictional status: the torturers were unconsciously carrying out the desire of the big Other.

14. See Reynold Humphries, "Caught in the act of looking. The opening sequence of Michael Powell's *Peeping Tom*," *Caliban* XXXII (Toulouse: Presses Universitares du Mirail, 1995). I shall never forget the experience of watching *Peeping Tom* for the first time late one Saturday night when I was a student. A noisy audience fell silent as the eye opened in the pre-credit sequence and you could hear a pin drop for the next one hundred minutes. Never have I seen so cowed an audience as those who rose at the end, put on their coats, and filed silently out. As a friend who saw the film with me remarked: "They should put *Peeping Tom* on every Saturday night to keep them quiet."

15. Conversely, the most alert filmmakers have also represented literally the death drive embodied by their characters. I am thinking of Al Roberts's drive across country in *Detour*, Marion Crane's drive to the Bates motel and the long, final sequence of *Se7en*. Significantly, Marion ends up at a place she did not consciously aim for, the motel which was to become her final destination.

16. Shooting for *My Little Eye* started in April 2001.

17. One of the businessmen in *Hostel II*, a deliberate caricature of Republican ideologues, at one point advances in slow motion towards his limousine. I refer readers to the documentary *How Arnold Won the West* (Alex Corke, 2004), where there is an identical shot of the new Governor of California leaving his home and advancing to be interviewed by journalists.

18. The recent *P2* is relevant here. The seemingly charming parking attendant, who turns out to be a sadistic psychopath, remarks revealingly at one point that nobody sees him, as if he did not even exist. In one remarkable scene he imitates Elvis, then dances with a huge teddy bear, as if

with a woman, which neatly condenses his need for recognition (in every sense of the word) and a total social and sexual alienation.

19. See "Top Bush aides directed torture from the White House," www.wsws.org, April 12, 2008.

20. It is useful to refer to a film that deals very much with torture but on a quite different mode from any of those cited: Michael Haneke's *Funny Games*. I would ask a question: why did the director choose to remake this particular film (a German-language film originally made in Austria in 1997) at this particular time (2007) in a particular foreign country, the United States? (The remake is called *Funny Games U.S.*). Because he was assailed by an overwhelming desire to become famous across the Atlantic? Because he was offered too much money to refuse? Because it's his favorite among his own films? I would suggest that to ask such questions is already to stress their general lack of pertinence. I am not privy to Haneke's reasons for remaking *Funny Games*, and even if I were, I would not be obliged to accept them at their face value. However, given that he is a highly self-conscious filmmaker (in the modernist, rather than the postmodernist, sense of the term), it seems likely that he felt that an American version would contribute in some way to the pervasive contemporary topic of torture.

WORKS CITED

Evans, Dylan. *An Introductory Dictionary of Lacanian Psychoanalysis*. London: Routledge, 1996.

Gordon, Bill. Review of *FearDotCom*. *Horror Fan Zine*, March 30, 2007. www.imdb.com (accessed August 29, 2007).

Hobson, Louis B. Review of *FearDotCom*. Jam!Movies, August 30, 2002. www.imdb.com (accessed August 9, 2007).

Hornaday, Ann. Review of *FearDotCom*. *Washington Post*, August 30, 2002. www.imdb.com (accessed August 9, 2007).

Humphries, Reynold. "Caught in the act of looking. The opening sequence of Michael Powell's *Peeping Tom*," *Caliban* XXXII. Toulouse: Presses Universitaires du Mirail, 1995. 39–53.

———. *The American Horror Film. An Introduction*. Edinburgh: Edinburgh University Press, 2002.

———. *The Hollywood Horror Film, 1931–1941. Madness in a Social Landscape*. Lanham, Md.: Scarecrow Press, 2006.

Jameson, Fredric. *The Geopolitical Aesthetic: Cinema and Space in the World System*. London: BFI, 1995.

———. *The Cultural Turn: Selected Writings on the Postmodern, 1983–1998*. London: Verso, 1998.

Kermode, Mark. Review of *FearDotCom*. *Guardian*, June 29, 2003. www.imdb.com (accessed August 8, 2007).

LaSalle, Mark. Review of *FearDotCom*. *San Francisco Chronicle*, August 30, 2002. www.imdb.com (accessed August 10, 2007).

Messier, Max. Review of *FearDotCom*. Filmcritic.com, 2002. www.imdb.com (accessed August 10, 2007).

Montgomery, Karina. Review of *FearDotCom*. USENET newsgroup, 2002. rec.arts.movies. reviews (accessed August 6, 2007).

Rechtshaffen, Michael. Review of *FearDotCom*. *Hollywood Reporter*, August 30, 2002. www.imdb .com (accessed August 5, 2007).

Skal, David. *Screams of Reason: Mad Science and Modern Culture*. New York: W. W. Norton & Company, 1998.

Tudor, Andrew. *Monsters and Mad Scientists. A Cultural History of the Horror Movie.* London: Blackwell, 1989.

Zizek, Slavoj. *Welcome to the Desert of the Real! Five Essays on September 11 and Related Dates.* London: Verso, 2002.

———. *Violence.* New York: Picador, 2008.

Part Two

THE USUAL SUSPECTS

Trends and Transformations in the
Subgenres of American Horror Film

TEENAGE TRAUMATA

Youth, Affective Politics, and the Contemporary American Horror Film

—Pamela Craig and Martin Fradley

Hollywood's teen-targeted material has mainly meant
teen protagonists coping with teen dilemmas in a teen milieu.
—THOMAS DOHERTY

Everybody's cursed—it's called life.
—ELLIE (Christina Ricci) in *Cursed*

Most of all: have fun, man!
—ALEX (James Urbaniak) in *Elephant*

TEEN HORROR AND THE CRITICS

Even on first viewing, perhaps the most striking elements of Gus Van Sant's hypnotic, haunting *Elephant* (2003) are the film's understated allusions to the stock character types, narrative preoccupations, and strangely resonant *mise-en-scène* of the American teen movie. As the camera tracks down suburban tree-lined avenues, through sterile and monotonously labyrinthine locker-lined school corridors, and via quasi-ethnographic snapshots of geeks, goths, jocks, arty-outsiders, beauty queens, and bespectacled ugly ducklings, the central imagery and thematic tropes of the Hollywood teen genre are uncannily familiar even for those of us for whom both the United States and the period of our own adolescence are another country entirely. More specifically for our purposes, it is *Elephant's* subdued expressionist motifs and opaque articulation of repressed dread and foreboding amid the banality of the everyday which intimate the generic terrain of the horror film. Indeed, *Elephant's* depiction of high school as an insidiously benign gothic space is characteristic of the thematic preoccupations of much recent American horror cinema. Perhaps most generically resonant, however, are the film's unnervingly fluid steadicam shots, coolly and methodically landscaping the internal geography of the high school, unveiling in turn the fragmented internal landscapes and psychosocial geographies of American adolescence as it too is endlessly refracted through the generic prism of what has become *the* key production trend in recent American horror cinema: the teen horror movie.

Of course, Van Sant's perversely beautiful and almost serenely nonjudgmental art-house *homage* to the gothic underside of the teen movie works precisely to defamaliarize this generic *mise-en-scène*. The affectless ambiguity and disquieting sense of alienation that characterize *Elephant* function in stark contrast to the melodramatic emotional lexicon of the contemporary teen horror film. Yet while *Elephant*'s allusions to numerous high school shootings in the United States (of which the Columbine massacre is only the most high-profile case) and its sustained neo-realist aesthetic—what the director self-consciously describes as "anti-entertainment" (Said 18)—seem implicitly to critique the high-concept excesses of recent teen horror, we argue instead that the passionate detachment of Van Sant's movie—that is, its simultaneous numbing of the subgenre's affective content and its defamiliarizing of the teen movie's central themes and imagery—actually strikes at the core of teen horror's contemporaneous generic evolution.[1] This thematic and aesthetic continuum between the leftfield products of the "independent" sector and the commercially lucrative field of mainstream teen horror is, we would argue, increasingly evident in other recent films which focus upon the emotional and psychosocial subalternity of youth. Critically acclaimed productions such as *Welcome to the Dollhouse* (1996), *The Virgin Suicides* (1999), *L.I.E.* (2001), *Donnie Darko* (2001), *Bully* (2001), and *Mysterious Skin* (2004) all underline in various ways the heterogeneous nature of contemporary cinematic depictions of young American adults, representations that are specifically filtered through the horrors of the late-capitalist gothic imaginary.

In critical terms, of course, the American horror film has lost much of the scholarly goodwill that it received from the 1970s through to the early 1990s, a state of affairs synopsized by Robin Wood's (2004) recent and mournfully rhetorical question: "Aside from *Day of the Dead* [1985] is there *any* American horror movie made since 1980 that could be championed as any sort of radical statement about our (so-called) civilization?" (xviii; original emphasis). As the esteemed *enfant terrible* of ideological film criticism (and, with his essay "An Introduction to the American Horror Film" [1979], one of the most influential scholars to ever write about horror cinema), Wood's concern with what he dubs the "degeneration" of the genre is both significant *and* symptomatic. For Wood, the American horror film has lapsed into a combination of baroque postmodern apathy—typified, perhaps, by the success of the glibly parodic *Scary Movie* cycle (2000–2006)—and an apparently reactionary agenda which, as he understands it, mirrors the decline of leftist politics and the emergent neoconservative hegemony in American culture more broadly. "Perhaps the new administration will goad people into a new sense of outrage," Wood muses with quiet fury, "but it may take the equivalent of the Vietnam War" (xiv).

Indeed, Wood's non-too-subtle allusion here to the disastrous military adventurism of the Bush administration (2001–2009) is symptomatic of the critical backlash that the American horror film has received in recent years. Moreover, it is precisely the supposed failure of the genre to articulate the real-world horrors of the present, as it has done so incisively in the past, which has led to a widespread sense of critical disillusionment with recent horror films, particularly when events both within and without American society are so ripe for expressive commentary and critique. One has only to look to the speculative critical fanfare that greeted Eli Roth's *Hostel* (2005) to witness the desperate search for cultural relevance in contemporary American horror. Certainly, *Hostel* and its (admittedly, marginally more interesting) 2007 sequel invoke, with varying degrees of obliqueness, some heavyweight topics, including, but not limited to, the specter of the holocaust, sex trafficking, violent pornography, and the amoral logic of late-capitalist consumer culture. But confident assertions of both films' post-9/11 resonance were, in our view, spectacularly overstated. While *Hostel* was enthusiastically self-promoted by Roth as a gruesome allegory of human rights abuses perpetrated by Americans in Guantanamo Bay and Abu Ghraib, any hint of political critique is soon undermined by the rabid xenophobia and casual misogyny that characterizes both films. Lacking even the reflexive self-awareness and bawdy comic intelligence of, say, *Eurotrip* (2004)—a film which similarly engages with the continental misadventures of American youth—both *Hostel* movies are dubiously cautionary tales that insistently warn domestic audiences of the apparently regressive dangers of the Old World.[2] While this is certainly indicative of a post-9/11 awareness of global anti-Americanism, the films do very little to dissuade their viewers of the fundamentally reactionary nature of such fears. In contrast to some of the more intelligent 1970s exploitation films which they ape, both *Hostel* and its sequel transparently encourage vengeful emotional identification with their surviving protagonists' violent retribution, something which only serves to underline the films' endless displacements and symptomatically paranoid logic.[3]

Implicitly, of course, this righteous discontent is methodological, for it is precisely the critical tools wielded by Wood—that is, an ideological critique predicated on a heavily politicized fusion of psychoanalytic theory and Marxist thought—which have become increasingly marginal both within and without in the academy. However, in terms of scholarly approaches to horror cinema, one has only to think of arguably the two most significant and influential critical studies of horror cinema since Wood's classic writing on the subject—namely, Carol Clover's post-Mulveyan *Men, Women, and Chainsaws: Gender in the Modern Horror Film* (1992) and Barbara Creed's Lacanian-Kristevan tome *The Monstrous-Feminine: Film,*

Feminism, Psychoanalysis (1993)—to see how their methodologies are more often than not inadequate to deal with the generic terrain of contemporary American horror cinema. Yet given its status as a key Hollywood production trend, in this essay we insist upon the continued validity of political-ideological criticism of the horror film; in particular, we are interested in the relationship between contemporary horror and its primary consumers: young adults. Although Wood argues that "the popularity of [horror] films with teenagers is vastly more interesting . . . than the films themselves ever are" (xviii), we would take issue with his blanket dismissal of the contemporaneous genre and suggest instead that Wood's emphasis on the continuing popularity of the horror film with a youth demographic (and, in turn, that demographic's representation on-screen) is central to understanding American horror in the last decade.

The widespread discontent with recent teen horror that we have been alluding to is exemplified by some recent examples of critical polemic which attempt to summarize the degraded status of the American horror film today. This brand of criticism is typically characterized by a combination of brooding cultural pessimism underscored by a gloomy nostalgia for the genre's low-budget oppositional heyday from the late 1960s through until roughly the late 1970s, a mythologized era usually situated somewhere between the release of *Night of the Living Dead* in 1968 and the likes of *The Hills Have Eyes* (1977), *Dawn of the Dead* (1978) and David Cronenberg's intelligent and unnervingly prescient exploitation output in the latter half of the 1970s. Not insignificantly, it was the extraordinary success of *Halloween* in 1978—a landmark film, which, depending on your ideological point of view, is either something of a formal high-water mark for the genre or a deeply reactionary proto-Reaganite denunciation of the women's movement—which established the teen "slasher" subgenre as *the* key horror production trend at this historical juncture; a trend to be later revived and reimagined, of course, as a commercially potent force in the 1990s. As a result of this apparent shift in contemporary horror's political trajectory, a critic such as David Sanjek (2000) bemoans both "the tone of ennui" (112) he considers to have belittled the genre and the "paltry or pacified" thematic and ideological dimensions of American horror of the 1990s (114). Mournfully citing Jonathon Lake Crane's dictum that to watch a horror film is to engage in a type of psychosocial "reality check," Sanjek suggests that any affective sense of the uncanny has been evacuated from recent horror—what he describes as the systematic "neutralization of the unusual or unsettling" (114)—substituted instead by a pro-hegemonic reinforcement of the sociopolitical status quo.

Indeed, even in one of the most cogent and least polemical of recent genre assessments, Andrew Tudor (2002) finds "sadly, precious few horror films with the power to disturb" or offer a perceptible "assault on horror movie sensibilities" (107). Elsewhere, British critic Mark Kermode (2003) sees the condition of contemporary

American horror reflected most clearly in the huge commercial success of *The Texas Chainsaw Massacre* (2003). "What emerges," argues Kermode, "is a bizarre conundrum":

> [A] film that wants to look like an authentic replica of a cheap, edgy slasher classic while attracting the kind of young audience that wouldn't watch a 30-year-old re-release if their lives depended on it. In short, what we have is hallmark 1970s horror product cunningly rebranded for a jaded 21st-century audience: a perfect example of a trend currently sweeping the horror genre. (13)

At the core of Tudor, Kermode, and Sanjek's respective arguments is both the positioning of 1970s horror as the generic benchmark against which contemporary horror is judged—and necessarily found wanting—rhetorically coupled with a broad contempt for the lucrative but "jaded" youth demographic who regularly pay to see and enjoy contemporary horror both within and without the local multiplex. Indeed, Kermode's dismissive tone is underlined by the implicit allusions to his own youthful savvy and the suggestive terminology he employs. The youthful consumers who helped *The Texas Chainsaw Massacre* remake take over $28 million in its opening domestic weekend are, in his view, a "sheen-saturated" and "wide-eyed, unknowing crowd" casually exploited by producer Michael Bay and director Marcus Nispel (14).[4] Contemporary "pre-packaged teen slashers" subsequently transform the brutal intelligence and scathing social commentary of low-budget 1970s classics into "spectacularly meaningless entertainment" (15), a process of rebranding which results in heavily front-loaded commercial properties that are "all form and no content" (16). Obviously bewildered by the "cynical modern sensibility" of this film, Kermode metaphorically holds his hands up in despair: "What the new *Texas Chainsaw Massacre* 'means' to its audience is anyone's guess":

> As a textbook disembowelling of a once unruly genre classic, it makes for depressing viewing. But as one of the most financially successful horror films of 2003 [...] it is a significant signpost pointing towards a genre future still dominated by the ghosts of the past, still treading the road that leads to nowhere. (16)

It barely needs pointing out at this juncture that Kermode's skeptical use of punctuation here reiterates that, for him, *The Texas Chainsaw Massacre* is practically devoid of *meaning* on a political or even subtextual level.

Despite our reservations concerning the reductive tendencies epitomized by this sweeping overview of the contemporary horror scene, in many ways we concur with Kermode's unapologetically polemical stance at this juncture. The pre-sold

Bay/Nispel reimagining of *The Texas Chainsaw Massacre* does indeed erase the disturbing exploitation aesthetic and sociopolitical fury of Tobe Hooper's esteemed 1974 original, offering as a poor substitute only the leeringly fetishized apparition of pneumatic starlet Jessica Biel. Even more symptomatic and historically contingent is the remake's most obvious deviation from the original when, in the film's concluding sequences, Biel's "final girl" valiantly rescues an abducted infant from the clutches of her persecutors. Serving no real narrative purpose other than to belatedly reveal a hitherto veiled maternal streak, this functions as a deeply conservative and wholly unnecessary plot alteration that only serves to underscore Susan Faludi's (2008) persuasive thesis concerning the reactionary gender politics and concurrent reinvigoration of "family values" rhetoric typifying American culture in the wake of 9/11. Yet while both Kermode and Sanjek are absolutely correct in highlighting the American film industry's preoccupation with attracting young adults toward their products and, in turn, Hollywood's regular depiction of terrorized youth on screen, we would suggest that mobilizing these trends as evidence for the supposed evacuation of politics from the genre is both misguided and frequently overdetermined. Indeed, it remains a truism that even while horror has suffered a dramatic decline in its critical standing it has nevertheless remained enduringly popular at both the box office and in all-important ancillary markets. Of course, for the genre's critics it is *precisely* the supposed absence of thematic depth or political relevance upon which the commercial potency of contemporary horror is predicated, an apathetic and ideologically torpid state of affairs Thomas Doherty has famously dubbed "the juvenilization of American movies" and which Paul Wells (2000) has more specifically defined as "the *McDonaldisation* of horror" (97).

The fusion of gothic themes with the youthful concerns of the teenpic is, of course, hardly a new phenomenon; nor, indeed, is the critical contempt casually directed toward such movies. In a typically cantankerous essay on contemporary teen films, for example, Wheeler Winston Dixon (2000) argues that the globally dominant youth audience requires that movies, as a commercial prerequisite, "must not partake of the real world, but rather of a construct having nothing to do with contemporary teen reality" (130). Continuing in appropriately apocalyptic tones, Dixon posits that the contemporary youth demographic wants "escapism without risk, and when it gets too close, they lose interest" (130). The remainder of his diatribe is worth quoting at length for its bleakly archetypal vision of youthful apathy and unwitting cultural dupery:

> Hyperreality is not the issue here; the key is *unreality*, unrelenting and unremitting. The movie viewer, ensconced in her/his seat in the darkness seeks above all to *avoid* reality, to put off for as long as possible the return to normalcy, when they push past the upturned boxes of popcorn and spilled sodas

and make their way through the doors into the world outside. But are they ever satisfied? The entire key behind contemporary genre films is to keep the viewer hooked, perpetually wanting more, to be satisfied yet still hungry for a return to the same world, the same characters, the same general plot line, with only minor variations. This explains why every cast member not killed in *Scream* (1996) is back for *Scream 2* (1997); contemporary narrative-driven audiences want continuity and predictability in their entertainment above all other considerations. Today's genre films are really serials, in which formulaic thrills and entertainment are dispensed in two-hour bursts, with the promise of more to come held out in the final scenes of each episode. Tangentially, it is no surprise that the major television networks are increasingly targeting teenage women as a major portion of their audiences for daytime soap operas. As with film sequels, it is the *seriality* of the daytime soap opera, the mixture of the familiar with a slight plot twist to keep the narrative from becoming too predictable, that draws in younger audiences. (130–31; original emphasis)

Leaving aside the weary sub-Adorno histrionics of this fevered critical salvo, what is most noticeable here is less the contempt for sequels and "seriality" (something which, of course, has long been endemic to the genre) and rather the almost laughably sexist preconceptions and abject critical horror at the supposed *feminization* of horror cinema. To this end, we would like to make two broad points at this juncture. First, we would strongly contest Dixon's blanket dismissal of both youth-oriented films and their allegedly wholesale escapist allure. Second, we want to highlight the (gendered) allusion here to the generic terrain of the soap opera. Indeed, building upon Peter Hutchings's recent (and pleasingly nonjudgmental) observation that *Scream* and its ilk are most productively understood "not as 'postmodern horror' but rather as 'teenage soap horror'"— (2004, 215), we would suggest that rather than contemporary horror simply failing to live up to generic expectations (a "failure," which is then systematically projected onto the supposedly apathetic political sensibilities of its youthful consumers), it is in our view more productive to understand recent developments in the American horror genre as another stage in the genre's perpetual evolution. Rather than the sociopolitical commentary of horror being undermined and/or betrayed by the soap operatics and narcissistic solipsism of intra-youth relations, we propose that this is simply another phase in the processual nature of the genre, a development that insists upon the (inter)personal being understood as always already *political*.

However, Dixon's illustrative use of the popular *Scream* cycle (1996–2000) is without doubt significant. We are certainly wary of marginalizing the fluid, processual nature of generic evolution at this juncture, and do not want in any way to claim—as many have done—special or revolutionary status for the *Scream* trilogy.

Indeed, as recent revisionist work has demonstrated, a fetishistic critical insistence upon claiming transformative status for individual movies is a trend that often afflicts genre studies. Both Mark Jancovich (1996) and Kevin Heffernan (2004) have demonstrated that canonical horror films such as *Psycho* (1960), *Rosemary's Baby* (1968), and *Night of the Living Dead* have regularly—and erroneously—had radical and/or innovative status projected upon them at the expense of more marginal (but no less interesting) contemporaneous films, exemplifying the kind of critical hyperbole that necessarily elides developments within the genre more broadly. Nevertheless, there *is* still much about the *Scream* cycle that is regularly presumed to be emblematic of teen horror in the last decade:

(i)   the films feature a recurring cast of highly photogenic young actors playing characters in a high school or college campus environment, many of whom are already familiar to audiences from youth-oriented television shows;[5]

(ii) they are set in a suburban and almost exclusively white, middle-class milieu;

(iii) generically, all three *Scream* films are characterized by a hybridized fusion of horror, comedy, and teen melodrama with a concomitant emphasis on interpersonal relationships, elements that are frequently attributed to the aesthetic sensibilities of screenwriter Kevin Williamson;[6]

(iv) finally, and most notoriously, the *Scream* trilogy offers their audience a knowing and reflexive commentary on the generic logic of the "slasher" film and a concomitant pop-Brechtian dynamic that underlines their appeal to the shared cinematic experiences and subcultural capital of youthful media consumers. In other words, Wes Craven's *Scream* franchise offers a densely intertextual experience that rewards and sustains the pleasures of repeat viewings in subsequent ancillary releases.[7]

As a number of commentators have suggested, however, the comically baroque generic model we have briefly sketched above is not by any means as hegemonic as is often presumed.[8] Furthermore, contrary to, say, Rick Worland's assertion that the *Scream* series "is about *almost nothing* except the often-simplistic formula of the slasher cycle of the early 1980s" (2007, 19; emphasis added), we would counter that this self-awareness demonstrates the ways in which contemporary teen horror reflexively understands that popular culture is a hugely important element in the cultural fabric of its audience's everyday lives. So while the box office success of *Scream* undeniably reinvigorated teen horror as a commercial property, this production trend has been more diverse and sophisticated in terms of narrative, tone, and thematic concerns than has often been recognized. Indeed, the genre continues to sustain itself via the perennial evolutionary dialectic between *familiarity* and *novelty*, with the representation of young adults functioning as the most fixed and unwavering element of recent years. Thus, whereas the rhetorical strategy employed by the critics cited above tends to emphasize the formulaic and homogenizing elements of recent teen horror, we prefer to focus upon the more interesting *differences* between individual horror texts. To paraphrase Lucy Fischer (1996), horror continues to offer expressionistic allegories of psychological and social *realities*, and for contemporary viewers the primary way these realities are communicated is through the hybridized generic lexicon and melodramatic emotional resonance of contemporary teen horror.

TEN YEARS OF TEEN HORROR: A (GUARDEDLY) OPTIMISTIC OVERVIEW

This is not to suggest, of course, that all contemporary teen horror necessarily warrants sympathetic reevaluation. In addition to the problematic *Hostel* films cited above, we would also suggest that a film like *Wrong Turn* (2003)—rather than simply being "about almost nothing"—is equally dubious as, among other things, a conservative and deeply paranoid class fable. Despite the intertextual nods to *The Texas Chainsaw Massacre*, *The Hills Have Eyes*, and *Deliverance* (1972)—the latter film even directly namechecked in the dialogue—the isolated rural setting and narrative trajectory of *Wrong Turn* lack the allegorical potency of its generic antecedents and subscribes to only the most tediously reactionary of horror *motifs*. While a number of recent films have offered (to varying degrees) more intriguing variations on the rural-horror theme—among them *The Blair Witch Project* (1999), *Jeepers Creepers* (2001) and its 2003 sequel, *Cabin Fever* (2003), *House of Wax* (2005), *Timber Falls* (2007) and, in particular, the intelligent remake of *The Hills Have Eyes* (2006)—*Wrong Turn's* schematic moral agenda and its regressive economies of gender, class, and race are practically bereft of any redeeming attributes.

Finding themselves isolated deep in the Appalachian region of West Virginia with their transport sabotaged, the recently graduated medical student Chris Flynn (Desmond Harrington) and a vacationing group of college friends—ostensibly headed by the willful Jessie (Eliza Dushku)—head into the woods to try and find a telephone. Meanwhile, as the rest of the party venture off, young couple Francine (Lindy Booth) and Evan (Kevin Zegers) wait with the stranded vehicles. Killing time as they await their friends' return, Francine is continually associated with an excessive orality: she repeatedly smokes cigarettes and marijuana and verbally initiates sex with Evan before descending to his crotch to perform oral sex. Later, while the couple attempt to salvage what they can from the damaged vehicles, Francine vocalizes to Evan that she can't find anything to eat in Chris's wrecked car while covertly stuffing confectionary into her mouth. The film's punitive agenda is made abundantly clear when, in a repeat of the film's opening tableau featuring the brutal and entirely unmotivated murder of an affluent young couple, Evan and Francine subsequently become the second pair of unwitting middle-class victims of the region's inbred "mountain men." Given that her murder takes places off-screen, our next glimpse of Francine is particularly overdetermined. As her bloody corpse is dragged into a rough shack that serves as home to the mountain men, a graphic close-up reveals that Francine's mouth and lower face have been grotesquely mutilated by a barbed wire noose wrapped around her head. Unceremoniously dumped directly in front of Chris and Jessie's eyeline as they cower unseen under a bed, Francine's body is then in turn crudely heaved onto a table and, for no apparent reason, methodically hacked to pieces by one of her lumpen assailants.

Lacking the self-reflexive humor of the *Scream* cycle or the sustained and impressively sardonic tone of *Cherry Falls* (2000), the absence of comedy in *Wrong Turn* is in some ways more typical of teen horror in the 2000s; yet it is this apparent seriousness that also confirms the film's ideological brutality. Indeed, the basic premise of a group of utterly unsympathetic rural subalterns preying on unsuspecting white middle-class holidaymakers is problematic in itself[9]; however, when the terrified young adults discover a hidden glade filled with unused vehicles belonging to earlier victims it transpires that the racially ambiguous mountain men lack even an economic motive to attack their victims. While this scene ostensibly functions to obscure the class paranoia at stake here, it also underscores the moral, ideological, and socioeconomic otherness of the *Wrong Turn*'s inbred underclass monsters. One might suggest at this juncture that *Wrong Turn*'s scenario—as well as its relative temporal proximity—suggests a bewildered and horrified kneejerk reaction to 9/11's violent assault on domestic security and Western late-capitalist culture more broadly. This may well be true on some (unconscious) level, but the film is nevertheless unrelenting in its systematic erasure of difference; indeed, the only obviously ethnically marked character, Carly (Emmanuelle Chriqui), is rapidly reduced to little more than a hysterical burden upon her white friends (and is later decapitated for her troubles). Meanwhile, survivors Chris and Jessie eventually form a tentatively platonic surviving couple, their chaste relationship almost entirely muting the sultry sexual ambiguity and charismatic postfeminist fortitude that Dushku brings from her iconic role in gothic teen-soap *Buffy the Vampire Slayer* (1997–2003).

As we hope our brief discussion of *Wrong Turn* serves to demonstrate, ideological analysis is still an essential tool when critically assessing the politics and affective investments of contemporary horror. Yet in our view, recent teen horror is usually more progressive than the likes of *Hostel* and *Wrong Turn* would suggest. Indeed, despite the dubious gender politics of those films perhaps the most welcome development in American horror has been precisely the shift toward the mode of female address which Dixon both identifies and immediately belittles.

While the assumption that young men constitute horror's key audience has been challenged in recent years, it is hardly insignificant that key critical interventions such as Clover's *Men, Women, and Chainsaws* and Creed's *The Monstrous-Feminine* both take for granted the assumption that horror is aimed primarily at the fears and desires of the hetero-masculine psyche.[10] Of course, this is due in no small way to the theoretical limitations of the psychoanalytic models of film spectatorship and identification which both Creed and Clover mobilize. But it is also perhaps indicative of shifts *within* the genre itself that these critics' important volumes increasingly seem anachronistic when dealing with much contemporary horror. As Valerie Wee (2006) notes in her analysis of the promotion, reception, and narrative strategies of the *Scream* trilogy, it is self-evident that their emotive soap operatics and "female-oriented perspective" (60) contributed enormously to the cross-gender appeal and commercial success of the cycle. Whereas key slasher franchises, from the late 1970s onward such as *Halloween, Friday the 13th* (1980), and *Nightmare on Elm Street* (1984)—all three continuing to the present day—tended to emphasize the return of the iconic monster in their promotional apparatus, the pre-publicity and DVD packaging for post-*Scream* franchises such as *I Know What You Did Last Summer* (1997–1998), *Urban Legend* (1998–2005), and *Final Destination* (2000–2009) instead foregrounded the troubled (and frequently female) teen protagonists and, implicitly, the films' empathetic focus on their physical, emotional, and psychological suffering, a trend which has since become practically the standard industry model in the promotion of teen-centric horror films.

With this overt courting of a female demographic also comes a refreshingly alert (post-)feminist sensibility which both refers back to and updates the proto-feminism of the slasher film's Final Girl from the late 1970s and early 1980s. As ever, then, recent teen horror adheres primarily to the genre's enduring emphasis on heightened subjective experience and psychological perception, appealing to *emotional* rather than objective realism. Thus, teen horror's allegorical pop-expressionist rendering of social experience affectively adheres to Hollywood's traditional melo-dramatic mode and its insistence upon on individualizing social trauma through emotive plotting and character-driven storytelling.

At their most straightforwardly subtextual, of course, victim-identified slasher films have always on some level addressed and expressionistically engaged with female anxieties concerning the threat of violent sexual assault. In more recent films, however, this trope becomes explicit: *Scream's* Sidney (Neve Campbell), *I Know What You Did Last Summer's* Julie (Jennifer Love Hewitt) and *Halloween H2o's* (1998) Laurie Strode (Jamie Lee Curtis) all exhibit recurrent symptoms including debilitating paranoia and anxiety attacks all-too-similar to those of the post-trau-matic suffering of victims of rape and domestic abuse. Even the largely comic plot of *Cherry Falls*—whose DVD cover gleefully foregrounds the film's high-concept fusion of *Scream* and *American Pie* (1999)—pivots upon a bleak back-story concerning the brutal gang rape of a young woman by, among others, the father of teen protagonist Jody (Brittany Murphy). The untrustworthiness of young men in recent teen horror is also underpinned by the genre's allusions to date rape. Having unknowingly dated and slept with the young man who raped and murdered her mother in the trilogy's first installment, by *Scream 3* the iconic Sidney is a hypervigilant, defiantly independent but ultimately reclusive loner. Armed with pepper spray and hidden away in a secluded Los Angeles safe house, Sidney now works as an anonymous telephone counsellor for the women's crisis center.[11] This generic preoccupation with the violent and/or sexual abuse of young women is also extended into other recent films such as *Hard Candy* (2005), *All the Boys Love Mandy Lane* (2006), and *Captivity* (2007) through to (the admittedly less teen-centric) remake of *The Amityville Horror* (2005) and the suggestively titled *An American Haunting* (2005), only the most recent in a series of horror texts preoccupied with domestic sexual abuse which arguably lead back to the influence of David Lynch's groundbreaking gothic soap opera *Twin Peaks* (1990–1991) and its big-screen prequel, *Fire Walk With Me* (1992).

This heightened emphasis on the potential horrors of heteronormativity also infuses the postfeminist sensibilities of some of the more intriguing examples of contemporary teen horror. *Valentine* (2001), for example, offers a sustained critique of normative masculinity from a female perspective, illustrating the everyday emotional, psychological, and sexual dysfunction of young manhood by emphasizing the ideological continuum between everyday chauvinism and the brutal violence enacted by female hero Kate's (Marley Shelton) neurotic, alcoholic boyfriend Adam (played, in a sharp piece of casting, by teen heartthrob David Boreanaz from *Buffy the Vampire Slayer* and *Angel* [1999–2004]). There is arguably a similar critical edge to the portrayal of selfish and immature youthful masculinities in *Cabin Fever* (2003), though, as in Eli Roth's other films, this is undercut by the filmmaker's neurotically persistent association of the female body with abjection. Considerably more interesting is the depiction of female homosociality in *The Craft* (1996), which, like its televisual cousin *Charmed* (1998–2006), is a supernatural parable of female friendship, gendered rage, and sublimated sexual energies that offers a clear and incisive rebuttal of straight white male heteronormalcy.[12] Alienated from male peers and their casual sexism, the film's self-styled "bitches of Eastwick" are symptomatic in their defiant reclamation of "witch" as a proto-feminist term of defiance, intelligence, and female independence from both men and, implicitly, the social and ideological panopticon of the heterosexual matrix.

Indeed, if most teen horror is resolutely heterosexual in outlook, *The Craft* exemplifies the contra-heteronormative thrust toward what Roz Kaveney dubs "the polymorphous portrayal of sexual chemistry" (2006, 6) that characterizes the most interesting contemporary teen movies. Although their difference from standards of normalcy is expressed primarily through the traditional channels of youthful self-expression—that is, through consumption and appearance—the young women find in each other and their supernatural bonds a joyous communal escape from both their dysfunctional family backgrounds and the dystopian space of high school.[13] While the film lacks the courage of its convictions and eventually revels in the subsequent collapse of their quasi-subaltern solidarity, it is the close friendship and gendered utopia of the film's midsection that lingers in most viewers' memories. Once again, however, the teen horror film offers a distinct female address while engaging effectively with emotive social issues via its fantastic pretext. The problems faced by the three central characters are illustrative in this respect: Nancy (Fairuza Balk) never escapes the trap of her lower-class background despite the death of her violent, alcoholic father; Rochelle (Rachel True) is repeatedly a victim of casual racism; and Sarah (Robin Tunney) is forced to fend off her duplicitous boyfriend when he attempts to rape her. Whereas the humorous critique of the social and sexual inadequacy of straight white masculinity in, say, *American Pie* eventually leads to a conservatively reassuring conclusion, *Valentine* and *The Craft* explicitly refuse this dubiously recuperative strategy, both remaining resolute in their gendered social perspective to the end.[14]

Of course, one can easily trace teen horror's ideological dissatisfaction with social definitions of gendered and sexual normalcy back to the subgenre's emergence in the 1950s. However, one key text—Brian DePalma's *Carrie* (1976)—functions in our view as one of the most important generic influences on the contemporary teen horror movie. *Carrie*'s scathing depiction of the horrors of high school socialization and its insistence upon the systematic internalization of institutionally sanctioned misogyny is articulated in emotionally hyperbolic tones, while its hybridized combination of horror, comedy, soap opera melodramatics, and exploitative teen drama mark it as a significant generic template. Certainly, *Carrie* is a key influence on *The Craft*, with which it shares a preoccupation with the sublimation of female anger and repressed sexuality, and also with *Valentine*, which openly alludes to the climactic prom scene from DePalma's film in its opening minutes. Films such as *The Faculty* (1998), *Welcome to the Dollhouse*, and *Elephant* also follow *Carrie* and *The Craft* in depicting middle-class suburbia and the high school environment as an oppressively institutionalized gothic space.

Having acquired a substantial cult following since its release, *Ginger Snaps* (2000) is another intriguing film that also updates and develops *Carrie*'s gendered horror paradigm.[15] A darkly witty tale of female lycanthropy, *Ginger Snaps* presents teenage female alienation as a troubled but distinctly oppositional subjective positioning in contrast to the oppressive conventions of feminine heteronormativity. As sisters Ginger (Katharine Isabelle) and Brigitte (Emily Perkins) pithily dismiss their milieu in unambiguously queer terms ("High school's just a mindless little breeders machine," Brigitte rasps, "a hormonal toilet"), the film ambivalently endorses their apparently self-willed refusal to begin their menstrual cycles and succumb to the abject social and physical prison of adult womanhood. *Ginger Snaps'* explicit references to genre classics such as *Cat People* (1942) and *Carrie* are not simply instances of smug postmodern posturing, however; the film deliberately engages with and celebrates the genre's long-term investment in subjectively expressing and empathizing with marginalized female experience. Thus, *Ginger Snaps'* vision of normative female heterosexuality as precisely a curse, a form of monstrous possession, offers an incisive critique of the limitations of gender roles and the (hetero)sexual double-standard ("A girl can only be a slut, bitch, tease, or the virgin next door," seethes Ginger), while the eponymous protagonist's dark wit and righteous social fury coupled with the film's mournful conclusion offer a compellingly bleak vision of gendered dis-ease. "I get this *ache*," Ginger confesses to her sister, "I thought it was for sex, but it's *to tear everything to fucking pieces.*"

Whereas Ginger's gendered rage and frustration is aimed at "everything," tearing more specific things to pieces is the thematic epicenter of Mitchell Lichtenstein's *Teeth* (2007). As an exemplar of many of the most compelling aspects of contemporary teen horror, *Teeth* offers a potent combination of deliciously black humor, graphic horror, and social critique in its often impressively sensitive portrayal of the emotional and psychological pitfalls of female adolescence, bodily insecurity, and sexual coming-of-age. As such, *Teeth* functions as an intelligent (post-)feminist movie mobilizing dark comedy and recurrent images of penile trauma to explore serious youth-oriented social issues, simultaneously literalizing, deconstructing, and celebrating the *vagina dentata* myth. Positively brimming with nuanced allusions to genre conventions and Freudian imagery and *motifs*, *Teeth* offers no shortage of incisive social commentary and meta-generic theoretical bite. Following the protagonist Dawn (Jess Weixler) through progressive mutation from a timid and defiantly virginal member of an evangelical chastity group to an independent and physically confident young woman, *Teeth's* satire of suburban sexual development moves beyond the relatively easy target of religious oppression and, much like *Carrie*, offers a sweeping critique of both the casual and institutionalized misogyny that Dawn encounters. From the film's opening tableau, in which an infant Dawn is coerced by her older stepbrother Brad (John Hensley) into "playing" I'll-show-you-mine-if-you'll-show-me-yours, *Teeth* presents growing up in American suburbia as, in no uncertain terms, a socio-sexual battleground. Although his early encounter with his sister's evolutionary defense mechanism leaves him (literally) scarred (and with a *penchant* for aggressive anal sex driven by latent castration anxiety),[16] Brad's contempt for women is represented as merely the most extreme form of the misogyny that characterizes the protagonist's social world. Indeed, with the exception of her stepfather, all Dawn's encounters with the normative masculine psyche are overwhelmingly negative: the apparently sensitive and caring would-be boyfriend Tobey (Hale Appleman) effectively attempts to rape Dawn after she is knocked unconscious as a result of his forceful and unwanted sexual advances; long-term admirer Ryan (Ashley Springer) poses as the sexually attentive hero who will conquer the "dark crucible" of femininity but, after plying Dawn with sedatives and champagne, is unveiled mid-*coitus* as a shallow and manipulative braggart; while Brad's long-term, quasi-incestuous desire for his stepsister is treated, like her other suitors, with suitably masticatory contempt. In one of *Teeth*'s most discomfiting sequences, a deeply insecure and anxious Dawn puts her faith in a medical examination in an attempt to clarify her physical abnormality. In keeping with the film's skeptical attitude toward the sexually exploitative duplicity of male figures, Dr. Godfrey (Josh Pais) is both hideously patronizing and lecherous (a cut reveals him covertly removing his surgical glove before carrying out an internal examination), and the entire procedure is sympathetically represented as humiliating, degrading, and physically painful. Indeed, the overall tone of *Teeth* is at once angry, tender, disturbing, and playful, and given the film's overt feminist (self-)consciousness it perhaps comes as no surprise that the most moving scenes in the film are, first, those between Dawn and her terminally ill mother; and second, the revelatory moment when Dawn comes face-to-face with the beguiling anatomical beauty of the female sexual organs in a previously censored textbook diagram (although, this time, reassuringly *sans* teeth).

In a fashion similar to the representation of the high school environment as an oppressive ideological prison in films like *Ginger Snaps* and *Teeth*, *The Faculty* offers a comically nightmarish depiction of the educational apparatus as the ideological epicenter of normative socialization. Like *Ginger Snaps*, *The Faculty* presents adults and adulthood as something terrifyingly "other" and *literally* alien, reworking the central conceit of *Invasion of the Body Snatchers* (1956) in which the transformation into one of "Them" is depicted as one of monstrously alienated conformity and the systematic annihilation of *difference*.[17] To this end, the saccharine conclusion in which the film's collective of heroically marginalized outsiders—including iconic young actors Josh Hartnett, Elijah Wood, and Clea DuVall—triumph over the alien invaders is delivered with a deliberate, almost Sirkian irony. As Timothy Shary (2002) and Andy W. Smith (2007) point out, all the lead characters surrender what made them interesting in the first place: the eternal nerd (Wood) becomes a sexually desired celebrity; the sexually ambivalent and ambiguously gendered tomboy Stokely (DuVall) enthusiastically embraces heteronormativity and embarks on a relationship with the film's requisite jock; and the intelligently rebellious outsider Zeke abandons pharmaceutical experimentation in favor of joining the football team. That the conclusion of *The Faculty* is effectively a satirical *homage* to the teen "classic" *The Breakfast Club* (1985) only confirms the film's ambivalent critique of the ideological colonization and crushing self-delusion imposed by normative social interpellation.

This use of intra-generational conflict as a metaphor for the eternal tension between social assimilation and individual autonomy is, of course, hardly a recent development in youth-oriented horror fare. Yet one the most interesting aspects of the genre in the last decade has been the insistent marginalization of adults from this youthful milieu. While parents and other authority figures have long been represented as bumbling, ineffectual, and conspicuously absent when needed the most, parental presence in the horror film has more recently become even less tangible. Of course, it has frequently been suggested that the supposed breakdown of the nuclear family unit as the core component of American society manifests itself in the *mise-en-scène* of contemporary horror, a world which is—in familial terms, at least—often fractured, dysfunctional, and emotionally awry. Symptomatic of this is recent teen horror's frequent representation of self-sufficient siblings at the heart of their narratives: *Ginger Snaps, Jeepers Creepers, House of Wax, Cursed, The Hamiltons* (2006), and *The Hills Have Eyes* all explicitly pivot around such relationships, for example. The opening section of *Jeepers Creepers*, featuring a protracted but stilted conversation between brother and sister Daryll (Justin Long) and Trish Jenner (Gina Phillips), is exemplary in its subtle intimations of domestic and interpersonal disquiet. Indeed, the belated appearance of the film's "reaper" is best understood on some level as a monstrous return of the emotionally repressed: a gothic manifestation of the unspoken tensions between the two characters. And just as *The Craft* ambivalently offered the girlfriends' proto-coven as a gendered escape from familial dysfunction, so too does Wes Craven's *Cursed* intimate a contra-heteronormative future for the family unit. At the film's conclusion, parentless siblings Ellie (Christina Ricci) and Jimmy (Jesse Eisenberg) have broken free of the lycanthropic curse that has haunted them and form an alternative familial collective with their pet dog and recently outed gay friend Bo (Milo Ventimiglia). Having rejected serial monogamy and vanquished her troubled relationship with her possessive and overbearing boyfriend Jake (Joshua Jackson), Ellie ends *Cursed* content and happily outside the strictures of the heterosexual matrix, functioning instead as the benevolent matriarch of a progressive and wholly inclusive *post*-nuclear collective. In *The Hamiltons*, however, this gothic reformulation of the nuclear family unit is presented in somewhat darker terms. Here, a group of vampiric and incestuous siblings strive to maintain domestic unity and economic survival by reducing their relationship to human beings *not* related by biology to one of predator and (necessary) prey. The film's critique of the primacy of blood-ties and its metaphors of social vampirism and reified alienation—epitomized by the siblings' murderously antisocial rejection of any moral or empathetic association beyond the ties that bind—systematically challenges the "normality" of the family unit. Just as the eldest sibling and would-be patriarch comically asserts that the Hamiltons are "just trying to be an ordinary family," the film offers an ambivalent and strangely melancholy assessment of the deep-rooted sociopathology involved in the pursuit of domestic and/or suburban normalcy.[18]

While teen horror's frequent evacuation of adults from its thematic *mise-en-scène* is certainly indicative on one level of the consistently narcissistic preoccupations of the teenpic, this structuring absence also necessarily allows its audience to vicariously work through collective fears and anxieties. The successful *Final Destination* franchise, for example, is notable for both its virtually adult-free fantasy universe and the series' gallows humor and progressively more gruesome aesthetic. However, it is clear that the morbid dread which underpins each of the films in the cycle returns compulsively to the same subject matter: premature death. Given the fantastic premise of the series—that "Death" can be cheated if one remains hyper-vigilant and works out its malevolent "design"—we would agree with Peter Hutchings's assertion that the *Final Destination* films function on one level as reassuring fantasies underpinned by youthful disavowal. What is perhaps most interesting about the cycle, then, is its insistence upon the terrifyingly banal manner in which young life can be casually snuffed out. As ever, horror ritualistically confronts its audience with the adult realities of mortality, grief, and psychological anguish, and to this end we would argue that the *Final Destination* series does indeed function on some levels as a melodramatic return of the Real which temporarily punctures the fantasmatic and insular bubble of affluent middle-class youth. By the third installment, the series was reflexively highlighting itself as a virtual thrill ride by opening with a spectacularly fatal rollercoaster accident, and while it is certainly true that the *Final Destination* films share with *Stay Alive* (2006) the internal logic of video games (wherein avoiding death is precisely a matter of skill, intelligence, and guile), it is their compulsive return to the spectacle—and aftermath—of unexpected death that marks their core appeal.[19]

Although we have attempted to offer a more optimistic summary of teen horror over the last ten years or so, it would be disingenuous to overlook some of the genre's more glaring limitations. Most obviously there is the almost unremitting *whiteness* of teen horror's on-screen representations of American youth. Somewhat notoriously, *Scream 2* opens with an arch and characteristically reflexive sequence in which two African American characters, Phil (Omar Epps) and Maureen (Jada Pinkett Smith), attend a theatrical screening of the movie's film-within-the-film, *Stab*. Echoing Sidney's racially blank dismissal of slasher films in the first film ("What's the point? They're all the same: some stupid killer stalking some big-breasted girl who can't act who is always running up the stairs when she should be running out the front door. It's insulting!"), Maureen complains that the film

will inevitably be a "dumb-ass white movie" and that "the horror genre is historical for excluding African-American elements." A few minutes later, both characters
are butchered in a theater filled with white audience members gleefully wearing
ghost-face masks. Given the humorously reflexive generic logic of the film, Maureen is ostensibly murdered due to her po-faced refusal to take the genre seriously;
however, there is also an unpleasant sense that she is killed precisely for the crime
of *speaking* race within the predominately white generic milieu she critiques. We
do not quite claim here that *Scream 2* is necessarily guilty of "ironic" racism at this
juncture, but in mobilizing this double move it *is* certainly guilty of a frustrating
incoherence on this subject. Indeed, when the film clearly suggests Maureen's vocal
discontent with the ideological shortcomings of horror films to be little more than
pseudo-political racial posturing—given Maureen's avowed stance, her boyfriend
understandably mocks her preferred viewing choice of a (*very* WASP-ish) Sandra
Bullock star vehicle—*Scream 2* seems even more culpable of hiding behind its own
inscrutable "ghost face."[20] (That Sidney's college roommate Hallie (Elise Neal) is
also black—and also meets a predictably bloody end—only adds to the politically
muddied water.)

Indeed, this problematic attitude to race seems largely endemic to recent teen
horror: *I Still Know What You Did Last Summer* (1998) is notable as one of the
very few teen horror films that contains central African American characters, while
Jeepers Creepers 2 is an intermittently interesting film that offers a critique of narcis-
sistically aggressive white masculinity and the subsequent racial tensions among the
film's stranded high school football team. Yet any sustained commentary on race is
casually displaced by the film's disappointingly relentless tone of homosexual panic
as the predatory reaper gazes desirously at the toned and athletic bodies of the fearful male protagonists. *Urban Legend* and *Halloween H20* (both 1998) feature African
American adults (played by Loretta Devine and L.L. Cool J) who survive the respective murderous onslaught; both, however, are little more than bumbling caricatures:
tokenistic figures whose primary function in the narrative is to (ineptly) protect
white teens. Such consistent generic limitations in terms of racial representation are
almost certainly why the preternaturally calm figure of Benny (Bennie Dixon)—the
sole African American student we encounter in *Elephant*—is so haunting: generically, we know he is doomed. As such, watching Benny's quietly determined stroll
toward his inevitable fate it is difficult not to see his wordlessly oneiric demeanor as
a direct allusion to the hypnotic Carre-Four's (Darby Jones) striking liminal presence in the fiercely intelligent and racially charged genre classic *I Walked With a
Zombie* (1943).[21]

It hardly needs stating that teen horror is also for the most part unrelentingly
and unapologetically middle class in both focus and sensibility. *The Craft* and *My
Little Eye* (2002) stand out as two of the few films to make the disparity between the

socioeconomic backgrounds of its protagonists a key thematic point in the narra-tive. *My Little Eye* is also arguably the forerunner in the recent cycle of films offering (with varying degrees of success) a critical look at the numbing reification and ethi-cal vacuity of late capitalism, a cycle not coincidentally preoccupied with the use and abuse of new visual and communication technologies and which includes the *Hostel* films, *Captivity* and *Vacancy* (both 2007), and George Romero's timely "teenifica-tion" of his ongoing zombie saga in *Diary of the Dead* (2007). The two films in the briefly popular *I Know What You Did Last Summer* cycle also offer the intriguing possibility that what really haunts the troubled teens is less guilt over their youth-ful transgressions *per se* and more their psychological inability (and, in the case of Freddie Prinz Jr.'s character, Ray, the *literal* socioeconomic inability) to transcend the socioeconomic trappings of the small working-class fishing town where they grew up. Eternally stalked by a menacing figure clad in industrial fisherman's garb, both films are best understood as affective psychodramas that indicate a some-what more emotionally realistic examination of class consciousness and socioeco-nomic guilt than can be found in, say, *Wrong Turn* or the equally hysterical *When a Stranger Calls* (2006).[22] Similarly, perhaps the most intriguing aspect of *My Bloody Valentine* (2009) is its generically uncharacteristic temporal shift from an initially hedonistic teen milieu. Indeed, the film's sustained depiction of a blue-collar small town characterized by socioeconomic entrapment for those selfsame youth now in thirty-something adulthood is infinitely more powerful than its banal quasi-slasher *motifs*. Elsewhere, in their neo-Orientalism and narrative actualization of (racist) urban myths both *Turistas* (2006) and *The Ruins* (2008) follow the *Hostel* movies in articulating a socioeconomically paranoid and distinctly xenophobic attitude to that which lies outside the boundaries of the United States. *Turistas*, in particular, opens with painfully crass visual shorthand for the presumed horrors of an impov-erished Latin America: stray dogs, poor transportation, and—worst of all—public breastfeeding. Meanwhile, it is barely coincidental that Kiko (Agles Steib), the sole Brazilian native to befriend the "arrogant gringo tourists," is a young man whose trustworthiness is signified primarily through his determination to "improve" (read: Westernize) himself by learning to speak English. While all of these films to an extent engage critically with the gulf between the casual affluence of their young protagonists and the everyday poverty and social deprivation they encounter abroad, the specter of global inequality and Western exploitation is rapidly exorcised when these "innocently" wealthy and attractive teens are assaulted by malevolent indigents from foreign lands. The conclusion of *Turistas* is emblematic in this respect, with one of the few survivors sagely advising another young tourist who wants to explore the inner country by bus to "take the plane" instead. Here be dragons, indeed.

Finally, just as the teen horror film's class and racial economies are symptomatic of Hollywood representation more broadly, so too are the genre's heterosexism and relentless fetishism of (in particular) young female bodies. While we have earlier noted the proto-queer subtexts evident in films such as *Ginger Snaps* and *The Craft*, a throwaway gag in *The Faculty* about a bootleg video in circulation featuring naked footage of Neve Campbell and Jennifer Love Hewitt is certainly indicative of the knowing exploitation mentality of contemporary teen horror and its foregrounding of attractive young stars. The promotional material for *Turistas*, for example, largely consisted of images of nubile bikini-clad twenty-somethings, while Elisha Cuthbert's—star of TV's popular *24* (2001–)—roles in both *House of Wax* and *Captivity* seem troublingly predicated on a systematically punitive psychosexual logic. Although *Captivity* offers a somewhat superficial critique of the beauty myth, and briefly attempts to draw parallels between the reification and objectification of the glamour industry and the brutal punishment enacted by the protagonist's torturers, the film as a whole is uneasily schizophrenic in tone. In one particular moment of misogynistic *Grand Guignol*, the imprisoned actress-cum-model Jennifer (Cuthbert) is force-fed blended entrails in a cruel parody of her earlier consumption of a nourishing health drink. Lacking the intriguingly perverse morality and ponderous ethical dimensions of the successful *Saw* (2004–) cycle to which it is clearly indebted, *Captivity*'s visual pleasure in foregrounding threats to Jennifer's physical beauty seems grounded in gleeful sadism and a clear delight in punishing female "narcissism." While the latter stages of the film attempt to displace this psychosexual gratification onto the warped psyche of Jennifer's assailants, their glibly Oedipal back-story—in a film overflowing with allusions to *Psycho*, it is no surprise that their animosity toward women stems from sexual abuse at the hands of their mother—only seems to add to the misogyny of the piece. Moreover, just as *Captivity* foregrounds its own reflexive interest in the cult of celebrity via its young starlet (Jennifer may as well *be* Cuthbert), so too does Paris Hilton's cameo in *House of Wax* offer a problematic dual address. In perhaps the most memorable sequence of a largely undistinguished film, Hilton's character meets her demise when she is orally impaled upon a lengthy metal rod. As the film cuts to a graphic close-up of Hilton's open mouth sliding suggestively down the bloody pole, her murderer also begins to film his victim's grotesquely sexual death-throes on a hand-held camera. In a scene that famously provoked cheers and applause from theatrical audiences, *House of Wax* alludes quite transparently—and vindictively—to the notorious celebrity's widely circulated "sex tape." Like Cuthbert's sadistic treatment in *Captivity*, however, the film's obvious relish at this point leaves the viewer, like poor Paris, with a bad taste in the mouth. This brief critique of *Captivity* and *House of Wax* is not to dismiss teen horror's engagement with youthful desire and sexual expression out-of-hand, however. Whereas Thomas Doherty sees recent teen films' attitude to sexual contact as being overshadowed by the specter of AIDS, we would suggest in contradistinction that films such as *Cherry Falls* offer a somewhat more liberal and celebratory vision of youthful sexuality, what we would tentatively (if, admittedly, somewhat reluctantly) dub a post-AIDS sensibility. Yet the genre is certainly not naïve on this point: films as diverse as *Cabin Fever, Cursed, Ginger Snaps, Teeth*, and the aforementioned *Cherry Falls* all deal with sexually transmitted infection (and the avoidance thereof) with varying degrees of opacity, wit, and intelligence.

CONCLUSION: LOOKING BACKWARD, LOOKING FORWARD

Just like the camera in *Elephant*, then, Hollywood's recent horror output insistently prowls the social, psychological, and emotional corridors of contemporary American youth. In contradistinction to critics of recent developments within the genre, we would argue that it is—at best—simply misguided to project leftist longings onto contemporary teen horror only, and inevitably, to find it wanting. Indeed, what is so striking about the hallowed horror films of the late 1960s and 1970s is less their articulation of any kind of coherent politically oppositional stance and more their (entirely symptomatic) outright nihilism. In other words, we suggest that the affective appeal of contemporary teen horror needs to be understood *on its own terms*—a hybridized generic lexicon, perhaps outside the critical remit of enthusiasts enamored with earlier stages in the American horror film's historical development.

However, one element of recent horror does strike us as being indicative of the necessity for cautious optimism where American horror's future is concerned. A recurrent trope in films that have emerged since the military invasions of Afghanistan and Iraq has been a melodramatic insistence upon the *innocence* of young Americans in the face of their various aggressors. While this does on some level indicate a form of sociopolitical disavowal, recent youth-oriented remakes of *The Fog* (2005) and *The Hills Have Eyes* foreground a refusal to be associated with the sins of the fathers and a resistance to the key horror *motif* of history repeating itself. If recent horror films—from *Scream* to *Elephant* and beyond—have often depicted the social experience of American youth as akin to being trapped *within* a horror movie, then the genre has also begun tentatively to indicate a way out, a way to escape the inescapability of the past. These gothic melodramas about youthful trauma may maintain that, to paraphrase *Cursed*'s Ellie, (social) life *is* a curse. But they also ensure that their engagements with this affective agenda follow the directive to "have fun," to work through their concerns via the reflexive serious play of youth culture. Like teen horror as a whole this stance certainly has its limitations, but it also offers cautious cause for optimism about the future direction of the genre and, hopefully, American culture more broadly.

NOTES

1. With the Virginia Tech massacre of April 2007 still fresh in the memory, it was reported that five people were shot (including the suicide of the perpetrator) at SuccessTech high school in Cleveland, Ohio, during the first drafts of this paper in early October 2007. There have been at least five reported shootings at U.S. educational establishments since then, including (most recently and most seriously at the time of writing) six deaths at Northern Illinois University in February 2008.

2. See Diane Negra, "An American Werewolf in London," *America First: Naming the Nation in U.S. Film*, ed. Many Merck (London: Routledge, 2007), for a lively discussion of the politics of "European misadventure" films.

3. See Kim Newman, "Torture Garden," *Sight and Sound* 16.6 (June 2006), for a useful commentary on *Hostel* and a summary of torture iconography in horror films more broadly. As he suggests, the final stages of *Hostel* are indicative of Roth's "lazy writing and direction, and any sense that an important issue is being touched upon gets lost [. . .] The veiled message is that torture is an atrocity when perpetrated on Americans but is justified when used by Americans against those they deem responsible for starting the conflict [. . .] which is perilously close to being George W. Bush's foreign policy than the premise for a box-office shocker" (31).

4. *The Texas Chainsaw Massacre* eventually grossed $80,148,261 at the domestic box office. Source: www.imdb.com.

5. For example, *Scream* featured Neve Campbell from *Party of Five* (1994–2000) and Courtney Cox from *Friends* (1994–2004); *I Know What You Did Last Summer* starred Jennifer Love Hewitt (also from *Party of Five*) and Sarah Michelle Gellar from *Buffy the Vampire Slayer*; Joshua Jackson from *Dawson's Creek* (1998–2003) stars in *Urban Legend*, *Cursed*, and *Scream 2*; *The Fog* featured Maggie Grace from *Lost* (2004–) and Tom Welling from *Smallville* (2001–); while *House of Wax* included key actors from *24*, *The Simple Life* (2003–2007), and *One Tree Hill* (2003–).

6. Williamson's teen-soap credentials were established in his work on the popular television show *Dawson's Creek*. In addition to writing *Scream* and *Scream 2* (and producing *Scream 3*), he also wrote screenplays for *I Know What You Did Last Summer*, *The Faculty*, and *Cursed*.

7. For a detailed discussion of "subcultural capital" and its centrality to contemporary youth culture, see Sarah Thornton, *Club Cultures: Music, Media and Subcultural Capital* (Cambridge: Polity Press, 1995); for more on the pleasures and (sub)cultural functions of repeat viewings and domestic technologies, see Barbara Klinger, *Beyond the Multiplex: Cinema, New Technologies, and the Home* (Berkeley and Los Angeles: University of California Press, 2006).

8. See Andrew Tudor, "From Paranoia to Postmodernism? The Horror Movie in Late Modern Society," *Genre and Contemporary Hollywood*, ed. Steve Neale (London: British Film Institute, 2002) and Peter Hutchings, *The Horror Film* (Harlow: Pearson Education, 2004). For a sympathetic reading of *Scream*—albeit one that relies heavily on the concept of postmodernism—see Kendall R. Phillips, *Projected Fears: Horror Films and American Culture* (Westport, Conn.: Praeger, 2005), 163–80.

9. We appropriate the term "subaltern" here from Antonio Gramsci, *Selections from the Prison Notebooks*, ed. Quintin Hoare and Geoffry Nowell-Smith (New York: International Publishers, 1971). Gramsci's use of the term has most frequently been read as a quasi-Marxist euphemism for the proletariat, but "subaltern" has a protean critical history and has also been taken to apply to other marginal social groups (such as sexual and ethnic minorities, for example), which would seem appropriate to *Wrong Turn's* "monsters" on a number of levels. We would like to

distinguish our usage at this specific juncture from elsewhere in the essay when the term is occasionally mobilized in reference to (middle-class) American youth. Given the expressionistic underpinnings of horror, "subaltern" is here intended as a subjective metaphor for the liminality and (perceived) marginality of adolescence and associated subcultural groupings.

10. See, for example, Isabel Cristina Pinedo, *Recreational Terror: Women and the Pleasures of Horror Film Viewing* (Albany: State University of New York Press, 1997); Brigid Cherry, "Refusing to Refuse to Look: Female Viewers of the Horror Film," *Identifying Hollywood's Audiences: Cultural Identity and the Movies*, ed. Melvyn Stokes and Richard Maltby (London: British Film Institute, 1999); and Valerie Wee, "Resurrecting and Updating the Teen Slasher: The Case of *Scream*," *Journal of Popular Film and Television* 34.2 (2006), on the pleasures of horror films for female viewers.

11. For more on the gender politics of the *Scream* cycle and its relationship to postfeminism, see Kathryn Rowe Karlyn, "*Scream*, Popular Culture, and Feminism's Third Wave: 'I'm Not My Mother,'" *Genders Online Journal* 38 (2003), http://www.genders.org/g38/g38_rowe_karlyn.html.

12. For an interesting discussion of *Charmed* and the relationship between "witchcraft" and communal postfeminism, see Hannah E. Sanders, "Living a *Charmed* Life: The Magic of Postfeminist Sisterhood," *Interrogating Postfeminism: Gender and the Politics of Popular Culture*, ed. Yvonne Tasker and Diane Negra (Durham, N.C.: Duke University Press, 2007).

13. Steve Bailey and James Hay, "Cinema and the Premises of Yuth: 'Teen Films' and Their Sites in the 1980s and 1990s," *Genre and Contemporary Hollywood*, ed. Steve Neale (London: British Film Institute, 2002), rightly note that, in recent teen cinema, "there is a post-liberal acceptance of the absolute primacy of the commodity system and that practices of self-development and self-discipline cannot be separated from this logic" (232). Their comment that the shopping mall has become "the metaphorical location for the assumption of a mature lifestyle" (227) is exemplified in the closing sequences of celebrated teen comedy *Superbad* (2007), where the central male protagonists reluctantly sacrifice the comforts of adolescent homosociality for their predetermined heterosexual trajectories amid the commodified interpellations of the shopping mall.

14. For more on the representation of masculinity in *American Pie* and other teen movies, see David Greven, "Contemporary Teen Comedies and New Forms of American Masculinity," *Cineaste* 27.3 (2002): 14–21.

15. For more on the cult reputation of *Ginger Snaps* and its sequels, see M. Barker, E. Mathijs, and X. Mendik, "Menstrual Monsters: The Reception of the *Ginger Snaps* Cult Horror Franchise," *The Cult Film Reader*, ed. Ernest Mathijs and Xavier Mendik (Maidenhead: Open University Press, 2008).

16. As reviewer Isabel Stevens notes, the film offers two broadly "realistic" explanations for Dawn's genital mutation: "the result of the nuclear power station that looms over the tree-lined streets, or a Darwinian case of adapt-to-survive" (78).

17. Similarly, Abel Ferrera's stylish and effective remake of *Invasion of the Body Snatchers*— *Body Snatchers* (1993)—reworks the central trope of the film directly in terms of the domestic, social and—given the film's setting on a military base and its temporal proximity to the Persian Gulf War—*national* alienation experienced by the film's young female protagonist, played by Gabrielle Anwar.

18. See Nathan Holmes, "Playing House: Screen Teens and the Dreamworld of Suburbia," *A Family Affair: Cinema Comes Home*, ed. Murray Pomerance (London: Wallflower, 2008), for an intriguing commentary on the ways in which American cinema has repeatedly depicted the "failed utopia" of suburbia as an expressionistic stage "upon which middle-class anxiety, desire, perversity, frustration and alienation are performed" (250).

19. That the spectatorial pleasures of the *Final Destination* series are marked by a fantasmatic generic economy of mastery/lack (akin in no small way to Freud's account of the infantile psychology at play in the *fort/da* "game") was underscored by the DVD release of *Final Destination 3*, which included a special feature allowing viewers to "change the course of the film and characters fates." Just like the *Final Destination* movies' narratives, then, the DVD insisted upon the possibility that youthful viewers can, if they so choose, "take control of the ride!"

20. This very postmodern sense of ideologically "having it both ways" is also typified by *Scream*'s now-iconic ghost-face mask derived from Munch's "The Scream" (1893). The mask serves as a witty comment on the casual commodification of (teenage) angst just as the *Scream* franchise itself commercially exploits that selfsame angst. Inevitably, the very mask made famous by the *Scream* franchise is now an ancillary product readily available to purchase outside the diegesis of the films.

21. For a fascinating reading of the racial politics of *I Walked With a Zombie*, see Alexander Nemerov, *Icons of Grief: Val Lewton's Home Front Pictures* (Berkeley and Los Angeles: University of California Press, 2005): 97–131.

22. James Morrison, "Hostages and Houseguests: Class and Family in the New Screen Gothic," *A Family Affair: Cinema Comes Home*, ed. Murray Pomerance (London: Wallflower Press, 2008), makes a compelling case for the "expedient synthesis of hysteria and smugness" which characterizes a recent spate of gothic-tinged American films concerned with assaults on the domestic sphere, which are, he argues, ideologically predicated on "a largely disavowed class consciousness" (190).

WORKS CITED

Bailey, Steve, and James Hay. "Cinema and the Premises of Youth: 'Teen Films' and Their Sites in the 1980s and 1990s." *Genre and Contemporary Hollywood*. Ed. Steve Neale. London: British Film Institute, 2002. 218–35.

Barker, M., E. Mathijs, and X. Mendik. "Menstrual Monsters: The Reception of the *Ginger Snaps* Cult Horror Franchise." *The Cult Film Reader*. Eds. Ernest Mathjis and Xavier Mendik. Maidenhead: Open University Press, 2008. 482–94.

Cherry, Brigid. "Refusing to Refuse to Look: Female Viewers of the Horror Film." *Identifying Hollywood's Audiences: Cultural Identity and the Movies*. Eds. Melvyn Stokes and Richard Maltby. London: British Film Institute, 1999. 187–203.

Clover, Carol. *Men, Women, and Chainsaws: Gender in the Modern Horror Film*. London: British Film Institute, 1993.

Creed, Barbara. *The Monstrous-Feminine: Film, Feminism, Psychoanalysis*. London: Routledge, 1993.

Dixon, Wheeler Winston. "'Fighting and Violence and Everything That's Always Cool': Teen Films in the 1990s." *Film Genre 2000: New Critical Essays*. Ed. Wheeler Winson Dixon. Albany: State University of New York Press, 2000. 125–41.

Doherty, Thomas. *Teenagers and Teenpics: The Juvenilization of American Movies in the 1950s*. Philadelphia: Temple University Press, 2002.

Faludi, Susan. *The Terror Dream: What 9/11 Revealed about America*. London: Atlantic Books, 2008.

Fischer, Lucy. "Birth Traumas: Parturition and Horror in *Rosemary's Baby*." *The Dread of Difference: Gender and the Modern Horror Film*. Ed. Barry Keith Grant. Austin: University of Texas Press, 1996. 412–31.

Gramsci, Antonio. *Selections from the Prison Notebooks*. Eds. Quintin Hoare and Geoffry Nowell-Smith. New York: International Publishers, 1971.

Greven, David. "Contemporary Teen Comedies and New Forms of American Masculinity." *Cineaste* 27.3 (2002): 14–21.

Heffernan, Kevin. *Ghouls, Gimmicks, and Gold: Horror Films and the American Movie Business, 1953–1968*. Durham, N.C.: Duke University Press, 2004.

Holmes, Nathan. "Playing House: Screen Teens and the Dreamworld of Suburbia." *A Family Affair: Cinema Comes Home*. Ed. Murray Pomerance. London: Wallflower, 2008. 249–62.

Hutchings, Peter. *The Horror Film*. Harlow: Pearson Education, 2004.

Jancovich, Mark. *Rational Fears: American Horror in the 1950s*. Manchester: Manchester University Press, 1996.

Karlyn, Kathryn Rowe. "*Scream*, Popular Culture, and Feminism's Third Wave: 'I'm Not My Mother.'" *Genders Online Journal* 38 (2003). http://www.genders.org/g38/g38_rowe_karlyn.html.

Kaveney, Roz. *Teen Dreams: Reading Teen Film and Television from 'Heathers' to 'Veronica Mars'*. London: I. B. Tauris, 2006.

Kermode, Mark. "What a carve up!" *Sight and Sound* 13.12 (December 2003): 12–16.

Klinger, Barbara. *Beyond the Multiplex: Cinema, New Technologies, and the Home*. Berkeley and Los Angeles: University of California Press, 2006.

Morrison, James. "Hostages and Houseguests: Class and Family in the New Screen Gothic." *A Family Affair: Cinema Comes Home*. Ed. Murray Pomerance. London: Wallflower Press, 2008. 189–201.

Negra, Diane. "An American Werewolf in London." *America First: Naming the Nation in U.S. Film*. Ed. Mandy Merck. London: Routledge, 2007. 119–213.

Nemerov, Alexander. *Icons of Grief: Val Lewton's Home Front Pictures*. Berkeley and Los Angeles: University of California Press, 2005.

Newman, Kim. "Torture Garden." *Sight and Sound* 16.6 (June 2006): 28–31.

Phillips, Kendall R. *Projected Fears: Horror Films and American Culture*. Westport, Conn.: Praeger, 2005.

Pinedo, Isabel Cristina. *Recreational Terror: Women and the Pleasures of Horror Film Viewing*. Albany: State University of New York Press, 1997.

Said, S. F. "Shock Corridors." *Sight and Sound* 14.2 (February 2004): 16–18.

Sanders, Hannah E. "Living a *Charmed* Life: The Magic of Postfeminist Sisterhood." *Interrogating Postfeminism: Gender and the Politics of Popular Culture*. Eds. Yvonne Tasker and Diane Negra. Durham, N.C.: Duke University Press, 2007. 73–99.

Sanjek, David. "Same as it Ever Was: Innovation and Exhaustion in the Horror and Science Fiction Films of the 1990s." *Film Genre 2000: New Critical Essays*. Albany: State University of New York Press, 2000. 111–23.

Shary, Timothy. *Generation Multiplex: The Image of Youth in Contemporary American Cinema*. Austin: University of Texas Press, 2002.

Smith, Andy W. "'These children that you spit on': Horror and Generic Hybridity." *Monstrous Adaptations: Generic and Thematic Mutations in Horror Film*. Eds. Richard J. Hand and Jay McRoy. Manchester: Manchester University Press, 2007. 2–94.

Stevens, Isabel. "Teeth." *Sight and Sound* 18.7 (2008): 78–79.

Thornton, Sarah. *Club Cultures: Music, Media and Subcultural Capital*. Cambridge: Polity Press, 1995.

Tudor, Andrew. "From Paranoia to Postmodernism? The Horror Movie in Late Modern Society." *Genre and Contemporary Hollywood*. Ed. Steve Neale. London: British Film Institute, 2002. 105–16.

Wee, Valerie. "Resurrecting and Updating the Teen Slasher: The Case of *Scream*." *Journal of Popular Film and Television* 34.2 (Summer 2006): 50–61.

Wells, Paul. *The Horror Genre: From Beelzebub to Blair Witch*. London: Wallflower Press, 2000.

Williams, Linda. "Melodrama Revised." *Refiguring Film Genres*. Ed. Nick Browne. Berkeley and Los Angeles: University of California Press, 1998. 42–88.

Wood, Robin. "Foreword: 'What Lies Beneath?'" *Horror Film and Psychoanalysis: Freud's Worst Nightmare*. Ed. Steven Jay Schneider. Cambridge: Cambridge University Press, 2004. xiii–xviii.

Wood, Robin. "An Introduction to the American Horror Film." *American Nightmares: Essays on the Horror Film*. Eds. Andrew Britton et al. Toronto: Festival of Festivals, 1979. 7–28.

TRAUMATIC CHILDHOOD NOW INCLUDED

Todorov's Fantastic and the
Uncanny Slasher Remake

—Andrew Patrick Nelson

"LOVED THE ORIGINAL, HATED THE REMAKE"

Long before and quite apart from the self-referential "rules" expounded in Wes Craven's *Scream* trilogy or the lesson-instilling "games" orchestrated by the Jigsaw killer in the *Saw* franchise, horror movies in general—and slasher movies in particular—have been in the business of helping viewers reconcile themselves to some of life's cold, hard facts. To cite a personal example: as I am not a virginal teenage girl, I know that the odds of my surviving an encounter with a masked, knife-, axe-, or chainsaw-wielding maniac are slim to none. Furthermore, I know that a willingness on my part to make self-conscious, self-deprecating references to popular culture and cinematic conventions—regardless of how such references may both thwart my chances of coital success and endear me to the audience—will do little to improve those odds.

Another important and rather more academic lesson I have learned in the school of slash-and-gash is how difficult it can be to appraise a remake on "its own merits" if you have seen the original. As a result, a critical tendency when dealing with remakes in general is to establish a pretense of objectivity, often by declaring an admiration for the original at outset. This tendency comes out most clearly— and, perhaps, honestly—in user comments and reviews found on Web sites like the *Internet Movie Database* and *Ain't It Cool News*, which manage to claim an outright distaste for the trend of remaking major horror movies while maintaining that each new remake has been given the benefit of the doubt and been viewed with an open mind. Yet in spite of such disclaimers, many reviews both professional and amateur proceed nonetheless—and usually unintentionally—to judge the new film in relation to the original.

It must be said that there are many other genres from which one could arrive at similar conclusions. Horror certainly has no monopoly on remakes, and thus no monopoly on the ways in which remakes are appraised. I would, however, argue that the tendency to judge remakes in relation to originals is part of a natural, cognitive process. We appraise all movies to some degree based on our experiences, be they from our everyday lives—"it just wasn't realistic" being a common criticism—or from other movies we have seen. A remake simply provides us with a more concrete background against which to measure a film. What is more, one could certainly argue that, in the case of the horror genre, this tendency is fed not only by a propensity for remakes but also a preponderance of sequels and, more generally, sets of expectations based on familiarity with the genre and its conventions. All genres have conventions, certainly, but there is a fair amount of truth to the old cliché that there is always an audience for horror—the notion that there exists a particular audience that frequents horror movies on a consistent basis.

None of this is particularly groundbreaking, of course, and so a more interesting question is how to productively examine and articulate the similarities and differences between remakes and originals while maintaining a degree of generic specificity. To that end, what I first propose to do in this piece is to carry out a comparative analysis of a recent horror remake and its original by adapting the critical approach employed by the literary philosopher Tzvetan Todorov in his seminal 1970 study *The Fantastic: A Structural Approach to a Literary Genre*. Following this, I shall expand my inquiry to consider the role of the fantastic in the broader cyclical contexts of both the original and the remake.

Making use of Todorov's articulation of the fantastic in the context of an examination of the horror movie is by no means an original conceit. Many syllabi for film courses on the horror genre feature Todorov's text, and several writers, including Noël Carroll and Dudley Andrew, have discussed the fantastic in relation to cinema. But what is at least halfway original—for reasons I shall detail in due course—is my choice of which films to examine.

TWO *HALLOWEENS*

Perhaps the most notorious, polarizing horror remake of recent years—in terms of both the very idea of attempting a remake and the realization of that notion—is heavy-metal-musician-turned-moviemaker Rob Zombie's 2007 remake of John Carpenter's 1978 film *Halloween*. From his effort at reimagining the origin of serial killer Michael Myers it is clear that Zombie understood the task he faced, even if his attempt at crafting a film that balances reverence for the original with updates and innovation—or perhaps his own personal vision—was not judged to be successful.

Rather than release the movie on or around October 31, where it would face stiff competition from *Saw IV*, the distributors of the new *Halloween* chose to open the film on the final Friday of August, which is considered by American studios to be the last weekend of summer. Despite receiving a drubbing by critics, *Halloween* took top spot at the box office, earning a respectable $26 million in its opening weekend before being dethroned the following week by another genre remake, *3:10 to Yuma* (James Mangold), thus beginning a quick slide into box office obscurity.

Before turning to an analysis of the two *Halloween*s, however, a brief introduction to some of Todorov's ideas about the fantastic is in order. Essentially, works of the fantastic involve what Todorov calls an uncanny event, a mysterious or strange narrative occurrence that provokes a "hesitation" in both the story's protagonist and the reader—or, in our case, the viewer. Writes Todorov:

> In a world which is indeed our world, the one we know, a world without devils, sylphides, or vampires, there occurs an event which cannot be explained by the laws of this same familiar world. The person who experiences the event must opt for one of two possible solutions: either he is the victim of an illusion of the senses, of a product of imagination—and the laws of the world remain as they are; or else the event has indeed taken place, it is an integral part of reality—but then this reality is controlled by laws unknown to us. Either the devil is an illusion, an imaginary being; or else he really exists, precisely like other living beings—with this reservation, that we encounter him infrequently. (25)

The fantastic can occur only so long as a hesitation between the two solutions is sustained. Hence, the fantastic exists on the frontier of two neighboring genres: the marvelous and the uncanny. In the former, the event in question is accounted for as supernatural in origin. In the latter, the event—no matter how unusual or disquieting it may be—is explained in terms of the laws of the natural world.

Here it is important to distinguish between Todorov's use of "uncanny" and the term's more familiar psychoanalytic usage subsequent to Sigmund Freud's influential 1919 essay on the subject. Oddly, Todorov makes no reference to his parallel use of the term, save for a single, brief aside, writing that "there is not an entire coincidence between Freud's use of the term and our own" (47). What is more—more confusing, potentially—he uses "uncanny" both as an adjective (viz., "uncanny event") to describe a particular narrative occurrence *and* as the proper name of one of the fantastic's neighboring genres.

Common to Freud's conception of the uncanny and Todorov's adjectival use is the idea of an experience or event provoking a feeling of uneasiness, where the familiar seems strange and the strange familiar. For Todorov, however, this sensation is not a symptom of a deep-seated neurosis—of the author or of one of the narrative's characters—that it then becomes the analyst's or the critic's task to interpret using the tools of psychoanalysis. Indeed, he cautions in his concluding chapter against such a procedure, warning "the too-direct application of a method in a realm other than its own results in the reiteration of the initial presuppositions" (152). Todorov is instead concerned with the *thematic and structural implications* of the "hesitation" that the uncanny event elicits. At stake is a work's generic classification—uncanny, fantastic, marvelous—based on which we can examine the work in relation to others like it.

Many stories deliberately delay—that is, hesitate—before ascribing events to either one of the two polar rationales. For example, the revealing at a tale's conclusion of a "mastermind" who has been clandestinely orchestrating seemingly paranormal happenings is a common plot device in both literature and film. In such instances, events that seem supernatural throughout a story receive a rational explanation in the end. Conversely, a narrative may conclude with an affirmation or acceptance of the supernatural—it really was ghosts, monsters, or the devil all along.

Recognizing these cases, Todorov further posits two transitory subgenres and conceptualizes their relationship using the following diagram:

The median line between fantastic-uncanny and fantastic-marvelous represents the fantastic in its pure state. As Todorov notes, few narratives sustain their ambiguity to the very end—that is, beyond the narrative itself—so as to achieve this pure state, but there are examples. One he cites is the Henry James tale *The Turn of the Screw*, which "does not permit us to determine finally whether ghosts haunt the old estate, or whether we are confronted by the hallucinations of a hysterical governess victimized by the disturbing atmosphere that surrounds her" (43).

My contention is that the original *Halloween* is an instance of the fantastic, but that the remake falls into the realm of the uncanny. Whereas Carpenter's movie sustains a fantastic hesitation as to the nature of its uncanny event by refusing to provide a tangible explanation for Michael Myers—the origin of his iniquity, the nature of his physical power, the motivation for his murderous actions—Zombie's picture instead opts to account for the killer's evil using pop psychology. As explained in the movie by the psychiatrist Dr. Samuel Loomis, Michael's adolescent psychopathy is the product of a kind of serial killer recipe: "Michael was created by a perfect alignment of interior and exterior factors gone violently wrong. A perfect storm, if you will. Thus creating a psychopath that knows no boundaries, and has no boundaries."

A recurring criticism of the remake of *Halloween* is that the film just isn't scary. This is one of the most damning judgments that can be leveled against a horror movie, especially if one subscribes to the notion of horror as "body genre," characterized by the elicitation of an intended affective response in the viewer. Personally, I am content to leave the matter of whether or not the remake is scary—or whether or not the original is, for that matter—to the individual viewer or critic. Of greater interest is *how* the remake attempts to induce this desired effect. To hazard a crude dichotomy: unlike Carpenter's original, Zombie's remake privileges shock over suspense. As opposed to tension built up in a sustained and formally minimalist fashion, visceral impact is instead favored throughout. This emphasis points to the remake's general orientation. Instead of mystery and suspense, we *see* and *know*.

In the original *Halloween*, after the famous, subjective-view opening murder of his older sister Judith by the young Michael Myers, the narrative has two foci: one is Laurie Strode and her high school girlfriends, who are stalked by the adult Myers after he escapes from Smith's Grove Sanitarium; the other, Dr. Loomis as he desperately tries to find his former patient. In the new version, we are given a greatly expanded back-story, depicting not only ten-year-old Michael's troubled home life before the horrific events of October 31, but also his subsequent psychological treatments by Dr. Loomis. Young Michael is also no longer content to simply murder his older sister. Before killing her, he slays his stepfather and Judith's boyfriend by catching them unaware—sparing only his baby sister "Boo"—in addition to having dispatched with a school bully earlier in the day. While in the sanitarium, he also murders a nurse, bringing his pre-teen body count to five. When Myers finally escapes from Smith's Grove Sanitarium after fifteen years' imprisonment, we follow him to a truck wash where he murders a trucker and steals his clothes. Only then, nearly an hour into the movie, does he proceed back home to Haddonfield.

Rather than Myers stalking his prey, the narration in the remake now follows Myers. Rather than being an entity—a "shape," as he was called in the end credits of the original film—Michael is a *character*. This is the central, defining premise upon which Zombie stakes his film, and it has both formal and thematic implications for the narrative.

To the remake's credit, continuity is created between Michael the deranged boy and Michael the adult monster in a detailed, systematic way. To cite one specific example: a striking shot from the film's first half has Michael, distantly framed between two rows of trees, silently stalking a school bully who beat him up earlier in the day. This view, including the distant framing of the killer, is graphically duplicated in the second half of the picture as Michael follows Laurie home. To cite a more general trend: during murder scenes in both halves of the movie, the same alternations in shot scale—quickly cutting between disorienting close-ups and long shots—are deployed to depict the killer in action, and "both" Michaels are consistently filmed from low angles, giving the impression of him bearing down on his victims. Achieving this spatial arrangement in the case of young Michael requires deliberate arrangements of the *mise-en-scène*, as each of his victims is larger than he himself is. Both Michael's stepfather and Judith's boyfriend are butchered when they are seated, allowing the adolescent killer to tower above each. The most striking image of the subsequent scene—during which Michael dons his signature white mask for the first time—is a distantly framed, low-angled shot of Michael, knife in hand, slowly walking toward his injured sister as she desperately tries to crawl away.

While this kind of attention to detail is noteworthy in its own right, it is ultimately in service of the aim of *characterizing* the murderous Myers—an aim that proves to be thematically problematic. The concomitant behavioral and representational continuity across the fifteen-year divide reinforces not only Michael's centrality to the narrative but also his humanity (as it were). In this way, the adult Michael's murderous actions are *the same* as his childhood atrocities, and they (presumably) stem from the same boyhood trauma.

The extended prologue of the new *Halloween* is clearly an attempt to offer something in the way of an explanation for Michael's rage. Although he has a loving relationship with his stripper mother (who is initially blind to his eccentricities), he has an abusive stepfather, is bullied at school, and tortures animals. Yet none of this is able to account for Michael's violent, juvenile dementia. If it were, Loomis would be able to treat him. But he isn't, so Michael's evil is, ultimately, unexplainable. So why the lengthy, gruesome prologue, if the film is going to retain the original's premise about the unintelligibility of evil? Again, the focus is not on the unknown but the known.

Consider how, in the remake, Loomis is more shaken by what the young Michael has done—five brutal murders—than what he *is*. In the original *Halloween*, Loomis looked into Michael's eyes and saw nothing but blackness. In the remake, Loomis sees the blackness in his patient's eyes, but ultimately characterizes them as "the eyes of a psychopath." As he later tells Sheriff Bracket, Myers is a "soulless killing machine driven by pure, animal instinct." The original *Halloween* does not explicitly imbue Myers with any supernatural qualities. That would come with time (and sequels—specifically, the pagan rituals of 1996's *Halloween: The Curse of Michael Myers*). Yet there is something undeniably otherworldly about the Shape, particularly in regard to the killer's improbable physical strength. As Todorov notes, a recurring theme of the fantastic is the existence of beings more powerful than men (109). An uncertainty as to the source of this power contributes to the hesitation characteristic of the genre.

Quite unlike the behemoth that he is in the remake, the original Myers is completely ordinary in stature and build. And yet he displays not only remarkable resilience but also near-superhuman strength, both of which the viewer is at a loss to explain. Adding to this ambiguity is the eerie elegance with which Myers carries out his violent acts. The gracefulness of the Shape's slow, stalking gait is one of the original *Halloween*'s best-known features, but even actions like lifting a hapless teenager off the ground by his throat and pinning him to the wall with a butcher knife are carried out with a certain methodical fluidity that belies their physicality—and increases the degree of uncertainty as to the nature of the film's uncanny event.

In the new *Halloween*, Michael's physical size is emphasized in a number of ways that erase all doubt as to the source of his strength. In the first place, the character is played by Tyler Mane, a muscular, 6'9" stuntman who towers over every other actor in the movie. The low-angle framing of Myers detailed above serves not only to accentuate this size difference but also to characterize it as threatening and overpowering. His is a looming presence overhead that explodes downward in savage bursts. It is not surprising, then, that the only scene in the movie's second half that portrays Myers as halfway vulnerable—his first meeting with Laurie, where he produces a worn photograph of himself holding his baby sister (a gesture Laurie fails to understand)—has him drop to his knees and slump to Laurie's level. Correspondingly, both characters in this scene are framed straight on at eye level.

The question of Myers's motivation for returning to Haddonfield and seeking out Laurie Strode is also answered. As the scene described above shows, Michael returns home in search of his baby sister. That Laurie Strode is actually the younger sister of Michael Myers is a familiar element of the *Halloween* storyline. The Shape's unrelenting quest to finish off his entire family—first his sister (in the first and second movies), then his niece (4, 5, and 6), and then his sister again (7 and 8)—sets in motion the narratives for each installment of the "original" series. This plot point is so enshrined in the series' mythology that it is easy to forget how this relationship, and all the thematic implications one can draw out of it, play *no part whatsoever* in the original film. It is not until *Halloween II* (Rick Rosenthal, 1981) that the familial relationship between victim and killer is (rather clumsily) tacked on, thus retrospectively positing a reason for Michael's pursuit of Laurie. In the first *Halloween*, the Shape's interest in Laurie—stalking her, isolating her by killing her friends, and then attacking—is largely unexplained. In an early scene, the Shape observes Laurie with young Tommy Douglas, and there is a sense that the killer identifies himself with Tommy, and thus equates Laurie with his murdered older sister. The point is left open, however. In contrast, Michael's homecoming in the remake is a perverse expression of a big brother's love—if we could call it that—for his baby sister. When she fearfully rejects him, unaware of their relation, Myers's rage spills over and he spends the final act of the picture chasing her.

While Loomis's ultimate inability to effectively treat Michael is a gesture in the direction of commentary on the unaccountable nature of evil, the dominant current of the remake flows unquestionably toward explanation and explication. The lengthy prologue of Michael's traumatic childhood shows us the origins of his iniquity, and the connection between the violent manifestations of his boyhood rage and his later atrocities is reinforced through formal continuity. Those same formal strategies are used to accentuate the adult Michael's already imposing physical size, erasing all questions as to the nature of his strength and resilience. Finally, further motivation for Myers's bloody homecoming is provided by the movie's adoption of the original series' conceit that Laurie is, in fact, the killer's baby sister. This, in sum, erases all hesitation that Myers may or may not be a supernatural phenomenon. Whereas the new Loomis believes he "failed" Michael by not being able to help him, the original Loomis knew he *couldn't* help Michael and dedicated himself to keeping Myers locked up.

With all of that said, a question remains: to what degree are these features the product of Zombie's authorial vision, as opposed to being symptomatic of larger trends and transformations in the horror film genre, American cinema, or even American popular culture at large? In order to properly consider this matter, we need to expand the focus of our inquiry to include an examination of the broader—and comparable—generic contexts of both the remake and the original *Halloween*.

SLASHERS

As much as Carpenter's *Halloween* is regarded, rightfully, as an important work of horror cinema—or cinema in general, really—it is also part of a larger phenomenon: a cycle of American horror films released in the 1970s and early 1980s that we now refer to as slashers. Although not without precedent within the horror genre—Carol Clover has noted affinities between the cycle and Alfred Hitchcock's 1960 film *Psycho* (16), while Andrew Tudor describes slashers as a "youth-focused" variant of a common "terrorizing" horror narrative (198)—the original *Halloween*, together with Tobe Hooper's *The Texas Chainsaw Massacre* (1974), has been held by most scholarship as one of the two movies that inaugurated the cycle by establishing its narrative and thematic conventions.[1]

In general, slasher movies concern teenage protagonists who, while partaking in a ritualized activity—babysitting, camping, prom night, a road trip—are terrorized by a villain unknown to them, who often goes about murdering the members of the group in a physical fashion using a variety of physical implements. The main protagonist of slasher pictures, as detailed most thoroughly by Clover in her seminal book *Men, Women, and Chainsaws: Gender in Modern Horror Film*, is often a virtuous (although not necessarily virginal) female.

A likely objection to this description of the cycle is how, by emphasizing aspects like physicality and materiality, it excludes one extremely popular movie that is frequently included in discussions of the slasher movie: Wes Craven's *A Nightmare on Elm Street* (1984). This is deliberate on my part. Without denying the similarities between the first *Elm Street* film and earlier horror movies like *Halloween* and *Friday the 13th* (Sean S. Cunningham, 1980), I would argue that the picture's emphasis on family—both the threat to the collective family unit and conspiratorial efforts by adults to protect their children from external threats—makes it more akin to movies like *The Omen* (Richard Donner, 1976) and Craven's earlier works *The Hills Have Eyes* (1977) and *Last House on the Left* (1972). As Pat Gill has observed, the imperiled teenagers in slasher pictures have "no hope of help from their parents" (18). Furthermore, the explicitly supernatural characteristics of *A Nightmare on Elm Street* make it both unlike the initial slasher movies and, as I shall detail shortly, part of a subsequent development in the horror genre.

By chance—or perhaps a more sinister force!—Zombie's *Halloween* is also part of a cycle of horror movies: in this case, a cycle of slasher remakes. Recent years have brought us new versions of *The Texas Chainsaw Massacre* (Marcus Nispel, 2003), *When a Stranger Calls* (Simon West, 2006), and *Black Christmas* (Glen Morgan, 2006). Looking ahead, a remake of *Prom Night* (1980) will be released in the spring of 2008, and updated takes on both *My Bloody Valentine* (1981) and *Friday the 13th* are currently in development.

Here we are presented with an opportunity to pose two further questions: Are any other movies from the original slasher cycle also examples of Todorov's fantastic genre? If so, is the uncanny nature of the new *Halloween*—with its more communicative narration and emphasis on overt display—common to other slasher remakes? A sampling of classic slasher films and their recent remakes sheds light on this question.

Black Christmas

In *Black Christmas* (Bob Clark, 1974) the members of a sorority house are terrorized over the Christmas holiday by "Billy," an unseen murderer who alternates between menacing the coeds with threatening, sexually explicit phone calls and killing them off, one by one. Although comparatively neglected in scholarship, *Black Christmas* is considered by some to be the first slasher film. Interestingly, it anticipates *Halloween* in a number of ways. For example, the movie makes extensive use of a mobile camera—here using a wide-angle lens, which creates a distorting effect—accompanied by heavy breathing to represent the killer's subjective point of view. What I would like to highlight, however, is the film's ending.

After finally determining that the threatening phone calls are "coming from inside the house!" the police rush to the sorority—but not before Jessica kills her boyfriend Peter, whom both she and the police believe to be the killer. A distraught

Jessica is then sedated and left to sleep in the darkened sorority house. Slowly, the camera tracks away from her room and moves down the hallway, stopping on the attic door. It opens a crack, and the scene cuts to the interior of the attic, where two of the killer's victims remain hidden. "Agnes, it's me Billy," comes the lispy voice of the killer, and as the camera pulls back, the phone inside the house begins to ring.

This conclusion is not unlike that of the original *Halloween*, where, after shooting Michael six times, Loomis looks over the balcony to the ground below, only to find that the Shape has vanished. As Todorov notes, endings like these are a common feature of the fantastic, because they restore at a story's very end the hesitation between a natural and abnormal explanation for the events described (51). To this I would add that it is important to distinguish between the endings of *Black Christmas* and *Halloween* and the more conventionalized horror conclusion that has the villain "come back" for one final attack. Such endings are less about sustaining fantastic hesitation than providing, as we shall see in a moment, one final shock or jolt before the credits roll. Moreover, they usually conclude a narrative in which there is no uncertainty as to the nature of the uncanny event.

As in the new *Halloween*, the *Black Christmas* remake furnishes the psychotic Billy with an extensive, explanatory back-story. Born with a rare liver condition that makes his skin yellow, Billy is loathed by his mother from the start. After witnessing them murder his loving father, young Billy is locked in the attic by his mother and her lover. He remains there for years and is only visited by his mother on one occasion—an occasion that has him sire his own sister. Eventually, Billy escapes from the attic, maims his sister cum daughter, kills his mother and stepfather, and makes Christmas cookies from their flesh before being apprehended by police. Like Myers, Billy escapes from a mental asylum after fifteen years' imprisonment, and he and his inbred daughter proceed to tag-team the helpless sorority sisters now residing in his house. The movie's final, *final* confrontation—after most of the characters are killed, the sorority house burns down, and the inevitable mix-up in the morgue— has Billy's daughter Agnes mounting one final assault on Kelli, the surviving female. Kelli pulls through, killing Agnes by frying her brain using a defibrillator.

When a Stranger Calls

Released in the wake of *Halloween*, *When a Stranger Calls* (Fred Walton, 1979) provides an alternative example of a film creating fantastic hesitation. The movie is most famous for its opening sequence, where a babysitter is terrorized by a series of anonymously placed phone calls that are ultimately, as in *Black Christmas*, revealed to be coming from inside the house. The babysitter survives the ordeal, but we learn that the two children sleeping in their upstairs bedroom have been brutally butchered by a mysterious killer, a man named Curt Duncan. Yet this episode only serves as the movie's prologue; the rest of the original *When a Stranger Calls* follows a private investigator as he tracks Duncan after—what else?—the psychopath escapes from a mental institution after years of incarceration. When the investigator, Clifford, visits the asylum he presses Duncan's former psychiatrist about why she was unable to treat the murderer. The psychiatrist looks Clifford in the eye and says, "Do you want to know how much we *really* understand of the human mind?"

Although *When a Stranger Calls* is ultimately an example of fantastic-uncanny, the introduction of this kind of doubt—that the uncanny event is attributable to forces beyond our comprehension—nonetheless contributes to a fantastic hesitation. The remake, however, contains no such hesitation, and instead expands the initial scenario of the threatened babysitter to fill its entire running time. Interestingly, the new *When a Stranger Calls* does the opposite of *Halloween* and *Black Christmas* by making its villain entirely anonymous. Yet the result is the same: there is no reason to question the uncanny nature of the killer.

The Texas Chainsaw Massacre

In terms of offering an explanation for its uncanny events, the remake of *The Texas Chainsaw Massacre* stakes out a middle ground between the exposition of the new *Black Christmas* and the anonymity exemplified by the *When a Stranger Calls* remake. Although his bloody butchering of wayward teenagers is facilitated and encouraged by his deranged backwoods family, Leatherface is not given the kind of traumatic childhood that shaped compatriots Michael Myers and Billy. Even so—and in a departure from the original film—the chainsaw-wielding maniac is depicted as horribly disfigured, hence his fondness for fashioning masks from the flesh of his victims (the trope of physical deformity being one of the oldest ways of denoting a character's evil inner nature).

In what could be seen as an inevitable development given the trend toward sequels and spin-offs exemplified in the original slasher cycle, the new *Texas Chainsaw Massacre* was followed by a prequel released in 2006. It should come as no surprise that *The Texas Chainsaw Massacre: The Beginning* (Jonathan Liebesman) furnishes a complete history for Leatherface (or Thomas, his given name), making him the deformed product of a botched abortion who is rescued and subsequently adopted by the cannibalistic Hewitt family.

Absent from the remake (and its prequel) are a number of admittedly minor elements that nevertheless add a degree of ambiguity to the original *Texas Chainsaw Massacre*, including an astrological subtext introduced early in the film. In one of the movie's first scenes, one of the teenagers, Pam, reads to the others from her *American Astrology* almanac. Initially, her gloomy prognostications about "Saturn in retrograde" are laughed at by her friends. But after a violent encounter with a hitchhiker, her reading of Franklin's horoscope, predicting a "disturbing and unpredictable day," elicits no laughter. Pam is then asked to read Sally's horoscope: "There are moments when we cannot believe that what is happening is really true. Pinch yourself and you may find out that it is."

As in *When a Stranger Calls*, the underlying theme that the events in question are the product of supernatural powers is not developed at any great length, yet the introduction of such an element has the effect of calling into question the degree to which the uncanny events that befall the characters can be explained by recourse to the laws of the natural world.

THE RETURN OF THE RETURN OF THE REPRESSED

While none of the other original slasher films that have been remade prove to be examples of the fantastic in the manner of *Halloween*, each nonetheless introduces elements that contribute to a fantastic hesitation. Mysterious villains, unresolved endings, and subtexts about the limits of rational understanding add degrees of uncertainty about the nature of a film's uncanny events, calling into question whether those events are the product of natural or supernatural forces. In contrast, the remakes work in a variety of ways to both quantify and qualify their disquieting phenomena, from positing origins for their villains through explanatory back-stories to providing conclusive endings. So if fantastic elements are characteristic to some original slasher movies yet not to their remakes, why is this so?

One approach would be to consider larger developments in the horror genre since the inauguration of the original slasher cycle in the 1970s. As I noted above, Noël Carroll has addressed the fantastic in his book *The Philosophy of Horror or Paradoxes of the Heart*. For Carroll, examples of the fantastic are *not* horror because, by his definition, horror requires a patently supernatural element. In the larger sweep of the genre, this is a perfectly reasonable condition. Yet, in the context of contemporary horror cinema, it would be overly exclusionary. Indeed, the only contemporary American horror movies of late to feature the paranormal tend to be remakes of Japanese and Korean films, and even this trend seems to be waning. We could also note how, in the original slasher cycle, there is a swift move away from fantastic equivocation—and, perhaps, away from the slasher proper—to either the uncanny or, more prevalently, the supernatural. Two of the more popular horror series of the mid- and late 1980s, *A Nightmare on Elm Street* and Clive Barker's *Hellraiser*, feature necromancy and supernatural villains. At the same time, even the *Halloween* and *Friday the 13th* series become increasingly supernatural—helping, in part, to explain how their respective monsters are able to return time and again. This tendency toward paranormal villains reverses in the late 1990s, signaled not only by the success of the *Scream* franchise (1996, 1997, 2000) and subsequent teen-oriented horror movies like *I Know What You Did Last Summer* (Jim Gillespie, 1997) and

Urban Legend (Jamie Blanks, 1998) but also by the failure of big-budget supernatural horror pictures like *The Haunting* (Jan de Bont, 1999) and *House on Haunted Hill* (William Malone, 1999).[2]

What are the implications of these developments? Horror, like all fiction, favors certainty over ambiguity—a fact implicit in Todorov's positing of the fantastic as but a thin line between bordering genres. This may seem an odd assertion to make about a genre that is, again, regularly classified and examined on the basis of its elicitation of an affective response in the viewer—specifically, feelings of apprehension and doubt (two words that are often synonymous with *un*certainty). Yet regardless of whether bizarre and horrific happenings are earthly or otherworldly in nature, the vast majority of horror films leave *no question* as to which of those two polarities is the definite cause of the uncanny event. Many stories and films may flirt with the fantastic over the course of their narratives, but most ultimately fall to either side of the median line between the uncanny and the marvelous.

A second, and more interesting, possibility would be to reflect on the ways in which the original slasher cycle has been thought about, and how this thinking continues to influence those who watch, write about, and even *remake* those pictures. The dominant method of examining film genres has traditionally been to interpret movies as reflections of the American cultural zeitgeist. Westerns represent the eternal struggle between the forces of civilization and wilderness. Film noir reflects postwar anxiety and a crisis of masculinity. In the case of horror movies, the influence of Robin Wood's pioneering 1979 essay, "An Introduction to the American Horror Film," continues to be strongly felt in scholarship on the genre. The monster that explicitly threatens the community within a particular horror picture is a vengeful representation of whatever the dominant ideology deems a subversive threat to American society—empowered women, communists, teenage sexuality, terrorists—and it is thus trying to "repress" in order to maintain control and stability. In this way, critical methodologies drawn, however broadly, from cultural studies and psychoanalysis—what Wood called the "confluence of Marx and Freud" (195)—continue to be employed. It is not suprising that movies have begun to regurgitate this theory to the point that the kinds of meanings arrived at through criticism of the original slasher movies are now explicitly built into their remakes.

Erin, the female hero of the new *Texas Chainsaw Massacre*, is in every respect the prototypical final girl—a virginal, resourceful tomboy with a maternal instinct who abstains from alcohol and drugs—albeit reverse-engineered from a watered-down version of Clover's theory. The Freudian overtones in traumatic childhood back-stories of the new *Halloween* and *Black Christmas* are so apparent as to make the application of any psychoanalytic theory redundant. Nevertheless, one could certainly anticipate a variety of alternate ways in which a critic might go about reading these films.

We could note, for example, how the current cycle of slasher remakes is part of a larger, late-2000s trend of Hollywood "looking back" to 1970s American filmmaking, both in terms of remaking pictures from that era but also setting new films in the seventies (e.g., *Zodiac* [David Fincher, 2007], *American Gangster* [Ridley Scott, 2007]). Many on the political left would no doubt see this hindsight as a reflection of how the cultural climate of the United States in the early twenty-first century is akin to the social unrest that the country experienced in the 1970s—that, for example, Iraq is the new Vietnam. Yet if the kind of fantastic equivocation observed in the movies of the original slasher cycle—particularly as it relates to the nature of evil—is taken to be the product of, say, cultural uncertainty, then the complete absence of this hesitation in the new cycle of slasher remakes undermines any links between 1970s and 2000s America one could wish to make based on the kinds of films produced in each decade.

An alternative route would be to read the trend in the new slasher movie toward attributing violence to social conditions as a repudiation of the idea that there exists such a thing as "pure" (and unexplainable) evil. This would, however, prove to be a very well worn path. Michael Ryan and Douglas Kellner argue that the violence in slasher films indicates real-world concerns like "heightened levels of anxiety in the culture, particularly with regard to family, children, political leadership, and sexuality" (168). Ryan and Kellner are writing about the *1970s and 1980s* slasher cycle, however—so including the original *Halloween*. In this way, earlier slashers that leaned toward depicting evil as unexplainable have nevertheless been construed as reflections of contemporaneous, extra-filmic social conditions and cultural anxieties. Certainly, "family, children, political leadership and sexuality" are just as much concerns today as they were in the late 1970s and early 1980s.

The problem with these attempts to account for the presence of the fantastic in Carpenter's *Halloween* and other original slasher movies is that traditional methods of genre analysis—principally those that read films as reflections of society—rely on *interpretation*. Interpretation is, however, at sharp odds with the fantastic. Indeed, it threatens its very existence. As detailed above, the fantastic depends on a dual hesitation: by both the characters within the story and by the reader. Yet this reader is not the one physically holding the book in his hand or sitting in a darkened cinema watching the movie. This reader is instead the one implicit in the text itself: a reader who Todorov says, "considers the world of the characters as a world of living persons" (30) and "reacts to events as they occur in the world evoked" (60). There is no longer a space for the fantastic if events are read allegorically, because the fantastic *requires fiction*. Consider: if Michael Myers and other slasher killers are the product of and powered by repressed psychosexual energy, as per the dominant psychoanalytic explanation, their superhuman resilience makes sense. After all, psychoanalysis has yet to tire of delineating the myriad ways in which we are all so gosh darned repressed, which means that the cultural engine that drives the slasher films' masked maniacs is fed by a bottomless barrel of fuel.

This matter is central to Todorov's project, which conceives of structure and meaning as two separate objects, implied by two distinct activities: poetics and interpretation. He writes, "[To the] poetician what matters is the knowledge of an object external to him, [while] the critic tends to identify himself with the work, [and] constitute himself as its subject" (142). It comes as no surprise that Todorov is critical of the propensity in psychoanalytic criticism to look beyond the text for meaning. He writes:

> When psychoanalysts have been concerned with literary works, they have not been content to describe them, on any level whatever. Beginning with Freud, they have always tended to consider literature as one means among others of penetrating an author's psyche. Literature is thus reduced to the rank of simple symptom, and the author constitutes the real object of study. (151)

Given the penchant for interpretation in genre criticism in general and horror criticism in particular, it is likely that for many nothing short of an all-encompassing psychoanalytic or cultural exegesis of either slasher cycle will suffice. Yet such explanations rely on extremely broad readings that neglect the formal and thematic specificities of the films in question. In contrast to an interpretive method that sees all violent, teen-oriented horror movies as reflections of social anxieties, the poetical approach espoused by Todorov (with its attention to form) enables us to not only detect important, overlooked developments within the slasher movie but also provides a productive framework for comparative analysis. Indeed, approaching the case of the two *Halloweens* in this manner has led to the recovery of one of the central, animating aspects of Carpenter's original: its thoroughgoing uncertainty. In this way, what Todorov's model ultimately provides is an indication of how a study attuned to structure—that is, concerned with describing themes and configurations rather than naming meanings—has the potential to shed new light on one of the darker, more blood-splattered corners of the schoolhouse of horror.

NOTES

1. See, for example, Carol Clover, *Men, Women, and Chainsaws: Gender in the Modern Horror Film* (Princeton, N.J.: Princeton University Press, 1992), 24, and Andrew Tudor, *Monsters and Mad Scientists: A Cultural History of the Horror Movie* (Oxford: Blackwell, 1989), 198.

2. An objection one might raise to this trajectory is the release of a number of successful American ghost movies around the turn of the century, including *The Sixth Sense* (M. Night Shyamalan, 1999), *What Lies Beneath* (Robert Zemeckis, 2000) and *The Others* (Alejandro

Amenábar, 2001). Each of these films is quite unlike those others mentioned—and the vast majority of horror movies—in that they are targeted at adult rather than teenage demographic, and also enjoy the concomitant benefit of being easily assimilated into neighboring genres like "thriller."

WORKS CITED

Clover, Carol. *Men, Women, and Chainsaws: Gender in the Modern Horror Film*. Princeton, N.J.: Princeton University Press, 1992.

Gill, Pat. "The Monstrous Years: Teens, Slasher Films, and the Family." *Journal of Film and Video* 54.4 (2002): 16–30.

Ryan, Michael, and Douglas Kellner. *Camera Politica: The Politics and Ideology of Contemporary Hollywood Film*. Bloomington: Indiana University Press, 1988.

Todorov, Tzevetan. *The Fantastic: A Structural Approach to a Literary Genre*. Trans. Richard Howard. Ithaca, N.Y.: Cornell University Press, 1975.

Tudor, Andrew. *Monsters and Mad Scientists: A Cultural History of the Horror Movie*. Oxford: Basil Blackwell, 1989.

Wood, Robin. "An Introduction to the American Horror Film." *Movies and Methods, Vol. II*. Ed. Bill Nichols. Berkeley and Los Angeles: University of California Press, 1985. 195–219. Rpt. from *The American Nightmare: Essays on the Horror Film*. Toronto: Festival of Festivals, 1979.

WHITHER THE SERIAL KILLER MOVIE?

—Philip L. Simpson

THE DEATH OF A GENRE?

Once upon a time, it seemed as if the serial killer genre had come to domi-nate American popular cinema. The genre's peculiar amalgamation of Gothic melo-drama and horror reached a critical zenith during the 1990s with the immensely popular and Academy-Award winning *The Silence of the Lambs* (1991), which in turn led to a proliferation of mainstream Hollywood films such as *Copycat* (1995), *Se7en* (1995), and *Natural Born Killers* (1994). Major Hollywood stars such as Anthony Hopkins, Jodie Foster, Brad Pitt, Morgan Freeman, and Sigourney Weaver headlined these productions, which introduced grisly on-screen mayhem to mainstream audi-ences that otherwise may never have attended a horror film. The popular "stalker" and "slasher" films of the 1970s and 1980s had been supplanted by the serial-killer genre. It seemed that the multiple murderer had "arrived" to stake out a lasting and lucrative place in cinema. By 1992, Su Epstein's multi-decade survey could catalog 155 different serial killers in film. The sheer ubiquity of these films led scholars such as Mark Seltzer to proclaim: "Serial murder and its representations . . . have by now largely replaced the Western as the most popular genre-fiction of the body and of bodily violence in our culture" (1).

Continuing into the late 1990s and early twenty-first century, serial killer films have been released on a regular basis. A partial list of these releases includes *The Bone Collector* (1999), *The Minus Man* (1999), *Summer of Sam* (1999), *Cell* (2000), *The Watcher* (2000), *American Psycho* (2000), *From Hell* (2001), *Hannibal* (2001), *Blood Work* (2002), *Red Dragon* (2002), *In the Cut* (2003), *Monster* (2003), *Suspect Zero* (2004), *Mindhunters* (2005), *Cry Wolf* (2005), *Perfume* (2006), *Scoop* (2006), *Disturbia* (2007), *Mr. Brooks* (2007), *Zodiac* (2007), and *Hannibal Rising* (2007). Many prestigious Hollywood names are associated with these productions. Actress Charlize Theron won the 2003 Best Actress Academy Award for her portrayal of serial killer Aileen Wuornos. Kevin Costner took on an uncharacteristically sinis-ter role as the titular lead in *Mr. Brooks*, wherein his serial-killing character enters a twelve-step program to break his addiction to serial murder and fights off the constant temptation to murder urged upon him by his imaginary alter ego Marshall, played by William Hurt. Other actors, such as Denzel Washington, Angelina Jolie, Owen Wilson, Keanu Reeves, Johnny Depp, Clint Eastwood, Ralph Fiennes, Edward Norton, Meg Ryan, Ben Kingsley, Val Kilmer, Jake Gyllenhaal, and Robert Downey Jr., all starred in films featuring serial murder. A number of acclaimed directors also took on serial killer projects, among them Spike Lee with *Summer of Sam*, Woody Allen with *Scoop*, and Clint Eastwood with *Blood Work*. Director David Fincher, famous for *Se7en*, returned to the genre with *Zodiac*, for the most part a critically well received examination of a journalist's obsession with determining the identity of an elusive San Francisco serial killer and what seems to be, according to Manohla Dargis, "an unexpected repudiation of Mr. Fincher's most famous movie, . . . *Seven*."

Real-life filmmakers were not the only famous names attached to serial killer films. The fictional character of Hannibal Lecter, who almost single-handedly helped launch the genre into prominence, also continued to appear in films in the new millennium. Producer Dino de Laurentiis, no doubt cursing himself for having passed on the film rights to *The Silence of the Lambs*, attempted to make up for a woeful financial miscalculation by commissioning a remake/prequel (*Red Dragon*), a sequel (*Hannibal*), and a prequel (*Hannibal Rising*), all based on the foundational work of Thomas Harris. Of *Hannibal*, Robert Cettl announced that "the critical and popular success of [*Hannibal*] legitimized the serial killer movie. It was no longer considered the domain of low-budget exploitation . . . Now, 'serious' filmmakers, even auteurs, increasingly used the serial killer film for message and money" (1). Writing in 2007, Geoffrey Macnab concurred: "Long associated with low-grade movies and straight-to-video fare, the genre has increasing mainstream appeal."

Yet in spite of what demonstrably seems to be producers' enthusiasm for serial killer films in the first years of the new millennium, popular and certainly critical taste does not necessarily seem to bear out the industry's fondness for the genre. Disappointed by *The Watcher*, among other films, Sara M. Fetters asks rhetorically: "is the serial killer genre as we know it dead? . . . Can this genre be revived?" Will Self goes so far as to claim that the film adaptation of *Hannibal* "terminates with extreme prejudice a whole genre, which will, I feel certain, come to be associated with the last decades of the 20th century, just as surely as Margaret Thatcher or the compact disc." As these comments suggest, in the few years since the release of *Hannibal*, the last serial killer "blockbuster" film in terms of box office revenue, times have changed.[1] Or, put another way, that was then, and this is now. If the serial killer movie was the new "Western," as Seltzer claimed, then the serial killer movie also seems to be fading from the cultural spotlight in much the same way as the Western did before it. Of the films on the preceding list, some did gross more than their production costs, such as *The Bone Collector*, *The Cell*, *Monster*, and *Disturbia*.[2] But none would qualify as a "blockbuster," generally acknowledged as a film that grosses over $100 million. The most recent high-profile serial killer films, *Hannibal Rising* and *Zodiac*, are no exceptions.[3] In mainstream Hollywood cinema, the serial killer story often seems derivative, exhausted, even dated in comparison to the cinematic emphasis on thinly veiled war allegories and the so-called torture-porn movement (best exemplified by the *Hostel* and *Saw* series) in horror since the terrorist attacks of September 11, 2001, and the American invasion of Iraq in 2003. As is evident in the commercial disappointments of fare such as *Mr. Brooks*, *Mindhunters*, *Suspect Zero*, or the aforementioned *Hannibal Rising* and *Zodiac*, the mainstream appeal of serial killer cinema may be on the wane since the "glory days" of the 1980s, 1990s, and early twenty-first century.

In many ways, the decline of the serial killer in film roughly parallels the disappearance, or at least the retreat from prominence, of the serial killer as the media's Public Enemy Number One. During the 1980s, a confluence of high-profile serial murder cases dominated public attention, especially that of the itinerant Henry Lee Lucas, whose claims about having killed hundreds of people nationwide were greeted with little skepticism. According to Philip Jenkins, the federal Justice Department, concerned with expanding its own role and budgets in the aftermath of the limitations placed upon it during the 1970s, greatly overstated the extent of serial murder. Jenkins elaborates:

> The "federal" view of serial murder asserted that serial murder was a vast menace, with some four to five thousand related fatalities each year, or up to a quarter of all American homicides. According to this view, the problem was novel, without historical precedent, and the threat potential was all the greater because killers were highly mobile, wandering freely between different states and jurisdictions. (14)

The popular journalistic and entertainment media, ever quick to capitalize on new trends, turned to the supposed murder epidemic as a source to generate audience interest. However, the Justice Department's sensational interpretations of the data became increasingly suspect (in part due to Jenkins's skepticism of the existence of a "serial killer epidemic"), and serial killers as figures of entertainment became seriously overexposed, toward the end of the 1990s.

While acknowledging the recent financial downturn of the mainstream releases, it is doubtless premature to pronounce the death of the serial killer film genre in the United States. Analysis of the current state of the genre shows it to have transmuted with the times, eking out a marginal hold in the mainstream commercial marketplace while flourishing in lower-budget "niche" cinema or the straight-to-video realm. Audiences have become so familiar with these stories that their conventions have become part of the cultural landscape, and filmmakers who wish to grab the attention of the genre-savvy audience must devise scenarios to fit the changing times. In other words, the genre may have entered into a period of recalibration, readjustment, and scaling back of expectations to succeed on levels other than vast box office take. The genre is looking back on its own past, now unavoidably through the prism of the dissonant post-9/11 global scene, and rewriting the classic narrative patterns to interrogate and reinvigorate their own assumptions and positions.

A large part of this transformation of the genre, as David Schmid argues, is to reclaim the serial killer as a reassuringly familiar, even archetypal American antihero within a cultural context of fear of the Middle Eastern Other (254). In fact, what is happening is nothing less than a redeeming or humanizing of the serial killer, in contrast to the mythologizing of the character during what can be considered the "classical" era of the genre when the archetype was cemented. As evidenced in this transformation, the formulaic conventions of the genre have proven themselves adaptable to changing historical conditions, thus allowing critics to make "historical and cultural inferences about the collective fantasies from one cultural period to another" (Cawelti 7). The serial killer story simultaneously defies containment within one historical era and bears the signature stamp of the specific cultural context in which it was created.

When viewed in this way, the genre has always been mutable—sensitive to the cultural changes of modernization. The genre owes its recent identification with "serial killers" to what Philip Jenkins calls the "media panic" over serial killers during the 1980s. Certainly, the term "serial killer," arguably coined by FBI profiler Robert Ressler during the 1970s, entered the popular lexicon for good at that time. But in another sense, a film genre built upon a plot framework of sequential murders committed by a psychosexually maladjusted antagonist dates back to Robert Wiene's *The Cabinet of Dr. Caligari* (1919). Surely, a genre that has ridden the mercurial flow of history and thus gone through many name changes has some life left in it yet.

Even if the recent crop of films has not yielded the financial return expected by its producers, there seems to be no shortage of new product. Indeed, David Schmid maintains that "the serial killer industry that existed in the United States before the attacks [of 9/11] has continued to flourish . . . Indeed, if anything, this industry is experiencing a boom" (246). One must qualify Schmid's statement in the light that many of the cinematic projects in development he cites as supporting evidence for this claim subsequently went on to achieve less-than-stellar revenues and reviews. Nevertheless, serial killer movies continue to be made.

Serial killer cinema in the United States has been undergoing a transformation over the past ten years to ensure its continued relevancy in the twenty-first century. The focus on transcendent, inexplicable evil found in the bulk of the earlier 1990s films gradually shifts to more politically pointed commentary in the late

1990s, particularly with some critical and social distance from the early-1980s conservative law-and-order ideology that helped construct the serial killer myth in the first place. The serial killer characters in the process of renegotiating their personal identities become more clearly emblematic of ideological concerns, or as Steffen Hantke phrases it, "the problem of identity, which is so closely linked to that of privacy, can take on national rather than personal proportions" ("The Kingdom"). Mary Harron's film *American Psycho*, for one, moves away from Gothic suspense altogether and utilizes the serial killer as a nihilistic, satirical character who epitomizes the moral bankruptcy of American consumer culture. Spike Lee's *Summer of Sam* takes another approach to the genre, in which the serial killer figures only in the background to symbolize the tension of an urban community always on the verge of an outbreak of violence, in this case a New York Italian-American neighborhood in the 1970s. In what looks for all the world like his earlier film *Do the Right Thing* (1989), remade as a serial-killer movie, Lee focuses on marginalized or "underworld" groups, where the serial killer is only the most extreme manifestation of a sick society and a pathological sense of alienation among the disenfranchised, the angry, and the lost. Geoffrey Macnab identifies Lee's film as following in a tradition established by Alfred Hitchcock's 1927 film, *The Lodger*, and concludes: "Ironically, most of the best serial killer movies aren't about serial killers. They are about the effect that a killer has on the community." In this sense, Harron's and Lee's films are dystopic visions of the corruption of American society, reified in the figure of the serial killer.

However, the genre has reinvented itself in the aftermath of the 9/11 attacks. The genre shows a marked trend toward heightening the degree of sympathetic bond between audiences and the lethal protagonists depicted on-screen. In many ways this claim seems counterintuitive. After all, wouldn't the social fear engendered by the terrorist attacks increase audience alienation from the serial killer? However, the claim makes more sense in light of several factors underlying this latest evolution. The first is that federal law enforcement now has a new bogeyman to gin up widespread public support for expansion of power: the Middle Eastern terrorist. The serial killer now seems almost quaint in comparison. Another factor may simply be that the genre has been in the public awareness for a long enough period of time now that any genre's tendency to interrogate its own conventions has in this case rewritten the preternaturally cunning serial killers of the classical era into ones more humanly accessible to the audience. Monsters, which serial killers in mainstream cinema have certainly been coded as, have always elicited audience sympathy through their freakish exceptionalities and pathetic loneliness. Audiences have always been coaxed through identification strategies to assume the killer's point-of-view and thus empathize with it. So why should it now be surprising that the cinematic serial killers are becoming even more humanized and comprehensible?

The *Showtime* television drama series *Dexter*, based loosely on the novels of Jeff Lindsay, constitutes an apex of sorts for this trend. The series debuted in October 2006. It centers on the character of Dexter Morgan, a serial killer who works for the Miami Metro police department as a blood-spatter analyst. Having been trained by his adopted policeman father to fake normal human emotions and channel his bloodlust, Dexter as an adult confines his killing to other killers. His job provides him with not only a means to find victims but a socially constructive outlet for his fascination with blood. He is well liked by most of his colleagues and maintains the façade of a loving relationship with his girlfriend Rita. The series enjoys critical and audience approval and has completed its third season as of this writing. When one considers that the audience is asked to identify and sympathize with a serial killer to an unprecedented extent, the success of the series is remarkable.

An additional factor may be at play here, one that Elisabeth Bronfen alludes to when she writes that "our enjoyment of Hollywood cinema is contingent upon a welcome familiarity with the imaginary geography it produces (its characters, its stories)" (20). Certainly, the serial killer, with a proven track record for eliciting a pleasurable *frisson* in audiences, is one of those familiar characters by this point in cinema history. One of the reasons for this audience comfort level is that the serial killer is a shadow manifestation of the American self-image of independence and innocence. These values have been tested sorely by the traumatic national events of the past several years. The notable embrace of the serial killer as hero may signify a nationalistic re-justification of the violence that has always been the shadow of American independence.

The genre flirtation with serial killer movies with a social conscience did seem to change in the aftermath of 9/11 and the American invasion of Iraq. As the nation moves forward into a frightening future haunted by the specters of resource scarcity, international isolation, environmental deterioration, and what seems like never-ending war, is it any wonder that a character so quintessentially American is going to be rehabilitated for film audiences searching for the comfort of the familiar in the contours of film geography? The result is fiction that, in Isabel Santaularia's words, "through the manipulation of fear and a closure that involves a restabilisation of the social order or a defence of the need to fight for its preservation— ultimately articulates a socially conservative discourse" (66). Edward J. Ingebretsen makes a related point: "[serial killers] *restore* a sense of immediacy and intimacy to relations that had been 'domesticated'—precisely because they place these under threat. . . . the existence of the domestic *fantasy* makes possible a certain organization of social facts and conditions, making them 'visible' in ways that subsequently can be politically useful" (33). To sum up, then, the serial killer in fiction performs a restorative function for the consuming audience. The filmmakers' strategies in facilitating this reconciliation between audience and serial killer are diverse, but certain patterns do emerge.

REWRITING THE PROFILE: FROM *THE CELL* TO *ZODIAC*

The duel between an exceptionally dedicated yet marginalized professional and an even more marginalized serial killer with a baroquely distinctive modus operandi remains a genre constant. The battle between good and evil inherent in such narratives, especially in a time of escalating international tensions and ubiquitous political rhetoric about the evil character of one's enemies, has built-in contemporary relevance. The closure, however temporary, typically provided by film narrative serves a therapeutic function in such times. The blurred metaphysical lines or moral ambiguity in serial killer stories, wherein the distinctions between the detective figure and the killer are often elided, do not detract from audience experience of these films and are, in fact, critical to producing narrative anxiety as a necessary prerequisite for the satisfying closure. Carl D. Malmgren explains this satisfaction:

> [Serial killer] fiction puts crime in brackets, giving readers a glimpse into the psychopathology of a decentered character even as that character is being neutralized by the procedures of the centered world of the police. Such a denouement is quite satisfying [...] insofar as it reassures us that the [...] forensic science of one world can disarm the unreason of the other. (179)

Of the anxiety inherent in the narratives, Barbara Fister writes that crime fiction is "a genre that deliberately exploits anxiety" by tapping "into topical social concerns using familiar formulas to produce suspenseful narratives" (43). The familiar serial killer film may also be said to exploit the anxiety of confronting the potential for evil within the self. Given the dramatic tension inherent in such a dynamic, it is likely that stories featuring a showdown between a serial killer and an equally obsessed investigator (often, but not always, a law enforcement agent) will continue to appear over the long term.

Films containing this dynamic, initiated by the breakthrough profiler film *The Silence of the Lambs*, are very much in the style of "gory, Italian-style detective drama—American *giallo*" (Worland 112–13). Some of these American *giallo* films, much like serial killers emulating the murderous careers of those who have gone before them, replicate and amplify the already hyper-signified thrills of *The Silence of the Lambs*. A film like *The Cell* is a typical example of "copycatting" of the template established by Demme's film, right down to using *Lambs* composer Howard Shore to score the film's music. The template can be summarized like this: the serial killer serves the narrative as both a pitiful freak and a terrifying threat. He is confronted by a courageous but vulnerable heroine committed to saving the lives of the innocent. The plot exploits any number of social anxieties, such as the long-term harmful effects of abuse inflicted upon innocent children. But *The Cell* also rewrites the template in intriguing ways that suggest movement away from demonization of the serial killer character even while preserving that legacy of the genre, like an insect fossilized in amber.

In *The Cell*, the heroine is gifted therapist Catherine Dean, who is committed to bringing a boy named Edward from a coma. To do so, she utilizes a new technology that combines psychotropic drugs with virtual reality to link her mind directly into Edward's. But at the request of FBI agent Peter Novack, she enters the mind of comatose serial killer Carl Stargher to find clues as to the location of an imprisoned woman. *The Cell*, taking a genre trend to an extreme, literalizes and visualizes what was only witnessed from the exterior before: the interiority of the killer's psychological spaces and the corruptive peril those spaces pose to the intellectual who would seek to enter them to gain information.[4] In Stargher's case, he dreams of himself in his coma as alternately a powerful Asian king and a fearsome demon: manifestations of a will to murder that threatens to kill Dean. If *The Silence of the Lambs* shows the serial killer's psyche as painfully uncovered by Clarice Starling and helpfully interpreted by her "it-takes-one-to-know-one" guide Hannibal Lecter, then *The Cell* physically places the heroine directly inside the topography of the killer's mind, truly a prison "cell" from which escape is difficult. A benign version of Lecter's manipulative psychiatrist, Dean brings the terrified little boy who still inhabits the labyrinth of Stargher's psyche into her own healing mind. Through doing so, she ultimately releases him from his earthly prison to find redemption. Having done so, Dean is now worthy of restoring the other innocent boy, Edward, to his waking life.

In the plot device of a race against time to save an otherwise doomed victim, *The Cell* follows faithfully the template of *The Silence of the Lambs*. However, *The Cell* amplifies a theme barely suggested in the earlier film—that early trauma and horrific child abuse creates a monstrous adult. As is demanded of a serial killer in such films, Stargher practices an elaborate if not outright Byzantine murder ritual, or signature, unique to him. He places kidnapped women in a large glass tank, waits for a period of time, and then drowns them. Part of the suspense of the film lies in discovering what trauma in Stargher's past gave its imprimatur to his bizarre methodology. As a boy, Stargher nearly drowned while being baptized in a river. He was abused by a father who beat the boy for breaking plates and playing with dolls. The young Stargher drowned an injured bird that he loved in order to keep it from meeting a worse fate at the hands of his cruel father.

Frozen psychosexually in place by this early trauma, the adult Stargher ritually drowns his victims as he did to the bird, bleaches them white to match the dolls he played with, and suspends himself from hooks clipped to steel rings in his back to provide the illusion of weightless rapture evocative of his baptism. Audience sympathy is further reinforced for Stargher by Agent Novack's stated belief that Stargher discards bodies in increasingly clumsy ways so as to ensure his eventual capture and cessation of the cycle of violence. The little boy still surviving within the adult Stargher asks Dean to drown him, which she initially refuses to do. But she soon realizes this is the only method to free him from his coma and the torment of his adult life. She grants his wish and then grieves for his death. While the "stop me before I kill again" theme is certainly not new to the genre, it is striking how much it is emphasized here, a necessary prerequisite for the heightened audience sympathy for the killer as a suffering being. *The Cell* does not celebrate the death of the serial killer, as did *The Silence of the Lambs*. Rather, the film challenges an audience to grant absolution to a killer and celebrate his salvation.

The film *Zodiac* takes a different approach to the story of an investigation into the crimes of a serial killer. The social anxiety strategically built into this film is the post-9/11 fear of terrorism, not the 1990s anxiety over ill effects of child abuse and victimization. Unlike the sympathetic killer of *The Cell*, the serial killer in *Zodiac* is largely off-stage and never conclusively known to the audience. So, the investigation to unmask the killer's identity takes center stage. Compared to the hallucinatory, fast-paced aesthetic of *The Cell*, *Zodiac* is deliberately realistic (an exception is the striking scene where the text of one of the killer's ciphers is superimposed on the walls of a newsroom) and almost leisurely paced. The time frame of the story is greatly expanded by covering a span of many years, from the late 1960s to the early 1980s. The running time (158 minutes) of the film favors methodical scene development and extended dialogue, so there is little artificially hyped sense of urgency. Rather, the countless details and time-consuming false or inconclusive trails of any lengthy investigation of an unsolved case are here on display.

Zodiac is a cerebral exercise in the methodology of solving a puzzle, or, as Amy Taubin says, "[It] is less a film about characters than about process—the process of mining and arranging information in search of the truth" (25). Those expecting a cathartic confrontation between investigator and serial killer will not get one, except for a brief staredown at the film's end. Director David Fincher constructs the antithesis of the typical film centered on a serial killer investigation. In Taubin's words, the film is "shaped to foil narrative expectations" (25). Fincher resists the temptation to replicate the adrenalin highs of his earlier success, *Se7en*. He is not only rewriting the genre to make his story fresh, he is attempting to deconstruct the genre that *Se7en* helped cement. The familiar genre touchstones are here for the genre-savvy audience to embrace, but they are presented in a realistic fashion.

One of the most recognizable touchstones is the dedicated, even obsessive investigator who has made it his life's work to pursue a serial killer. *Zodiac* primarily hinges upon the character of Robert Graysmith, a *San Francisco Chronicle* cartoonist and self-proclaimed amateur sleuth who commits to a quest, at great personal and professional risk, to uncover the identity of northern California's mysterious Zodiac killer. Graysmith is watching from the office sidelines when a series of letters, some in cipher and purportedly written by the killer, are mailed to the newspaper editorial staff. Graysmith takes it upon himself to begin obsessively working leads on the case. He strikes up an unlikely alliance with a *Chronicle* reporter, Paul Avery, to share theories and information about the case. Avery's function in the narrative is to represent everything that Graysmith is not: a flashy, arrogant, debauched, and privileged member of the journalistic inner circle, in contrast to Graysmith's straight-arrow outsider. Yet Avery quickly self-destructs and suffers exile under the stress of the investigation. He ultimately loses his job at the respected newspaper and descends into the professional nadir of writing for the tabloids—perhaps an inevitable end, given the legitimate newspaper world's fascination with the lurid details of the Zodiac case.

The failure of the journalistic investigatory apparatus now evident, it is left to outsider Graysmith to carry on the investigation on his own time in the film's second half. His amateur sleuthing parallels the officially sanctioned city police investigation spearheaded by Chief Inspector Dave Toschi. It does not take much genre savvy to know which investigation will ultimately unmask Zodiac. Graysmith's extralegal status allows him to take shortcuts that Toschi never could, so it is Graysmith who eventually puts it all together, with Toschi as a reluctantly admiring audience of one, to reveal the likely identity of Zodiac. Yet precisely because Toschi has no hard evidence, Zodiac remains officially unidentified and the narrative finally frustrates audience desire for the traditional closure of the "detective versus serial killer" story. Fincher destabilizes the climactic "unmasking" even more by noting in the end title cards that the DNA of Graysmith's favorite suspect, Arthur Leigh Allen, did not match the DNA on file for the Zodiac killer. Through this kind of evocation of the ambiguity of real life, the film situates itself within the realistic tradition.

One of the social anxieties most dramatized in *Zodiac*'s use of the serial killer template is that of family values in conflict with professionalism. In the span of years that the film covers, Graysmith is initially single but then marries and becomes a family man. However, he continuously neglects wife and children in fevered pursuit of the shadowy, taunting killer. Of Graysmith's single-mindedness, Manohla Dargis writes: "Domestic tranquility, it seems, can't hold a candle to work, to the fanatical pursuit of meaning and self discovery." Ryan Gilbey concurs: "Cinema commonly applauds single-mindedness in its heroes, but *Zodiac* shows the cost of it, too" (45). The threat Graysmith poses to his own family's unity is bad enough, but when it becomes publicly known that Graysmith is working on a book about the murders, he begins to receive frightening anonymous calls at his home. This double threat to the sanctity of family, aided and abetted by the detective's own obsession, is well known to any regular viewer of the serial killer genre. What is different this time is Fincher's restrained, realistic approach to the story of a journalist covering a crime story. The film is very much in the style of Alan J. Pakula's *All The*

President's Men (1976). Like Woodward and Bernstein, Graysmith's persistence is rewarded with completion of his book. He achieves certain knowledge of Zodiac's identity, a discovery that not even Toschi, hampered by the limitations of his official role, could uncover.

The vulnerability of family is not the only social phobia that *Zodiac* exploits. There is much here in the film to resonate with anxiety-ridden audiences in the post-9/11 era. The faceless Zodiac killer traumatizes the entire region of northern California, striking safely at random victims from anonymity. His crimes are unthinkably brutal, such as when he stabs repeatedly two bound and helpless young lovers by the side of an idyllic lake. He co-opts the media as an unwitting accomplice in terrorizing citizens by sending the *Chronicle* chilling and taunting messages he knows will be broadcast far and wide to audiences that would have never otherwise heard from him (evoking memories of the periodic messages from Osama bin Laden delivered to the Western media, or the by-now-almost-forgotten and still unsolved "anthrax" letters of 2001). He proves frustratingly elusive, such as the time when police see him fleeing the scene of the cabdriver's murder but nevertheless escaping because of a flawed suspect description. Even when Graysmith begins to narrow in on the individual whom he believes to be the killer, the suspect remains largely inaccessible and unknown to society at large. To an audience accustomed to a sense of a continuing siege mentality since 2001 and frustrated by the national inability to capture the chief architect of the 9/11 attacks, the Zodiac killer of the 1960s and 1970s is perceived as much as terrorist as he is serial killer. The inability of the police as agents of the American state are as helpless to prevent and solve the crimes as the U.S. Government was to prevent 9/11. But the film is ultimately consoling because Graysmith, as a hard-working individualist in the tradition of the American national archetype, succeeds in solving (or apparently solving) a mystery that the marshaled resources of the state apparatus cannot solve.

THE JOURNEY OF THE HERO IN THE FILMS OF THOMAS HARRIS

The adaptations of Thomas Harris's prequels and sequels—for example, *Hannibal, Red Dragon,* and *Hannibal Rising*—constitute another distinct movement in the evolution of the genre: the completion of the transformation of the serial killer from feared object of evil to hero and subject of sympathy. The films continue the narrative arc of turning a cannibalistic serial killer from a caged supporting character into central protagonist and romantic hero who serves as the narrative's dual object of identification and desire.

Ridley Scott's *Hannibal* establishes Hannibal Lecter as an audience-friendly, gallant medieval knight willing to endure great tribulation for the love of his lady,

Clarice Starling. The film plays with the dark promise implied in *The Silence of the Lambs* by bringing Starling and Lecter together in a transcontinental courtship (although not taking it as far as Thomas Harris's source novel). Lecter proves himself worthy of love in the finest tradition of courtly romance. For years, he pines for Starling in his exile in Florence, establishing the lovesickness essential to such a hero. He demonstrates his willingness to risk his own liberty and life by sending Starling a note of cheer when her career is jeopardized by a botched police raid and the antagonism of her professional nemesis, Paul Krendler. As a devoted romantic hero should, he not only braves but defeats every obstacle thrown his way by the extralegal conspiracy set in motion by the villainous Inspector Pazzi and Mason Verger. He travels across the ocean to reunite with Starling. Aided by his lady fair in a critical moment of great peril, he escapes the wild beasts (specially trained man-eating swine) of a sacrificial arena and carries the wounded, swooning Starling in his arms in an iconic image of patriarchal romantic dominance.

His courtship culminates in a surreal romantic dinner in which he dissects the brain of the still-living Paul Krendler, thus eliminating Starling's prime enemy. He indirectly expresses his love for Starling by asking her: "Would you ever say to me, 'Stop. If you love me, stop'?" She replies, "Not in a thousand years." Lecter responds to the rebuff with obvious affection for her integrity: "'Not in a thousand years.' That's my girl." He is ever the spurned potential lover, suffering for his love but unwilling to relinquish it.[5] Rejected by Starling, he nevertheless proves the depth of his love for her by sacrificing his hand (or at least part of it) to Starling rather than hurt her when she handcuffs him to detain him for the imminent arrival of law enforcement. The audience is coerced by the net effect of all these textual elements to applaud Lecter's escape at the film's climax—an escape by boat which Starling is now in the power position to stop but, perhaps swayed by some involuntary feeling for him, does not. Lecter is borne away over the waters, Arthur-like, to his wounded exile in a far-off exotic land (in this case, somewhere in Asia). He is doubly wounded, both in body and heart. But like King Arthur and as the film's last image of his signature wink promises, he will doubtless return someday. The film paints a portrait of the serial killer as a gallant, even chivalrous protagonist whom the audience wants to see rewarded for his romantic ardor, even if he does not ultimately win "his" girl.

Perhaps the most narratologically forced instance of the trend to valorize Lecter is found in Brett Ratner's remake, *Red Dragon*, in which the role of Lecter is noticeably expanded and spotlighted as much as possible within the constraints of a source novel where an imprisoned Lecter occupies an even more marginal position than he does in *The Silence of the Lambs*. The mixed critical and public reaction to the film *Red Dragon* seemed to, in some way, capture the mood and tone of a culture ever so slightly turning away from its attraction to mainstream serial killer cinema.

Complicating matters, Dino de Laurentiis, the producer of Ratner's film, also produced the novel's first adaptation, *Manhunter* (1986). The original performed financially poorly at the time but has since gone on to garner a highly devoted public and critical following. The remake quickly polarized fans of the original production and those who wanted to see a more faithful adaptation of the source novel. Brett Ratner defended his film in *USA Today* by first commenting on the poor financial performance of *Manhunter*: "Nobody saw the movie . . . It was at the box office for, like, one weekend" (qtd. in 4D). He then addressed the aesthetic differences between the two films: "[*Manhunter*] stays in the *Miami Vice* '80s thing . . . It's very stylized. I made *Red Dragon* to be more of a timeless movie" (qtd. in Bowles 4D). Tom Noonan, the first actor to play serial killer Francis Dolarhyde, offers a contrarian view of the remake: "It doesn't feel great that they're remaking it . . . But I've quit being surprised by the greed of Hollywood" (qtd. in Bowles 4D).

Undoubtedly commercial calculations did support the decision to proceed with the remake. A related factor behind that decision is the opportunity for Anthony Hopkins to reprise his signature Lecter role one more time. For this purpose to work, however, the screenplay must invent more scenes for Lecter than originally existed in the novel. Consequently, the film moves unevenly between the story of serial killer Francis Dolarhyde's lethal search for romantic love (which serves as one of two primary narrative foci in the novel) and that of the psychological and verbal sparring between profiler Will Graham and Lecter.

This expansion of screen time for Lecter is evident in the film's opening scenes. Dramatizing and revising scenes only briefly alluded to in the source novel, the opening establishes a late-night collaboration between FBI profiler Will Graham and Baltimore psychiatrist Hannibal Lecter, whom no one as yet suspects of being the very serial killer ("the Chesapeake Ripper") that Graham is stalking. When Graham realizes the truth, a fight ensues in which Graham is seriously injured and Lecter is shot and apparently dies, his eyes glazed and wide open. He is next seen laid out on a slab as if for burial in a basement dungeon, a setting familiar to the audience as the cell he occupies in *The Silence of the Lambs*. But he resurrects to speak to Graham. Lecter appears in the film in several more scenes, during which he offers Graham in drips and drabs a profile of the "Tooth Fairy" killer, primarily to continue to inflict psychological harm upon the investigator Lecter nearly killed. Through coded correspondence with Dolarhyde, Lecter even provides the killer with Graham's home address so that Dolarhyde may then target Graham's family at the film's climax. The cumulative effect of all these scenes, both within the context of the film and the audience's presumed extra-textual knowledge of the other Lecter films, is that Lecter has risen from the dead to exert superhuman influence upon events even from the limbo of his confinement. If one considers the trilogy of films united by the commonality of Hopkins as Lecter, it is in *Red Dragon* that Lecter achieves his apotheosis as a character and manipulates events from a privileged zone set far apart from the society of men and women.

Noticeably missing is the sexual and romantic tension between Starling and Lecter, so the film must content itself with the heavy burden of any prequel in doggedly establishing the earlier manifestations of storylines and character behaviors and predilections already known to the audience. Therefore, *Red Dragon* spends much screen time establishing Lecter's unique culinary predilections, his sly verbal manipulation, his reptilian tics and mannerisms, and his brutality masked by a façade of Old World courtesy—all of which have already been on display in *The Silence of the Lambs* and *Hannibal*, deployed in the service of a Gothic flirtation with Starling. With Will Graham as a foil to Lecter instead of Starling, it is tempting to conclude that audiences must have been disappointed. Certainly the film's below-expected box office take (a tad shy of $93 million and short of the anticipated blockbuster revenues) provides an indirect measure of that possible disappointment. Recognizing its own structural deficit, the film concludes with a scene that provides a direct bridge to *The Silence of the Lambs*, wherein the ever-annoying Dr. Chilton announces to Lecter in his cell that a woman far too pretty to be an FBI agent is there to see him. The scene is too little too late for those who miss Starling. So *Red Dragon* as a story-of-origins ultimately frustrates those who wish to see how the murderous romantic hero came to be Starling's demon lover. Lecter as a remote, godlike being directing the fall of every sparrow just does not satisfy without his foil, Clarice Starling.

Going back to the beginning of the Hannibal Lecter story is the etiological narrative conceit of *Hannibal Rising*, a film which again may have suffered financially for a structure that does not allow for the presence of Clarice Starling and instead offers a sexually charged but chaste relationship with Lecter's Japanese aunt-by-marriage. That aside, the transmogrification of Lecter from villain to protagonist is completed in this film, or as Kim Newman writes, "There's no longer even a pretence that Lecter is anything but a hero" (64). The extreme suffering of the youth is offered by way of mitigation for the excessive crimes of the older man on display in *The Silence of the Lambs* and *Hannibal*. *Hannibal Rising* is exculpatory in intent, in much the same way as the *Star Wars* prequels humanize Darth Vader. The story provides a context for understanding the seemingly incomprehensible brutality of the mythic, older Lecter. By situating Lecter's childhood and formerly indistinct nationality within a precise historical time and place (Lithuania during World War II), the film accounts for the otherwise inexplicable Old World manner and speech of Lecter in the other film installments.

But more than that, the World War II setting allows the film to explain to an audience just how Lecter became a murderous cannibal. The intent is doubtless to compel the audience to sympathize with Lecter, an otherwise incomprehensible icon of evil, as the product of his environment. Additionally, within the larger cultural context of the Iraq war, the film subtly suggests that wartime cruelty inflicted on civilians by a powerful aggressor nation carries with it a heavy karmic debt that survivors of the carnage may come back to inflict upon the author of the destruction. Given the divided American response to the war at the time of the film's release, such a textual reading would not necessarily be off-putting to a large segment of the viewing audience.

A sketchy outline of the formative traumatic events in Lecter's life was given in Thomas Harris's novel *Hannibal* but did not make it into that film. However, in the film *Hannibal Rising*, the story reappears and is expanded. This prequel argues essentially that Lecter, however monstrous his actions are, is human, and that there is some degree of causality between childhood trauma and adult pathology.[6] This humanizing project is nevertheless overlaid upon a mythological structure similar to what Joseph Campbell popularized in his discussions of the hero's quest in *The Hero with a Thousand Faces*. Lecter's starting point on his journey is his privileged childhood in Lithuania. However, he is soon orphaned by the intrusion of Hitler's armies upon his idyllic rural estate. This abrupt and savage expulsion from the domestic sphere begins the nightmare story of Lecter's lifelong exile from human society. With his younger sister Mischa, he is held captive in the Lecter country hunting lodge by a renegade band of local soldiers, led by a despicable fellow named Vladis Grotas (the villain of the story). The starving soldiers eventually slaughter and eat Mischa. Lecter barely escapes this early descent into a personal hell, but retains no conscious memory of what happened to his sister. The remainder of the story, and the hero's quest, hinges upon his journey to recover this memory and, once recovered, act upon it.

Raised in a Russian orphanage during the Stalin era and suffering from terrible nightmares, he leaves on his own from the orphanage and finds his way to the home of Lady Murasaki, his Japanese aunt in France. Murasaki tutors him in the attitudes and combat styles of martial arts, thus helping set the stage for his future highly stylized murders. His deep reservoir of rage is soon directed at those who commit acts of rudeness, especially those against important women in his life. His first, initiatory murder is that of the obese and vulgar Paul the butcher, who makes the fatal mistake of insulting Lady Murasaki. Following this murder, Lecter is dogged by his shadow double, a French detective named Popil, who is also a survivor of wartime atrocities. In his officially sanctioned capacity, Popil brings war criminals to justice, a laudable project that Lecter will soon, in his own inimitable extralegal way, parallel. The similarities between the two men further predispose the audience to accept Lecter as a hero questing to redress a grievous wrong.

As further befits a culture hero, Lecter travels to the underworld, in this case the subterranean recesses of his own mind, to seek revelations necessary for completion of his journey. After witnessing a condemned criminal's reaction to sodium pen-tathol, Lecter decides to inject himself with the drug to access his repressed memo-ries of what happened to his sister. By so doing, Lecter returns to the most trau-matic event of his life—thus a metaphoric descent into hell. In this drug-induced, visionary state of mind, Lecter remembers what happened to his sister and brings the knowledge back to his conscious life. So armed, he returns to Lithuania to sys-tematically track down the killers of his sister. One by one, he eliminates his former tormentors and eats portions of them in a dispensing of poetic justice worthy of Dante Alighieri.

The film's climactic confrontation, of course, is with Grotas, whose villainy as a human trafficker competes with that of grotesquely scarred child-molester Mason Verger in the audience's collective memory of the Lecter films. It is interesting that within the context of these films, the exploitative evil of Grotas and Verger makes Lecter's brand of evil noble or at least just in comparison. Lecter's victory over Gro-tas frees him to travel to Canada and the New World, in a parody of the journey of European immigrants, to claim the life of the last of the soldiers who ate his sister. The film concludes with the iconic image of a diabolically smiling Lecter winking at the camera, positioned from the point of view of the next victim and, by exten-sion, the audience. This familiar mocking gesture links the young Lecter to the old and invites the audience to be consumed by this elegant monster from a foreign, war-torn land. Because Lecter is so familiar, even beloved, the masochistic audience welcomes the invitation.

THE BIOPICS: FROM *MONSTER* STRAIGHT TO VIDEO

Another genre movement has been to dramatize the lives of some of the notorious real-life murderers that complemented and reinforced the rise of the serial killer movie in the first place—Ted Bundy, Aileen Wuornos, Jeffrey Dahmer, Ed Gein, Albert DeSalvo, Richard Ramirez, John Wayne Gacy—to produce what may be called the serial killer "biopic." These films are returning to the source, as it were, for the serial killer screen narrative. It is a move, of course, that replicates the ori-gin of the genre in the first place in drawing so much on real-life cases for creative inspiration.[7] But the move also provides support for Annalee Newitz's thesis that "serial killer stories are preoccupied with realism" and "originate in literary natural-ism." Newitz elaborates: "many of these stories are based in fact or have a pseudo-documentary feel to them [...] the realist's urge to get at some kind of social truth haunts every story in the pantheon of serial killer tales" (15). At the same time, she concludes, the serial killer tale also often disavows its social concerns through the signature narrative insistence that in death is truth. The finality and mystery of death thus frequently trumps any social agenda that may be stated or implied by the narrative events.

Undoubtedly the most preeminent of these pseudo-documentaries or biopics is Patty Jenkins's *Monster*, based on the life of convicted Florida murderer Aileen Wuornos and starring a nearly unrecognizable Charlize Theron in an Oscar-winning performance. However, many less well-known films, such as *Ed Gein* (2000), *Ted Bundy* (2002), *Dahmer* (2002), *Nightstalker* (2002), *Gacy* (2003), *Green River Killer* (2005), *Rampage: The Hillside Strangler Murderers* (2005), *Boston Strangler* (2006), *Albert Fish* (2007), and *Ed Gein: The Butcher of Plainfield* (2007), fuse factual biography of notorious killers and horror convention to revisit the territory of the serial killer biopic as established by earlier genre works such as the well-known *Henry: Portrait of a Serial Killer* (1986) or a more obscure entry such as *Dahmer: The Secret Life* (1993). The majority of these films (with the notable exception of *Monster*) were made on low budgets, cast with relatively unknown actors, and released directly to video—an acknowledgment on the part of the producers that these biopics typically serve a narrowly defined market niche and do not constitute viable theatrical releases, let alone blockbusters.[8] Given the recent record of the mainstream serial killer films, the biopic producers may be making the smartest economic bet of all.

While not one of the "founding" members of America's most recognizable class of serial killers, Aileen Wuornos is nevertheless significant in that the media of the early 1990s was quick to brand her as the "first female serial killer." What is typically meant by this label is that Wuornos's murders were popularly believed to be sexually motivated in the same way as those committed by males. Wuornos, a prostitute, was arrested in 1991 and convicted in 1992 for the murders of seven men across central Florida. At her trial, she defended her actions as justified self-defense against "johns" who had turned violent on her. The courtroom jury (as well as the social jury represented by the media) discounted her claims and condemned her to death. The vehemence with which American society initially judged Wuornos is explained by Miriam Basilio: "The use of Wuornos to redefine the category of criminal deviance known as the serial killer to include women occurs at a time when women's greater social mobility is causing anxiety in conservative sectors of American society." Wuornos, a lesbian prostitute with no fixed address and a self-confessed record of murderous violence, tapped into these sectors' greatest fears. For all of these sins, she was first demonized and then punished.

Hence, the title of Jenkins's film: *Monster*. If media representations tended to deny Wuornos her humanity, Jenkins's film invokes that distancing strategy through the title and then reverses it with a plot that ostensibly humanizes Wuornos and creates sympathy for her hopeless, tragic quest for fame, power, wealth, and love. Rather than becoming President of the United States, as she fantasizes about, she becomes a media "monster" and "the first female serial killer," an arguable assertion in light of the numerous documented cases of females who commit multiple murders over time.[9] Rather than securing steady white-collar employment, she can obtain money only through selling sexual favors to men that she despises and will eventually turn her rage against. Rather than finding her soulmate, she suffers betrayal when her female lover, Selby, testifies against her at her trial. All she aspires to is domesticity and love and acceptance, but what she achieves is social exile and notoriety followed by death. The catalog of woes suffered by Wuornos leads Thomas Doherty to place the film within the woman's melodrama genre (4). From this perspective, then, *Monster* attempts to forge audience emotional connection to Wuornos and de-mystify the "monster" label. The serial-killer-as-protagonist trend is definitely embodied in the film.

However, *Monster* also disavows its protagonist by rendering her lesbian love story the site of uncanny horror for the audience. The developing relationship between Wuornos and Selby takes place within the context of escalating violence targeted against men. The juxtaposition readily lends itself to audience identification of lesbianism as a source of warped sexuality leading to murder. Terri Ginsberg labels the film as repressive, even fascist, in its effect. She argues that, in the storyline, "'queer' and 'perversion' are the same." Perversion in this context not only refers to lesbian sexuality but the perversion of the natural order of victimology, in which a female prostitute from a social class frequently brutalized by men turns the tables and kills males. Witnessing such "unnatural" acts may produce alternating levels of voyeuristic titillation and anxiety within a mainstream audience—impulses that must be denied and exorcised through Wuornos's ritual trial and condemnation at the end of the film. The serial killer biopics tend to conclude with similar expurgations of the serial killer main character, perhaps so that the audience may walk away without anxiety and residual guilt from sampling the menu of atrocities on display for most of the running time of the typical biopic.

These biographical films cover the spectrum of America's most recognizable serial killers. Often using only the killers' names as title is an indicator that the filmmakers have every confidence there is enough name recognition for each serial killer to ensure an audience within the niche defined by the straight-to-video distribution model. Ed Gein in particular is significant in that his crimes, quite modest by today's standards of serial-killer crimes, influenced an entire generation of earlier American writers to mythologize him and his then-unimaginable deeds in a variety of fictional narratives that resonate within the culture even today. Thus, a cinema-literate culture may not know exactly who Gein was, but they do know well the films—*Psycho*, *The Silence of the Lambs*, *The Texas Chainsaw Massacre*—based in part on his actions and may be expected to respond to another film marketed as the story of the "true life" Norman Bates or Buffalo Bill or Leatherface. Though not an inspiration for fiction in the same way as Gein, Ted Bundy is remembered in extensive true-crime literature and media reportage as a mythic sexual predator, hiding behind a pleasant mask of heterosexual normalcy that allowed him to rape, beat, kill, and/or dismember scores of women for years over a huge geographical range. Then there is Jeffrey Dahmer, one of the most recognizable names coming out of the 1990s, immortalized in the mass media as a "real-life" Hannibal Lecter. Dahmer constitutes the closeted, homosexual mirror image of the roving heterosexual Bundy—a trap-door spider as opposed to a wolf.

The cinematic hagiographies focused on these killers are a gloss on the high (or low) points of their lives, as well as creative interpretations of what motivated the killers and what metaphysical and/or cultural implications may be drawn from study of their actions. In terms of genre, the films occupy an ambiguous positioning somewhere between art and exploitation, with only *Monster* largely escaping the "exploitation" charge by virtue of the illustrious names associated with its production.[10] One need only compare the generally favorable critical response to *Monster* to the derisive reviews for films like *Ted Bundy* or *Ed Gein*. For example, critic Mike D'Angelo, in reviewing *Ted Bundy*, calls that biopic an "amalgam of trash and pretension" that "fits snugly within a burgeoning genre some call 'artsploitation.'" Jeffrey Sconce's coining of the term "paracinema," and Joan Hawkins's elaboration upon it, is also applicable here, in that both critics discuss genres outside of the mainstream that rely on extreme affect (arousal or revulsion) over intellect. Because of the emphasis on body over mind, such films are typically dismissed by critics who would otherwise champion the pushing of conventional boundaries in art. Like pornography and gory slasher films, one is on reasonably safe ground in grouping the serial killer biopics under the rubric of "paracinema."

The realist aesthetics of the serial killer biopics differ significantly from their more expressionistic genre cousins. The biopic aesthetic tends to visualize the story with a minimum of flourish and a decided lack of brand-name stars (except for Charlize Theron) whose celebrity might otherwise distract the audience. There are few shots that call attention to their artifice, although again *Monster* through its technical virtuosity manages to escape the "paracinema" label for the critics. A good example of a shot that calls attention to itself in *Monster* is the dizzying 360-degree camera shot that captures the breathlessness of Lee and Selby's roller-rink date in *Monster*. Overall, however, the studied lack of pretension becomes the films' biggest pretension. The editing pace is generally methodical, even languid—very much a reaction against the expressionistic, shock-cut, rapid-fire, blurred, asynchronous, or otherwise fractured sequences in mainstream serial-killer thrillers (such as *The Cell*) that have come to signify the monstrous point of view of the outwardly nonmonstrous killer, a point made by Steffen Hantke ("Monstrosity Without a Body"). There is little of the repetitive, pseudo-sexual buildup and release of suspense so much a staple of mainstream thrillers. The aesthetic result is pseudo-documentary in its denial of the conventional methods used to manipulate the audiences of thrillers. The serial killer biopics are subversive of the slick and expensive stylistics of conventional Hollywood product, while still indulging in the escalating portrayal of violence typical of "psycho" cinema both high and low budget.

The serial killer biopics occupy an ambiguous niche between "true crime" narratives and works of fiction. Two of these films, *Ed Gein* and *Bundy*, purport to tell the true story of each killer through brief but authentic video footage and still photographs intercut with extended dramatizations in a style that manages to be both deliberately artificial and doggedly realistic at the same time. The newspaper and photographic records of crime scenes and legal proceedings provide the films with a frame of reality, while the dramatizations of villainy crafted around actors who physically resemble the killers lead the voyeuristic audience into the otherwise inaccessible details of the killers' lives and crimes only hinted at it in the official documents. The two films also stick closely to the known facts of the cases, changing only victims' names. Any speculative scenes, flashbacks, or dialogue are quite logical extrapolations from those known facts. The film *Dahmer* eschews the archival material in favor of a more fictionalized and less factually bound approach to the title character, while still retaining overall fidelity to some of the well-known highlights of Dahmer's criminal career. The films in aggregate convey the now-clichéd banality of evil through recreations of the killers' mundane daily lives juxtaposed with the most heinous moments of their criminal careers. It could even be argued that the films themselves are banal in structure, theme, and execution and thus come by the aesthetic and affective effect honestly.

The overall genre trend, then, has been toward a solid domestication of the serial killer. The spectacular mainstream success of the genre in the last years of the twentieth century, accelerated into hyper drive with the complicity of law enforcement agencies with a vested interest in promulgating the myth of the serial killer, has now so entrenched it in the culture that the latest narratives are engaged in a project of revisiting, interrogating, revising, and reinventing the endlessly permeable genre. The fictional serial killers are as familiar and welcomed in the current climate as an old friend, perhaps fallen on hard times but still beloved. It is likely, then, that audiences will continue to see more of the serial killers at the local cineplexes. The killers' eyes will no doubt continue to glare malevolently at consumers from the covers of DVDs in the Best Buy stores.

NOTES

1. *Hannibal* earned $165,092,266 in release. By comparison, its follow-up film, *Red Dragon*, earned $92,955,420 (*The Numbers*).

2. *The Bone Collector's* budget was $48 million and box office gross $66,488,090; *The Cell's* budget was $35 million and box office gross $61,280,963; *Monster's* budget was $5 million and box office gross $34,469,210; *Disturbia's* budget was $20 million and box office gross $80,106,701 (*The Numbers*).

3. *Hannibal Rising* earned $27,669,725; *Zodiac*, $33,080,084 (*The Numbers*).

4. Films like Bruce A. Evans's *Mr. Brooks* and James Mangold's *Identity* (2003) take a slightly different but no less extreme approach in that they project the interior space of the psycho killer out into the exterior world in the form of murderous alter egos, which both the killer and the audience can see and hear.

5. It must be noted that in Thomas Harris's source novel, Lecter and Starling do dine together on Paul Krendler's brain, become lovers, and abscond together as fugitives to South America. Lecter accomplishes this feat of corrupting Starling first by isolating her and then brainwashing her into compliance with his wishes through powerful drugs and hypnotic suggestions. The filmmakers rejected Harris's ending as too alienating for the audience, and instead chose to portray Lecter as a rejected lover.

6. Of course, longtime readers of Harris's source fiction should not be surprised by this theme. The film adaptations have tended to minimize or eliminate altogether the narrative importance in Harris's fiction of early trauma in the creation of criminals. For Harris, serial killers are fossilized in psychological place by the formative events of their early youth—angry children in dangerous adult bodies and possessed of adult strength and cunning.

7. Philip Jenkins, one of the pioneering critics of the cultural construction of serial murder, comments upon this type of cross-fertilization between fact and fiction: "As we see the constant creation and recycling of media accounts, the proliferation of texts and images, . . . it is difficult not to describe this process as compulsive, irresistible, obsessive, lacking any natural ending" ("Catch Me," 15).

8. According to Jon Silver and Frank Alpert: "Each year, fewer than half of the total films produced even receive a theatrical release; most go straight to video or are made for TV"; "Digital Dawn: A Revolution in Movie Distribution?" *Business Horizons* 46.5 (September–October 2003): 57–66.

9. See Michael Newton's *Bad Girls Do It: An Encyclopedia of Female Murderers* (Port Townsend, Wash.: Loopanics, 1993).

10. Interestingly, Leslie Felperin takes *Monster* to task for being too polished or glossy: ". . . in its own movie terms, there's something bogus about *Monster*. Like its swaggering star, hips out and thumbs hooked in her belt loops, the film walked the indie-movie walk with its impeccably gritty mise en scene . . . But . . . *Monster's* script is clean-edged and fussily neat . . . [Wuornos's] voiceover . . . sounds airlessly literary and knowing"; Felperin, "Monster (rev.)," *Sight and Sound* 14.4 (April 2004): 59.

WORKS CITED

Basilio, Miriam. "Corporal Evidence: Representations of Aileen Wuornos." *Art Journal* 55.4 (Winter 1996): 56–62. Academic Search Premier. Brevard Community College, Cocoa, FL. http://web8.epnet.com (accessed October 18, 2005).

Bowles, Scott. "*Red Dragon* vs. *Manhunter*: The Gloves Come Off." *USA Today*. October 7, 2002.

Bronfen, Elisabeth. *Home in Hollywood: The Imaginary Geography of Cinema*. New York: Columbia University Press, 2004.

Campbell, Joseph. *The Hero with a Thousand Faces*. 1949. New York: Barnes and Noble Books.

Cawelti, John. *Adventure, Mystery, and Romance: Formula Stories as Art and Popular Culture*. Chicago: University of Chicago Press, 1976.

Cettl, Robert. *Serial Killer Cinema: An Analytical Filmography with an Introduction*. Jefferson, N.C.: McFarland, 2003.

D'Angelo, Mike. "*Ted Bundy* (rev.)." *Time Out New York*, April 12, 2003. http://www.timeoutny .com/film/363/363.film.bundy.rev.html.

Dargis, Manohla. "Hunting a Killer as the Age of Aquarius Dies." *New York Times*, September 7, 2007. http://www.movies.nytimes.com.

Doherty, Thomas. "Aileen Wuornos Superstar." *Cineaste* 29.3 (2004): 3–5.

Epstein, Su C. "The New Mythic Monster." *Cultural Criminology*. Eds. Jeff Ferrell and Clinton R. Sanders. Boston: Northeastern University Press, 1995.

Felperin, Leslie. "*Monster* (rev.)." *Sight and Sound* 14.4 (April 2004): 59.

Fetters, Sara M. "Seattle's International Film Festival: Part 5: SIFF Day 6—Ticket Longings and Serial Killer Dread." *Features*. Movie Freak. 2001. September 13, 2007. http://www.moviefreak .com/features/siff2001/seattlefilm05.htm.

Fister, Barbara. "Copycat Crimes: Crime Fiction and the Marketplace of Anxieties." *Clues* 23.3 (Spring 2005): 43–56.

Gilbey, Ryan. "Watching the Detectives." *New Statesman*, May 21, 2000, 45.

Ginsberg, Terri. "Lesbian Violence as Fascist Crusade in *Monster*." *Genders Online Journal* 43 (2006). http://www.genders.org/g43/g43_ginsberg.html.

Hantke, Steffen. "'The Kingdom of the Unimaginable': The Construction of Social Space and the Fantasy of Privacy in Serial Killer Narratives." *Literature/Film Quarterly* 26.3 (1998): 178–95. Wilson Web. Brevard Community College, Cocoa, FL. http:vnweb.hwwilsonweb.com (accessed January 6, 2004).

———. "Monstrosity Without a Body: Representational Strategies in the Popular Serial Killer Film." *Postscript* 22.2 (January 2003): 34–54.

Hawkins, Joan. *Cutting Edge: Art-Horror and the Horrific Avant-Garde*. Minneapolis: University of Minnesota Press, 2000.

Ingebretsen, Edward J. "The Monster in the Home: True Crime and the Traffic in Body Parts." *Journal of American Culture* 21.1 (Spring 1998): 27–34.

Jenkins, Philip. "Catch Me Before I Kill More: Seriality as Modern Monstrosity." *Cultural Analysis* 3 (2002): 1–17.

———. *Using Murder: The Social Construction of Serial Homicide*. New York: Aldine De Gruyter, 1994.

Macnab, Geoffrey. "Still Making a Killing." *The Independent*, May 4, 2007. Look Smart. http:// findarticles.com (accessed September 28, 2007).

Malmgren, Carl D. *Anatomy of Murder: Mystery, Detective and Crime Fiction*. Bowling Green, Ohio: Bowling Green University Popular Press, 2001.

Newitz, Annalee. *Pretend We're Dead: Capitalist Monsters in American Pop Culture*. Durham, N.C.: Duke University Press, 2006.

Newton, Michael. *Bad Girls Do It: An Encyclopedia of Female Murderers*. Port Townsend, Wash.: Loompanics, 1993.

The Numbers: Box Office Data, Movie Stars, Idle Speculation. http:www.the-numbers.com/movies (accessed November 7, 2007).

Santaularia, Isabel. "'The Great Good Place' No More?: Integrating and Dismantling Oppositional Discourse in Some Recent Examples of Serial Killer Fiction." *Atlantis* 29.1 (June 2007): 55–67.

Schmid, David. *Natural Born Celebrities: Serial Killers in American Culture.* Chicago: University of Chicago Press, 2005.

Sconce, Jeffrey. "'Trashing' the Academy: Taste, Excess, and an Emerging Politics of Cinematic Style." *Screen* 36.4 (Winter 1995): 371–93.

Self, Will. "That's All Folks! (Or the Death of the Serial Killer Genre)." *The Independent,* February 11, 2001. Look Smart. http://findarticles.com (accessed September 13, 2007).

Seltzer, Mark. *Serial Killers: Death and Life in America's Wound Culture.* New York: Routledge, 1998.

Silver, Jon, and Frank Alpert. "Digital Dawn: A Revolution in Movie Distribution?" *Business Horizons* 46.5 (September–October 2003): 57–66.

Taubin, Amy. "Nerds on a Wire." *Sight and Sound* 17.5 (May 2007): 24–26.

Worland, Rick. *The Horror Film: An Introduction.* Malden, Mass.: Blackwell, 2007.

A RETURN TO THE GRAVEYARD

Notes on the Spiritual Horror Film

—James Kendrick

PENDULUM SWINGS: THE RETURN OF "QUIET HORROR"

In the summer of 1999, M. Night Shyamalan's *The Sixth Sense* became an unexpected smash hit, earning $293 million at the domestic box office, which made it the second-highest grossing film of the year behind George Lucas's much-anticipated *Star Wars: Episode I—The Phantom Menace*. Even with its memorably creepy and intriguing trailer that all but guaranteed the pop-culture permanence of the phrase "I see dead people," no one expected *The Sixth Sense* to become the phenomenon it did. After all, the horror genre had not produced a major blockbuster since the 1970s, when *The Exorcist* ruled the box office in 1973 and *Jaws* dominated it in 1975. The film's star, Bruce Willis, had anchored the Michael Bay/Jerry Bruckheimer hit *Armageddon* (1998) the summer before, but he was hardly a sure bet given that his track record was also littered with recent disappointments such as *Last Man Standing* (1995) and *The Jackal* (1997). And, at the time, few people had heard of the writer/director M. Night Shyamalan. Even fewer knew how to pronounce his name.

As it turned out, *The Sixth Sense* was just the beginning of a cycle of spiritually minded horror films that were especially evocative in tone and theme of the mid-eighteenth-century Graveyard School of poets, whose focus on themes of death, human mortality, spirituality, gloom, and melancholy prefigured the eighteenth-century Gothic novel and helped to lay the foundation of the horror genre.[1] This cycle included such films as *Stir of Echoes* (1999), *What Lies Beneath* (2000), *The Gift* (2000), *The Others* (2001), *Frailty* (2001), *Dragonfly* (2002), *White Noise* (2005), and *The Exorcism of Emily Rose* (2006), all of which moved away from a focus on graphic violence and instead created a backbone of terror, dread, suspense, and spiritual contemplation. I am thus using the term "spiritual" to refer to matters that are often referred to as supernatural—those things that are beyond the explanatory scope of rational and scientific understanding. However, the spiritual goes beyond the supernatural in the assumption that there is meaning in that which we cannot explain in material terms, usually related to issues of life and death and what follows our existence in the physical world. This is in keeping with a general etymological development of the terms during which *supernatural* has come to describe anything that is above the natural, whereas *spiritual* has a direct connection to the human spirit, that is, the idea that being human transcends mere material existence. The spiritual is, in some way, sacred.

The supernatural/spiritual horror film has a long history in the American cinema and has, in some sense, always run parallel to materialist horror. But the cycle of films that emerged in the wake of *The Sixth Sense* is particularly important and worthy of attention because, not only was it extremely concentrated, but it marked a decided shift in the horror genre as it was currently constituted, which served a dual function. First, in terms of the films themselves, it refreshed the genre by returning it to its initial emphasis on the psychological and the spiritual over the material and physical. This is a quite different development from the one traced by Jerrold E. Hogle in his analysis of the Gothic at the end of the twentieth century. "Terror can return," Hogle argues, "in a fantasy that deliberately strives to point out *the body*, indeed the most primal and destructible possibilities of the body, and thereby recover it from earlier Gothic disembodiments and the dissolution of it into myriad simulations, large and small" (160).

Second, in economic terms, this shift in the genre attempted to mainstream horror films (a historically marginalized genre associated with independent studios and B-level production values) by giving them a potentially broader audience via their typical PG-13 ratings and more conventional emotional resonances. The box office success of *The Sixth Sense* showed that horror movies could be hugely profitable if geared toward a mainstream audience, rather than the niche audience composed primarily of adolescent boys that had been the primary consumers of contemporary horror in the 1980s. Thus, the visual excesses associated with violent horror were toned down, eliminating one of the primary critiques of the genre ("It's too gory!") and subsequent roadblocks to larger audiences. It is telling that, of the nine films listed earlier, six were rated PG-13 and only three of them were rated R. And even the three R-rated films (*Stir of Echoes, Frailty*, and *The Gift*) studiously avoid the kinds of graphic violence that tended to characterize horror films of the previous decade.[2]

However, this cycle has been relatively short-lived, especially since, in recent years, increasingly graphic horror and torture movies like the *Saw* series (2004–2008) and the *Hostel* films (2005/2006), as well as violently intensified horror remakes like *The Texas Chainsaw Massacre* (2003), *The Hills Have Eyes* (2006), *Halloween* (2007), and *Friday the 13th* (2009), have become the new rage. While this might suggest that the horror genre's embrace of the spiritual at the turn of the twenty-first century was a brief, temporary detour en route to its final resting place in the physical, it is more likely another arc in the constant evolution of the genre, which over the decades has swung back and forth with varying degrees of force between the visceral and the suggestive, the graphic and the contemplative, the material and the spiritual.[3]

THE HORROR FILM IN THE 1990S

The widespread popularity of *The Sixth Sense* was particularly surprising because, by the summer of 1999, the mainstream horror genre did not appear to have room for moody, elegant, supernatural films aimed at a wide audience. At that time, the horror genre, which was on an upswing from virtual nonexistence in the early 1990s, was known primarily for a series of self-conscious updates of the slasher film, a subgenre that had all but dominated horror in the 1980s. The slasher film has been defined by Carol Clover as "the immensely generative story of a psycho killer who slashes to death a string of mostly female victims, one by one, until he is subdued or killed, usually by the one girl who has survived" (21). Steeped in formula, these films developed into long-running franchises aimed at primarily teenage audiences: *Friday the 13th* (eight installments between 1980 and 1989); *Halloween* (five installments between 1978 and 1989); *A Nightmare on Elm Street* (five installments between 1984 and 1989). The seemingly endless string of sequels, spin-offs, and rip-offs reinforced the perception of most critics and moral watchdogs that such films were bankrupt artistically, if not morally, further shoving the horror genre into the illicit margins of cultural detritus.

Thus, by the early to mid-1990s there was a perception that the horror genre was all but dead. A 1994 article in *Daily Variety* questioned the future of horror films, suggesting that recent box office failures and a significant drop-off in home video sales of horror titles portended the end of a "tired" genre that had been recently glutted with "mediocre product" (Klady 13). This is despite the fact that, similar to the efforts of Stanley Kubrick and Paul Schrader in the early 1980s, the early 1990s had witnessed a concerted effort by well-regarded filmmakers to reclaim the horror genre with big-budget, star-studded, "intellectual" horror films that were, in effect, grandiose Gothic fantasies. The trend kicked off with Francis Ford Coppola's audacious reimagining of *Bram Stoker's Dracula* (1992), a financially successful film that merged music video romanticism with ample gore and a film-lovers' cavalcade of references to old-school filmmaking techniques.[4] It was followed by a more serious and less popular take on *Mary Shelley's Frankenstein* (1994), which Coppola produced after handing the directorial reigns over to British director Kenneth Branagh, who at the time was best known for his Shakespeare adaptations. That same year saw the release of Mike Nichols's urban werewolf satire *Wolf* and Neil Jordan's lavish adaptation of Anne Rice's *Interview With the Vampire*, which caused no end of controversy in the casting of megastar Tom Cruise as the infamous vampire Lestat.

In the mid- to late 1990s, the genre was dominated by the reemergence of the slasher film in updated, postmodern guise (Wee). While intertextuality and self-referentiality had been elements of the horror genre for years (Brophy), it was especially foregrounded in the so-called postmodern slasher film. *Scream* (1996), which was written by young newcomer Kevin Williamson but directed by genre veteran Wes Craven, led the way in self-consciously playing with the basic parameters of the slasher film by introducing self-aware would-be victims as a filmic reflection of the young, media-savvy, self-aware audience. If the endless sequels of the 1980s had begun to alienate even the most devoted horror fans, *Scream* drew them back by playing to their preexisting knowledge about the genre. Interestingly, Craven had ventured into similar waters two years earlier with *New Nightmare* (1994), an imaginative spin-off from his popular *A Nightmare on Elm Street* franchise in which those involved with making the original movie, including star Heather Langenkamp and Craven himself, played themselves being terrorized by the series' bogeyman Freddy Krueger, who had broken free of his celluloid prison and infiltrated the "real world." *New Nightmare* was not a hit with audiences, perhaps because it was *too* self-reflexive, or perhaps because fans were simply tired of seeing Freddy Krueger after six films in fewer than ten years.

Scream, however, was a huge success both critically and commercially. It featured a cast of popular young stars, many of whom were drawn from television (including Drew Barrymore, Neve Campbell, and Courtney Cox), and it stroked its viewers' egos by playing to their preexisting genre knowledge. It earned $103 million at the U.S. box office, a rarity for even the most popular horror films, and was, therefore, not surprisingly followed by two sequels, one in 1997 and one in 2000. It also led to an avalanche of new teen horror movies and sequels whose producers hoped to cash in on *Scream*'s success: *I Know What You Did Last Summer* (1997) and its 1998 sequel *I Still Know What You Did Last Summer*, *Disturbing Behavior* (1998), *The Faculty* (1998), *Urban Legend* (1998) and its 2000 sequel *Urban Legends: Final Cut*, and *Final Destination* (2000) and its two sequels (2003 and 2006). The striking similarity of the promotional posters used to advertise these films, which invariably involve some arrangement of the main characters in front of the looming image of the film's killer, suggests just how akin the films are in both their approach to horror and their desired audience.

The new flurry of horror films also led to the resurrection of several dormant franchises, including *Halloween* (1998's *Halloween H20: Twenty Years Later*, which brought original star Jamie Lee Curtis back into the series, and 2002's *Halloween: Resurrection*), *Friday the 13th* (2001's *Jason X*, which sent the hockey-mask-wearing slasher into space), and *Child's Play* (1998's *Bride of Chucky* and 2004's *Seed of Chucky*, both of which are dark, tongue-in-cheek comedies). As the last two examples suggest, there was an air of self-parody growing in the horror genre, especially after the release the Wayan Brothers' *Scary Movie* (2000) and its three sequels, not to mention a decade of "Treehouse of Horror" episodes on *The Simpsons*. The majority of these teen-centric horror films, despite their sometimes clever postmodern trappings, fell victim to the same criticisms inflicted on 1980s slasher films: tired commercial garbage whose cheeky self-referencing was just a thin façade to hide an otherwise uncomplicated and incessantly perverse fascination with creative means of violent death.

Thus, because the genre was glutted with films that focused primarily on violence, with no consideration as to what happened after the knife (or axe . . . or saw . . . or meat cleaver . . .) had been sunk, *The Sixth Sense*, which was released just three years after *Scream* had self-reflexively rewritten the horror genre, appeared to be something new and different. With its reverently hushed tones, burnished cinematography, and air of grave sincerity, it was a horror movie for people who didn't like horror movies. More important, it was a horror movie that asked to be taken seriously in its evocation of life after death. It had human characters, rather than cardboard victims, and it dealt with relationships, both familial and spiritual. For many it was an emotional experience, wringing a wide spectrum of responses; audiences both jumped in their seats and welled up with tears at the end, even as they marveled at the narrative gymnastics that unfolded so fluidly in the unexpected twist ending. And it didn't feature a single teenage character or knife-wielding psychopath.

Rather than focusing on the earthly, physical fears of sudden bodily damage, *The Sixth Sense* focused on the afterlife. What happens after we die? What is the relationship between the living and the dead? What, in fact, is the nature of death itself? These are questions that are certainly not new to the horror genre; in fact, according to some histories, such questions are the very root of the genre, which began with the Graveyard School of poets in the mid-eighteenth century. In turning to such issues, *The Sixth Sense* paved the way for a cycle of horror films that returned to the genre's spiritual roots in the graveyard.

THE GRAVEYARD SCHOOL

Although there are traces of what we would now consider "horror" in works as ancient as Homer's *The Odyssey*, the origins of the contemporary horror genre are usually traced back to late-eighteenth- and early-nineteenth-century English Gothic literature, especially Mary Shelley's *Frankenstein* (1818) and Dr. John

Polidori's *The Vampyre: A Tale* (1819), "two of the most enduring outgrowths of the traditional Gothic tale of terror" (Tropp 28).

The term "Gothic" has a long and somewhat conflicted history of shifting meanings, beginning with reference to the medieval German tribes known as "Goths." As a result, in English the term "Gothic" came to refer to all things primitive, chaotic, superstitious, and excessive—essentially those negative qualities associated with the "Dark Ages" from the perspective of the seventeenth-century Enlightenment, which prized reason, logic, and rationality. However, Gothic history was rewritten in England in the mid-eighteenth century to celebrate those primitive qualities that had previously been dismissed as contrary to civilization (Punter and Byron 7–8).

The connection between the Gothic and the horror genre derives from the use of the word *Gothic* to describe a literary movement that began in the late 1700s as a reaction against neoclassicism and is variably viewed as either the predecessor of Romanticism or a simultaneous variant of it. While the generally agreed-upon first Gothic novel is Horace Walpole's *The Castle of Otranto* (1764), the best-known works of the "High Gothic" period were written between 1790 and the 1820s, which "is very nearly synchronic with the Romantic period" (McEvoy 19). Regardless of how it is dated, Gothic literature produced many novels and stories built around recurring images, motifs, and themes that would come to be associated with the horror genre: an emphasis on the past, the exploration of the aesthetics of fear, and the merging of fantasy and reality (Spooner and McEvoy 1). Even more obvious are the formal qualities that include supernatural elements and settings that emphasize death and decay. It is also worth noting that, as David Punter points out, Gothic fiction lends itself quite readily to psychoanalytic thought, which has been one of the most oft-utilized critical approaches to the inner workings and subtexts of the horror genre.

However, to truly understand horror we need to dig back deeper into history, past the Romantic and Gothic traditions to which it is typically traced, to the Graveyard School of poets, whose contributions to the horror genre have been consistently understated, if not ignored. If horror is usually traced back to Gothic literature, then Graveyard poetry must be considered one of its deeper roots, given the fact that, as Punter and Byron note, "it prefigures the Gothic novel in several ways" (10), most notably in its rejection of the ideal of rational understanding and its emphasis on the sublime. While Edmund Burke's *Origin of Our Ideas of the Sublime and Beautiful* (1757) is often referenced as the first significant connection between sublimity—in which the mind reels in the presence of something greater than itself—and terror, the Graveyard poets were exploring such ideas in verse several decades earlier. For example, Punter and Byron interpret Thomas Parnell's "A Night-Piece on Death," which was first published in 1722, as follows: "To learn wisdom, it is necessary to take a quicker and more frightening path, which is the path not of reason but of intense feeling [. . .] from prolonged and absorbed meditation on [life's] extreme limit: death" (11). Thus, the Graveyard poets were among the first to recognize that deep insights into life could only emerge from ruminating on death, which meant that such insights were inextricably linked to terror.

Parnell and the other Graveyard poets emerged primarily in England in the first half of the eighteenth century and spread via imitation to other European countries and across the ocean to New England before falling beneath the shadow of the Gothic and Romantic writers they helped inspire. The influential nature of their works can be seen in Samuel Taylor Coleridge's discussion in his *Biographia Literaria* (1817) of Friedrich Schiller's play *The Robbers* (1781). Coleridge notes that the German translation of Edward Young's nine-volume graveyard poem *The Complaint; or Night-Thoughts on Life, Death, and Immortality* (1742–1745) was one of the three most popular books in Germany in the years before Schiller wrote his play and that Schiller clearly borrowed "the strained thoughts, the figurative metaphysics, and solemn epigrams" of Young's poem and then added "horrific incidents, and mysterious villains [. . .] the ruined castles, the dungeons, the trap-doors, the skeletons, the flesh-and-blood ghosts" (183–84; see also Miles 11). Furthermore, Coleridge also traces these devices to Walpole's *The Castle of Otranto*, the first Gothic novel. Thus, in this instance we can see a clear lineage from the Graveyard poets to English Gothic literature to German drama. Despite such influence, though, the Graveyard poets are no longer read as frequently as their Gothic followers. Nevertheless, their work remains crucial to understanding where the horror genre derived much of its iconography, even if the genre as a whole has largely discarded the Graveyard poets' thematic underpinnings of spirituality.

Although the writers included under the label "Graveyard School" worked independently of each other, they collectively established much of the fundamental imagery of the modern horror genre decades before it made its way into English Gothic literature. Initially inspired by medieval funeral elegies and the use of melancholy in English poetry, these writers were among the first to focus their attention on death, darkness, ruins, and decay—"everything, indeed, that was excluded by rational culture" (Botting 32). Poems such as the aforementioned "A Night-Piece on Death" and *The Complaint; or Night-Thoughts on Life, Death, and Immortality*, as well as Robert Blair's *The Grave* (1743) and Thomas Gray's "Elegy Written in a Country Churchyard" (1751) were among the first to be set in graveyards and feature Death as a character. They established the skin-crawling use of such lasting images as ravens, creepy yew trees, decomposing bodies, skeletal remains, and dank crypts, all of which would feed the fervid imaginations of everyone from Edgar Allen Poe to George A. Romero.

It is not as though such images had never occurred in other forms of art and literature prior to the poets of the Graveyard School. Rather, what makes their contribution so crucial to the formation of the horror genre was their coupling of such images not just to the frightening nature of death itself, but to whatever it is that comes after. This was partially because their work appeared at a historical moment when attitudes regarding death were in transition:

> The new attitude found death frightening, but that wasn't and isn't the worst. The worst is just what the Graveyard poets and their precursors held up as death's negation: the hope or belief that the dead will rise, bodies and all, on the Day of Judgment. Trust in that rising gave way, within two generations of the Graveyard poets, to a fear that has not abated: that the dead will rise and in fact do rise, all the time, the moment you turn your back on them. (Kendrick 21–22)

Thus, while the poems were often graphic in their descriptions of death and decay, the purpose of the Graveyard poets' work was intently spiritual, as virtually all of it came from clergymen who likely drew inspiration from the graveyards they saw out the windows of their church dwellings every day (Cameron 15–20). As the literary historian Walter Kendrick notes, "Though the horrors they invoked were those of the flesh, they desired to admonish the spirit" (10). In other words, they had a specifically didactic purpose in visually illustrating for readers the logical ends of physical materiality in the hopes of turning their attention to eternal spiritual matters.

The underlying theme of Graveyard poetry, then, is that life is redeemed by the promise of an afterlife. While the poems tend to focus on the gruesome, physical details of death, which is frequently personified as a frightening physical presence, the goal is to encourage the reader to ponder the transient nature of life on earth and the temporary pleasures it affords. Many of the poems read like sermons in verse form, warning against sinfulness and a godless existence and encouraging readers to transcend their earthly fears of the ugliness of death through faith in the afterlife. In fact, Kenneth Walter Cameron suggests that Graveyard poetry was a conscious and direct response to the eighteenth-century rise of deism and atheism, which forced pastors and priests to find "potent illustrations for frightening their people into the path of virtue and faith" (18).

Interestingly, the Graveyard School's poems served a dual, and somewhat contradictory, function. As we have seen, their poems reinterpreted the physicality of death in spiritual terms, positing graveyards and corpses as objects on which to meditate in order to understand the redeeming nature of the afterlife. However, as Kendrick points out, they also paved the way for turning the grotesquerie of death into aesthetic appreciation. Kendrick particularly notes how Parnell's "A Night-Piece on Death" differed from its predecessor, the funeral elegy, by detaching grief from a specific individual's death and turning it into poetry that could be sold for profit. This process continued into subsequent Gothic literature, which drew from the Graveyard poets' horrific imagery, but discarded the spiritual content, resulting in a literature that stressed how "there is something inherent in our very mortality that dooms us to a life of incomprehension, a life in which we are forever sunk in mysteries and unable to escape from the deathly consequences of our physical form" (Punter and Byron 12). Thus, even though the avowed intention of the Graveyard poets was to encourage their readers to consider spiritual issues by bringing them face-to-face with the gory realities of death and decay, they also began the process by which modern horror would eliminate such concerns in favor of gross-out thrills, "until tombs and skulls lost whatever connection they once had to anybody's real death and became the icons of a new kind of entertainment" (Kendrick 14).

THE INTERSECTION OF THE SPIRITUAL AND THE PHYSICAL

It is not surprising that the horror genre took a more spiritual turn at the end of the 1990s because, at the time, it seemed that the entire American film industry was caught up in fin-de-siècle-inspired renewal of spirituality and religion that infiltrated virtually every genre. In the early 1990s, there had been a brief cycle of life-after-death films led by *Ghost* (1990) and *Jacob's Ladder* (1991), both of which were written by Bruce Joel Rubin, but it wasn't until the end of the decade that this theme kicked into full gear. Kevin Smith played with Catholic doctrine in his comedy *Dogma* (1999), while *A Life Less Ordinary* (1997) made screwball antics out of angelic intervention; the romantic melodrama was given a spiritual twist when an angel falls in love with a mortal in *City of Angels* (1998) and a man in heaven tries to save his suicidal wife's condemnation to hell in *What Dreams May Come* (1998); *Contact* (1997) went beyond usual science fiction trappings to ruminate on the existence of God, the essence of faith, and the conflict between science and religion; meanwhile, *Spawn* (1997), one of the few comic book heroes to make it to the big screen in the late 1990s, was forged in hell; even an Arnold Schwarzenegger action vehicle was recast in religious-spiritual terms in the apocalyptic *End of Days* (1999). In this sense, then, it seems all the more natural that the horror genre, whose roots can be traced back to the church graveyard, also took a spiritual turn.

However, it is important to note that, like the films just mentioned, the majority of spiritual horror films released at this time did not adhere to any particular spiritual tenets or religious beliefs. Most likely for the sake of avoiding controversy and selling as many tickets as possible in the process, the spiritual nature of these films was kept deliberately vague in terms of religious affiliation—a sort of "grab bag" approach that borrows liberally from Christianity, Judaism, Buddhism, and various

New Age belief systems without specifically citing any well-known figures, texts, or creeds.[5] So, unlike the Graveyard poets, whose works were specifically Christian in theology and intent, Hollywood films in the late 1990s, and many horror films in particular, took a generally open, abstract approach to issues of spirituality, borrowing liberally from many theological schools without adhering to any one.

"You Don't Know So Many Things"

This spiritual turn in the horror genre took a number of different forms, but they all hinged on the intersection of the physical and spiritual worlds, the purpose of which was usually to impart the idea that the spiritual world has something important to tell us. In this respect, spiritual horror films employ the same Freudian concept of "the return of the repressed," which is often identified as a crucial component in modern horror by numerous scholars. While Robin Wood has most memorably linked repression to cultural issues such as race, gender, and sexuality, here it becomes a mode for thinking about spirituality—not just how the spiritual dimension had been largely repressed in horror films in favor of visceral physical violence throughout the 1980s and 1990s, but also how characters within the films themselves tend to repress or deny the existence of the spiritual. The most incisive example and direct model for so many subsequent horror films is *The Exorcist* (1973), which dared to take seriously the idea of demonic possession and place it in direct opposition to medical science. Throughout the film the idea that twelve-year-old Regan's changes in behavior have a supernatural explanation are repressed in favor of medical and scientific tests that are intent on finding neurological illness, but are ultimately shown to be fruitless. Similarly, characters in the spiritual horror films of the late 1990s resist, at least initially, the invasion of their rational, physical realities by the spiritual realm.

This operation is clearly at work in *The Sixth Sense* via the character of Dr. Malcolm Crowe (Bruce Willis), whose profession in psychology immediately marks him as a rational man who adheres to scientific, medical principles in attempting to help mentally disturbed children. And, while his work has earned him accolades and praise from his community and peers—most notably from the mayor of Philadelphia, who has awarded him "The Mayor's Citation for Professional Excellence"—it does not equip him to deal with children who have the supernatural ability to see ghosts; that is, children whose consciousness can connect simultaneously with the physical and spiritual realms.

Malcolm's inability to diagnosis his patients in anything other than rational, scientific terms results in a literal return of the repressed in the form of Vincent Grey (Donnie Wahlberg), a former child patient who breaks into Malcolm's home and shoots him and then himself in a fit of emotional desperation. The torment endured by Vincent as a result of his never being able to come to terms with his special gift

of seeing dead people—something that both Malcolm and the audience don't realize until well into the film—serves as a warning about the dangers of ignoring the
spiritual in favor of the physical. "You don't know so many things," is the first thing
Vincent tells Malcolm, a clear indication that the good doctor's medical training has
ill-equipped him to help people like Vincent whose spiritual torment is written off
in meaningless medical terms ("possible mood disorder"). This statement could very
well be seen as the calling card of spiritual horror films, admonishing the self-aware
audience that they know, in fact, much less than they think.

Malcolm's eventual realization that his new patient, ten-year-old Cole Sear
(Haley Joel Osment), can truly "see dead people" (the gift with which Vincent was
also "cursed") emboldens Malcolm to help the boy understand and make peace
with this connection, rather than trying to "cure" him. In other words, he finally
accepts the spiritual and its role in our physical world, which means that, at its
core, *The Sixth Sense* is a conversion narrative, which is typical of supernatural
horror films.[6] However, the difference is that Malcolm not only accepts the existence of the supernatural, but is at peace with it; that is, he discovers that it is not
something to be feared, but rather embraced. Malcolm is not immediately open
to this possibility, as he resists believing Cole when the boy first confides in him,
preferring instead to assess his seeing dead people as "visual hallucinations, paranoia, and some kind of school-age schizophrenia." The fundamental element of
Malcolm's repression of the spiritual is his inability to realize that he is, in fact, a
ghost himself, one of the ones Cole says "don't know they're dead"; thus, the film's
final moments following this grand realization mark his complete acceptance of
realms outside the physical and his connection to them. The irony is that the conversion is complete—Malcolm believes in life after death—only after he has made
the transition.

We can see conversion narratives operating in several other films, as well,
including *Stigmata* (1999), *Dragonfly* (2001), and *The Exorcism of Emily Rose* (2005),
all of which feature characters who are self-professed atheists until they come face to
face with the invasion of the material world by the spiritual. For example, the central
character in *Dragonfly* is Dr. Joe Morrow (Kevin Costner), a successful Chicago
doctor who is mourning the death of his wife Emily (Susanna Thompson), who
was killed in Venezuela while on a Red Cross relief mission to help sick children. It
is established early on that Joe is an atheist who does not believe in an afterlife, but
following a few strange, seemingly supernatural occurrences, including several child
patients in the pediatric oncology ward who all draw the same squiggly cross symbol and tell Joe that they have spoken with Emily during near-death experiences,
he becomes convinced that her spirit is trying to reach him. Thus, like Malcolm,
Joe is converted into a belief in life after death through direct experiences with the
supernatural.

Similarly, Frankie Page (Patricia Arquette), the young hairdresser in *Stigmata*, and Erin Bruner (Laura Linney), the hard-driving attorney in *The Exorcism of Emily Rose*, are both opened to the possibilities of God and an afterlife when their lives are directly affected by the supernatural. Interestingly, both films present their encounters with the supernatural in violent, frightening terms: Frankie is struck with the stigmata, the sudden appearance on her body of Christ's wounds, and Erin is stalked in her apartment by a threatening, unseen force. Yet their experiences put them at odds with organized religion, specifically the Catholic Church, which is at pains to maintain control over how the spiritual is experienced. Thus, unlike the Graveyard School of poets, these films are explicitly anti-clerical, even as they reify the existence of something beyond our rational understanding. *Stigmata* is particularly troubling in this respect, as it willfully confuses elements of Catholic dogma to suit its own narrative ends, such as presenting the stigmata, traditionally understood as a physical manifestation of a deep spiritual connection to God, as a virus-like form of demonic possession that can be passed on from a religious object and manipulated by dark forces.

The Dead Won't Stay Dead: Justice from beyond the Grave

By far the most popular narrative in spiritual horror is a variation on this "return of the repressed" theme in which an unjustly murdered person makes contact with the living in order to solve the mystery of his or her death. The frequency with which this particular narrative appeared over a short period of time in *The Sixth Sense*, *What Lies Beneath*, *Stir of Echoes*, and *The Gift*, as well as its use as purposeful misdirection in *Dragonfly*, illustrates its potency. It plays a crucial role in *The Sixth Sense*, although it doesn't develop until the final third of the film. By this point, the relationship between Cole and Malcolm has already been firmly established, as has the nature of Cole's special "gift": his ability to see dead people, not all of whom realize they are dead and many of whom have proved threatening to him, both psychologically and physically (his withdrawn nature being evidence of the former, while vicious red welts on his arms and body represent the latter).

Cole is eventually drawn into the death of Kyra Collins (Mischa Barton), a child his age who died under mysterious circumstances. Kyra's ghost differs from the others Cole has come across because she seeks him out. Cole's other run-ins with ghosts—at least the ones we see in the film—are all linked to the place of their deaths. Thus, we assume that the angry, abused housewife and the teenager who accidentally shot himself with his father's gun, both of whom Cole encounters in his mother's apartment, were previous tenants, just as the bicyclist with the broken neck at the end of the film is seen near the site of her deadly accident and the women accused of being witches hang from the rafters in the courthouse-turned-schoolhouse. Kyra, however, lived and died in the suburbs a lengthy bus ride away from Cole's urban apartment, which suggests that she has somehow sought him out, suspecting that he would be willing to go to her funeral and unearth the truth of her death. Cole does this by discovering a video recording that accidentally caught Kyra's mother poisoning her soup in a willful effort to keep her sick, an act that explains the young girl's death not as the result of a lengthy, inexplicable illness, but as the sad result her mother's psychological disorder.

Kyra's various ghostly appearances are both frightening and sad, which underscores Shyamalan's vision of the interaction between the spiritual and the physical realms. The ghosts Cole sees are frightening because they are not part of his world, but they each in their own way reflect the shortcomings of life on earth. Thus, in true Graveyard School fashion, the ghosts of *The Sixth Sense* each represent some form of sin and shortcoming, whether it be careless parenting, spousal abuse, infanticide, or political persecution.

This operation is at work in several other spiritual horror films as well. In *What Lies Beneath*, a supernatural thriller directed by Robert Zemeckis—while he waited for Tom Hanks to lose weight and grow out his hair and beard for his role as a man stranded on an island in *Cast Away* (2000)—the ghost of a murdered college student begins haunting the home of Norman and Claire Spencer (Harrison Ford and Michelle Pfeiffer), whose seemingly perfect life, best embodied in their elegantly appointed, but comfortably homey lakefront estate, is a façade for dark secrets. When the film begins, they are taking their daughter to college for the first time, and Claire is left with empty-nest syndrome. Taking one of many pages from Alfred Hitchcock, the first third of the film is willfully misleading as it borrows a scenario from *Rear Window* (1954) in which Claire watches their neighbors through binoculars because she suspects the husband, who works at the same university as Norman, to have murdered his wife.

However, it soon becomes clear that the focus of the film is supernatural, as the presence of a mysterious woman becomes undeniable, at least to Claire. A particular picture falls to the floor, the front door breathes itself open, a bathtub upstairs mysteriously fills itself with steaming water, voices whisper in the dark. These events happen only to Claire, and Norman is less than understanding because he feels that Claire's experiences are simply a way for her to bring attention to herself and distract him from his work. Not knowing whether these experiences are real or imagined, Claire becomes determined to find out who the ghost is and what she wants. The narrative is turned on its head at the end when she discovers that the girl whose ghost is haunting the house was murdered by her own husband, which shifts the source of fear from the spiritual to the physical. However, the role of the spiritual realm is heightened in the film's climax as the murdered girl's ghost literally takes her murderer down with her, emphasizing that, as Kendrick notes, "the dead will rise and in fact do rise, all the time, the moment you turn your back on them" (21–22).

CONCLUSION

By returning to the original roots of the horror genre that were initially laid down by the eighteenth-century Graveyard poets—which included themes of death, human mortality, spirituality, gloom, and melancholy to underpin images of carnage and decay—horror filmmakers in the late 1990s returned the genre to a more contemplative terrain. One consequence of this shift was an increase of respectability for horror in general. For the first time since the early 1970s, some horror films were being taken seriously by the popular critical community. *The Sixth Sense* received such widespread critical praise that it was recognized by the industry via nominations for six Academy Awards, including the top awards of Best Picture, Best Director, and Best Original Screenplay. While none of the subsequent spiritual horror films reached that level of critical consensus, many mainstream film critics gave these films uniformly good notices, although the praise tended to subside as more and more tonally and thematically similar films appeared at the box office, each amping up the potentially maudlin emotional nature of ghosts speaking to the living. By the time *Dragonfly* limped into theaters in February 2002, the *Washington Post* critic Stephen Hunter could describe it as "touchy-feely-creepy-icky" (C05).

Part of the reason for these films' critical acceptance and widespread popularity is arguably their focus on broadly spiritual matters, rather than abject physical horror. They include just enough horrific imagery, foreboding music, and jump-in-your-seats moments to qualify as horror in most people's minds, but without the gore and splatter effects that had defined horror films over the previous two decades. This is not surprising, as critics have long drawn a line of demarcation between supernatural horror and violent horror, with the former being associated with respectable high culture while the latter is generally associated with disrespectable low culture. Ivan Butler addresses this directly in his classic work *Horror in the Cinema* when he writes:

> Almost any degree of horror will prove acceptable to an audience provided it appears to fit into the context and not to be gratuitously thrown in to satisfy their own presumed taste for violence. When a spectator of normal sensibility revolts it is invariably because the film seems to be indulging in beastliness for its own sake, to be *enjoying* cruelty. (18)

As Gregory Waller points out in his introduction to *American Horrors*, Butler's book, as well as Carlos Clarens's *An Illustrated History of Horror and Science-Fiction Films* and S. S. Prawer's *Caligari's Children: The Film as Tale of Terror* are "based on the assumption that truly effective horror is always indirect and suggestive, leaving the horrific primarily to the viewer's imagination" (7).

Yet, such a restrained approach to horror is generally short-lived, as filmmakers seek to draw attention to their films by pushing the envelope and showing in detail what others have left to the imagination. Thus, just as the works of the Graveyard poets were quickly subsumed by the more sensational and less spiritually minded Gothic writers that followed them, the sudden rise of the spiritual horror film in the late 1990s was matched by a similarly rapid fall as audiences turned their attention to a new wave of graphically violent horror films that made increasingly visceral gore the centerpiece of the genre once again. Led by James Wan's *Saw* and epitomized most directly in Eli Roth's *Hostel*, this new development has become so popular that a name was even been coined for the new group of directors who have made their mark with such films: "The Splat Pack."[7] The reasons for this shift are myriad, ranging from audience and critical fatigue of the increasingly similar spiritual horror films, to a general movement in film aesthetics toward a more intensified and hyperkinetic visual approach that favors visceral thrills over contemplative interiority, to cultural issues such as the war in Iraq and its associated images of torture at Abu Ghraib. Perhaps it is because imaginary scenarios of supernatural apocalyptic turmoil tied to the year 2000 have given way to the more mundane, though no less horrific, realities of a world torn by strife, terrorism, and war, and as they tend to do, horror films have responded accordingly. Whatever the reason, it seems that the spiritual has largely taken a backseat, but as the history of the horror genre shows us again and again, nothing can be repressed forever.

NOTES

1. For a more detailed discussion, see Walter Kendrick, *The Thrill of Fear: 250 Years of Scary Entertainment* (New York: Grove Weidenfeld, 1991), 10–22.

2. Although the story in *Frailty* is, for example, about a man who believes God has commanded him to kill demons hiding in human form with an axe, director Bill Paxton keeps virtually every bit of bloodshed off-screen.

3. For example, one can note a decided swing in the genre between the Universal horror films of the 1930s and the Val Lewton-produced horror films for RKO in the 1940s. As Carlos Clarens argues, Lewton's films "stand out as chamber music against the seedy bombast of the claw-and-fang epics of the day" (*An Illustrated History of Horror and Science-Fiction Films: The Classic Era, 1895–1967* [New York: De Capo Press, 1967], 111).

4. *Bram Stoker's Dracula* earned $82 million at the domestic box office, making it the fifteenth-highest grossing film of the year in U.S. theaters. Significantly, the only other traditional horror film to crack the top fifty of the year was *Candyman* (49th).

5. For example, much of the heaven-and-hell scenario in *What Dreams May Come* (1998) is based on traditional Judeo-Christian notions of immortal life after death, but certain aspects are slightly twisted or bolstered with a New Age mentality and aspects of other religions. For instance, despite the existence of heaven and hell, reincarnation is still an option, and although the movie admits the existence of God, he is still left as an uninvolved abstraction, someone

who, even to those souls in heaven, is still "up there" and has no interaction with them. Heaven itself is essentially individualistic, where each soul creates his or her own utopian universe in which to spend eternity. The film also avoids explicitly stating the criteria that determine who goes where. Although a large majority of the film takes place in a hell (most of the characters go out of their way to avoid referring to it by that word) that is filled with many lost souls, there is never any explanation of what they did to cause their damnation. Similarly, Stephen Hunter in the *Washington Post* described *Dragonfly* (2002) as "essentially an endorsement of a generic, nondenominational afterlife—Heaven without brand names" (C05).

6. For a more detailed discussion, see, for example, Carol Clover, *Men, Women, and Chainsaws: Gender in the Modern Horror Film* (Princeton, N.J.: Princeton University Press, 1992), 66.

7. This moniker for such directors as Eli Roth, Rob Zombie, Alexandre Aja, and James Wan was coined by Alan Jones in the online magazine *Total Film*.

WORKS CITED

Botting, Fred. *Gothic*. London: Routledge, 1996.

Brophy, Philip. "Horrality: The Textuality of Contemporary Horror Films." *Screen* 27.1 (January–February 1986): 2–13.

Butler, Ivan. *Horror in the Cinema*. New York: Kinney, 1967.

Cameron, Kenneth Walker. "The Church and the Graveyard School." *Historiographer of the Episcopal Diocese of Connecticut* 19 (February 1957): 15–20.

Clarens, Carlos. *An Illustrated History of Horror and Science-Fiction Films: The Classic Era, 1895–1967*. New York: De Capo Press, 1967.

Clover, Carol. *Men, Women, and Chainsaws: Gender in the Modern Horror Film*. Princeton, N.J.: Princeton University Press, 1992.

Coleridge, Samuel Taylor. *Biographia Literaria Volume II*. Ed. J. Shawcross. 1817. London: Oxford University Press, 1907.

Hogle, Jerrold E. "The Gothic at Our Turn of the Century: Our Culture of Simulation and the Return of the Body." *The Gothic*. Ed. Fred Botting. Woodbridge, U.K.: D. S. Brewer, 2001. 153–80.

Hunter, Stephen. "Dances With Dragonflies: Kevin Costner Hits the Mawk. Splat!" *Washington Post*, February 22, 2002, C05.

Kendrick, Walter. *The Thrill of Fear: 250 Years of Scary Entertainment*. New York: Grove Weidenfeld, 1991.

Klady, Leonard. "Once Popular Genre Looks into the Face of B. O. Death: Scary Future for Horror Pix." *Daily Variety* (April 11–17, 1994): 13.

McEvoy, Emma. "Gothic Traditions." *The Routledge Companion to Gothic*. Eds. Catherine Spooner and Emma McEvoy. London: Routledge, 2007. 7–9.

Miles, Robert. "Eighteenth-Century Gothic." *The Routledge Companion to Gothic*. Eds. Catherine Spooner and Emma McEvoy. London: Routledge, 2007. 10–8.

Punter, David. "Narrative and Psychology in Gothic Fiction." *Gothic Fictions: Prohibition/Transgression*, ed. Kenneth W. Graham. New York: AMS Press, 1989. 1–28.

———, and Glennis Byron. *The Gothic*. Oxford, England: Blackwell, 2004.

Spooner, Catherine, and Emma McEvoy. "Introduction." *The Routledge Companion to Gothic*. Eds. Catherine Spooner and Emma McEvoy. London: Routledge, 2007. 1–3.

Tropp, Martin. *Images of Fear: How Horror Stories Helped Shape Modern Culture (1818–1918)*. Jefferson, N.C.: McFarland, 1990.

Waller, Gregory A. "Introduction." *American Horrors: Essays on the Modern American Horror Film*. Ed. Gregory A. Waller. Urbana: University of Illinois Press, 1987. 1–13.

Wee, Valerie. "The *Scream* Trilogy: 'Hyperpostmodernism,' and the Late-Nineties Teen Slasher Film." *Journal of Film and Video* 57.3 (Fall 2005): 44–61.

Wood, Robin. "An Introduction to the American Horror Film." *Planks of Reason: Essays on the Horror Film*. Ed. Barry Keith Grant. Lanham, Md.: Scarecrow Press, 1984. 164–200.

Part Three

LOOK BACK IN HORROR

Managing the Canon of
American Horror Film

AUTEURDÄMMERUNG

David Cronenberg, George A. Romero, and the Twilight of the (North) American Horror Auteur

—Craig Bernardini

THE AUTEUR IS A ZOMBIE

To the average mainstream video consumer accustomed to Blockbuster or Hollywood, the independent, "alternative" video store must appear a sort of Borgesian nightmare. Where the chains wallpaper their stores with new releases and shelve "older" films broadly by genre (drama, comedy, horror), the independents subdivide and re-categorize relentlessly. Foreign films may be divided by country—logical enough, given the larger selection than in the chains—and then divided again by genre (e.g., "J-horror"). There will probably be a large "Cult" section, organized according to a manager's whim. And then there is the defining feature of the alternatives: the "Directors" section, invariably organized alphabetically, where the alphabet is understood to be the great leveler of the global cinematic canon. Generic comedies and dramas, which together with new releases form the bulk of the chain video stores' wares, are the alternatives' leftovers.

Auteur theory, it appears, did its job too well: the force that impelled film into the academy has survived a series of attempts on its life, often by reinventing itself in the guises of its would-be assassins.[1] Perhaps, as Peter Wollen once suggested, the theory's resilience is a product of its particular relevance to America. After all, it was those rugged individualists carving out territories inside the relatively more hospitable terrain of genre (territories already settled, of course, but only by the heathen), and circling their wagons against the hostile glare of the studios, whose canonization caused such a scandal. Ironically, the author's death was pronounced at the moment when he was deemed to have arrived in Hollywood: the so-called director-as-superstar era (Wood, *Hollywood* 87). And if academics and film journalists have never managed to end their ambivalent, five-decade love affair with the auteur, it should come as no surprise that many liberally educated members of the general public (i.e., those who took a few film courses in college) remain enamored. In fact, I would speculate that a series of developments—the greater access to production information through the Internet; DVD packages featuring commentary tracks by "star" directors; and critics like Leonard Maltin appending a by-director section to the end of his immensely popular *Video and Movie Guide*—has fixed the auteur in the minds of more American moviegoers than at any time since the theory was first espoused.

It is true that contemporary film criticism and journalism have a more sophisticated conception of the auteur than did those French mavericks who wielded him as a polemical hammer half a century ago. As the theory has accommodated itself to structuralism and poststructuralism, the auteur has devolved from transcendent cause to a "bundle of libidinous energies" set forth by psyche/society (Wexman 7), and finally to a "commercial strategy for organizing [audience] reception," a "shell" of "material publicity" which has "effectively vacated the agency of a metaphysics of expressive causality and textual authority" (Corrigan 104, 118). To an extent, these academic resurrections of authorship have responded to broader cultural and technological shifts in production and consumption that have impacted, and continue to impact, the way texts are produced and consumed, and hence the way authorship is experienced by the broader public. And yet, if the auteur has indeed fallen from cause to commodity, I would argue that what is marketed is the nostalgia for authority itself. That is, in a time of fragmented authorship (Browning 40) and even more fragmented (hyper)consumption (Corrigan 27–29), the auteur appears as a harbor of stable meaning and authority, evoking a nostalgia similar to that Timothy Corrigan identified in contemporary audiences for lost collective rituals (15). Corrigan also notes that the auteur originally served to attract audiences to theaters by giving film a "romantic aura" that distinguished it from television (102). With the latter-day impact of television and home-viewing technologies on film production, however, film and auteur have come to reside in an interzone between the former's romantic aura as art, and the purely commercial "producer's medium" of television. Film, so to speak, is unable to die and become "just TV"; it "lives" like *Videodrome*'s Brian O'Blivion . . . only now in letterbox.

The vacated agency of the romantic auteur, the limbo between (living) art and (dead) image—what could be more reminiscent of the zombie? It is a particularly fitting figure for those directors who have staked their artistic claim in the horror genre. Here, what fascinates me is not so much film culture's and criticism's continued preoccupation with the auteur, as the manner in which not genre per se, but the *horror* genre impinges upon a director's status as an auteur.[2] For while auteur theory served to rescue *some* genre cinema from the prejudice that *all* genre cinema was mindless fodder, the auteur label has always sat least easily with horror. Hitchcock was never called a "suspense auteur," or Ford a "Western auteur." But "horror auteur"—that "oxymoronic montage of the idiosyncratic and conventional"

CRONENBERG, ROMERO, TWILIGHT OF AMERICAN HORROR AUTEUR   163

(Hantke 182)—is commonly employed to describe that group of directors who, taken together, formed a sort of shadow equivalent of the "superstars." Today, a director who makes one or two moderately interesting horror films is quickly labeled a "horror auteur" (most recently, Larry Fessenden of *The Last Winter*) and compared to the 1970s patriarchs. This is at once a fine instance of the marketing of auteur nostalgia, and a further indication that the contemporary horror director's auteur status remains circumscribed by the genre.

An example: when I tried to find a Cronenberg movie at Tower Video (the only alternative video store in Salt Lake City, where I went to graduate school), I could go to either of two sections: "Cult" or "Directors." In the "Cult" section were all of Cronenberg's early movies up through *Videodrome* (1982). In the "Directors" section were Cronenberg's later films. There are multiple ironies here. While it is true that Cronenberg deliberately turned to commercial genre filmmaking with *Shivers* (1975), it has been argued that Cronenberg's aesthetic was "closer" to his personal vision in his earlier films than in later ones. Cronenberg wrote every film up through *Videodrome*; since *The Dead Zone* (1983), he has chosen either to adapt a preexisting work or to revise a screenplay.[3] More disturbing, the cult/director division here cleaved Cronenberg's career into low-budget independent and bigger-budget, sometimes studio-financed projects—a typical bias toward moneyed horror films as being more "serious," hardly the conception of cinema one would associate with an alternative video store. The director's turn to "art" movies, generally agreed to have begun with *Dead Ringers* (1988), had thus managed to redeem his better-budgeted projects, but not his earlier "exploitation" films. This is not to say that there aren't aesthetic and thematic differences between "early" and "late" Cronenberg films, but rather that at least one alternative video market could not reconcile the grotesque violence and low budgets of Cronenberg's early, highly original films with the idea of the auteur—at least, not until Cronenberg had made enough "late" movies that the earlier genre films had been sufficiently diluted. (I confess that, every time I rented a movie at Tower, I would surreptitiously move the early Cronenberg films from the "Cult" to the "Directors" section—an indication more of my own hang-up with legitimizing the horror genre than with auteur theory.)

Fast forward fifteen years, to Kim's Video, New York's alternative mini-chain. Today—or maybe just in New York, at the Morningside Kim's—the complete Cronenberg corpus is available in the "Directors" section, on both tape and DVD. But when I go to the R's . . . Rohmer . . . Rossellini . . . where is Romero? Romero, it turns out, is shelved in the "Cult" section, though a special subset of this section called "Cult Directors," which seems to be reserved largely for washed-up horror directors—Tobe Hooper is there—or ones who have gone more mainstream, I guess, like Wes Craven. I could swear that Romero used to be in the "Directors" section. But time has not been kind to Romero. The Romero zombie may be the single most recognizable icon of the horror genre today, but the man who made the stumbling, flesh-eating ghoul famous and worthy of reams of critical scrutiny seems to have joined them in anonymity. Thus, as Cronenberg is retroactively dubbed an auteur and finds his early horror movies moved from the "Cult" section to their rightful place in the "Directors" section, Romero is demoted from the "Directors" section to the "Cult" section, albeit to a special wing, in the select company of his peers. God forbid that, in five years, he finds his films dispersed throughout the "Horror" section, organized alphabetically by title, of all things.

I don't mean to suggest that the organization of a director's output in the alternative video market is the best measure of his or her current stature. At the same time, these markets do shape, and are shaped by, the public perception of a director's oeuvre. Considered in this light, the fall of George A. Romero is as dramatic as the rise of David Cronenberg.

I have chosen to focus on these two directors as much for their early similarities as for their inverted career trajectories since the 1980s. Both rose to prominence around the same time—Romero somewhat earlier with the big splash (or splatter) of *Night*, though it was a relationship with the genre he would not consolidate until a decade later. Both were credited with revitalizing, and even reinventing, horror in the 1970s and early 1980s. Both were viewed as mavericks, independents working outside the Hollywood system and against the genre grain. And both were dubbed auteurs in the same year, 1979: Romero by *Film Comment*, and Cronenberg, in a telling double negative ("Cronenberg is nothing if not an auteur"), by Robin Wood. But where Cronenberg rose to increasing international prominence after *The Fly* (1986), Romero's own interaction with the studios was less than genial, and by the midnineties he had largely stopped working, making only one, undistributed film in the years between *The Dark Half* (1993) and *Land of the Dead* (2005). I would argue, however, that their popular/critical divergence—and Romero's recent return—has less to do with the success or failure of each director's encounter with the studios than with the evolution of the genre, perceptions of each director's relationship to the genre, and the interplay between the genre and history.

Contemporary media have given directors a greater opportunity than ever before to become the custodians of their legacy, and David Cronenberg has been particularly canny in this regard. The auteur mystique that surrounds him—the fact that every next movie is anticipated as a "Cronenberg movie"—is partly indebted to this. Even though Cronenberg's cinematic identity was forged through his early horror films, it has become paradoxically more reified as he has distanced himself from the genre—a paradox which Cronenberg himself has expressed through the figure of the outsider in disguise. In this sense, *A History of Violence* (2005) might be Cronenberg's *most* "Cronenberg movie" to date: the self-made Tom Stall, a monster hidden in the mainstream, is perhaps the clearest analogue to the director of any of his protagonists; and the film's interrogation of the American myth of self-making takes on the subsidiary role of interrogating Cronenberg's identity as an auteur. *Violence* can be read as a desperate attempt and ultimate failure to assert the integrity of identity (human, artistic) against the fragmented/fragmenting conditions of authorship; and it is this despair and longing that resonate with the audience's nostalgia for the lost integrity of the patriarch, both familial and cinematic. To a somewhat lesser extent Romero has also participated in fashioning his own cinematic image, in this case as a small businessman, political progressive, and movie-lover—which goes a long way toward explaining, together with the persistent bugbear of modest box office, his retreat from cinema for much of the 1990s. But I am more interested in exploring the way in which the road back to the *Dead* series was paved by the confluence of two forces: the sharpening of the historical moment on the one hand, and the recent spate of Romero-inspired zombie films on the other. Together, they have given Romero the opportunity to make a "cinematic comic book" that is at the same time a political weapon—albeit a characteristically ambivalent one, where nostalgia for a kinder, gentler capitalism masquerades as revolution, and where the leap forward from a genre mired in parody is legitimized by a step backward to social-allegorical tradition. Overall, while Cronenberg's movies have come to exhibit that staid minimalism we expect from a "mature" director of international stature, Romero's latest marks just the opposite: a joyful yet dour return to the exuberance of his genre's g(l)ory days.

THE SELF-FASHIONING OF DAVID CRONENBERG (AND TOM STALL)

It used to be a running gag uniting the hundreds of interviews with David Cronenberg: *He looks different from what I expected.* Even as late as 1999 the critical establishment seemed unprepared to confront the director in person. Its envoys would arrive loaded down with silver bullets and crucifixes and holy water. Didn't they know that these fetishes descend from the very gothic tradition from which the director had worked to distance himself? And when they found instead a "college professor type" (Blackwelder), or a "dental student" (Rodley xiii), or, most famously, "a gynecologist from Beverly Hills" (Scorsese 47), did they imagine they heard, in that Canadian accent, a hint of Lugosi?

If the gag still seems fresh, maybe Cronenberg has something to do with it. He is hardly averse to identifying himself with his films, even as he maintains that the work of art may not be revealing about its creator at all (Grünberg 26; Rodley 152). Art, he argues, is "of you, but it's not you. It's not identical with you" (Grünberg 148). To a point, Cronenberg just wants to dissuade critics from looking to crude autobiography for answers—as Grünberg does, ironically enough, when he mythologizes the director as "a monster . . . born from [the] hypocritical self-restraint and . . . repressive social consensus [of Puritan Toronto]" (10). But if the "monster born from repression" formula is hardly adequate to describe the director or his work, the figure of Cronenberg-as-monster resonates beyond Grünberg, echoing the title of William Beard's ever-expanding study. It is not this monster that interests me, however, so much as another "monster," born of the tensions between and within two interpretive economies, genre and auteur, which alternately disguise and reveal each other, and between and against which the director attempts to fashion himself.

Cronenberg's rise to critical and (less consistently) commercial prominence can be understood in light of metamorphoses in both his oeuvre and his directorial persona: from cult horror-movie director to maker of arthouse-*cum*-mainstream films (Beard 471; Lowenstein 166). Such metamorphoses, however, imply continuities against which the director's "evolution" or "progression" can be measured (Black-welder; Rodley xix). For Adam Lowenstein, for example, Cronenberg has evolved from art-inflected horror to horror-inflected art; but all the director's films inhabit a generic between-space where the untenable distinctions between genre and "art" cinema are revealed.[4] Like Lowenstein, Jonathan Crane argues that Cronenberg's later films retain elements of horror, but locates the early films' generic impurity in their affinity with science-fiction—not to attempt to "claim" early Cronenberg as sci-fi, but to note that the early films drew from both generic discourses to produce a hybrid Crane calls "science embodied" (65). And Cronenberg himself famously described *The Brood* as his version of *Kramer Vs. Kramer*, or family melodrama reconfigured as horror (Scorsese 47).

From his earliest days as a commercial filmmaker, then, Cronenberg has troubled the idea of genre as a pure, stable category; even horror, his mother-genre, had to be remade *from the outside*. From horror 'zines to academic journals, Cronenberg has repeated the same story: that he has "never been a genre buff" (Porton 8), that he "didn't think of [him]self as genre-specific" (9), and that he only began making horror films because the genre seemed like "a natural fit" (9) for his thematic preoccupations. The darker aspects of human nature and society that Cronenberg treats—aging, media control, disease—have always brought his films within the orbit of the genre; but it was the *literalizing* of these in the grotesque body that once earned him the label of "Canada's King of Horror." (This is why the word "literally" occurs perhaps more than any other in criticism of Cronenberg's early films.) Conversely, it is almost entirely on the basis of the absence of the grotesque body that his departure from the genre has been judged. As Beard so aptly put it in his first film-by-film treatment of Cronenberg's oeuvre, "the moment Max [Renn]'s slit appears . . . it is a Cronenberg movie, and there is no going back" ("Mind" 66). The near-disappearance of the monstrous body has left critics to wrestle for the few crumbs of grotesquerie Cronenberg's early style has left behind, as when, in the most recent edition of *The Artist as Monster*, Beard lovingly describes Yvonne's teeth in *Spider* as "prominent, yellowish, [and] gapped" (488).

Cronenberg's propensity to generic hybridity, however, also needs to be measured against shifts in genre and cinema since he began making commercial films. Crane, for example, has argued that the horror genre's "system-wide collapse into parody" (63) in the 1990s was incompatible with the director's tragic vision. And what Crane says of horror in the nineties, critics like Robin Wood have extended to commercial cinema as a whole. For Wood, "hybridity" is too strong a term to describe the flattened cinematic landscape of today, where genre cinema has become "self-conscious pastiche" and Hollywood's efforts more and more homogenized (*Hollywood* xxxv). In such a transformed landscape, the horror film has either become more openly parasitical upon tropes that were once alien to it (and vice-versa), or has self-consciously gazed backward to a perhaps imagined time of greater generic stability.[5]

It would be logical to assume that the bleeding out of the violence of Cronenberg and other "body horror" directors' films into cinema as a whole, coupled with the decrement of the grotesque body in Cronenberg's own films, would have weakened the director's cinematic identity. Paradoxically, just the opposite is true. Beard, whose last edition of *The Artist as Monster* runs to almost six hundred (wonderful) pages, has as little difficulty telling us what makes "a Cronenberg film" in 2006 as he did in 1983, with or without stomach slits. (And he is by no means alone; the title of J. Hoberman's review of *Eastern Promises* in the *Village Voice*: "Still Cronenberg.") In a 1999 *Cineaste* interview, Cronenberg explained his early involvement with horror in classical Hollywood terms: the genre helped him to pass off his grim, abstract meditations about mortality in the commercial arena—something his late respectability has allowed him to do without the fetters of genre. Purified of the "generic" elements of his filmmaking identity, his true cinematic personality has been allowed to blossom; he has been left a sort of transcendent, self-referential being, his oeuvre a genre unto itself, as every good auteur desires it to be (Rodley 59). As such, Cronenberg doesn't "do" genre pictures anymore—he would argue that he never really did. Cronenberg does *Cronenberg* pictures.

And yet, while Cronenberg claims that leaving behind the trappings of horror has given him the opportunity to express himself more directly, he has done so ever more *in disguise*. Cronenberg articulated this paradox as early as 1982, when he was on the cusp of domestic recognition for *Videodrome* and only a few, albeit frustrating, years away from commercial Hollywood success with *The Fly*: "The more accepted you become in your society and the more a part of the establishment you become," Cronenberg said to Piers Handling and William Beard, "the more tenuous your grip on your 'insideness' becomes"; and, in response to their surprised follow-up: "I am [still an outsider]. I'm just much more in disguise" (195). True to his words, as his international reputation has grown over the last two decades, with the attendant bigger budgets and gigs on film juries that such respectability bestow, his image as a maverick seems to have grown in direct proportion. This is not just the phenomenon of the *enfant terrible*, of celebrated notoriety. As Cronenberg phrases it, the more fully he embraces mainstream, genre, and America, the more completely he remains a maverick Canadian independent; and the more "unoriginal" he *appears* to be, the more his true originality is confirmed. Hence the odd double-move that has characterized Cronenberg's evolution "away" from horror: toward self-revelation on the one hand, and toward yet-greater disguise on the other.

As the foregoing suggests, Cronenberg's aura as arch-auteur is as much proactive self-invention as it is a retrospective construct of critical analysis (Wollen 602). Indeed, he has grasped better than most of his colleagues the way in which a director can participate in fashioning the public mirror in which he wishes to be viewed. If there is, as Robin Wood once wrote, "a dislocation between the intellectual pretensions (what [Cronenberg's] films say they are about) and the repulsive and obsessional imagery (what they actually do)" ("Dissenting" 134), I would argue that this dislocation is at least partly a product of Cronenberg's own eagerness to say what his films are about. Cronenberg becomes the central text for interpreting "Cronenberg," to the point that the critic is occasionally unsure whether he is responding to the work or the man, so thoroughly is our perception of his oeuvre shaped by his presence. Lowenstein may be right that Cronenberg is parodying this auteur mystique by "appearing" as a disembodied voice in *Crash* (171); but if so, he is doing it as the purest self-parody, in full knowledge of the way he has himself participated in its construction.

Key to the creation of the Cronenberg mystique—his cinematic "I am that I am"—is the denial of any cinematic influences (e.g., Rodley 23, 72).[6] Cronenberg is less loath to admit philosophical and literary influences; but even here he resorts to biological and other, more monstrous metaphors, such as fusion, ingestion, and parallel evolution (Browning 39, 53; Rodley 153; Grünberg 127). Their loosely scientific air, however, does not hinder the director from investing his conception of influence with quasi-metaphysical heft, as when he speaks of "becoming" Hemingway (Breskin 69), or Burroughs "writing" *Naked Lunch* (Browning 39). In this way, his literary precursors become less influences than equals, or doubles; Cronenberg, like Burroughs, becomes an original creative artist in his own right (cf. Beard, *Monster* 540).

In this way, Cronenberg's mid-1980s turn to adaptation and revision is easily recuperable within his purported creative economy. This has little to do with the less-mined vein of auteur theory which dictates that, by being thrown back on pure cinema, Cronenberg became a true artist, the screenplays just "catalysts" for his unique vision (Wollen 600). Rather, it is because Cronenberg retains, or has claimed that he retains, a strong writerly presence in many of his later films. Beard, for example, reminds us that *Naked Lunch* is only nominally an adaptation, and that *Dead Ringers* bears little resemblance to the original.[7] But *Dead Ringers* was also a *collaborative* adaptation, one which Cronenberg claims was so effective a fusion that he no longer fully remembers who wrote what (Bloch-Hansen 55). What's more, fusion quickly shades into ingestion. For Cronenberg is also quick to emphasize the director's preeminent role in deciding every aspect of the film, from script to score to special effects (Garris, "3" 26; Timpone 21). Like his literary influences, the director appears to "consume" the filmmaking apparatus as well, from the scriptwriter down to the best boy. Every frame teems with *his* vision. It is just such a mystique Beard invokes when he asserts even adaptations like *M Butterfly* and *Crash* exhibit the director's "150-proof authorial presence" (424).

A few reactions to *The Dead Zone* may help illustrate how Cronenberg's turn to adaptation and more "mainstream" filmmaking can be recuperated through the concept of the auteur-in-disguise. The film was praised by writer Philip Nutman because the director had "managed to impose his own vision to such a degree that the end result is undeniably a Cronenberg film" (172); by Serge Grünberg for "really [being] a Cronenberg film," to the point that the script "doesn't feel [. . .] Stephen King-inspired" (77); by Robin Wood because it had "released [Cronenberg] from his constricting personal obsessions" ("Nightmares" 115)—that is, those that qualified him as an auteur; and by George Romero because the director had effaced himself, thus allowing the film to remain a faithful translation of King's novel (Gagne 123). Such contrary opinions could only be arrived at if these critics and filmmakers had a very clear idea of what a "Cronenberg movie" does or does not look like [. . .] yet none of them could agree about what that means. This seems the essence of the Cronenberg paradox, and perhaps also speaks to the mystique of the auteur more broadly: as soon as the director's name is stamped on a film, normality can always be perceived as transgression in disguise, absence construed as directorial presence. But Cronenberg's own words on the film are, as usual, the most revealing. Admitting some anxiety about the turn from writing to adaptation, Cronenberg reassured himself, "I had to assume that through the accumulation of thousands and thousands of details that go into making a film, I would be there" (Rodley 113). Like Yvonne's teeth in *Spider*—and God, and the Devil—the auteur is in the details, at once the transcendent presence behind the film and atomized in its every frame, an accumulation of material facts that becomes, by some miracle of alchemy or critical theory, a coherent whole.

Ironically, another example of Cronenbergian disavowal of influence is the director's constant reference to his "Canadianness," where Canada exists only as an *absence*—not just the absence of explicitly Canadian settings within the films (Knee

34), but the absence of any coherent national framework for reading them. There is something perverse about positing "Canadianness" as a shared, public frame of reference, and then withdrawing it in the same stroke by claiming "Canadian" means that the proper, indeed the only, frame of reference is the private one of the film-maker-artist. Even autobiography is withdrawn from its public, historical context, since the director reveals that his family invented their own version of what it meant to be middle-class Jews in Toronto (Rodley 3). Like "Canada," they seemed to have provided the budding artist with an environment in which self-making was possible and legitimate.

Jim Leach has noted that Cronenberg emphasizes his Canadianness in part by calling himself an "exile from American culture" (482). But the Canadian is only the vehicle here; the tenor, once again, is the idea of Cronenberg-as-outsider—not just the Canadian as outside America, but the independent filmmaker as exile from Hollywood. Beard has noted the importance of the outsider trope to Cronenberg's perception of himself as "a kind of romantic hero who must brave the depths of the unconscious" (*Monster* ix). Cronenberg is the outcast, the derelict who, in the later films, resolves into the figure of the artist (xi), and who remarked to Grünberg, "Spider, c'est moi" (qtd. in Beard 490). He is the one whose dangerous ideas have been "censored" and "banned" by ideologues and governments on both ends of the political spectrum (Porton 5)—this *because* his films are as devoid of historical and ideological influences as cinematic ones; because they "go back to the voice that spoke before all these [social, ideological] structures were imposed on it" (Rodley 158). Cronenberg is—if we are to take his arguments for the meanings of his films seriously—a much-misunderstood, much-maligned figure. We may not go as far as Martin Scorsese once did, saying that Cronenberg "has no idea what his films are about"; but there is some justice to this, given how many critics have contested Cronenberg's stated intentions about his representations of technology and sexuality, and their relationship to human liberation and identity creation.[8] Conversely, many of Cronenberg's apologists seem to swallow whole the director's pronouncements about his films, to the point that he appears the mythic obverse of Robin Wood's early caricature: a champion of artistic and sexual freedom, enemy of dogma, theory, and ideology (Rodley xxiv). What his apologists and detractors alike seem to miss is the importance of misapprehension to the Cronenberg mystique. Taken together, the director's feeling that his films are both transgressive *and* misunderstood only further reinforces his aura of otherness.

Cronenberg has more than once invited comparison between himself and his heroic but myopic father figure-scientists, like Raglan in *The Brood* (Chute 42). But in his connection to Raglan, I would stress the myopic as much as the heroic. For if Cronenberg is Raglan, then his texts are Nola Carveth; and it is their dangerous generativity—their ability to self-augment, to create new meanings without the

intervention of their father-author—that Cronenberg appears to resent. The director also compares himself to Nola: the films are children of his own rage, projections
of his own unconscious. It is a telling wish, and not just for the idea of partheno-
genesis, which speaks so clearly to Cronenberg's desire for total originality. For what
defines the brood, according to the film, is their identity with their mother; as mere
embodiments of her repressed wishes, they expire when those wishes are fulfilled.
Thus, even as Cronenberg acknowledges that a film "has a life of its own that [. . .]
go[es] beyond what you consciously planned" (Garris, "2" 27), the emphasis is not
on the brood as a figure for textual indeterminacy and free-play, but an invitation to
the audience to decipher their father-creator's unconscious.

The simultaneous desire for misapprehension and unitary meaning helps
explain Cronenberg's long-standing ambivalence about horror: the genre appears as
both a monstrous mother in whose grotesque body he can hide, and hide his audience from, "the terrible truth," and as a cinema capable of confronting that "only fact
of human existence," the body (Rodley 158, 59; Porton 9). The genre thus figures the
double-move between revelation and disguise. The dark corners and stripped veneer
and other shoddy gothic imagery with which Cronenberg clutters his musings on
Truth are themselves but metaphors of unmasking; the films' "proximity to [. . .]
our unconscious" (46) Grünberg praises is but censorship by another name; there is
no "literally." For this reason Cronenberg can never definitively leave the genre and
appear "as himself," tear through the monstrous veil to reveal the *Ding an sich*. Like
horror, the "global cinematic artist" is but another veil hiding a monster.[9] Cronenberg's career is thus less a descent toward some great and final unmasking than a
pageant, a horizontal movement between masks, or masks *within* masks: monsters
disguising monsters.

Cronenberg once wore the mask of horror, the outsider genre, to disguise and
protect the outsider within. Today, horror itself has become something monstrous
to the director, a reminder of an "old" self hidden under the mask of international
recognition. Cronenberg claims he reacts with "horror" to his old movies (Grünberg
48), and of himself as a young man, he remarks, "I'm a completely different creature" (Grünberg 94).[10] In good gothic fashion, the new and improved Cronenberg
is haunted by the specter of his monstrous past. But the monster here isn't only the
younger self as gothic Other whose repression predicates its inevitable return; it is
also the composite body of the auteur who, at the same time that he asserts his radical difference from himself, insists that these previous incarnations can be assembled into a coherent whole. The entomological metaphors Cronenberg employs to
describe aging (Grünberg 94) are also a fitting evocation of the tension between
sameness and difference that characterizes artistic growth. If each film sloughs off
the previous to become something wholly new, to what extent can it be understood
as a fragment of an overarching vision? To what extent is the pupa, the butterfly,

the maggot the fly? Cronenberg wishes to be both the consistent controlling presence *impersonating* a series of cinematic selves, and to *be* each of those selves, to make himself anew with each film. His dilemma, then, is to assemble a coherent identity from ostensibly heterogeneous incarnations which threaten to fragment his cinematic body to such an extent that the "hidden" auteur is never quite able to unify it—except, perhaps, *as* a monster. This is why, even as Cronenberg's films revel in fragmentation, they seem deeply nostalgic for truth, wholeness, and the romantic auteur: that missing piece, the Piece of pieces, held by the protagonist, the director's stand-in, like that bloody shard of glass up Spider's sleeve.

A History of Violence is remarkable for the way it puts so many of the aforementioned features of Cronenberg's career—generic hybridity, disguise, and self-authorship—into play. A sort of obverse *Long Kiss Goodnight* or *True Lies*, *Violence*'s generic inheritance is complex even for Cronenberg; critics have inventoried elements of film noir, road movie, at least two distinct Western subgenres, "serious art film meditation," and "it-came-from-within horror" (Taubin 26; Fuller 13; Lim). All of these come wrapped up inside the "mainstream adult thriller" *Violence* was marketed as, and which certainly describes its origin: a 32-million-dollar studio vehicle which Cronenberg initially took on as a sort of hired gun (Taubin 26). *A History of Violence* was perceived by critics to work on two levels: genre thriller *and*—what else?—"Cronenberg movie." A mass, "Red State" audience might be fooled into believing that this was an action flick about defending family values against evildoers; but those of us who know it's *Cronenberg* see a different film. In this regard, *Violence* is really the director's apotheosis: Cronenberg, the outsider-in-disguise, has hidden a dark message inside the candy coating of a big-budget Hollywood thriller—a film that is itself about a man who disguises his darkness from the American mainstream, and about a country that hides its darkness from itself. It is the clearest allegory of Cronenberg's perception of his role as an artist—clearer, I think, than *Spider*; Cronenberg could just as appropriately have said, "Joey, c'est moi." *Violence* is thus at once Cronenberg's most American film—in big budget, comic book origin, and setting—and, precisely *because* of this, his most transgressive: the Canadian "outsider" tearing through the mythic veil of Middle America; the monster invited to sit down to dinner.

Critics such as Philip Nutman and Tim Lucas argue that the family has been an "abiding concern" of Cronenberg's cinema. But *A History of Violence* and *Spider* are his most explicit treatments of the family since *The Brood*—with the difference that *Violence* examines the social construction of the American family. Of course, there are two families here: Tom Stall's, the nuclear family of Midwestern American myth; and Joey Cusack's, "The Family" of the Eastern mafia, as mythologically and cinematically American as the former. The latter is the former's shadow, a parody of Tom's plain domestic happiness . . . or perhaps just the opposite is true. ("Home sweet home," Ruben says of Richie's mansion when he and Joey arrive together.) Essential to the latter, too, is not just the mythic violence of the gangster, but the extended patriarchal family that operates as an economic unit.[11] The nuclear family may have supplanted the patriarchal clan, but The Family remains its unacknowledged residue—and it remains thus in the contested figure of the father. For the father, who runs the family business, is the end product of the primitive accumulation of those earlier fathers, of the force and fraud of countless generations of fathers who enabled Tom, for all his Christ-like "going into the desert" to "kill Joey," to become a small-business owner. Tom Stall may be the essence of the self-made man—not just the businessman, but the one who existentially remakes himself, who pulls his *identity* "up by his bootstraps"—but all self-made men were "made" men first, as sure as Jay Gatsby was. As mafia don Carl Fogarty remarks when he tries to give Tom a one-hundred-dollar bill, "It shouldn't be any problem for *you*." Like America historically, Tom/Joey's impossible task is to separate The Family from the family, the made from the self-made, by violently suppressing the former. His inability to do so threatens to tear his family apart, since it reveals the violence at the origin of family making, and indeed of identity making.

Ironically, self-made Tom Stall probably couldn't survive without his wife's income; *Violence*'s opening gives us the impression that Stall's Diner is slow on a good day. But if Edie supports Tom financially, Tom performs a much more important function for Edie: he sustains her belief in mythic America. Edie comes across as a hard-nosed realist and modern; Tom, by contrast, is a throwback to an older America. He pines for drive-ins, of all things. Tom is *too* American, in the same way his son is too much the wimp, the school bully too much the bully. Edie loves Tom Stall *because* he is an American icon. And Edie, too, is perfectly willing to transform herself into an American myth (cheerleader, high school sweetheart) to seduce her mythic husband.

Or does Edie love Joey Cusack, the mythically violent gangster with whom she has violent sex on the Stalls' stairs? We might ask the same question of the town of Millbrook. For it is Tom's classic American heroism—his unbridled violence—that brings Millbrook out to applaud. Not Tom Stall, but Joey, the made man, brings in the clientèle . . . and Edie, too. Violence is good for business; it makes people nostalgic for that old America, which Tom sells by the cup ("It really is very good coffee, Joey . . ."). As for Edie, she will begin to role-play just like her husband—will come to recognize that role-playing has always been the stuff of family life, as ridiculous as the grown-up cheerleader who seduces "Tom Stall."

Joey may be an artist of violence, but like Cronenberg, his chief artistic act is self-creation: *Tom Stall* is a work of art. Yet, as Beard has noted about the existential drama that forms the heart of Cronenberg's films, *Violence*'s attempt at self-creation fails: the hero's "fragile ego" disintegrates over the course of the film; the exposure of his act of self-creation makes it unclear whether it can be sustained; and Edie's learning the truth about Tom's past leaves the couple alienated from each other and from themselves. Richie Cusack may momentarily represent what is disavowed for the purpose of catharsis in the combat between "bad" and "good" brothers à la *Scanners*; but the ridiculous ease with which Tom dispatches him and his idiot crew suggests only more disavowal. It is significant that Richie is fumbling with his keys, locked out of his "nice" house, when Joey opens the door and puts a bullet through his head. The true owner has arrived: Richie is as much an intruder as were the "bad men" on Tom Stall's front lawn, and Joey/Tom is finally *really* living the American dream. For all the iconicity of Tom's *Marathon Man*-esque throwing of his gun into the water and washing himself at the end of the film (in Richie's pond, no less), the Stalls are in no way now safe to continue living their fiction. Knowledge that it *is* a fiction has undermined them. The "bad men" (and women) are not in the East, but in the kitchen, sitting around the family table.[12]

Violence's ending is also remarkable from the perspective of the genre in which the film purports to be working. One of the chief tropes of the action thriller, for example, is that of the male hero who, moments after brutally killing scores of bad men, returns home to his family with light step and beaming smile. Tom's homecoming is anything but this. The Monster has sat down to dinner, and, for all the world, we can still see the blood on that ever-more-ridiculous flannel shirt. He looks haunted; his wife and son seem embarrassed, or terrified. But dinner is served, so what can anyone do except pass the potatoes? The discourse of horror similarly undermines the mainstream thriller by forcing the audience to question their "complicit[y] in the exhilaration" of the film's violence (Cronenberg, qtd. in Lim). The few moments of grotesquerie—mainly shots of wounded bodies—are there to remind us of the end product of Joey Cusack's brutality. If these scenes are not "unshowable" in the early Cronenberg sense, or "unfilmable" like the novels of Ballard and Burroughs, they are unshowable in another way: excluded by the conventions of the genre. They are the missing scenes from any Hollywood action-thriller, where the hero's violence is sanitized and the villain's is fawned upon. In *Violence*, villain and hero are one. Thus the film's grotesques are not narcissistic self-reference, bones thrown to the old horror crowd. Rather, Cronenberg's horror legacy allows him to manifest the repressed content not just of a psyche, but a *genre*—which is the American psyche writ large. Once again, Cronenberg is the monster unleashed upon mainstream Hollywood, tearing through the mythic veil of convention to expose the mythic violence behind.

In Tom/Joey, Cronenberg finds a linchpin between the American obsession with self-making and his own. Ironically, in undermining America's chief myth, he similarly undermines the attempts at independent self-fashioning that have characterized his career. With *Violence* Cronenberg reveals that self-making is itself a violent act, one that requires the violent suppression of the past and its violent substitution by a present. For if Joey was violent, Tom's attempts to keep his past at bay are similarly violent, and the film's escalating violence reflects his increasing failure to do so. This is the ambiguity that Andrew Britton identified in the figure of the monster between the return of the repressed and the return of repression (41). Such a troubling irresolution is a signature of Cronenberg's cinema, its paradoxical claim to unity: problem and solution, liberation and repression, "are more intimately connected than radically opposed" (Lowenstein 157). As such the Cronenbergian "gothic" neither reinforces traditional binaries nor offers a progressive alternative. Beard has commented that Cronenberg's heroes can find no happy medium between release and repression. By suggesting that release and repression are indistinguishable in their violence, *Violence* explains why this is so. For if the entire economy of repression/release is meaningless in *Violence*'s universe, and perhaps in Cronenberg's as well, how can there possibly be "a road to health and wholeness"?

GEORGE A. ROMERO'S CELESTIAL CITY OF THE DEAD

The earliest adult photo of David Cronenberg I encountered (on page 165 of *The Shape of Rage*) shows the director with shoulder-length hair shooting the short "From the Drain" at the University of Toronto. Stuffed with actor, assistant, light, and camera into a tiny bathroom, the picture expresses the sort of cramped intimacy I have always associated with art-film circles. The earliest photo I know of George A. Romero is the one on page 10 of Paul Gagne's *The Zombies That Ate Pittsburgh*. Described as "an early publicity photo for Latent Image," it shows a clean-shaven young man in a turtleneck and blazer poised before a movie camera and holding an open script in his hand. The calm expression belies nothing of that hunger to make a feature film which Romero has since said characterized his emotions at that time. But in a broader sense, it was the sole purpose of this little artifact of self-promotion: Latent Image's work shootingtelevision commercials was to be Romero's foot in the door.[13] Although these two photos were taken under totally different circumstances, they express a foundational difference in the identities of these two filmmakers. True, both went to college in the heady sixties, and Cronenberg, too, describes that hunger to make a commercial feature. But Romero's roots in advertising, and the formation of Latent Image in the mid-1960s—his immediate introduction into the *business* of filmmaking—could not be more different from Cronenberg's origins in Toronto's art film underground, or, for that matter, his later soliciting of government money to make his first commercial feature.

If Cronenberg has always insisted on being called an artist, his films art, Romero has preferred less lofty terms: entertainment, comic books, "penny dreadfuls." His is the more traditional story of the budding horror filmmaker in terms of his early exposure to the genre and to genre cinema (Gagne 8, 11). And despite occasionally feeling trapped by the genre label, be it by contractual stipulations or poor box office returns (Gagne 119, 169), Romero has declared an affinity for horror—*and* for genre filmmaking, *and* for filmmaking per se—that Cronenberg never has. Romero seems to have reconciled himself to his eternal return to horror with the same boyish enthusiasm he holds for filmmaking more broadly: that tinkerer's appeal to movies as a craft that we associate with Romero's films even today, and that I would argue distinguishes his visual style from Cronenberg's as well.

That said, Romero's cinematic persona is not without its own ambivalences and contradictions. In his own efforts at self-fashioning, he has tended to foreground his identity as a small businessman and political progressive. These are the two heads of the axe he has always had to grind about Hollywood. He has never claimed to have any illusions about how the big studios operate, or what their real interests are; corporations, like zombies, act according to their natures. He has only declared the wish that there were more alternatives for independents (Gagne 59–60). Nor has he ever expressed a conflict with the idea of profit—he is, after all, a businessman—so long as profits are small and tidy; again, it's the big boys and their blockbusters that have ruined the chances for independents to work and thrive (Gagne 59–60). From Hollywood, Romero's kvetch easily extends to contemporary America: the withering of cities, the planned obsolescence of new construction, the death of American industry and the middle-class wage (Gagne 74–75, 159).

As a businessman, then, when Romero kvetches about "the system," he does so with a greater or lesser degree of ambivalence.[14] One gets the impression that Romero can never quite reconcile the dissonance between the way the system is *supposed* to operate and the way it *does*. On one end of the spectrum is the Romero who is nostalgic for a saner, more ethical capitalism that purportedly allowed the small, independent producer to make his "tidy profits," the laborer his middle-class wage, and each to go home to his bourgeois family. On the other end is the Romero with the (understandable) desire to overthrow a "bullshit" system that screwed him out of his money for *Night of the Living Dead*, forced him to spend the next decade crawling out of the red rather than declaring bankruptcy (again: sanity, ethics), jacked every movie he released (thanks to the summer blockbuster, the problems of small distributors, the illegal purchase of the *Dead* franchise, etc.), and finally throttled his artistic independence. This is the Romero who has suffered a complete loss of faith in American capitalism and experiences a Woodian "savage joy" at the system's ultimate unsalvagability. His films tend to oscillate between these two extremes. The clearest expressions of the latter—creative tantrums of a sort over a system that doesn't work the way it's "supposed" to—are those in the *Dead* series.

Wood has expressed disappointment with all of Romero's films outside the *Dead* series, and clearly considers the latter to be the truest and most successful reflection of Romero's political temperament. Romero himself seems to corroborate this in interviews, although the syntax is ambiguous: when Romero says the series is the place where he "can show most how [he] see[s] the world" (qtd. in D'Agnolo-Vallan 23), he could be speaking less about the particular content of the message than the legibility of the form in which he works. It is difficult to imagine that *Knightriders* or *Martin*, which Romero has singled out as his favorite and most personal films, represent any less Romero's "real" perspective. Romero *is* a brilliant satirist of contemporary capitalism and patriarchy; but to argue that he writes and directs without a degree of ambivalence about the so-called American way is, I think, to caricature his oeuvre. More than Cronenberg, Romero is a contemporary Melville—one who, as Hawthorne once said of him, "can neither believe, nor be comfortable in his unbelief" ("Melville"). Hawthorne's ostensible subject was religion, but it could just as easily have been the American religion of free enterprise. Wood might criticize *Knightriders* for being "the archetypal liberal American movie" (*Hollywood* 168); but it is difficult not to conclude that Romero is the archetypal liberal American director, torn, as Bob Martin once figured it, between King Billy, the uncompromising idealist, and Morgan, "pleased by the cheers of the crowd, the rewards of a good business deal, and perhaps even a bit tempted by the glitter and gaudiness of show-business success" ("*Knightriders*" 66).

Romero's image as a maverick is a product of the mystique that developed around his refusal to work in Hollywood. As such, Romero's cinematic persona is inextricably tied to his identity as an independent businessman, and his legend and legacy are due as much to the success of Laurel, the company he founded with Richard Rubinstein in 1973, as to his films. The financial vicissitudes of being an independent in an age of conglomerates—digging up investors, deferring payments, and all the other seat-of-your-pants solutions independents find to get films made—certainly account for the themes that have obsessed Romero throughout his career: his quixotic exuberance for tilting at the windmills of corporate power (a trope best represented by Billy in *Knightriders*, but also by the hodgepodge of radicals and androgynes scattered throughout his films); and its obverse, the emptiness, greed, and oppression that characterize traditional authority (the military in *The Crazies*, Cuda of *Martin*, Rhodes in *Day*, *Knightriders*' fat cop, and so on). The tendency to frame his narratives in these terms also accounts for the propensity to read Romero's films as allegories both of the general struggle of the disenfranchised against consolidated economic power, and the specific struggle of the independent artist against the Hollywood behemoth. The clear allegorical bent of the individual films has also invited critics like Tom Allen to read the director's career as a meta-allegory, a "cautionary tale" about "what it takes for an independent to survive in an industry dominated by the Hollywood studio system" (xi). Romero is thus a sort of saint, whose life, like his work, points to an obvious moral. In this regard, his absence from cinema throughout most of the 1990s is an artistic statement in itself.

Romero claims that he did not begin his career as a conscious allegorist, and has expressed surprise at critics' willingness to read messages into *Night of the Living Dead*, generally attributing the meanings that did "creep in" to the historical moment: "It was 1968, man. *Everybody* had a 'message'" (Gagne 38). But the response to *Night* seems to have made Romero more conscious of the symbolic power of the zombie. By *Dawn*, Romero had a clear grasp of both the zombie's traditional significance and the way it could be put to work for social allegory; as he told Dan Yakir the year after *Dawn*'s release, he liked zombies because of their class identity as workers: they were the ones who "went out to pick the sugar cane" while "Lugosi lived in a castle" (60). Tellingly, in the same interview Romero also revealed that the seed of his scripts was the message, or "underbelly,"[15] claiming that "the surface doesn't matter." "Fantasy," he observed, "has always been used as parable, as socio-political criticism" (61). Shortly after, Romero seems to have about-faced again, to his earlier position that the message was largely unconscious (*Hollywood* 115); and by the time of Gagne's chronicle he was arguing that the desire for the film to have social significance could "interfere" with its "comic-book surface" (Gagne 38). In his most recent interviews, Romero has continued to play both sides: he has taken to calling the "message" of *Dawn* "too precious," suggesting again that underbelly had trumped surface (qtd. in Lee 68); on the other hand, he couldn't "pitch" the idea for *Land* because it was just an idea, about "people ignoring the problem in a post-9/11 world" (Curnutte).

My purpose here is not to "catch Romero out" by comparing statements he has made about the *Dead* films at different points in his career. Rather, I want to suggest that, as about business, he has always expressed a certain ambivalence about allegory, that tension between surface and depth, comic book horror film and socio-political message, the latter of which Romero has consistently referred to as their underbelly: a perfect, visceral term; a message written in gore. Since *Dawn*, critics have tended to look at the zombie films as all of an allegorical piece. But such a foreshortened perspective on the series tends to distort the individual films by seeing the earlier installments only in light of later ones, obscuring a crucial difference: that Romero has become more concerned with the "message," the *Dead* films more "belly," with each installment (Pinewood interview). That *Night* was understood in a variety of political contexts does not mean that critics expected *Dawn* to carry a "message." Only after *Dawn* had been digested as a satire of consumerism (and this certainly wasn't true for all critics, many of whom still saw it only as an ultraviolent horror film) did audiences come to expect a moment-specific "message" from the third *Dead* film. Ironically, *Day* was dogged by critics for being *overly* talky and philosophical, and I would speculate that Romero's comments in 1986 about the dangers of sacrificing surface to message were a response to *Day*'s trouncing by critics. But while the crew of *Day* referred to that film as "Zombies in the White House," even *Day* was not greeted with the sort of "what-will-Romero-have-to-say-about-Bush?" fanfare that *Land* was. Indeed, it would have been inconceivable for *Day* to be received with comments like "*Land of the Dead* will speak volumes to John Stewart's fan base" (D'Agnolo-Vallan 24), or to be included off the bat in a *Village Voice* article about films that respond to the "war on terror" (J. Hoberman's "Unquiet Americans"). Thus, *Land* reflects anything but a chastened Romero. Like Christian in *A Pilgrim's Progress*, Romero appears to have reached his allegorical apotheosis, a place of equipoise between message and form—a sort of celestial city of the dead.

What is remarkable about *Land*, however, is that Romero has not had to sacrifice the comic book surface; if anything, it has returned in a much grander style than was evident in the claustrophobic *Day*. To understand how *Land* can succeed so well on both "levels," we need to look beyond Romero's evolution as a socially conscious filmmaker, or consciousness on the part of the critical establishment about how to read the *Dead* films, and examine how historical developments and the post-*Day* developments of the genre have affected the production and reception of *Land*. In terms of the former, the use of the zombie as a lens through which to view the historical moment (counterculture, commodity culture, fascism) is well understood. In this regard, *Land* is obviously a response to the sharpening of global tensions around the neoconservative agenda and the "war on terror," as well as the (neo-)liberal capitulation to corporate interests that lay the groundwork for the neoconservative rise to power. In such a time, it is only fitting that Romero should return to the zombie, a figure closely associated with imperialism. What interests me more than the particular *content* of the historical moment, however, is the *form* through which that content is reflected. Perhaps Romero would say the same thing about 2005 that he said about 1968—perhaps, that is, we have reached another historical moment when having a message is a given: "It's 2005, man. *Everybody* has a 'message.'" Recent articles enumerating references to the Bush administration in recent Hollywood fare would seem to bear this out (Chang; Dargis). And yet, "underbelly" or "allegory" hardly seem the right terms to describe *Land*, so fully has the sociopolitical commentary been incorporated into the narrative. More than 1968 all over again, 2005 is a time of cartoon politics, a time when seemingly *everything* is "political," and yet nothing has any depth. What better time, then, to return to the grand comic book style? Cronenberg's comment about the politics of *A History of Violence*—that realpolitik "interbreeds" with genre and myth—takes on new life in *Land*. American politics has become a dead ringer for Romero's zombie world, *Land* a literalization of the comic book moment. In such a world, fantasy is no longer parable, but a slightly tweaked version of reality. In such a world, comic book revolution suddenly comes to seem not only fantastically *possible*, but *inevitable*.

Just as important as the comic book historical moment to *Land*'s collapsed allegory is the changed generic landscape in which it was produced. There is a tendency to see Romero's departure from filmmaking as a consequence not of his late disappointments with Hollywood, but of horror's retrenchment in the 1980s; as with Jonathan Crane on Cronenberg, the sense is that the genre morphed to such an extent that it could no longer accommodate the director's vision—hence the failure of *Day*. But if the genre gets blamed for Romero's departure, it might as well also be credited for his return—not because the genre has become again what it was in the 1970s (despite apparent efforts to that effect), but because the postmodern playfulness that has characterized the genre since the 1990s has proven to be fertile new ground for Romero's vision.

As the father of the stumbling, flesh-eating ghoul, Romero can claim the wave of zombie films following *Night* as his patrimony. His most important contribution to the subgenre, however, was to make the zombie viable again as an allegory for American society. Most recent zombie fare—including much of the late *Resident Evil*-driven deluge—has capitalized on the zombie not to update its symbolic significance, but to utilize it for postmodern play. This is clearest in the case of outright parody. No one, for example, could understand *Shaun of the Dead* without knowing Romero's series; a particular incarnation of the filmic zombie is being parodied. But *Shaun* is only the most obvious in this regard, since parody has also crept into ostensibly "straight" zombie films, and since audience expectations for zombie films continue to be built almost entirely from the bricks and mortar of Romero's *Dead*. This turn to parody and the sort of thoughtless generic incest that seems to motivate much recent zombie fare has left many critics, and Romero himself, groaning about post-*Scream* generic exhaustion, with the zombie as its appropriate motif: a dead genre can only cannibalize its own past and regurgitate it for an increasingly "knowing" audience, what Jonathan Crane has called "the vampiric, intertextual feint, the sneering look back" (61) of postmodern horror.

And yet, we could look back a decade before *Scream* and find a similar anxiety about the *Dead* series itself, with the simultaneous release of Romero's *Day*, slammed as an empty rehashing of earlier Romero, Romero himself accused of "running out of ideas," and *Return of the Living Dead*, which got a lot of mileage out of its characters trying to use the knowledge gained from Romero films to combat zombies. The issue is not cannibalism, which is a trait of all genres, but rather the manner in which the past is used. Barry Keith Grant, for example, has noted that each time Romero confronts "his own monstrous offspring" (202), it is a chance for the director to re-direct the subgenre's evolution—that is, not to reward audiences' "knowingness" about zombie films, but to extend, rethink, and perhaps even "correct" the tradition he helped to invent. While I largely agree with Crane and Grant about the 1990s' generic drift and Romero's avoidance of it, what is once again remarkable about *Land of the Dead* is the way that it capitalizes on this trend rather than merely repudiating or capitulating to it. The zombie Romero returns to in 2005 is a subtly different figure from the social-allegorical monsters of *Night*, *Dawn*, and *Day*. It has been so thoroughly *de*constructed and *re*constructed over the last decade that it is no longer a zombie (i.e., a stumbling, moaning, flesh-eating being from which the audience recoils). It is a walking trope. Horror audiences in the 1970s and 1980s might have gotten a message about consumerism or patriarchy by "reading" *Dawn* or *Day*, even if those messages seem "precious" in hindsight. But the audience for *Land* arrives with that trope called "zombie" already present in its mind, ripe to be plucked from its self-reflexive limbo and put back to work as social allegory. *Land* doesn't need to be read; it has no *subtext*. Its meaning is manifest in the figure of the "zombie." Once again, surface (rollicking horror-adventure) and message (war on terror, class struggle) collapse onto one another. Thus where Romero once blamed the failure of *Day* on competing with *Return of the Living Dead*'s spoof (Gagne 167), with *Land* he has turned the recent run of zombie pastiche to his profit.

Land of the Dead was thus made possible by the convergence of two inverted historical processes: toward fantasy in American politics, and toward self-reflexivity in the genre. At the same time that the allegedly "real" sociopolitical content becomes indistinguishable from the comic book fantastic, the fantastic figure of the zombie, fired in the kiln of 1990s generic self-reflexivity, becomes a transparent window onto social reality.

The imbrication of genre and history is apparent from *Land*'s opening credit sequence: a grainy, black-and-white montage of corpses punctuated by staticky radio transmissions reporting human-on-zombie violence is delivered following the title, "Some time ago . . ."; the film proper begins following the title "Today." For all its apparent difference, *Land* immediately announces *its* present as *our* present; generic and historical time merge. Of course, *Land*'s society will soon appear eerily familiar: tiny ruling class, balkanized underclass, loss of civil liberties, and so on. Of note here, too, is the efficiency with which Romero delivers subgeneric history: that a series of unconnected images and voiceovers is sufficient to place the viewer in the historical-generic "now" says as much about the economy of genre cinema per se as it does about its audience, for whom the conventions of the Romero zombie film are known by rote.

Land begins in "Uniontown," a suburban version of Cronenberg's Millbrook, with the difference that everybody is dead, night to Millbrook's radiant morning. True to the series, *Land*'s dead seem once again to be condemned to parody the labor or leisure that dominated their lives. But significant differences will soon appear between these zombies and their predecessors. The film continues the series-long trend toward humanizing the monsters, offering us a zombie leading man, complete with close-ups and choice wardrobe (Murray). Although Romero always stressed the zombies' working-class identity, here their connection to labor is explicit. They appear, as Stuart Klawans put it, as a Pageant of Trades (44): the black gas station attendant, the butcher with his cleaver. Finally and, given their new class-consciousness, logically, *Land*'s zombies are also nascent radicals. If the zombies were never really "pure motorized instinct," as "Frankenstein" said in *Day*, but pure motorized *ideology*, as Wood might put it, *Land* charts their transition from nostalgia for small-town capitalist America to longing for a revolutionary future. In this context it makes sense to ask two questions: Is "a zombie world" possible? And if so, what would it look like?

Big Daddy, the aptly named revolutionary zombie patriarch, continues the leadership role of African Americans from other *Dead* films. It is Big Daddy who takes the first step into the water separating Uniontown from the city, Big Daddy who shows the butcher that his ordinary cleaver can be a tool for class revolt. Big Daddy tries to rescue his fellow zombies from human marauders, a sympathy hardly exhibited by most of the film's human characters, who relentlessly cannibalize one another. Most important, it is Big Daddy who shows the zombies how flimsy are the walls erected around class privilege—not because of some fantasy of class mobility, but because such barriers, as much as the "instinct" to consume, are ideological.

By making the zombie characters types, Romero does with them what he always has with the human characters in his comic book cinema. Riley, the hardy Irish working-class hero; Cholo, the Hispanic immigrant full of bravado; Kaufman, the sneering capitalist: as types, the human characters clearly mirror not only the zombies, but one another. Cholo, for example, is very much Kaufman's creation: a monster of capital, it is fitting the two should die locked in embrace. For all Cholo's disparaging of his father's faith in the American dream—the father whom he symbolically kills by shooting an arrow into a zombie futilely pushing a lawnmower in circles—Cholo retains his father's desire for class mobility. It is only after Cholo is bitten and transforms that he recognizes the "other half" is not the zombies, but the ruling class. If Cholo and Kaufman violently undermine the American dream, Riley is a more ambiguous figure.[16] Riley wants *out* rather than *up*, and he has compromised himself as much as Cholo has to get what he wants. He has no faith in revolution—in anything, really, except himself. He is the loner, the American individualist who would rather ride off into the sunset than help Malachy, the organizer, build a new society. And yet, he *does* intend to build something—only "out there," away from *this*, from "people": in *Land*'s world, to the north, where there is, as Kaufman puts it, nothing. North becomes the new mythical West to be tamed and settled. In essence, Riley isn't all that different from Romero: the tinkerer creating for the powers-that-be until he gets enough money to strike out on his own, with his crew of loyalists, the old days of Latent Image or Laurel, when filmmaking was a family endeavor.[17]

By setting dead Uniontown in the suburbs, *Land* also updates the social geography of the *Dead* films. If up through the 1980s the suburbs were cannibalizing the cities, the last ten years have seen this trend reverse itself, as the wealthy have flooded back into an increasingly unaffordable, gentrified center, while the poor have begun a slow march to an ever-more-degraded periphery. Inside Fiddler's Green, *Land*'s high rise for the WASP and wealthy, "Life goes on in the grand old style." At least, that's what the television tells the Green's residents. But the glitch in that commercial, unnoticed except by the movie audience, reminds us that Fiddler's Green can appear natural only to those inhabiting the collective fiction that there is no outside.[18] As Riley notes, the wealthy are as trapped as the poor, and by the very same barriers they have erected, which, at the end, become terribly real—because they have made them so; because, like all of Romero's doomed characters, they can imagine nothing else. "Dine in," says the television. The zombies do.

Wood and Waller have remarked on the significance of Peter's giving up his rifle to the zombies at the end of *Dawn*. There is no such capitulation in *Land*: the human heroes ride away armed to the teeth; Big Daddy marches off with Peter's rifle strapped to his back. But if *Land* does not reject violence, it does reject spectacle, and makes a firm distinction between the two—between, that is, gore and fireworks. This is crucial because, over the last twenty years, horror movie gore has generally been equated with fireworks: pure spectacle that distracts the audience from real issues (Grant 202; Sanjek 114; Crane 59). In speaking about the *Dead* films, Romero has generally treated the Grand Guignol aspect as an essential part of the zombie film aesthetic, but otherwise unrelated to the "underbelly"—at best a "spoonful of gore" to help get the political medicine down the audience's throat. (Not for nothing Richard Rubinstein once called the gore effects in the *Dead* series "the moneymakers" [Gagne 5].) In 2000, however, Romero offered a retrospective justification of the zombie films' gore: as in the surgery scenes in *M*A*S*H*, the comic book surface is punctured by a splash of "cold water in the face," "a wake-up call" (Pinewood interview). This comment, however, might be better understood as a *prospective* justification of the violence in *Land*; for to a greater degree than the previous films, *Land* is a meditation on the relationship between audience and spectacle.

The fireworks are aligned with one sort of violence: they allow the human-on-zombie "massacre" to go on unimpeded, and as such they are symbolic of the kind of spectacle that distracts working people "from conscious recognition of their own oppression" (Williams). As is always the case in *Land*, the tenor is as important as the vehicle: the fireworks are *patriotic* spectacle. Conversely, the fireworks stop zombie-on-human violence, or revolutionary violence, which, more than the first kind, is the visceral, Grand Guignol violence associated with zombie films—not violence, but *gore*. Romero explicitly marks this distinction twice in the film: at the beginning, when Big Daddy crushes the severed head of a zombie that can't take its eyes off the fireworks; and again at the end, when the fireworks fail to distract the zombies as they close in upon a crowd fleeing Fiddler's Green. The sadistic, spectacular glee of Cholo's gang's motorcycle antics, so reminiscent of the end of *Dawn*, is replaced by a haunting, subdued score and cross-cutting between the zombie feast and Riley and his crew, its audience. The gulf between spectacle and message—between violent entertainment as sedative and violence as the terrible price of class oppression, the terrifying catharsis of revolution—has never been deeper.

The code for shooting off fireworks is also telling: "put some flowers in the graveyard." As Kim Paffenroth observes, we are back in the opening scene of *Night* (120). Romero's survivors have always had to learn to move beyond nostalgia for the traditions of a dead society. The denizens of Fiddler's Green do not ("Thank God," says one well-dressed man when fireworks appear, about to be consumed for God and country). In *Land*, it is the zombies who learn to move beyond the dead rituals of patriotic celebration and the deadening routine of small-town life. Thus, for all the incipient nostalgia of Uniontown, the answer to our initial question—what would a zombie world look like?—is: *Nothing like Millbrook.*

But has Riley, too, learned to move beyond? Riley enables Romero to distance himself from the film's most radical political implications—not just the zombies' revolutionary violence, but the similarities between Riley and Cholo-Kaufman. Riley's escape following the latter two's joint immolation effectively disavows that small and big capitalist are necessarily only different points along the same vector of capital accumulation. Moreover, post-apocalyptic fantasy always imagines a quasi-colonialist "outside" to escape to, where moral order can be restored and profits can be tidy. But the ironic lesson of Romero's career, and of the rather paltry 17 million studio dollars *Land* garnered by riding on the serendipitous coattails of a few blockbusters, is that such "outside" places only exist in Hollywood movies. In a system driven by the greatest gain for the smallest number in the shortest possible time, no "two-dollar window" can last for very long. Perhaps this is why every fantasized "outside" always looks suspiciously like the inside; and what Vivian Sobchack once remarked about families and patriarchy in the 1970s and 1980s sci-fi film holds true for the zombie film, too: nostalgia for how things used to be is reimagined as entirely new and projected into the future.

POLITICS OF NOSTALGIA

The fireworks that close *Land* are also a celebration: of the long-anticipated end of the *Dead* tetralogy, and even more, of Romero's return from the cinematic other side. *Land* may be less a capstone than a new beginning, as the more recent *Diary of the Dead* (2008) capitalizes even more fully on self-reflexivity for social critique.[19] It is only fitting that Romero should take a leading role in the post-parodic reanimation of the zombie. But there is a certain irony, too, as if only the rightful ruler restored to the throne usurped by Parody could ensure that the sub-genre's social-allegorical fertility was secure. Here again, that ambivalence between nostalgia and revolution, as the genre's break with the cycle of meaningless repetition is effected through a return to tradition.

Although Cronenberg did not suffer the decade-long dry spell that Romero did, *Eastern Promises* (2007), together with *A History of Violence*, also suggests that the director has entered a new phase in his career, one that uses generic costumes to deconstruct genre, and through it the myths on which genre thrives. Where *Violence* exorcised the American family, and America itself, of its pretensions to nature and God-given essence, *Promises* sets the former's ambiguities between family and Family in a new global context. These two films are more explicit about their socio-political milieux than any of Cronenberg's previous films except *M Butterfly*—although the director would no doubt consider this veneer for his metaphysical obsessions. True to form, *Promises* continues to explore the problematic of disguise and/as self-making.

The horror films of the 1970s have been championed for expressing deep-seated anxieties about capitalism and patriarchy. In this regard, it is ironic that while some contemporary horror directors busy themselves with seventies pastiche, the "old auteurs" are engaging with the present. It is a bit churlish of me, however, to spot-light these two filmmakers without emphasizing that the genre as a whole is nudg-ing toward a political Renaissance (D'Agnolo-Vallan 24; "Horror"), and that some young directors are looking backward not as unthinking participants in a broader cultural fixation on the 1970s, but for models and inspiration. Perhaps we really *are* in a new moment of "ideological crisis," when the "full significance" of the genre is beginning to re-"emerge" (Wood, *Hollywood* 118).

For those of us for whom Cronenberg and Romero are as the prophets Isaiah and Ezekiel were to William Blake, it is difficult to watch their recent films without a touch of nostalgia for their generic patriarchal authority and for a time when making movies outside the Hollywood system seemed less compromised, and not yet fully co-opted as a Hollywood fantasy itself; before the boundaries between center and periphery, power and powerlessness, were blurred; and before the oppressive condi-tions of production were obscured by an ideology of creative consumer liberation. Perhaps it's not that 2005 is 1968 all over again, but that those who were making movies in 1968 see a renewed potential in 2005 for political engagement, while those who started making horror movies in the last decade look at 2005 and can only feel nostalgic for a 1968 they never experienced: a politics of pastiche and nostalgia.

NOTES

1. As Andrew Sarris remarked in 1977, auteurism was never so much a theory as a tendency, "more a mystique than a methodology" (29). Sarris should know: in his seminal "Notes on the Auteur Theory in 1962" (in *Film Theory and Criticism*, 4th ed., ed. Gerald Mast, Marshall Cohen, and Leo Baudry [New York: Oxford University Press, 1992]), he defined the auteur for American readers less by what it is than by what it is not: beyond the tangible elements of technical competence or even style (although the boundary between the latter and the auteur is hardly distinguishable); "not quite" *mise-en-scène*, "not quite" worldview; "interior meaning" partly "imbedded in the stuff of cinema," the "intangible *difference* between one personality and another" (587; my emphasis). The auteur is thus more than just the essentially cinematic element of filmmaking: he is purity distilled from impurity, a coherent, individual identity from a collaborative art form, and the halo of art around the edges of commerce. Even as the auteur strained against the rise of more systematic critical schools whose stated goal was demystification, the auteur proved to have a near-magical tenacity. This is clearest in Peter Wollen's (mis)appropriation of structuralism in the service of the theory it was intended to supplant—a sort of attempt to rescue auteur theory from itself; "The Auteur Theory," *Film Theory and Criticism*, 4th ed., ed. Gerald Mast, Marshall Cohen, and Leo Baudry (New York: Oxford University Press, 1992). Bordwell has written extensively on film criticism's perennial urge to "save auteurism" by attaching it to other, contradictory modes of reading; see *Making Meaning* (Cambridge, Mass.: Harvard University Press, 1989), particularly chapters 3–4; 43–102.

2. Ian Conrich has traced the way a "prozine" like *Fangoria* consolidated its identity, and the identity of the genre, around the sort of "body horror" with which directors like David Cronenberg and George A. Romero would come to be associated; see Ian Conrich, "An Aesthetic Sense: Cronenberg and Neo-Horror Film Culture," *Modern Fantastic: The Films of David Cronenvberg*, ed. Michael Grant (Westport, Conn.: Praeger, 2000). But *Fangoria* was just as important, I think, for the way in which it responded to the more general trend in the film industry toward the director as an independent creative artist, and participated in the construction of the "horror auteur" for a genre audience. Although special effects were to become its particular fetish, *Fangoria* devoted more text to interviews with writers, producers, and (above all) directors than had *Famous Monsters*, the flagship genre publication for many years previous. As the magazine grew over the first half of the 1980s, *Fangoria* would devote an ever-increasing amount of space to a small cadre of visionary directors, including Cronenberg and Romero. For this reason, the horror fan, moreso than other moviegoers, is predisposed to understand horror as a director's cinema: to see a *Cronenberg* movie, a *Romero* movie. The tendency to append these directors' names to their movie titles is case in point, and mirrors a similar trend in art-cinema advertising; see David Bordwell, "Authorship and Narration in Art Cinema," *Film and Authorship*, ed. Virginia Wright Wexman (New Brunswick, N.J.: Rutgers University Press, 2003), 42–49. For some interesting corroborating evidence of this "horror auteur" phenomenon, see Paul Wells's summary of his "Spinechillers" survey findings, in *The Horror Genre* (New York: Wallflower, 2004), 27–35.

3. *eXistenZ* (1999) is the sole exception. I am aware that this irony depends on whose auteur theory one subscribes to: the genre director working with another writer's material who is thus forced to express himself in purely cinematic terms, or the writer-director who works with a recognizable set of themes—a confusion that reflects the fog of mystique around the auteur more generally. Film criticism has tended to prefer theme to style (Bordwell, *Making Meaning*, 79), and post-classical Hollywood, "auteur" has come to imply *writer*-director. Romero would probably

support a "semantic" version of auteur theory, since he has spoken about the way the cost of the medium hampers the development of an original style; Paul R. Gagne, *The Zombies That Ate Pittsburgh* (New York: Dodd, Mead & Company, 1986), 7.

4. *Dead Ringers* is an understandable but somewhat problematic choice for a turning point. One thinks, for example, of Sid Scheinberg's (at Universal studios) argument that *Videodrome* should be marketed as an art film, a decision with which Cronenberg agreed; see Chris Rodley, *Cronenberg on Cronenberg* (Boston: Faber and Faber, 1992), 59; and Bob Martin, "On the Set of *The Dead Zone*," *Fangoria* 26: 42–44). For further discussion of this tension/hybridity between art cinema and horror, see Steffen Hantke, "Genre and Authorship in David Cronenberg's *Naked Lunch*," *Twentieth-Century American Fiction On Screen*, ed. R. Barton Palmer (Cambridge: Cambridge University Press, 2007), 164–79, esp. 173; William Paul, *Laughing, Screaming: Modern Hollywood Horror and Comedy* (New York: Columbia University Press, 1994), 369.

5. Even by the early 1980s, Leo Braudy argues, horror had "become the dominant genre, even invading with its images and motifs films that are otherwise not really 'horror' films" (1), such as the police thriller; in Gregory Waller, "Introduction," *American Horrors*, ed. Gregory Waller (Chicago: Illinois University Press, 1987), 10. It is a trend that has continued apace (witness the *Saw* series, whose killer's macabre inventiveness owes as much to the Faustian experimenters of sci-fi as to slasher movies, and whose sequel potential must be starting to make Jason nervous). Nor have other genres been reticent to adopt horror's graphic violence and apocalyptic quasi-supernaturalism: the Western (*The Proposition*) and the disaster film (*The Day After* and the *War of the Worlds* remake) are two examples. Conversely, horror has hardly been immune to adopting the conventions and elements of other genres, such as the survival adventure (*The Last Winter*, *The Descent*). And bladder effects and prosthetics have found their way (back?) into FX-laden comedies, like the *Men in Black* franchise. Regarding the backward gaze, I would point to the return of the big-budget supernatural and the current "retro-obsession" (Corrigan's term) with the 1970s more generally—from *Grindhouse*, pastiche's nadir, to the remakes of *The Hills Have Eyes* and *Dawn of the Dead* and the phenomenon of Rob Zombie.

6. One generic feature of the Cronenberg interview is the moment when the interviewer compares the film under discussion to someone else's, or mentions that it bears the marks of another filmmaker, only to have the director challenge or reinterpret this. Another is the tale of originality vindicated. In the interview on the *Shivers* DVD, for example, the director recounts a story about being accused of "stealing" Dan O'Bannon's parasite idea from *Alien*, and then straightening out his accuser. It certainly helps to explain his dislike for the film, which he once described as "a man in a crocodile suit chasing a bunch of people around a room" (qtd. in Bob Martin, "The Brood and Other Terrors," *Fangoria* 3 (December 1971): 13)—this after remarking that it was devoid of subtext (!). He would probably also disavow the debt Jonathan Crane has identified to earlier sci-fi, just as the comparison between *Star Wars* and *Scanners* Handling and Beard make in their 1982 interview was immediately recuperated by the director, who noted that both films are influenced by classical texts; Serge Grünberg, *David Cronenberg: Interviews with Serge Grünberg*, rev. ed. (London: Plexus, 2006). In the same interview, Cronenberg recounts a story about being accused and then vindicated of stealing the story idea for "Transfer" (1966), his first short. Today, his auteur status universally confirmed, there is far less at stake in admitting influence as when he was struggling to forge his artistic identity. In some rather stark reversals from earlier interviews, he has spoken to Grünberg about his interest in low-budget horror and his early filmgoing experiences (17–18, 29), and has repudiated his earlier impatience with directors who did not write their own screenplays; see Ira Nayman, "Definitely a David Cronenberg Film: An Interview with David Cronenberg," *Creative Screenwriting* 6.2 (1999): 71–73.

7. For Beard, "to imply some leaching away of authorial originality [in Cronenberg's turn to adaptation] . . . is a canard" (*Monster*, 423). Then again, the real "canard" may be the claim to authorial originality itself: *Dead Ringers*, for one, seems to bear greater resemblance to the novel than Cronenberg would care to admit. See Mark Browning, *David Cronenberg: Author or Filmmaker?* (Bristol: Intellect, 2007), 81–109, 201.

8. One wonders whether Cronenberg has a tendency to overstate his case in the polemic surrounding his films, or if he just does it to shock; to say the endings of *Shivers* or *Videodrome* are "happy" hardly does justice to the ambivalence which Cronenberg's most sensitive readers have noted in all of his films, and which Cronenberg himself, when he is not backed into a corner, has acknowledged. Cronenberg's much-touted "balance," his ability to see both sides of an issue (once again attributed to his numinous Canadianness), tends to vanish when he feels his films are being attacked; in the 1999 *Cineaste* interview, he speaks in more measured terms about the ambiguity of the images of liberation in his films. But the problem of the representation of liberation as monstrosity is endemic to the genre as a whole. Wood returned to this in "Neglected Nightmares" (*Hollywood from Vietnam to Reagan . . . and Beyond* [New York: Columbia University Press, 2003], 97), where he calls for the death of Dracula, and by extension of a genre which had "served [its] purpose" (100) of releasing repressed energy.

9. Perhaps this is the meaning of Cronenberg's combined reference to Melville and Whitman as literary kindred spirits (Tim Lucas, "The Image as Virus: The Filming of *Videodrome*," *The Shape of Rage: The Films of David Cronenberg*, ed. Piers Handling [New York: Zoetrope, 1983], 155). They died within a year of each other, one the consummate outsider forgotten by his time, the other the most popular poet of his day. Taken together, they represent the fantasy of being at once inside and outside of one's own time, of mainstream popularity and transcendent, misunderstood artistry.

10. For example, the conceived and executed bleeding potato that never appeared in *Spider* because the director decided it was "from some other movie" (Pinewood interview)—that is, an *early* Cronenberg movie.

11. For a somewhat fuller discussion of this, see Mary Campbell's remarkably suggestive "Biological Alchemy and the Films of David Cronenberg," in *Planks of Reason: Essays on the Horror Film*, ed. Barry Keith Grant (Metuchen, N.J.: Scarecrow, 1984), 307–20.

12. The father-son relationship is similarly denied closure. The bloody father-son hug directly after young Jack Stall has killed Fogarty foreshadows another troubling embrace: Richie hugging Joey. Like the deadly embraces in *Rabid*, these embraces between male relatives seem to pass the virus of violence along.

13. The Romero of circa 1966 has almost nothing in common with the image of the director that had crystallized by the late 1970s: bearded, bearish, holding a cigarette instead of a script, and wearing that trademark lucky scarf. The Romero of today is similarly transformed—so much so that, the first time I saw a picture of him post-*Land of the Dead*, I did not recognize him. He has aged inordinately in the fifteen years since the publicity stills for *Two Evil Eyes*: wizened, hair white, and for the first time sporting glasses, enormous glasses that sit heavily on his face. Compare this, once again, to Cronenberg, who was already wearing his trademark glasses (the smug intellectual) in the midsixties. He has since lost them, but it has only increased the intensity of his gaze; and despite his claims to complete transformation, the features and expression remain unmistakably Cronenberg. He has aged with a sort of calm assurance—odd for one for whom mortality has been a central artistic preoccupation.

14. A similar ambivalence destroyed the 1970s auteurs who went to Hollywood with aspirations of remaking the system; and in this light it is tempting to think of Romero as an

image of what Francis Ford Coppola's career might have looked like had he never gone west. The term "romantic entrepreneur," which Timothy Corrigan applies to Coppola (108), fits Romero as well, if read with a Pittsburgh accent; see Corrigan, *A Cinema without Walls: Movies and Culture after Vietnam* (New Brunswick, N.J.: Rutgers University Press, 1991). Matt Becker finds the same ambivalence operating in all the seventies "horror auteurs": all self-described hippies, all looking for the big hit, and all walking a fine line between spectacular and oppositional violence; Becker, "A Point of Little Hope: Hippie Horror Films and the Politics of Ambivalence," *The Velvet Light Trap* 57 (Spring 2006): 42–59. They thus closely mirror the second wave of the New Hollywood, the so-called brutalists, as the inception of a more jaundiced view of the counterculture; see Peter Biskind, *Easy Riders, Raging Bulls* (London: Bloomsbury, 1999), 314.

15. Conversely, when Yakir asked Romero about the thematic significance of the suburban home in *Martin*, Romero immediately turned his answer to the home's visual appeal. Romero may or may not write his films message-first, but what often comes through in interviews is a fascination with *surface*.

16. By allowing the Irish laborer of yesteryear to rub shoulders with today's largely Latino working class, Romero has once again capitalized on postmodern pastiche, in this case to assert the invariant of an immigrant laboring class across different moments in American history, and perhaps to join "today" with a time when class divisions were more deeply felt and consciously understood.

17. It is ironic that Romero's characters are always looking to get to Canada, that "nothing" space where self-creation is more than just a myth, and where directors like David Cronenberg seem to have had the opportunity to do just that. Or perhaps Canada is the place where a benevolent government subsidizes independent filmmakers? Regardless, it seems significant that Romero now makes his home in Cronenberg's native city.

18. The underclass is hardly better, having their pictures taken while fake-screaming beside a chained zombie, inured as the audiences of today to the zombie's revolutionary potential. In this respect it is only too fitting that the makers and stars of *Shaun of the Dead* are present here. For all Romero's expressed admiration for *Shaun*, it is *Land*'s mission to help liberate the zombie from this generic status quo.

19. *Diary*'s protagonists are film students shooting a horror movie, and the film itself is cobbled together from intradiegetic video footage. According to Romero, *Diary* was "inspired . . . by a desire to address not the terrors of modern life, but the relentless impulse to record them," itself a product of feelings of helplessness in the face of the seriously "fucked" state of the world. See Nathan Lee, "Videocam of the Dead," *Village Voice*, September 19, 2007, 66, 69.

WORKS CITED

Allen, Tom. Introduction. *The Zombies That Ate Pittsburgh*. By Paul R. Gagne. New York: Dodd, Mead & Company, 1986. xiii–xiv.

Beard, William. "The Visceral Mind: The Major Films of David Cronenberg." *The Shape of Rage: The Films of David Cronenberg*. Ed. Piers Handling. New York: Zoetrope, 1983. 1–80.

———. *The Artist as Monster: The Cinema of David Cronenberg*. Rev. Ed. Toronto: Toronto University Press, 2006.

———, and Piers Handling. "The Interview." *The Shape of Rage: The Films of David Cronenberg*. Ed. Piers Handling. New York: Zoetrope, 1983. 159–99.

Becker, Matt. "A Point of Little Hope: Hippie Horror Films and the Politics of Ambivalence." *The Velvet Light Trap* 57 (Spring 2006): 42–59. *Project Muse*. Mina Rees Library, New York, New York, December 1, 2007.

Biskind, Peter. *Easy Riders, Raging Bulls*. London: Bloomsbury, 1999.

Blackwelder, Rob. "Metaphor Man." *Splicedwire*. 1999. http://www.splicedonline.com/features/cronenberg.html (accessed November 15, 2007).

Bloch-Hansen, Peter. "Double Trouble." *Fangoria* 78 (October 1988): 52–55.

Bordwell, David. "Authorship and Narration in Art Cinema." *Film and Authorship*. Ed. Virginia Wright Wexman. New Brunswick, N.J.: Rutgers University Press, 2003. 42–49.

———. *Making Meaning*. Cambridge, Mass.: Harvard University Press, 1989.

Breskin, Robert. "The David Cronenberg Interview." *Rolling Stone* February 6, 1992, 67–70+96.

Braudy, Leo. "Genre and the Resurrection of the Past." *Shadows of the Magic Lamp*. Eds. George Slusser and Eric S. Rabkin. Carbondale: Southern Illinois University Press, 1985. 1–13.

Britton, Andrew. "The Devil, Probably: The Symbolism of Evil." *The American Nightmare*. Eds. Robin Wood and Richard Lippe. Toronto: Festival of Festivals, 1979. 34–42.

Browning, Mark. *David Cronenberg: Author or Film-maker?* Bristol: Intellect, 2007.

Campbell, Mary B. "Biological Alchemy and the Films of David Cronenberg." *Planks of Reason: Essays on the Horror Film*. Ed. Barry Keith Grant. Metuchen, N.J.: Scarecrow, 1984. 307–20.

Chang, Justin. "George A. Romero's *Land of the Dead*." *Variety*, June 19, 2005. http://www.variety.com/review/VE1117927425.html?categoryId=31&cs=1 (accessed December 1, 2007).

Chute, David. "He Came From Within." *Film Comment* 16.2 (1980): 36–39, 42.

Conrich, Ian. "An Aesthetic Sense: Cronenberg and Neo-Horror Film Culture." *Modern Fantastic: The Films of David Cronenberg*. Ed. Michael Grant. Westport, Conn.: Praeger, 2000. 35–49.

"Considering Horror Panel." *Pinewood Dialogues*. American Museum of the Moving Image, June 17, 2007. http://www.movingimage.us/pinewood/index.php?globalnav=dialogues&sectionnav=detail&program_id=280 (accessed January 15, 2008).

Corrigan, Timothy. *A Cinema without Walls: Movies and Culture after Vietnam*. New Brunswick, N.J.: Rutgers University Press, 1991.

Crane, Jonathan. "A Body Apart: Cronenberg and Genre." *Modern Fantastic: The Films of David Cronenberg*. Ed. Michael Grant. Westport, Conn.: Praeger, 2000. 50–68.

Cronenberg, David. Interview. *Pinewood Dialogues*. American Museum of the Moving Image, February 10, 2003. http://www.movingimage.us/pinewood/index.php?globalnav=dialogues&sectionnav=detail&program_id=241.

Curnutte, Rick. "There's No Magic: A Conversation With George A. Romero." *The Film Journal*, December 1, 2007. http://www.thefilmjournal.com/issue10/romero.html.

D'Agnolo-Vallan. "Let Them Eat Flesh." *Film Comment* 41.4 (2005): 23–24.

Dargis, Manohla. "Not Just Roaming, Rising Up." *New York Times*, June 24, 2005. http://www.nytimes.com/2005/06/24/movies/24rome.html (accessed December 1, 2007).

Fuller, Graham. "Good Guy, Bad Guy." *Sight and Sound* 15.10 (2005): 12–16.

Gagne, Paul R. *The Zombies That Ate Pittsburgh*. New York: Dodd, Mead & Company, 1986.

Garris, Mick. "Landis, Cronenberg, Carpenter: A Panel Discussion of Fear on Film, Part 2." *Fangoria* 20: 26–29.

———. "Landis, Cronenberg, Carpenter: A Panel Discussion of Fear on Film, Part 3." *Fangoria* 21: 26–29.

Grant, Barry Keith. "Taking Back the *Night of the Living Dead*." *Dread of Difference*. Ed. Barry Keith Grant. Austin: Texas University Press, 1996. 200–212.

Grünberg, Serge. *David Cronenberg: Interviews with Serge Grünberg.* Rev. ed. London: Plexus, 2006.

Hantke, Steffen. "Genre and Authorship in David Cronenberg's *Naked Lunch.*" *Twentieth-Century American Fiction On Screen.* Ed. R. Barton Palmer. Cambridge: Cambridge University Press, 2007. 164–79.

Klawans, Stuart. "Alien Nation." *Nation,* August 18, 2005, 44–47.

Knee, Adam. "The Metamorphosis of *The Fly.*" *Wide Angle* 14.1 (1992): 20–34.

Leach, Jim. "North of Pittsburgh: Genre and National Cinema from a Canadian Perspective." *Film Genre Reader II.* Ed. Barry Keith Grant. Austin: Texas University Press, 1995. 474–94.

Lee, Nathan. "Videocam of the Dead." *Village Voice,* September 19, 2007, 66, 69.

Lim, Dennis. "The Way of the Gun." *Village Voice,* December 13, 2005. http://www.villagevoice .com/film/0538,flim1,67990,20.html (accessed November 15, 2007).

Lowenstein, Adam. *Shocking Representation.* New York: Columbia University Press, 2004.

Lucas, Tim. "The Image as Virus: The Filming of *Videodrome.*" *The Shape of Rage: The Films of David Cronenberg.* Ed. Piers Handling. New York: Zoetrope, 1983. 149–59.

Martin, Bob. "On the Set of *The Dead Zone.*" *Fangoria* 26: 42–44.

———. "*The Brood* and Other Terrors." *Fangoria* 3: 13–15.

———. "*Knightriders.*" *Fangoria* 12: 17–19+66.

McLarty, Liann. "Beyond the Veil of the Flesh." *Dread of Difference.* Ed. Barry Keith Grant. Austin: Texas University Press, 1996. 231–52.

"Melville and Nathaniel Hawthorne." *The Life and Works of Herman Melville.* July 25, 2000. http://www.melville.org/hawthrne.htm (accessed October 1, 2007).

Murray, Rebecca. "George Romero Talks About *Land of the Dead.*" *About.com.* http://movies .about.com/od/landofthedead/a/deadgro62105.htm (accessed December 1, 2007).

Nayman, Ira. "Definitely a David Cronenberg Film: An Interview with David Cronenberg." *Creative Screenwriting* 6.2 (1999): 71–73.

Neale, Stephen. "Questions of Genre." *Film Genre Reader II.* Ed. Barry Keith Grant. Austin: Texas University Press, 1995. 159–86.

Nutman, Philip. "The Exploding Family." *Cut! Horror Writers on Horror Film.* Ed. Christopher Golden. New York: Berkley Books, 1992.

Paffenroth, Kim. *Gospel of the Living Dead: George Romero's Visions of Hell on Earth.* Baylor, Tex.: Baylor University Press, 2006.

Paul, William. *Laughing, Screaming: Modern Hollywood Horror and Comedy.* New York: Columbia University Press, 1994.

Porton, Richard. "The Film Director as Philosopher." *Cineaste* 24.4 (1999): 4–9.

Rodley, Chris. *Cronenberg on Cronenberg.* Boston: Faber and Faber, 1992.

Romero, George A. Interview. *Pinewood Dialogues.* American Museum of the Moving Image, January 11, 2000. http://www.movingimage.us/pinewood/index.php?globalnav=dialogues& sectionnav=detail&program_id=244.

Sanjek, David. "Same as It Ever Was." *Film Genre 2000: New Critical Essays.* Ed. Wheeler Winston Dixon. Albany: State University of New York Press, 2000. 111–23.

Sarris, Andrew. "Notes on the Auteur Theory in 1962." *Film Theory and Criticism.* 4th ed. Eds. Gerald Mast, Marshall Cohen, and Leo Baudry. New York: Oxford University Press, 1992. 585–88.

———. "The Auteur Theory Revisited." *Film and Authorship.* Ed. Virginia Wright Wexman. New Brunswick, N.J.: Rutgers University Press, 2003. 21–29.

Scorsese, Martin. "Scorsese on Cronenberg." *Fangoria* 32 (january 1984): 46–47.

Sobchack, Vivian. "Bringing It All Back Home: Family Economy and Generic Exchange." *American Horrors*. Ed. Gregory A. Waller. Chicago: Illinois University Press, 1987. 175–94.

Taubin, Amy, "Model Citizens." *Film Comment* 41.5 (2005): 24–28.

Timpone, Anthony. "David Cronenberg: Lord of *The Fly*." *Fangoria* 57 (September 1986): 21–24.

Tudor, Andrew. "Genre." *Film Genre Reader II*. Ed. Barry Keith Grant. Austin: Texas University Press, 1995. 3–10.

Waller, Gregory. Introduction. *American Horrors*. Ed. Gregory Waller. Chicago: Illinois University Press, 1987.

———. *The Living and the Undead*. Chicago: Illinois University Press, 1986.

Wells, Paul. *The Horror Genre*. New York: Wallflower, 2004.

Wexman, Virginia Wright. Introduction. *Film and Authorship*. Ed. Virginia Wright Wexman. New Brunswick, N.J.: Rutgers University Press, 2003.

Williams, Tony. "*Land of the Dead*." *Rouge* 7 (2005). http://www.rouge.com.au/7/land_of_the_dead.html (accessed December 1, 2007).

Wollen, Peter. "The Auteur Theory." *Film Theory and Criticism*. 4th ed. Eds. Gerald Mast, Marshall Cohen, and Leo Baudry. New York: Oxford University Press, 1992. 589–605.

Wood, Robin. "Cronenberg: A Dissenting View." *The Shape of Rage: The Films of David Cronenberg*. Ed. Piers Handling. New York: Zoetrope, 1983. 115–36.

———. *Hollywood From Vietnam to Reagan . . . and Beyond*. New York: Columbia University Press, 2003.

Yakir, Dan. "Morning Becomes Romero." *Film Comment* 15.3 (1979): 60–65.

HOW THE MASTERS OF HORROR MASTER THEIR PERSONAE

Self-Fashioning at Play in the *Masters of Horror* DVD Extras

—Ben Kooyman

Masters of Horror (2005–2007) is a television anthology series that debuted on October 28, 2005, on U.S. cable network Showtime and ran for two seasons. Each season comprises thirteen self-contained hour-long episodes, each directed by a different "Master of Horror": a director deemed to have made a significant contribution to the horror genre. The show and the special features attached to its subsequent DVD releases (director interviews, tributes from past collaborators, commentaries) are exercises in self-fashioning for contemporary horror filmmakers; that is, they provide a site where directors can fashion and master their public personae. The *Masters of Horror* project is an attempt to bestow prestige upon genre practitioners: it asserts that auteurship exists within horror cinema, and that the genre deserves greater critical respect.

However, the DVD special features are sites of tension between self-fashioning and self-sabotaging impulses that materialize throughout the self-fashioning process, while the selection process behind the series—who is involved and why—calls into question the legitimacy of the title of Master of Horror. This chapter offers a deconstructive analysis of both the Master label and the self-fashioning motifs that run through the DVD extras, and will explore tensions circulating around and within the project, with a particular focus on directors Stuart Gordon and John Landis, their season-one episodes, and the accompanying DVD paratexts. Ultimately, I wish to suggest that the assortment of tensions constituting the series is dialectical.[1]

SIR GARRIS AND THE GRISLY KNIGHTS

The following promotional passage is an example of typically hyperbolic advertising for the series that appeared in a trailer for the show's second-season DVD releases:

> They are possessed by the dark . . .
> They share an obsession for terror . . .
> 13 all new terrifying tales . . .
> 13 visionary directors . . .
> 13 hours of mind altering fear . . .
> From the Emmy Award winning anthology . . .
> Masters of Horror[2]

This passage proclaims that the Masters of Horror are visionaries obsessed with terror and possessed by darkness who will, if given the opportunity, alter your mind. Such exaggerated assertions position the filmmakers as real-life equivalents of the director of *La Fin Absolue du Monde*, the fictional film that triggers insanity at the center of John Carpenter's episode "Cigarette Burns" (2005). This sort of hyperbole continues a tradition of horror movie advertising dating back to the Universal monster movies of the 1930s starring the likes of Boris Karloff; while the appropriation of this style is perhaps deliberately ironic, when taken at face value it complicates our consideration of the Master denomination, especially given its incongruity with the more tongue-in-cheek origins of this denomination (and, indeed, a number of the episodes).

Masters of Horror arose, humbly enough, from a series of bimonthly dinners in which horror filmmakers got together and, half-jokingly and half- knowingly, labeled themselves the "Masters of Horror." The series itself was masterminded and spearheaded by one of these Masters, Mick Garris, best known for directing the television miniseries of *The Stand* (1994) and *The Shining* (1997). Garris recalls how the dinners came about, and by extension how the show came into being:

> For a long time, a lot of us who worked in the genre, film directors, had been saying, "Oh, we ought to get together sometime, it would be great [to] do this" [. . .] It took weeks to schedule a night where everybody could make it. So we had a dozen guys—John Landis, John Carpenter, Guillermo del Toro, Tobe Hooper, and so on—and we all had such a great time, that a couple of months later we did another one and it took me an hour to put it together. I've been wanting to do an anthology series for a long time, so this kind of eased the way. (Wilson)

The directors who contributed to the show's first season were Garris, John Carpenter, Stuart Gordon, Don Coscarelli, John Landis, Lucky McKee, Larry Cohen, Joe Dante, John McNaughton, Dario Argento, Tobe Hooper, William Malone, and Takashi Miike.[3] While each episode of the series is completely distinct, the episodes are linked together as a series by the same introductory credit sequence, which features drops of blood raining down on a blank white screen, a skull floating toward the camera, a baby doll coming to life and smiling malevolently, and other assorted signifiers of horror.[4] There is also some continuity in the behind-the-scenes crew, including Greg Nicotero and his special effects house KNB.

The title of Master immediately raises a variety of deconstructive impulses in both the aficionado and the academic. No matter how tongue-in-cheek the Master denomination may have originally been, the fact remains that it immediately generates high expectations for an audience. In an essay on horror "event" movies like *The Mummy* (1999) and *Hannibal* (2001), Phillip L. Simpson asserts that an event movie "becomes or sustains a cultural force" (86). *Masters of Horror* fits these criteria: the series was marketed on the premise that it united "visionary" directors and gave them complete creative freedom to unleash their imaginations without censorship restrictions, which generated buzz online and in print media (both mainstream and horror-oriented). The *Masters of Horror* imprint generates expectations, and thus invites both consideration and deconstruction from the outset, starting with the Master label upon which the series was founded.

The Master label asserts each director's mastery of the genre for mainstream audiences; however, the loaded nature of this label invites more discriminating viewers to call into question the grounds on which a director can be canonized as a Master of Horror. Established horror auteurs such as John Carpenter are relatively secure in their entitlement; others are much less so. Lucky McKee directed the well-received *May* (2002) but had not delivered an extended or consistent body of work that could be deemed necessary for qualification as a Master prior to his canonization. McKee's position is thus more akin to that of apprentice than Master. William Malone's body of work is larger, but his most recent feature films, *House on Haunted Hill* (1999) and (especially) *FearDotCom* (2002), were both critically lambasted. In the case of Garris, his aforementioned Stephen King adaptations were maligned by both King fans and cinephiles (though were praised by King himself), while earlier efforts like *Critters 2: The Main Course* (1988) and *Psycho IV: The Beginning* (1990) actually undermine and deride the title of Master. Meanwhile, both John McNaughton and John Landis have delivered classic films often associated with the horror genre—*Henry: Portrait of a Serial Killer* (1986) and *An American Werewolf in London* (1981), respectively—but the bulk content of their filmographies is outside the horror genre, a fact which complicates their inclusion.

A critique of the series in the *Washington Times* asserts that the show "purports to let horror's brightest stars scare us anew. The fact is, the horror genre has precious few stars in its galaxy" (Yourse). While this critique is emblematic of the mainstream in its dismissive and disparaging attitude toward the genre, it nonetheless touches on a raw nerve evident in the show's creative assembly line. The Master label implies the existence of a stable canon of horror filmmakers, an assertion that proves to be flawed on closer inspection. The title of Master thus generates all sorts of questions about discrimination in the assembling of the show's talent pool, questions that ultimately affect our response to the series. For instance, all of the directors who have contributed to the show are men, and all but three of them (Takashi Miike, Ernest Dickerson, and Norio Tsuruta) are white. This sexual and racial exclusion is undoubtedly symptomatic of the dominant position of white males within the Hollywood film industry. The recent reincarnation of *Masters of Horror* on NBC, *Fear Itself* (2008), addressed this gender discrimination somewhat superficially by including one female auteur, Mary Harron, the director of *American Psycho* (2000).

In some of the print advertising for the series, the show was sold on the basis of the Masters' previous films rather than their names, the publicity department perhaps wisely realizing that names like Don Coscarelli and Larry Cohen do not automatically signify films like *Phantasm* (1979) and *It's Alive* (1974) for most mainstream audiences. One such print advertisement went as follows:

> Their wildest dreams are your worst nightmares
> 13 original one-hour movies from the directors of
> Halloween
> The Texas Chainsaw Massacre
> Poltergeist
> The Stand
> An American Werewolf in London
> The Howling
> Phantasm
> Re-Animator
> It's Alive

The very idea of *Masters of Horror* is based upon canonizing specific individuals responsible for quality horror films. However, this advertising instead capitalizes on the name recognition of these horror films, and the series is sold through the movies—*Halloween* (1978), *The Howling* (1981), *The Texas Chainsaw Massacre* (1974)—rather than the individuals who directed them, the supposed Masters. The directors are nameless entities in this advertisement, represented by just one (in

Tobe Hooper's case two) of their feature films. Each film title represents a self-contained and highly regarded text, whereas a director's name would signify a larger body of work that may or may not sustain the same level of reverence as an isolated text. Even worse, a director's name may draw either blank responses from those outside horror fandom or interrogative responses (such as the one presently being mounted) from those within. This publicity decision, thus, makes sense, but still undermines the thrust of the project.[5]

Obviously the terms and conditions of each director's contribution to the genre were relatively flexible, and directors were not required to have made prolonged, sustained contributions to the genre of a consistently high quality. Veteran directors and emerging directors alike, not to mention directors who generally work outside the genre but nonetheless have made some sort of contribution, are present. As such, McNaughton, Landis, and McKee are canonized as Masters based upon their few acclaimed contributions to the genre rather than sustained bodies of horror work, while Garris and Malone are canonized as Masters due to the tenure of their work in the genre. Such flexibility, however, still raises eyebrows. In the featurette "Imprinting: The Making of Imprint" (2006), Takashi Miike jokes that "I think they thought, Ok, he directed *Audition*, let's ask him" (Oneda). Meanwhile, a contributor to the Internet discussion group *Horror at Indiana: Horror in Film and Literature* comments in a post that "I think that general selection process for being a 'Master' of horror is that you either know Mick Garris or just agree to be on the program" (Swindoll). These criteria certainly apply to Landis, who served as executive producer on Garris's directorial debut, the television family movie *Fuzz Bucket* (1986), and appears in several of Garris's films.

While the presence of certain directors and the absence of others calls into question the legitimacy of the title of Master, we cannot afford to ignore the matter of simple logistics. Ultimately, the final roll call for *Masters of Horror* is dependent on a variety of factors. By way of example, both George Romero and Roger Corman were lined up to direct episodes but dropped out due to extenuating circumstances and were replaced by McNaughton and McKee.[6] Would the series have been more or less authentic if Romero and Corman had participated? Whatever the case, the final assortment of directors was ultimately contingent upon matters of availability, scheduling, interest, and financing.

All this begs an obvious question: just how easy is it to become a Master of Horror? Just how few qualifications can a filmmaker get away with while still fitting the criteria? While *Fright Night* (1985) and *Child's Play* (1988) director Tom Holland has some claim to the title of Master, do Ernest Dickerson and Rob Schmidt, who were likewise canonized as Masters in the show's second season, really deserve canonization on the basis of the Snoop Dogg vehicle *Bones* (2001) and *Wrong Turn* (2003), respectively? How vested are Garris's own interests here? Is Garris using the project to canonize himself as a Master of Horror alongside the likes of Dario Argento and Tobe Hooper, while fleshing out the numbers needed to justify the project with anyone who may have directed a halfway decent horror film?

Value judgments aside, the whole *Masters of Horror* enterprise can be read as an exercise in self-fashioning. The term itself is derived from an early book by the New Historicist literary scholar Stephen Greenblatt, *Renaissance Self-Fashioning: From More to Shakespeare* (1980). In this book, Greenblatt analyzes the careers of Tudor England artists and luminaries Thomas More, William Tyndale, Thomas Wyatt, Edmund Spencer, Christopher Marlowe, and William Shakespeare and considers how these individuals fashioned their identities through artful processes which blurred the distinctions between reality and fiction, between life and text. The term self-fashioning describes these processes. We can see self-fashioning at work in *Masters of Horror*, with each filmmaker using their episode, their DVD special features, and the Master label to fashion themselves as important horror directors; indeed, as Masters of Horror. My key interest in self-fashioning resides in Greenblatt's observation (no doubt a product of New Historicism's roots in post-structuralist nihilism) that "any achieved identity always contains within itself the signs of its own subversion or loss" (9); that is, subversion is interiorized within the orchestrated identity of the artist. This internalized subversive force materializes constantly throughout *Masters of Horror*, in relation to the self-fashioning of individual directors and within the foundations of the show as a whole. Its exploration will form the thrust of this essay.

Self-fashioning is hardly new to the horror genre. The most entrepreneurial of horror directors would undoubtedly be William Castle, whose films during the 1950s and 1960s were accompanied by various extra-textual gimmicks: life insurance policies, flying skeletons, electric shocks, and so forth. Castle's showmanship and theatricality left a lasting impression on Stuart Gordon.[7] The director identifies *The Tingler* as an important film from his younger years (P. Martin, "Damnation"), thus inviting association with Castle and aligning his own work with Castle's highly theatrical style of filmmaking.[8]

The William Castle tradition of showmanship and theatricality still continues today in the genre, and we can see instances of this from several of the Masters of Horror. Take, for instance, *John Carpenter Presents Body Bags* (1993), an anthology of three short horror films in which Carpenter plays a wacky coroner in a morgue who introduces each segment.[9] Meanwhile, Takashi Miike makes a cameo appearance in Eli Roth's *Hostel* (2005), a film heavily associated with Miike's own *Audition* (1999). Miike plays a satisfied customer leaving the warehouse where abducted travelers are brutally tortured, thus inserting himself into the American torture-porn tradition, upon which *Audition* was a major influence.[10]

These examples, however, are fairly broad instances of performative self-fashioning in the genre. More commonly, DVD special features provide filmmakers with a platform for performative self-fashioning: to inform and educate audiences on the making of a film, to frame and shape a viewer's perception and reception of the material, and to fashion themselves through commentaries, interviews, and so on.

Given the level of self-fashioning that takes place around rather than within artistic texts, it comes as little surprise that the individual episodes of *Masters of Horror* contribute very little to the self-fashioning process. Though the episodes act as showcases for each filmmaker's directorial skills, these showcases are compromised by budgetary and casting limitations, shooting conditions, and other restrictions. In addition, each episode varies in quality, and some suffer from the tight financial and shooting restrictions more than others. As such, the special features attached to the show's DVD releases are far more exemplary exercises in self-fashioning, and go further to justify and validate the Master status of each director. Veteran horror directors like Carpenter and Argento use these special features to genealogize their oeuvres and to canonize themselves as legitimate artists, while emerging directors and non-horror directors strive to insert themselves within this evolving genealogy.

DVD features serve as useful paratexts. According to Gerard Genette, paratexts are "all those things which we are never certain belong to the text of a work but which contribute to present—or 'presentify'—the text" (qtd. in Allen 104). Furthermore, their function, according to Genette, is "to ensure for the text a destiny consistent with the author's purpose" (qtd. in Allen 107). Paratexts stand on the threshold of a text and shape our reading of that text. In this respect, DVD special features certainly qualify and operate as paratexts. The paratextual material on the *Masters of Horror* DVDs is shaped by both the Masters themselves and other behind-the-scenes personnel. Genette points out that paratexts can be both autographic (created by the author/director) and allographic (created by others), but I would argue that DVD special features are both. Although much of the supplementary material on DVDs is not directly shaped by the director of the titular text, these special features are mostly consistent with the intentions of the text they accompany. In the case of the *Masters of Horror* paratexts, each Master remains a guiding, synthesizing presence, and the supplementary material provided to honor these directors is tailored to fashion them as legitimate horror movie Masters.

Horror films have often been maligned in respectable critical circles, and the *Masters of Horror* DVD project attempts to address this situation; its special features are fashioned to legitimize horror filmmakers as auteurs and to establish that genre practitioners are worthy of such credentials. As such, the DVD special features that accompany the *Masters of Horror* episodes will be the main objects of analysis in this chapter, and the next two sections will specifically explore the self-fashioning of two particular filmmakers, Stuart Gordon and John Landis. Both Gordon and Landis, aged sixty-two and fifty-nine, respectively, have made significant contributions to the genre, though Gordon's body of horror work is decidedly more substantial, and both seek recognition as Masters of Horror through *Masters of Horror*.[11]

However, the DVD special features are also sites of tension between self-fashioning and self-sabotaging impulses, and in these textual supplements we glimpse the "subversion or loss" of their subject's "achieved identity" (Greenblatt 9). The main self-fashioning and self-sabotaging motifs to be explored throughout this essay are: each director's courting of association with illustrious predecessors, and their attempts to contextualize their work within broader artistic movements inside and outside horror cinema; the selective and discriminatory manner in which each director recollects his career; the extent of, and level of authority attached to, each director's posturing as a horror Master; and the strategies and techniques employed by both the directors and the makers of the special features to shape each director's self-fashioning, and the materials and testimonials selected for this intent.

The focus of my analysis will be the special features that accompany the season-one DVD releases of Gordon's "Dreams in the Witch House" (2005) and Landis's "Deer Woman" (2005). The core special features which accompany each disc include: a twenty- to twenty-five-minute interview with each director in which he recounts his career, as well as his experiences working on *Masters of Horror*; a "Working with a Master" featurette in which previous collaborators (actors, producers, writers) wax lyrical on their experiences working with the director;[12] a short making-of segment which unobtrusively observes typically amiable directors on typically pleasant sets with typically dedicated crews; short interview segments of about five minutes in which the lead actors recount their experiences working on the episode; and audio commentaries by members of the cast and crew. Gordon shares his commentary with lead actor Ezra Godden, while Landis is absent from the "Deer Woman" commentary, which features, instead, actors Brian Benben and Anthony Griffith.[13] My analyses of Gordon and Landis will concentrate primarily on material taken from the director interviews and tribute featurettes. The Landis and Gordon director interviews are both directed by Anchor Bay's Perry Martin (who also directs equivalent interviews with Argento, Carpenter, Dante, and Coscarelli), while frequent Anchor Bay contributor Frank H. Woodward handles their "Working with a Master" tribute featurettes (and equivalent tributes for most of the other first-season directors).

CASTLE FREAKS AND WITCH HOUSES: STUART GORDON

From his breakthrough film, the cult classic *Re-Animator* (1985) onward, Stuart Gordon's body of work has been consistently interesting and provocative, not to mention varied. Gordon's oeuvre contains both horror movies like *From Beyond* (1986), *Dolls* (1987), *The Pit and the Pendulum* (1991), *Castle Freak* (1995), *Dagon* (2001), and *King of the Ants* (2003), and uneven sci-fi/action movies like *Robot Jox*

(1990), *Fortress* (1993), and *Space Truckers* (1996). In "Dreams, Darkness & Damnation: An Interview with Stuart Gordon" (2006), the director comments that he had "always liked horror movies, ever since my parents refused to let me see them" (P. Martin, "Damnation"). This equation of horror with forbidden fruit appears to fuel Gordon's work in a number of ways: his films gorge themselves on violence and nudity and pursue broad excess, and a sense of mischief and playfulness runs through the likes of *Re-Animator* and *From Beyond*.

Gordon's season-one *Masters of Horror* contribution, "Dreams in the Witch House," is consistent with the director's body of work: the film's tone is broad and theatrical, and Gordon is generous with its violent and sexual content. By extension, it is tied to Gordon's previous work through the presence of Gordon's frequent writing partner Dennis Paoli, frequent composer Richard Band, and *Dagon* lead actor Ezra Godden, and through its connection to horror author H. P. Lovecraft. The featurette "Dreams, Darkness & Damnation" stresses Gordon's ongoing association with Lovecraft, as well as his early history as a theater director—a history that Gordon returned to recently with his film of playwright David Mamet's *Edmond* (2005)—two qualities which play an important role in Gordon's self-fashioning. "Working with a Master: Stuart Gordon" (2006)—featuring interviews with producer Brian Yuzna and actors Godden, Jeffrey Combs, Barbara Crampton, Ken Foree, and Carolyn Purdy-Gordon—also stresses these qualities.

Yuzna, Combs, and Crampton each discuss Gordon's theatrical background and draw attention to the fact that Gordon works closely with actors before production in a process akin to theater rehearsals (Woodward, "Gordon"). Combs also notes that each Stuart Gordon film has an "audience participation quality to it" (Woodward, "Gordon"), and that the seeds of this quality stem from Gordon's theater work. Reference is made to a theater piece Gordon directed in 1968 at the University of Wisconsin's Screw Theatre called *The Game Show*, a grim piece in which audience members (actors planted throughout the audience) were brought on stage and tortured.[14] Purdy-Gordon, who is Gordon's wife and has collaborated with her husband on stage and screen, comments that she broke up with Gordon for three months after first seeing the play because she felt it was "morally irresponsible of him to put people in that much fear" (Woodward, "Gordon").[15] A portrait of Gordon as provocateur is being painted, just as Gordon's horror movie (i.e., low-art) oeuvre and its intentions are being aligned with his theatrical (i.e., high-art) background.

Gordon himself discusses his tenure as artistic director of Chicago's Organic Theatre Company—a tenure spanning from 1970 to 1985—in "Dreams, Darkness & Damnation." The director cites his early association with Mamet, whose first play, *Sexual Perversity in Chicago*, Gordon staged in 1974, to further establish his credibility as a theater practitioner. However, Gordon also notes that he clashed with the

Organic Theatre Company over his plans to direct *Re-Animator* (P. Martin, "Damnation"). Thus, while Gordon refers to his theatrical background in order to feed off its high-art status (this status a symptom of an elitist and somewhat contrived high-art–low-art dichotomy) and to give himself credibility and prestige as an artist, he also distances himself from this medium which was ultimately too conservative for his horror movie ambitions. But according to Anchor Bay DVD producer Perry Martin, Gordon's theatricality can still be glimpsed in his work, such as in the theatrical special effects used throughout "Dreams in the Witch House" (Gordon, Godden, and Martin). Indeed, the action of the episode takes place predominantly in one location and features a small ensemble of actors, qualities that also reflect a theatrical inclination.

Horror luminary H. P. Lovecraft's influence on contemporary horror fiction, both cinematic and literary, is substantial.[16] Gordon has courted association with Lovecraft throughout the course of his career by adapting Lovecraft's work to the screen: *Re-Animator, From Beyond, Dagon*, "Dreams in the Witch House," and the forthcoming *The Thing on the Doorstep* are all Lovecraft adaptations.[17] Gordon has also, to a lesser extent, courted association with Edgar Allan Poe through his adaptations of *The Pit and the Pendulum* and, for *Masters'* second season, "The Black Cat" (2007). Thus, long before *Masters of Horror*, Gordon courted association with other recognized Masters of Horror and sought to be aligned with their oeuvres. The series gives Gordon an opportunity to continue this creative alignment, and (according to the *Masters* Web site) to "confirm his place as the premiere director of Lovecraft's tales of terror" ("Season 1").

Gordon's numerous allusions to Lovecraft throughout the *Masters of Horror* special features transcend simple matters of tribute. Gordon uses his theatrical pedigree to legitimize himself as an artist, but he must also legitimize and provide justification for his shift from the high-art, highbrow medium of theater to the low-art, lowbrow medium of low-budget filmmaking: low-budget horror filmmaking, no less. As such, it makes sense that Gordon devotes considerable time to discussing Lovecraft, because Lovecraft's literary reputation and respectability act as justification and validation for Gordon's artistic journey from theater to film. Lovecraft was used to validate Gordon's decision to leave theater in the mid-1980s, and Lovecraft is used once again to validate this decision for *Masters of Horror* viewers. The conflict with the Organic Theatre Company over Gordon's direction of *Re-Animator* provides some foundation for Gordon to endorse the horror film over the stage, but does not deny Gordon the significant prestige which association with the theater generates.

In "Dreams, Darkness & Damnation," Gordon validates himself and his oeuvre through the literary gravitas of Lovecraft, while simultaneously demonstrating a level of mastery over the author. He argues that "Lovecraft can be very cinematic. It's a question of taking the right story. A lot of his stories are very internal and would not be easy to adapt, but there are a lot of them that are action-packed" (P. Martin, "Damnation"). By highlighting the difficulty of adapting Lovecraft, Gordon draws attention to his own recognized success in negotiating these complexities in the likes of *Re-Animator* and *From Beyond*. Elsewhere, Jeffrey Combs similarly grants Gordon mastery of Lovecraft with his observation that Lovecraft had little investment in his original 1922 story "Herbert West: Re-Animator" (Woodward, "Gordon"). This observation highlights Gordon's mastery of the text; namely, his ability to extract success from material the author himself thought disposable.

Gordon draws attention to Lovecraft's fear of women in both "Dreams, Darkness & Damnation" and his audio commentary, and informs us that this anxiety materializes all throughout Lovecraft's work. Gordon thus places the blame for the inherent misogyny of "Dreams in the Witch House" on Lovecraft's shoulders and points out that he himself inserted the single mother character, Frances, into the story, thus improving on Lovecraft, whose only female character in the original story was the witch (Gordon, Godden, and Martin). Gordon also exhibits mastery over Lovecraft by using the inclusion of this female character to transform Ezra Godden's character Walter into a symbolic manifestation of Lovecraftian anxiety, torn between binary opposite representations of women as witches and beautiful mothers (Gordon, Godden, and Martin). On another level, by entering into discourse on the issue, Gordon uses Lovecraft's fear of women to absolve himself of, or perhaps artistically validate, the misogyny he has been accused of throughout his career.

Gordon also comments that "Lovecraft had been writing for pulp magazines and, like Poe, died young and in complete obscurity. Now people are saying that Lovecraft is the greatest horror writer of the twentieth century" (P. Martin, "Damnation"). A parallel emerges here with the maligned status of horror filmmakers in the mainstream, a collective to which Gordon himself belongs and a situation which *Masters of Horror* strives to remedy. Gordon's observation thus validates the purpose of the series and inserts the participating directors within a longer history of struggling horror artists. More pertinently, Gordon's comments on Lovecraft's recent popularity and prestige draw attention to his own smarts in recognizing the cinematic value of Lovecraft, as well as his own part in the increased appreciation of the author. In his "Dreams in the Witch House" commentary, Gordon has the following exchange with Perry Martin, after describing the efforts of Lovecraft's friends and associates to keep stories like 1933's "Dreams in the Witch House" in circulation after the author's death:

GORDON: Thanks to them, people are still, you know, reading Lovecraft and . . .

MARTIN: And thanks to you.

GORDON: Well, to some small degree. I mean, some of the stories were out
of print, like "Re-Animator" was when I did the film, you know, twenty
years ago. (Gordon, Godden, and Martin)

Gordon points out that movies have contributed to enthusiastic critical and scholarly reevaluations of Lovecraft; as a filmmaker heavily associated with Lovecraft,
Gordon thus inserts himself in a movement which has kept Lovecraft's work alive
and helped stories like "Herbert West: Re-Animator" see print again.

Gordon also points out that Lovecraft purists get angry watching his adaptations because of their frequent nudity (Gordon, Godden, and Martin). While there
is no nudity in Lovecraft, Gordon asserts that he uses nudity to explore the fear of
reproduction and monstrous sexuality running through the Lovecraft oeuvre (Gordon, Godden, and Martin), thus demonstrating discursive mastery over Lovecraft
scholars and other aficionados. However, while he enjoys playing the part of provocateur, the director also suggests that the opposition between himself and the
purists may be decreasing. Reception to "Dreams in the Witch House" at the 2005
H. P. Lovecraft Film Festival in Portland, Oregon, was positive, according to Gordon, and many purists felt his episode was the closest in spirit to Lovecraft of all
Gordon's adaptations, which pleased the director (Gordon, Godden, and Martin).
Gordon also feels himself advancing closer and closer toward a Lovecraftian plane,
citing the moment in his episode when Walter recognizes the dimensional gateway
in his apartment as his most Lovecraftian directorial moment to date, calling it "pure
Lovecraft" (P. Martin, "Damnation"; Gordon, Godden, and Martin). This is perhaps
the most explicit instance of Gordon attempting to genealogize himself alongside
and through his predecessor.[18]

The self-fashioning that occurs in and around "Dreams in the Witch House" is
actually fairly consistent with recent patterns in Gordon's work. Much of Gordon's
recent work shows a strain of self-fashioning intent, and a conscious return toward
both his theatrical and cinematic roots: the Organic Theatre Company was responsible for staging the earliest work of David Mamet, and Gordon returned to Mamet
in 2005 with *Edmond*; Gordon's *Masters of Horror* episodes "Dreams in the Witch
House" and "The Black Cat" continue the director's courting of Lovecraft and Poe,
respectively; and two of Gordon's future projects, *The Thing on the Doorstep* and
House of Re-Animator, mark returns to Lovecraft and, in the case of the latter film,
to the franchise where his film career began.

A BRAZILIAN DEER IN CANADA: LANDIS AND HIS HORROR AMIGOS

On the cover art adorning the American-release DVD jacket for "Dreams in the
Witch House," Gordon's appearance is grim, like a nightmarish mug shot, suggesting

barely contained fury. A number of the photos and stills sprinkled throughout the special features, often of Gordon at work directing on previous film sets, contain similar posturing on Gordon's part. This aggressive posturing is appropriate for a Master of Horror, though somewhat incongruous with the director's mild-mannered interview style, as well as with some of the observations made by collaborators throughout the special features, especially those made by Carolyn Purdy-Gordon.[19]

In sharp contrast with the picture of Gordon gracing the cover of "Dreams in the Witch House," the picture of John Landis on the U.S. cover of "Deer Woman" goes for a different quality altogether. Landis is smiling mischievously, even somewhat puckishly. The photos and stills peppered throughout the "Deer Woman" supplementary features similarly reflect Landis's style of square goofball chic. Furthermore, while Gordon's interview style is reserved and contained, Landis is animated and self-consciously wacky. This persona is in tune with Landis's "Deer Woman," which, in turn, is relatively in tune with the bulk of his oeuvre. Landis is, after all, a comedy director by trade. This incongruity permeates Landis's participation in *Masters of Horror*: his status in relation to the horror genre is ambiguous and uncertain, and his self-fashioning in large part acknowledges and responds to this generic anxiety and uncertainty, though neither is ever completely exorcised.

Landis's comedy catalog includes the cult classics *Kentucky Fried Movie* (1977), *National Lampoon's Animal House* (1978), and *The Blues Brothers* (1980), as well as broader mainstream fare like *Trading Places* (1983), *Spies Like Us* (1985), *The Three Amigos* (1986), and *Coming To America* (1988), starring high-profile comedic actors like Dan Aykroyd, Chevy Chase, and Eddie Murphy. In comparison, his horror output is limited to the popular *An American Werewolf in London* and the vampire movie *Innocent Blood* (1992), both of which are often seen more as comedies than horror movies. Landis's season-one *Masters* episode "Deer Woman," written by his son Max Landis, fits in with the director's previous horror ventures by incorporating plenty of humor, and Landis, like Gordon, plays to his own creative strengths throughout.[20] In addition to his output as director, Landis has also appeared as an actor in a number of films, including movies by his fellow Masters of Horror: *Spontaneous Combustion* (1990) for Tobe Hooper; *Psycho IV*, *Sleepwalkers* (1992), *The Stand*, and *Quicksilver Highway* (1997) for Mick Garris; and the forthcoming *Parasomnia* (2009) for William Malone.[21]

In "Animal Hooves: An Interview with John Landis" (2006), the title of which is obviously a play on Landis's seminal *Animal House*, Landis highlights and draws attention to the ambiguity of his position as a Master of Horror, but simultaneously fetishizes his status as outsider. He muses:

> How would I describe my episode? Silly. The premise of the film, it's utterly ridiculous, and I like that. But I think it's a problem when the monster becomes a joke, because the horror film stands and falls on whether the

monsters are scary. Even in *Abbot & Costello Meet Frankenstein*, which is probably the best monster comedy, the monsters are treated with great respect. And the approach is similar to "Deer Woman," because that is what interests me, to be as realistic as possible dealing with an essentially preposterous subject. (P. Martin, "Hooves")

Landis embraces his position as outsider while using this outsider status to critique the horror form, as he does above, which has the effect of privileging his insight and thus affording him an appropriate level of mastery. Also, by citing *Abbot & Costello Meet Frankenstein* (1948), Landis aligns his own film "Deer Woman" alongside that seminal horror comedy feature.

Elsewhere, Landis states that "Deer Woman" is "very much influenced" by the classic Jacques Tourneur horror film *Cat People* (1942) (P. Martin, "Hooves"). Both revolve around female monster-figures who are heavily sexualized, and Landis's film features a scene in which his protagonist Dwight Faraday (Brian Benben) believes he is being stalked down a dark street, in homage to a similar scene in *Cat People*. While the corresponding scene in *Cat People* ends with the engineered shock of a bus screeching into frame, the equivalent scene in "Deer Woman" ends with genuine peril, with a mugger bursting into frame to assault the hero. According to Landis, "it's not a false scare, it's a real scare" (P. Martin, "Hooves"). Landis thus exhibits mastery over Tourneur with his "real scare" as opposed to Tourneur's "false scare," though the foundations of this distinction (what makes the former false and the latter real) are debatable.

In addition to aligning "Deer Woman" with *Cat People* and *Abbot & Costello Meet Frankenstein*, Landis also refers to his own *An American Werewolf in London* throughout, thus genealogizing "Deer Woman" alongside *American Werewolf* and, by association, *American Werewolf* alongside Landis's other illustrious horror/comedy-horror predecessors. Furthermore, Landis uses *American Werewolf* and its success and reputation to justify creative decisions made for "Deer Woman," and to validate his ambiguous, incongruous place as a Master of Horror:

I don't consider *An American Werewolf* a comedy. It is a horror film. It's pretty funny, but the humour is used really to heighten the horror. Again the approach is to be as realistic as possible, dealing with a preposterous subject. To startle someone is fun but it's not necessarily what I like to do. I'm not interested in going Boo! It takes more skill to make them care about the fate of the characters, to create genuine suspense, to create suspension of disbelief, [to] take something that's not real and to make it real. (P. Martin, "Hooves")

"Deer Woman" contains probably the most explicit instance of intertextual self-referencing in the entire *Masters of Horror* series. In a scene in which Faraday defends his absurd hunch on the murder case before his superior, he refers to brutal animal attacks in London in 1981 to back him up. Interestingly, Landis says he was reluctant to include this in-joke, saying, "You know what I didn't like? The reference to *An American Werewolf in London*. I went 'Oh that's obnoxious, we have to take it out!' and Mick Garris said 'No, that's great, people like that stuff, keep it in!' So it's in, but it was written by Max, it's in because of Mick" (P. Martin, "Hooves"). Landis reads this self-referential in-joke as "obnoxious" and displaces responsibility for it onto his producer and his son, but the moment still serves to validate Landis's "Deer Woman" through the prestige of *American Werewolf*.

While footage from and references to the Masters' previous films are used in the special features to demonstrate their subjects' mastery of the genre, works by other artists are also heavily referenced, to place the Masters' films and oeuvres within a larger pop-culture canon. We see this self-fashioning motif most obviously in Gordon's references both to Lovecraft and his own theatrical pedigree, as well as his early love of horror movies and William Castle. In the case of Landis, this is most evident in his attempts to canonize his horror work alongside the likes of *Abbot & Costello Meet Frankenstein* and *Cat People*. Landis also attempts to align his comedy work alongside the output of Hollywood comic luminaries. He considers *Spies Like Us* his variation on the Bob Hope and Bing Crosby *Road* movie formula, and *Coming to America* his variation on the Ernest Lubitsch stylized comedy formula (P. Martin, "Hooves"). The director thus continues a pattern of defining his own films in relation to critically successful, archetypal Hollywood texts, each with the dream factory's requisite dazzle and polish.[22]

Though he highlights the incongruity of his Horror Master status with his wider body of work as a comedy director, Landis nonetheless embraces this status and uses his outsider position to advance his cause. He comments that "I've made 22 pictures but most of them are not horror films, so I think it's amusing to be called a Master of Horror . . . These guys have quite a body of work of horror films and I'm flattered to be in their company" (P. Martin, "Hooves"). Landis goes on to praise some of the other season-one episodes directed by his colleagues:

> Stuart Gordon's is really one of the better Lovecraft adaptations I've ever seen. I've seen Mick's, I've seen Don's, I've seen some of John Carpenter's, and I've seen all of Dario's. They're really different. Joe Dante, he took advantage of this opportunity to do something important. I took advantage of this opportunity to do something silly. (P. Martin, "Hooves")

Landis celebrates the company he is keeping and draws attention to the diversity of material on display. However, he also draws attention to the even greater difference and distance between himself and his fellow Masters, by pointing out that he used the opportunity "to do something silly" (P. Martin, "Hooves"). This is reinforced visually in the featurette by a cut to one of the more ludicrous moments in Landis's film (P. Martin, "Hooves"). Also, while Landis praises the diversity of texts produced by his colleagues, elsewhere he asserts his own originality over the other efforts, saying he chose the Deer Woman as his monster because "I knew that a lot of the guys would be doing serial killers and maniacs" (P. Martin, "Hooves"). Thus, while Landis praises the differences between the various *Masters of Horror* episodes, he also distances his own feature from a body of episodes, which, by his account, draw from the same slasher myth pool. Landis thus fashions himself as exotic outsider from the position of privileged insider.

Through fetishizing and reinforcing this status as exotic outsider, Landis sets up a certain critical distance between himself and the horror genre. This position permits Landis to be a Master of Horror while also giving him license to critique the genre from the outside, as a Master of non-Horror unwilling to regurgitate serial killer and maniac clichés. Ironically, the domain of serial killers is the very territory which Landis himself visits in his season-two *Masters* episode, "Family" (2006).

One convention which Landis does critique through "Deer Woman" is the inherent misogyny of the genre. Landis expresses particular satisfaction with a scene in "Deer Woman" where an American Indian tells Faraday the myth of the Deer Woman, only to then dismiss it as a misogynistic legend (P. Martin, "Hooves"). Landis's film thus draws from horror movie conventions in which the monster is gendered feminine—films that equate women and power with monstrosity—while simultaneously deconstructing the misogyny of not only these films but of the genre in general. Landis's approach, though perhaps slighter than my analysis has given it credit for, proves an interesting counterpoint to Gordon, who uses a witch, another monstrous female, as the villain of his episode with little critical or ironic commentary on the matter.

One of the more interesting self-fashioning gestures performed by Landis in the making of the episode was the hiring of his son Max as screenwriter. Landis, in addition to fashioning himself as a Master of Horror, uses the occasion to genealogize his nineteen-year-old son, in his professional scriptwriting debut, alongside the show's prolific writers. The gallery of scribes responsible for the episodes includes the likes of Dennis Paoli, Sam Hamm, and David J. Schow, while the pool of source material from which some of the episodes were adapted includes work by the likes of Lovecraft, Richard Matheson, Clive Barker, and Joe R. Lansdale.[23] Landis also appears to be fashioning his son after his own image. Most significantly, Landis wrote the original screenplay for *American Werewolf* in 1969 at the age of nineteen, while his son wrote the screenplay for "Deer Woman" at the same age. The echoes do not end there. Landis entered the industry at a relatively young age and worked as a gopher on the major studio war comedy *Kelly's Heroes* (1970).[24] Likewise, Max received his first professional industry gig (on *Masters of Horror*) while fairly young, under his father's tutelage. Just as his father's movie directing-writing debut was a monster comedy about a rampaging gorilla called *Schlock* (1973), Max's professional scriptwriting debut was a monster comedy about a killer with deer hooves. Finally, just as his first project *Schlock* was financed by a benevolent uncle, who gave the fledging director $50,000, Landis benevolently helped set up his son's first creative endeavor in the film business.

Max Landis is one of many guests who appear on "Working with a Master: John Landis" (2006) to praise Landis, alongside actors Brian Benben, Robert Loggia, Jenny Agutter, Don Rickles, and Dan Aykroyd, special-effects make-up artist Rick Baker, and horror-fantasy luminary Forest J. Ackerman. While the likes of Combs, Crampton, Foree, and Yuzna (on the Gordon featurette) possess strong horror genre credentials, only Baker, as *American Werewolf's* special-effects make-up mastermind, and Ackerman, celebrated editor of *Famous Monsters of Filmland* (1958–1983), have similarly strong genre connections on the equivalent Landis featurette. Combs and Foree practically drip iconic genre history (Foree is best known for his role in Romero's *Dawn of the Dead* [1978]), but the case is less so with the likes of Rickles and Aykroyd, so participants are forced to work harder to establish Landis's horror credentials.

Aykroyd identifies Landis as an avid reader of horror magazine *Fangoria* (1979–present), while Ackerman makes reference to Landis's love of Bela Lugosi and Boris Karloff (Woodward, "Landis"). Much is made, naturally, of *An American Werewolf in London.* The feature opens with the following tantalizing extract from Landis's original script for *American Werewolf,* dated from 1969: "The metamorphosis from man into beast is not an easy one. As bone and muscle bend and reform themselves, the body suffers lacerating pain. We can actually see David's flesh move" (Woodward, "Landis"). Much is also made of *Innocent Blood,* his work on Michael Jackson's *American Werewolf*–inspired music video for *Thriller* (1983), and his contribution to another self-fashioning anthology project, *Twilight Zone: The Movie* (1983). However, the treatment of *Twilight Zone* is somewhat selective: Aykroyd and Baker talk about the opening scare prologue featuring Aykroyd and Albert Brooks, but no mention is made of Landis's controversial story segment, which led to the accidental deaths of actor Vic Morrow and two young child actors, an incident which saw Landis tried for involuntary manslaughter.[25]

While *American Werewolf* star Agutter says, "I don't really think of him as being a horror movie director" (Woodward, "Landis"), Benben argues, though not with great conviction, that "John's made his bones in the horror genre, for sure, you know, the horror slash comedy genre. I think, you know, I think he's up there with all those guys" (Woodward, "Landis"). Ultimately, the "Working with a Master" featurette struggles to paint a convincing portrait of Landis as a horror director, though all participants sing their director's praises accordingly.

In the Gordon featurettes, footage and stills are shown from the likes of *Re-Animator*, *Dolls*, *From Beyond*, *The Pit and the Pendulum*, *Castle Freak*, *Dagon*, and even *Robot Jox*. Footage and stills on the Landis featurettes come predominantly from *Schlock*, *American Werewolf* naturally, and *Innocent Blood*. Brief snippets are shown from his more popular comedies, while in the case of lesser comedies like *Oscar* (1991), *Beverly Hills Cop 3* (1994), and *The Stupids* (1996), we see only fleeting poster art. Like *Twilight Zone: The Movie*, *Innocent Blood* occupies an awkward position in the Landis featurettes. As a horror comedy—one of only a few Landis features with horror content—it is required to flesh out and support the argument that John Landis is a Master of Horror. At the same time, its position is awkward because the film was not particularly successful.

Landis advocates for *Innocent Blood*, arguing that it was "a little too out there for people" (P. Martin, "Hooves"). The director discusses the film on "Animal Hooves" right after discussing *American Werewolf*. Referring to *American Werewolf's* horror comedy formula, he states that "I did it once more on *Innocent Blood*" (P. Martin, "Hooves"). Landis thus strategically aligns the less-successful latter film alongside the more-successful former film, in hope that some of the former's residual prestige will rub off on the latter. This echoes some of the promotional material for *Innocent Blood*, which declared, "The legendary director that brought you *National Lampoon's Animal House*, *The Blues Brothers*, *An American Werewolf in London*, *Trading Places*, and *Coming to America* brings you the dark comedy horror film from the undead" (IMDb, "Innocent Blood"). Landis's associates, however, are not particularly generous toward the film: Max Landis says the film is "not one of his most successful movies," while Don Rickles is less diplomatic, calling the film a "giant bomb" (Woodward, "Landis").[26]

Landis's feature film career degenerated over the course of the 1990s thanks to the likes of *Innocent Blood*, *Oscar*, *Beverly Hills Cop 3*, *The Stupids*, and *Blues Brothers 2000* (1998). As such, the opportunity for self-fashioning presented by *Masters of Horror* would have held considerable appeal for Landis.[27] The series also presents a valuable opportunity for Landis to step outside the realm of comedy: the director laments in his interview featurette that he has been pigeonholed as a comedy director (P. Martin, "Hooves"). In the aftermath of "Deer Woman" and his season-two episode "Family," Landis is currently attached to a project in development called *Ghoulishly Yours, William M. Gaines*, a biopic of the EC Comics publisher responsible for titles like *Tales from the Crypt* and *Vault of Horror* (both 1950–1955); this suggests that the *Masters of Horror* experience has enabled Landis to break away from the constraints of genre typecasting. Furthermore, just as Gordon's recent work harks back to an earlier phase of his career, we can elucidate similar self-fashioning intent from Landis's involvement with *Masters of Horror*. The shooting conditions for "Deer Woman" closely resembled the shooting conditions for his debut feature *Schlock*. *Schlock* was shot over the course of ten days in, according to the director, the "hottest summer in California history" (P. Martin, "Hooves"). Likewise, each *Masters of Horror* episode had a tight shooting schedule of only ten days.[28]

BULLSHIT OR DEERSHIT: INTENTIONS, TENSIONS, QUESTIONS

In an ideal world, each episode of *Masters of Horror* would attest to its director's mastery of horror, but in most cases these demonstrations of mastery are compromised. Interestingly, four issues of a *Masters of Horror* comic book series accompanied the show, capitalizing on horror fandom across both media. Horror comics are currently in vogue, and a number of companies have adapted horror movie franchises into comic book form. For example, Wildstorm, a division of DC Comics, has produced comics based on *The Texas Chainsaw Massacre*, *A Nightmare on Elm Street*, and *Friday the 13th*. Wildstorm editor Ben Abernathy insists that "in comics, we're not constrained by Hollywood concerns like budgets or locations, only by our imaginations" (Dickholtz 8).[29]

Unfortunately, the Masters of Horror themselves *are* constrained by Hollywood concerns. The legitimacy of each director's claim to the title of Master of Horror falls upon a larger body of work, which the *Masters of Horror* episodes complement. It is this body of work which the special features strive to pay tribute to, while simultaneously feeding off this work's intertextual energy. The extra-textual supplements—especially the director interviews and tribute featurettes, but also on-set cast interviews, making-of shorts, and commentaries—aid veteran directors in historicizing themselves as legitimate artists. These paratexts also allow emerging directors, as well as filmmakers on the fringe of the genre, to insert themselves within this evolving genealogy of Masters. Gordon, a noted horror director who has gone largely unrecognized in the mainstream, is formally canonized as a Master of his craft, while Landis, a filmmaker pigeonholed as a director of comedies with broad appeal, uses the project to stabilize his difficult position in the genre.

This, at least, is the idealized scenario. Unfortunately, the title of Master proves to be somewhat self-sabotaging. The DVD project attempts to address the maligning of horror in respectable critical circles, but amid this celebration of the genre there are unintentional disparaging voices, voices which undermine the thrust of the enterprise. Landis himself is one of those voices, dismissing much of the genre as the domain of "serial killers and maniacs" (P. Martin, "Hooves") even as he pursues recognition as a horror auteur. In his "Dreams in the Witch House" commentary, Gordon states, "I don't like these movies where you've got obnoxious teenagers getting slaughtered by a guy in a hockey mask" (Gordon, Godden, and Martin). Gordon's dismissive gesture does little to promote the genre, falling once again upon stereotypes. Meanwhile, Landis's leading man Brian Benben points out (in an on-set interview) that "the script had a lot of texture for a horror episode" (Altherr). This statement, while highlighting the deconstructive texture that Landis and his son bring to the episode, undermines the overall intention of the series to demonstrate the genre's inherent sophistication.[30]

The maligning of the genre and the vague criteria for canonization as a Master of Horror call into question the intended audience of the project. Are the *Masters of Horror* DVD special features aimed at engaging horror aficionados or mainstream consumers? Is the series preaching to the converted or converting the unconverted? The "Dreams in the Witch House" and "Deer Woman" extras would hold considerable appeal for fans of Gordon and Landis, who would already be familiar with the directors' career trajectories, would recognize snippets from their movies, and would recognize the likes of Combs and Crampton from these films. At the same time, these special features are partly calibrated toward audiences who are unfamiliar with their work, to educate them on these auteurs, to validate their canonization as Masters, and to help viewers of a more mainstream persuasion justify watching a horror program. However, the interiorized maligning of the genre and the loaded nature of the Master denomination invite discriminating viewers, both inside and outside horror fandom, to interrogate the Master denomination on the basis of tensions within the self-fashioning.

Landis stresses his position as exotic outsider while using the genre credibility of *American Werewolf* to canonize himself alongside more-established practitioners of the horror genre. Gordon fashions his persona by courting association with Lovecraft and emphasizing his theatrical pedigree. However, their self-fashioning is ripe with contradictory gestures, transforming the documentary/behind-the-scenes supplements into sites of tension between these conflicting impulses. Though Landis and the makers of these featurettes celebrate his displacement from the horror genre, at the same time they must nonetheless validate Landis's position as a Master of Horror. They ultimately strain in doing so, as the awkward treatment of *Innocent Blood* and half-hearted handling of *Twilight Zone: The Movie* attest. The latter in particular proves problematic: in shying away from the subject matter, neither Landis nor the makers of these featurettes project a completely honest portrait of Landis as an artist. While Gordon stresses his theatrical background, he must also maintain a distance from it to avoid shining a disparaging light upon his horror filmography. Lovecraft is used to bridge that distance, and also to validate Gordon's move from theater to film, but his association with Lovecraft likewise proves a site of contradictory impulses: Gordon reveres his Master predecessor while simultaneously attempting to exercise mastery over him, a gesture symptomatic of Harold Bloom's "anxiety of influence." Ultimately, these self-sabotaging gestures destabilize the scaffolding of the Master label.

While each director is clearly engaged in self-fashioning activity, we must question to what extent they are mastering their own personae or having it mastered for them. As indicated earlier, DVD paratexts are both autographic and allographic, and the self-fashioning gestures of the directors are subject to behind-the-scenes manipulation. In the director interviews, each director talks the audience through their careers and their passions, but this dialogue is shaped by the featurette directors, series producers, and so forth. This binary opposition—the filmmaker as both active subject of the featurette and passive subject within/to the featurette, the Master subject and the Mastered subject—does hint at a level of diplomatic subordination on these directors' parts.

The Masters of Horror participate in and benefit from this endeavor, but Mick Garris does so especially: each successfully orchestrated entry into the Master canon strengthens and secures his own self-appointed position as Master of that canon, Master of ceremonies, Master of the Masters of Horror. However, the Masters and their Master are not the only beneficiaries—creative and commercial—of *Masters of Horror*. Starz Media/IDT Entertainment benefits from the endeavor, as does Starz Media Entertainment/Anchor Bay, an imprint already well known for its horror catalog. Perry Martin and Frank H. Woodward also benefit from the enterprise: Garris himself was a film documentarian early in his career, producing making-of documentaries for the likes of Dante's *The Howling*, Carpenter's *The Fog* (1980), David Cronenberg's *Scanners* (1980), and Rick Rosenthal's *Halloween II* (1981); the *Masters of Horror* special features, thus, offer their makers the opportunity to fashion themselves after Garris.

Showtime also benefits from their involvement with the series. A *Variety* review of the series' debut proclaimed, "Although Showtime has waded into the competition to launch prestige dramas, there's something to be said for recognizing the many subscribers who still look hopefully to pay TV for good old-fashioned helpings of nudity and violence" (Lowry). This review praises Showtime for embracing and catering to the horror demographic, while—much like Landis, Gordon, and Benben—simultaneously disparaging the horror genre itself. In another *Variety* piece, Denise Martin notes that "Showtime will shell out more money than some of the B-movie auteurs are used to getting" (D. Martin). Not only is this observation inaccurate, it generalizes and perpetuates that all the participating directors, and by extension all horror directors and horror movies, are B-grade. Such comments are at odds with the network's and the producers' marketing of the show as both genre landmark and cultural event.

In 2008, *Masters of Horror* migrated from Showtime to NBC and was reinvented under the title *Fear Itself*. Garris was forced to resign from proceedings due to behind-the-scenes complications, but both Gordon and Landis remained onboard and contributed episodes, "Eater" (2008) and "In Sickness and in Health" (2008), respectively. The only other Masters to remain onboard were second-season recruits Brad Anderson, Ernest Dickerson, and Rob Schmidt. Max Landis also served as a writer on the new series. *Fear Itself* was produced by Lions Gate, a company that in recent years has garnered credibility with horror aficionados (particularly those of the younger set) through its association with the *Hostel* and *Saw* (2004) franchises. The presence of Darren Lynn Bousman—director of *Saw II* (2005), *Saw III* (2006), and *Saw IV* (2007)—as one of the show's new recruits serves to accentuate ties between Lions Gate's previous horror successes and the new series. However, the conscious decision not to overemphasize the credentials of the contributing filmmakers this time around seems to indicate an increased awareness of the critical ambivalence surrounding the Master denomination.

In an essay analyzing the Internet discussion group *Horror at Indiana: Horror in Film and Literature* (a group briefly cited earlier in this chapter), K. A. Laity discusses, among other things, the impetus of the group—an impetus that exists, I would argue, among all aficionados and scholars of the genre "toward creating an authoritative (hegemonic) view of horror works; however, this political elitism is constantly challenged by the similarly strong drive toward recognizing, even valorizing, the visceral, and decidedly non-intellectual, qualities as well [...] The variability of any 'authority' keeps the field contested" (173–74).

Masters of Horror, I would argue, is an explicit manifestation of this tension between our desire for hegemonic closure, a sealed and uncontaminated horror elite, on the one hand, and an open discourse on the other. The unstable criterion for the title of Master is frustrating, but this lack of authoritative closure is not completely negative. There are other problems surrounding the series: numerous contradictory impulses arise and circulate throughout the self-fashioning process, with each director's orchestrated identity vulnerable to the internalized "signs of its own subversion and loss" (Greenblatt 9); each episode is compromised in its demonstration of its Master's mastery; and the knee-jerk maligning of the genre is ever-present outside and interiorized within proceedings. However, these tensions ultimately contribute to a more productive discourse.

With the American horror movie mainstream currently dominated by remakes of classic American and recent Asian horror films, franchise-expanding sequels, and exercises in torture porn, the prospect of admired horror directors creating original material holds considerable appeal. However, a number of issues call into question the legitimacy of *Masters of Horror*'s Master denomination, and a number of conflicting impulses are at play in the self-fashioning of each director. These impulses materialize predominantly in the show's special features and paratexts, which are essential to the self-fashioning process, but also materialize elsewhere. However, while these self-sabotaging tensions are never completely resolved, their circulation within and across the texts is ultimately dialectical: they raise important questions about what constitutes auteurship in the horror genre—a question open to the academic, the aficionado, and the artist—and how auteurship is established through extra-textual supplements. Hopefully the *Masters of Horror* DVD project and its numerous positive incongruities will contribute to further academic consideration of the horror genre and will expand critical discourse in the field.

NOTES

1. Some brief background on the program's DVD history might be useful. The first season's episodes were originally released as individual DVDs in the United States, but have subsequently been re-released in double-feature packs, in two collected volumes each containing six episodes, and in a deluxe fourteen-disc box set in appropriately gothic mausoleum packaging. As this considerable effort on the part of Anchor Bay—now Starz Media, after IDT Entertainment (to which Anchor Bay belonged) was purchased by them in 2006—suggests, the promotion of horror movie auteurship, for which there is clearly a significant consumer market, is not without vested material interests or compensation. Second-season episodes have also been released individually and in collections in the United States, but my focus throughout this paper will be on first season releases. The Australian-release discs are used in my analyses throughout and are for the most part identical to the American discs, though there are minor variations. In the case of "Dreams in the Witch House" (2005) and "Deer Woman" (2005), the discs I will be using predominantly throughout this chapter, the stills/storyboard galleries, trailers, and DVD Rom features that accompany the American discs are not present on their Australian equivalents. As such, these particular features will not be touched upon in this chapter.

2. The Emmy citation, incidentally, is a rather creative promotional use of the accolade. The show won only one Emmy, for Ed Shearmur's opening title music.

3. Miike's controversial episode, "Imprint" (2006), was deemed too horrific to be screened on U.S. television. The episode was never aired, but has been released on DVD.

4. Actor Brian Benben, in the commentary for John Landis's "Deer Woman," jokes during the bloody opening credits that "this is where you really need a sponge" and muses that there is "more DNA there than [at] the O.J. trial"; see Brian Benben and Anthony Griffith, commentary, "Masters of Horror: Deer Woman," *Masters of Horror: Collector's Edition One* (Anchor Bay Entertainment, 2006).

5. On a side note, it is worth noting the absence of *May* (2002), *House on Haunted Hill* (1999), *Henry: Portrait of a Serial Killer* (1986), *Suspiria* (1977), and *Audition* (1999), among others, and thus the exclusion of their respective directors.

6. By extension, a number of directors who had participated in Mick Garris's original dinners, including Guillermo del Toro, Eli Roth, Tim Sullivan, and Rob Zombie, are not involved in the series.

7. Gordon is not alone in his appreciation of Castle. Three of his fellow Masters of Horror—John Landis, Joe Dante, and William Malone—appear in the documentary *Spine Tingler: The William Castle Story* (2008).

8. Gordon also cast actor Guy Rolfe as the benevolent/malevolent doll-maker in his film *Dolls* (1987). Rolfe played the villainous Baron Sardonicus in the William Castle film *Mr Sardonicus* (1964), a film Gordon talks affectionately about in the *Dolls* audio commentary.

9. Carpenter directed two of the *Body Bags* (1993) shorts, while the third is directed by Tobe Hooper, who makes a more-subdued acting appearance.

10. Shimako Iwai, author of the novel *Bokkê, kyôtê* from which Miike's "Imprint" (2006) was adapted, plays a brutal torturer in "Imprint," perhaps following in Miike's footsteps.

11. Significantly, both directors returned for the show's second season, as did Tobe Hooper, John Carpenter, Dario Argento, Joe Dante, and of course Mick Garris. On the other hand, Don Coscarelli, Larry Cohen, John McNaughton, Lucky McKee, William Malone, and Takashi Miike did not return for the second season; their places were filled by Tom Holland, Ernest Dickerson, Rob Schmidt, Brad Anderson, Peter Medak, and Norio Tsuruta. Gordon and Landis also returned for the show's reinvention under the title *Fear Itself* (2008).

12. These "Working with a Master" featurettes are typically fawning. For instance, on "Working with a Master: Stuart Gordon" (2006), Ken Foree calls Gordon "a pioneer" and "an inventor" while Barbara Crampton proclaims that Gordon "will always take chances and will always push the envelope"; Frank H. Woodward, dir., "Working with a Master: Stuart Gordon," *Masters of Horror: Collector's Edition One* (Anchor Bay Entertainment, 2006). Meanwhile, on the featurette "Working with a Master: John Landis" (2006), Landis's niche as a comedy director gives interviewees greater license to plant their tongues in their cheeks, particularly comedian Don Rickles, who jokes that "I don't know how he skyrocketed to become a director [. . .] He was a lovely guy then. Now he's changed, you know, has a few bucks and he sits in his estate and blows smoke to the mountains"; Frank H. Woodward, "Working with a Master: John Landis," *Masters of Horror: Collector's Edition One* (Anchor Bay Entertainment, 2006). At the same time, Rickles calls Landis "a very intelligent man," while Forest J. Ackerman praises the director as "a real human being" (Woodward, "Landis").

13. It is worth noting that there are some variations from disc to disc. For instance, "Dreams in the Witch House" features a special-effects segment, while the Landis episode features old footage from an episode of Z Channel's *Fantasy Film Festival* (1980). In this archival footage, the young John Landis is interviewed by the young Mick Garris. Landis and Garris discuss Landis's *National Lampoon's Animal House* (1978) and preview Landis's forthcoming *The Blues Brothers* (1980), and Landis alludes to another upcoming project, a horror comedy called *An American Werewolf in London* (1981). Similar archival interviews also appear on the discs for Garris's own "Chocolate" (2005), in which he interviews Roger Corman, and Joe Dante's "Homecoming" (2005), in which Garris interviews Dante about his recent film *Piranha* (1978). These archival interviews demonstrate the ongoing solidarity between these Masters of Horror.

14. The "audience participation quality" (Woodward, "Gordon") which Combs alludes to and the inventive staging of *The Game Show* (1968) could both be traced in part back to Gordon's appreciation of William Castle.

15. Gordon comments in both "Dreams, Darkness & Damnation" (2006) and his audio commentary that Purdy-Gordon also threatened to divorce him after seeing the finished product of "Dreams in the Witch House" on the grounds that it was too extreme; Perry Martin, dir., "Dreams, Darkness & Damnation: An Interview with Stuart Gordon," *Masters of Horror: Collector's Edition One* (Anchor Bay Entertainment, 2006).

16. During his lifetime Lovecraft's work was only published in pulp magazines, and the author died in relative obscurity. However, Lovecraft's status and respectability have risen over the course of time and he is now acknowledged as a master storyteller and a luminary of genre fiction. This reflects the driving force behind *Masters of Horror*: pulp authors (or auteurs) striving for recognition and respectability, qualities that Gordon seeks especially through his association with Lovecraft.

17. Although their ties with Lovecraft are less direct, *Castle Freak* and the proposed fourth *Re-Animator* film, *House of Re-Animator*, are also derived from the author's work.

18. Gordon's constructive use of the DVD commentary proves an interesting counterpoint to Landis, who declined to do a commentary for "Deer Woman" and who stated in a 2002 interview that "I don't like those usually" when pressed on the topic of audio commentaries; Scott Hocking, "The Wolf Man: John Landis," *Region 4*.11 (2002): 44–45. Landis has done only three commentaries, for his early films *Schlock* (1973) and *Kentucky Fried Movie* (1977) and for his documentary *Slasher* (2004). Gordon, meanwhile, has been more prolific in contributing commentaries to his films. In addition to his "Dreams in the Witch House" commentary, Gordon has provided commentaries for DVD releases of *Dolls*, *Re-Animator* (1985), *From Beyond* (1986), *Space Truckers* (1996), *Dagon* (2001), *King of the Ants* (2003), *Stuck* (2007), and season two's "The Black Cat" (2007).

19. Gordon's wife spends much of the time pointing out her Horror Master husband's own aversions to horror. She especially revels in an anecdote about how Gordon "got so woozy that he had to sit down and put his head between his knees" after their terrier nipped its paw on some glass and began bleeding (Woodward, "Gordon"). Gordon also "got queasy and wound up not being able to eat and had to go put his head between his knees" (Woodward, "Gordon") on the set of *Dolls* while having lunch with his wife as grisly make-up was applied to her. The director proved similarly averse to being with actor Jonathan Fuller in his grisly make-up on the set of *Castle Freak* (1995) (Woodward, "Gordon"). Such observations are at odds with the promotional picture's image of the director. Gordon himself, in "Dreams, Darkness & Damnation," owns up to his cowardly ways, commenting that "I'm like the biggest coward of them all. My wife is always kidding me about this. There have been times when I've had to get up and leave a horror movie in the middle" (P. Martin, "Damnation"). But Gordon comments further that "I know what scares me, so that is very helpful, I think, to scaring others" (P. Martin, "Damnation"). Gordon's own vulnerability and sensitivity to horror are thus reconceptualized by the director as a positive asset that contributes to his mastery of the genre.

20. It is worth noting that *Masters of Horror* is not the first anthology project that Landis has participated in. Landis was involved, most notoriously, with *Twilight Zone: The Movie* (1983), alongside fellow Master of Horror Joe Dante, George Miller, and Steven Spielberg. Warner Bros. intended to call the film *Steven Spielberg Presents The Twilight Zone*, which would have calibrated the self-fashioning aura of the project most heavily in Spielberg's direction; Spielberg declined the gesture, perhaps wisely for him given the aftermath of the project (*Steven Spielberg's Amazing Stories* [1985–1987], however, is a rather more explicit example of a filmmaker striving to mythologize themselves through the collaborative anthology format). For a good overview of the controversy surrounding Landis's participation in *Twilight Zone: The Movie*, see Tony Crawley, *The Steven Spielberg Story* (New York: Quill, 1983), 143–49. Another anthology project Landis participated in was *Amazon Women on the Moon* (1987), again alongside Dante and several others. Like *Masters of Horror*, the results of both projects were somewhat mixed. Stuart Gordon also expresses appreciation of the *Masters of Horror* anthology style, having been a fan of television shows like *Twilight Zone* (1959–1964) and *The Outer Limits* (1963–1965) (P. Martin, "Damnation").

21. By extension, a number of fellow Masters of Horror appear in Landis's films: Larry Cohen appears in *Spies Like Us* (1985), Joe Dante in *Oscar* (1991) and *Beverly Hills Cop 3* (1994), Dario Argento in *Innocent Blood* (1992), and Garris in *The Stupids* (1996).

22. This activity is not confined to *Masters of Horror*. Both Gordon and Landis also court association with their illustrious predecessors and contemporaries outside the *Masters of Horror* special features. Gordon, appropriately, waxes lyrical on Lovecraft's achievements in the documentary *The Eldritch Influence: The Life, Vision, and Phenomenon of H. P. Lovecraft* (2003). In addition to making appearances in films directed by fellow Masters, Landis has also waxed lyrical quite prolifically in recent times on the works of other horror and fantasy figures. Over the past few years, he has contributed to documentaries on Mario Bava, Edgar G. Ulmer, Val Lewton, Ray Harryhausen, and Forest J. Ackerman, among others. Both Gordon and Landis also make appearances in the recent documentaries *Spine Tingler: The William Castle Story* and *Dead On: The Life and Cinema of George A. Romero* (2008). Carpenter, Argento, and Garris also appear in the Romero documentary while, as mentioned earlier, Dante and Malone appear in the Castle tribute. Another recent documentary Landis participates in is even closer to home: *Beware the Moon: Remembering "An American Werewolf in London"* (2008).

23. But while the series draws on material from the likes of Lovecraft, Barker, and Matheson, this material is used in service of the directors and their self-fashioning, rather than the directors working in service of the material. While Max Landis gains recognition for his participation in the project, his work is carried out in service of his father's self-fashioning (and his father in turn does not hesitate to extend the horizons of his own authorship/auteurship by pointing out his own minor polish on the script). An obvious point of comparison here would be a recent TV series inspired by *Masters of Horror* called *Masters of Science Fiction* (2007), in which science-fiction authors—such as Harlan Ellison, Robert A. Heinlein, and Walter Mosley—are the "Masters" of the form rather than the directors adapting their work. This is not the case with *Masters of Horror*, where authorship (or, more precisely, auteurship) is reserved for the director.

24. Landis also worked as a stuntman on movie sets in Europe, including the set of *Once Upon a Time in the West* (1968), a film co-written by fellow Master of Horror Dario Argento.

25. An interesting aside: Baker mentions that originally he and Landis were to feature in the opening segment (Woodward, "Landis"). This jokey gesture would have been an interesting instance of self-fashioning on both their parts, especially for Landis in light of the notoriety the movie ultimately earned him.

26. As an indication of the film's maligned position in the Landis canon, the film currently holds a 5.2 rating on Rotten Tomatoes, a 5.8 rating on IMDB, and a C grade on Box Office Mojo. By comparison, the more popular *American Werewolf* scores 7.4, 7.4, and B, respectively, on these popular Web sites.

27. In addition to seeking auteur recognition for himself in the horror genre, Landis may well be seeking wider recognition for directors in general across all genres. In the *Fantasy Film Festival: Mick Garris Interviews John Landis* (1980) segment, Landis complains: "It's an odd thing with the critics. I don't think they know what they're talking about most of the time . . . A case in point is a movie now out called *Coal Miner's Daughter*, which is directed by a friend named Michael Apted. It's a wonderful movie, it really is, and all the reviews praise Sissy Spacek's performance & Tommy Lee Jones, rightfully so because they're wonderful, and very few of them say anything about Michael"; Steven A. Wacker, "Fantasy Film Festival: Mick Garris Interviews John Landis," *Masters of Horror: Collector's Edition One* (Z Channel, 1980).

28. Having said that, Landis—after working on big-budget Hollywood popcorn movies for so long—is unable to do justice to the tight budget and short shoot, especially compared to some

of the other directors (Gordon, Takashi Miike, and Don Coscarelli, for example) more recently accustomed to low-tech filmmaking. It is worth noting that Gordon's and Landis's conscious returns to former artistic territory are by no means isolated. For example, Tobe Hooper is currently in pre-production on *From a Buick 8*, which will be Hooper's third adaptation of a Stephen King text: his previous King adaptations are *Salem's Lot* (1979) and *The Mangler* (1995). The project is being produced by Mick Garris, who is also directing an adaptation of King's *Bag of Bones*; in an artistic flirtation reminiscent of Gordon and Lovecraft, Garris has courted association with King through *Sleepwalkers* (1992), *The Stand* (1994), *The Shining* (1997), *Quicksilver Highway* (1997), *Riding the Bullet* (2004), and *Desperation* (2006). Meanwhile, one of Dario Argento's recent films, *La Terza Madre* (2007, aka *Mother of Tears*), completes the director's Three Mothers trilogy that began with *Suspiria* (1977) and continued with *Inferno* (1980), and Argento's next film, *Giallo* (2009), takes the director back to his giallo roots. These are just three instances of horror directors actively fashioning, or re-fashioning, their personae by reengaging with earlier material.

29. The *Masters of Horror* comic series adapted Gordon's episode into comic book form, as well as Coscarelli's episode "Incident On and Off a Mountain Road" (2005). The *Masters* comics are on the whole lacking in texture, and Wildstorm's subsequent cancellation of their aforementioned monthly horror titles suggests that the medium, though not constrained in terms of imagination, cannot capture the fundamentally cinematic quality of Leatherface & Co's adventures.

30. Showtime's decision not to screen Takashi Miike's "Imprint" also damages the veneer of the show. While on the one hand it highlights the extreme content of Miike's episode and validates his status as a Master (and valorizes him over his American colleagues, whose episodes were not too extreme for broadcast), the gesture is also an emasculating one: Miike is emasculated of his Master status by having his episode banned from broadcast.

WORKS CITED

Allen, Graham. *Intertextuality*. London: Routledge, 2000.
Altherr, Bo, dir. "On set with Brian Benben." *Masters of Horror: Collector's Edition One*. Anchor Bay Entertainment. 2006. DVD. Madman, 2006.
Benben, Brian, and Anthony Griffith, commentary. "Masters of Horror: Deer Woman." *Masters of Horror: Collector's Edition One*. Anchor Bay Entertainment. 2006. DVD. Madman, 2006.
Butane, Johnny. "Lionsgate Behind Masters 3!" *Dread Central*, August 12, 2007. http://www .dreadcentral.com/index.php?name=News&file=article&sid=2836 (accessed September 23, 2007).
Crawley, Tony. *The Steven Spielberg Story*. New York: Quill, 1983.
Dickholtz, Daniel. "Wildstorm Slasher Comics: Freddy, Jason and Leatherface's New-est Line." *Fangoria* 258 (November 2006): 8.
Gingold, Michael. "*Fear Itself* episode/talent line-up announced." *Fangoria.com*, March 4, 2008. http://www.fangoria.com/news _article.php?id=6053 (accessed March 6, 2008).
Gordon, Stuart, dir. "Masters of Horror: Dreams in the Witch House." *Masters of Horror: Collector's Edition One*. IDT Entertainment. 2005. DVD. Madman, 2006.
———, Ezra Godden, and Perry Martin, commentary. "Masters of Horror: Dreams in the Witch House." *Masters of Horror: Collector's Edition One*. Anchor Bay Entertainment. 2006. DVD. Madman, 2006.

Greenblatt, Stephen. *Renaissance Self-Fashioning: From More to Shakespeare*. Chicago: University of Chicago Press, 1980.

Hocking, Scott. "The Wolf Man: John Landis." *Region* 4.11 (2002): 44–45.

"Innocent Blood (1992)." *IMDb: The Internet Movie Database*, September 23, 2007. http://www .imdb.com/title/tt0104511.

Laity, K. A. "From SBIGs to Mildred's Inverse Law of Trailers: Skewing the Narrative of Horror Fan Consumption." *Horror Film: Creating and Marketing Fear*. Ed. Steffen Hantke. Jackson: University Press of Mississippi, 2004. 173–90.

Landis, John, dir. "Masters of Horror: Deer Woman." *Masters of Horror: Collector's Edition One.* IDT Entertainment. 2005. DVD. Madman, 2006.

Lowry, Brian. "Masters of Horror." *Variety*, October 25, 2005. http://www.variety.com/ awardcentral_review/VE1117928675.html?nav= reviews (accessed September 23, 2007).

Martin, Denise. "Very scary prospect: Showtime nabs helmers for horror anthology." *Variety*, March 30, 2005. http://www.variety.com/article/VR1117920261.html?categoryid=1236&cs=1 &query=%22masters+of+horror%22+%22denise+martin%22 (accessed September 23, 2007).

Martin, Perry, dir. "Animal Hooves: An Interview with John Landis." *Masters of Horror: Collector's Edition One*. Anchor Bay Entertainment. 2006. DVD. Madman, 2006.

———, dir. "Dreams, Darkness, & Damnation: An Interview with Stuart Gordon." *Masters of Horror: Collector's Edition One*. Anchor Bay Entertainment. 2006. DVD. Madman, 2006.

"Masters of Horror on Showtime." *Showtime*, September 23, 2007. http://www.sho.com/site/ mastersofhorror/home.do (accessed September 23, 2007).

Oneda, Hidetoshi, dir. "Imprinting: The Making of Imprint." *Masters of Horror: Imprint*. Anchor Bay Entertainment. 2006. DVD. Madman, 2007.

"Season 1: Dreams in the Witch House." *Masters of Horror.net*, September 23, 2007. http://www .mastersofhorror.net/ (accessed September 23, 2007). Path: Season 1; Dreams in the Witch House.

Simpson, Philip L. "The Horror 'Event' Movie: *The Mummy, Hannibal,* and *Signs*." *Horror Film: Creating and Marketing Fear*. Ed. Steffen Hantke. Jackson: University Press of Mississippi, 2004. 85–98.

Swindoll, Jeff. "Various: MOH, EC Comics, etc." Online posting, March 30, 2007. *Horror at Indiana: Horror in Film and Literature*. https://listserv.indiana.edu/cgibin/waiub.exe?A2=ind 0703&L=horror&T=0&F=&S=&P=15751 (accessed September 23, 2007).

Timpone, Tony. "Mick Garris exits *Fear Itself*; episode details." *Fangoria.com*, January 16, 2008. http://www.fangoria.com/news_article. php?id=5936 (accessed March 6, 2008).

Wacker, Steven A., dir. "Fantasy Film Festival: Mick Garris Interviews John Landis." *Masters of Horror: Collector's Edition One*. Z Channel. 1980. DVD. Madman, 2006.

Wilson, Staci Layne. "Masters of Horror Text Interviews." *Horror.com*, July 14, 2005. http://www .horror.com/php/article-870-1.html (accessed September 23, 2007).

Woodward, Frank H., dir. "Working with a Master: John Landis." *Masters of Horror: Collector's Edition One*. Anchor Bay Entertainment. 2006. DVD. Madman, 2006.

———, dir. "Working with a Master: Stuart Gordon." *Masters of Horror: Collector's Edition One*. Anchor Bay Entertainment. 2006. DVD. Madman, 2006.Yourse, Robyn-Denise. "Oh, the Horror." *Washington Times*, October 27, 2006. http://washingtontimes.com/ entertainment/20061026-090540-5286r.htm (accessed September 23, 2007).

"THE KIDS OF TODAY SHOULD DEFEND THEMSELVES AGAINST THE '70S"

Simulating Auras and Marketing Nostalgia in Robert Rodriguez and Quentin Tarantino's *Grindhouse*

—Jay McRoy

ILLUSORY "AURAS" AND THE "GRINDHOUSE EXPERIENCE"

In his 1936 essay, "The Work of Art in the Age of Mechanical Reproduction," Walter Benjamin posits cinema as a nexus of scientific, aesthetic, economic, and political practices that effectively sublimate bourgeois conceptualizations of a work's "aura" to a process of simulation that ultimately "emancipates the work of art from its parasitical dependence on ritual" and "authenticity" (224). This formulation, however, meets its postmodern inversion in one of contemporary U.S. horror cinema's more conspicuous trends—the application of digital technology as a means of reconstructing an idealized, historically specific viewing experience marked, visually, by the material conditions of distressed celluloid and, audibly, by the pop and hiss indicative of damaged analogue soundtracks. An increasingly popular conceit, as evidenced in the films of directors such as Rob Zombie and Alexandre Aja, this digital manipulation places their films into a critical, nostalgic, and meta-cinematic dialogue with low-budget U.S. horror and exploitation films of the 1970s, revealing a desire to recapture, albeit in the most superficial and paradoxical ways, attributes connected with antiquated modes of cinematic exhibition and reception.[1] Consequently, in its fetishization of an imaginary "authenticity," contemporary U.S. horror cinema's affinity for imitating and/or reimagining the "look" and "feel" of an increasingly obsolete viewing experience conjures up the ghost of Benjamin's already immaterial "aura," complete with the ritualistic, authoritative, and hierarchical structures that allegedly vanished with the emergence of art's technological reproducibility.

Of these recent exercises in cinematic nostalgia, Robert Rodriguez's and Quentin Tarantino's *Grindhouse* (2007) emerges as perhaps the most metacinematic and overtly aestheticized. Supplemented by a compilation of bogus satirical trailers directed by Rodriguez, Eli Roth, Edgar Wright, and Rob Zombie, the majority of *Grindhouse* is comprised of two truncated features: Robert Rodriguez's archetypal zombie splatterfest, *Planet Terror*, and Quentin Tarantino's meta-cinematic paean to B-movie muscle car flicks and low-budget proto-slasher films, *Death Proof.* Together, Rodriguez and Tarantino endeavor to reproduce an increasingly obsolete viewing experience for contemporary cineplex audiences. Specifically, their ambitious collaboration aims to replicate the historically, technologically, and geographically specific "feel" of viewing exploitation films, often in the form of damaged or incomplete prints, within a spatially and temporally specific locale, namely the derelict, often financially imperiled, urban theaters that "flourished" in the 1960s and 1970s before slowly vanishing from the North American landscape with the emergence and proliferation of video cassettes and cable television channels. Far too impoverished to compete with the emergence of multiplexes boasting numerous large screens, increasingly sophisticated sound systems, and the support of major studios, these smaller, often independently owned movie theaters booked such marginalized fare as European art films, soft-core erotica, Italian cannibal films, spaghetti westerns, Asian martial arts extravaganzas, and sloppily constructed genre pictures ranging from biker films and blaxploitation features to splatter films and "Women in Prison" movies. In other words, out of sheer economic necessity, grindhouse theaters screened works that their wealthier, corporate-managed competitors would never consider booking out of a fear of offending a substantial percentage of the middle-class market share they quickly came to dominate. As Jane Mills notes, grindhouse cinema offered: "pure exploitation joy [. . .] Kung Fu, Sex, Revenge, Murder, Blood Gorged Frames, Fast Cars, Fast Women, and a pumping pulsing soundtrack that makes your dick or nipples hard" (para. 26). Consequently, these decaying urban theaters catered to audiences hungry for films created, in the words of Ephraim Katz, "with little or no attention to quality or artistic merit, but with an eye to a quick profit, usually via high-pressure sales and promotion techniques emphasizing some sensational aspect of the product" (446). Additionally, due to the economic constraints governing their operation, these inner-city venues, like the prints they screened, evidenced varying degrees of disrepair. Indeed, the venues' shabby confines contributed to the overall viewing experience, attracting eclectic audiences of die-hard cinephiles looking for "edgier" films with controversial or sensationalistic subject matter.

By their own admission, Robert Rodriguez and Quentin Tarantino are filmmakers very much inspired by their own grindhouse experiences. Works like *El Mariachi* (1992), *Desperado* (1995), *From Dusk Till Dawn* (1996), and *Once Upon a Time in Mexico* (2003) illustrate the influence of spaghetti westerns and gore-soaked horror flicks on Robert Rodriguez's highly stylized vision. Similarly, Quentin Tarantino's cinematic output wears its grindhouse trappings on its metaphorical sleeve; 1992's *Reservoir Dogs*, for instance, owes a pronounced debt to Ringo Lam's violent crime drama, *City on Fire* (*Long hu feng yun*, 1987), while the aesthetics of 1970s blaxploitation films inform both *Pulp Fiction* (1994) and *Jackie Brown* (1997). Famously, the two features Tarantino directed immediately prior to his contribution to *Grindhouse*, *Kill Bill: Vol. 1* (2003) and *Kill Bill: Vol. 2* (2004), provide a veritable checklist of stylistic and narratological trappings common to exploitation genres, from the choreographed mayhem of the *chambara eiga*, or samurai film, to the ultra-violence of gritty rape-revenge sagas.

Illustrative of the impact of exploitation films upon Robert Rodriguez's and Quentin Tarantino's creative sensibilities, *Grindhouse* marks one of the more remarkable, as well as one of the more paradoxical genre experiments in recent years. As contemporary filmmakers working within the Hollywood system, their gestures toward reproducing the "grindhouse experience" certainly seems suspect, especially if one understands the "grindhouse experience" as dependent upon both the spatial and temporal specificity of the film's exhibition *and* the physical materiality of distressed celluloid. Furthermore, if, as Walter Benjamin claims, the "criterion of authenticity ceases to be applicable to artistic production" in the age of its mechanical reproducibility, then Rodriguez and Tarantino's attempt to simulate the "aura" of grindhouse cinema is a futile project from the very start. In the paragraphs to follow, this chapter examines *Grindouse* as a text that deploys cutting-edge digital technologies to (re)produce a viewing experience with which only a fraction of the film's vast audience can directly relate. Using *Death Proof*, Quentin Tarantino's contribution to *Grindhouse*, as a case study, I will posit that structural (i.e., visual, aural, narratological) logics informing Rodriguez's and Tarantino's mammoth cinematic venture exist to *produce* rather than *stimulate* nostalgia. Lastly, through a close reading to two of *Death Proof*'s most violent sequences, this study interrogates whether the film's carnage functions as merely a fetishistic celebration of violence for violence's sake, or whether a potentially progressive social critique can be pried from the gruesome marriages of flesh and steel.

"TAKE A PICTURE, IT LASTS LONGER": (IN)AUTHENTICITY IN THE AGE OF MECHANICAL REPRODUCTION

Mechanical reproducibility did not commence with the advent of photography. Long before the potential to create an infinite number of prints from a single negative rendered claims to a celluloid-based image's "authenticity" moot, moulds and

printing presses had already jeopardized the "uniqueness" of *objets d'art*, from ceram-
ics to books and printed illustrations. Nevertheless, as Walter Benjamin deftly illustrates in his groundbreaking essay on "The Work of Art in the Age of Mechanical
Reproduction," photography and its inevitable spawn, the cinema, provided new
and increasingly popular avenues by which artists could engage creatively with
their world without being permanently "imbedded" within a "fabric of tradition"
or dependent upon a "presence" made manifest by the confluence, during a specific
time and within a given space, of the singular spectator and the unique work of art.
In this sense, viewing a photograph or watching a film differs from visiting an art
gallery or attending a play. "In the theater," Benjamin claims, "one is well aware of
the place from which the play cannot immediately be detected as illusory. There is
no such place for the movie scene that is being shot" (232). In other words, like a
painting that evokes reverence or awe as a result of its "authenticity" (its existence
as a valued/invaluable one-of-a-kind cultural artifact), the performance by an actor
before her audience is unique; it cannot be performed in exactly the same way twice.
As an art form largely contingent upon its mechanical reproducibility, cinema further dissipates the concept of the aura through the process of editing and its impact
upon the spectator's understanding of the *mise-en-scène*. Since its "illusory nature" is
"of the second degree, the result of cutting" (232), the film actor's performance differs significantly from that of the stage actor. Mediated by the camera and variably
manipulated during post-production, the film actor's performance—and, hence, her
impact upon her audience—diverges from that of the stage actor in that spectator
"need not respect the performance as an integral whole. Guided by the cameraman,
the camera continually changes its position with respect to the performance" (228).
For Benjamin, film's eradication of the "aura" constitutes a crucial transformative
moment in the history of art and visual representation. Motion pictures do not
share painting's ritualistic value—the notion that one must go to a specific museum
to view a certain painting from an individual's private collection. Films, by contrast,
are created to be reproduced.[2]

In their attempt to replicate the "grindhouse experience," Rodriguez and Tarantino effect a curious reversal of Benjamin's withering aura in the age of art's mechanical reproducibility. More specifically, they deploy several key strategies to evoke the
"tone" and "feel" of grindhouse cinema. They mimic the narrative conceits of easily
recognizable exploitation film genres. In the case of *Planet Terror*, Rodriguez creates a zombie/splatter film in the tradition of George Romero's *Dead* franchise and
Lucio Fulci's *Zombie* (1979), complete with clever in-jokes and intertextual references aimed at viewers "in the know." Similarly, Quentin Tarantino's *Death Proof*
evidences an avid cineaste's knowledge of the cult genres he skillfully intertwines—
most notably the high-octane car chase / "crash 'em up" film (e.g., Peter Yates's *Bullit*
[1968], *Dirty Mary Crazy Larry* [1974], and Paul Bartel's *Death Race 2000* [1975]),

and the ubiquitous splatter film/ultra-violent rape-revenge narrative (e.g., Meir Zarchi's *I Spit On Your Grave* [1978] and Abel Ferrara's *Ms .45* [1981]). Furthermore, through strategic technological manipulation of their films' footage during post-production, a process facilitated by simple special-effects tools available in most high-end digital editing suites, Rodriguez and Tarantino (as well as the directors of *Grindhouse's faux* trailers) simulate the material conditions of distressed celluloid. Thus, in addition to removing random frames and excising passages of their short features to suggest the inadvertent absence of crucial film reels, Rodriguez and Tarantino adorn their work's *mise-en-scène* with intentional scratches and splices, overexposures, and the random insertion of similarly damaged stock footage. Even the film's digital soundtrack is meticulously mixed so that artificial pops, crackles, hisses, and awkward voice-overs imitate the sound of a poor analogue recording. Rodriguez and Tarantino mobilize these computer-generated embellishments to create the illusion of "authenticity," the impression that what appears on screen approximates the "look" and, perhaps more problematically, the "feel" of attending a grindhouse theater.

It is precisely through these specific optical and auditory illusions that Rodriguez and Tarantino conjure up the ghost of Benjamin's already immaterial "aura," complete with the ritualistic and authoritative structures that allegedly vanished with the emergence of art's technological reproducibility. By directly linking their film's aesthetic with the experience of watching damaged motion pictures within North American grindhouse theaters, Rodriguez and Tarantino invest their work with the task of reproducing a sensation remarkably similar to the "aura" Benjamin links with the cult/ritualistic practice of viewing a socially valued work of art within a museum. Of course, Benjamin could never have anticipated a film like *Grindhouse*, although he almost certainly would have viewed the rampant application of digital technologies as bringing his "expectations of cinema [...] to fruition," especially given the ease with which digital technologies lend themselves to an aesthetics of "variability, manipulability [sic], dispersion, excess and hybridity" that ultimately imperils notions of "authenticity" and, quite possibly, "auteurity' (Daly, para. 1–3).[3] Rodriguez's and Tarantino's invocation of a grindhouse "aura," then, is one fraught with ironic inversions and irreconcilable paradoxes. By attempting to evoke the particularities of a temporally and spatially specific mode of "viewing" through the application of digital technology, *Grindhouse* gestures toward reestablishing the very "parasitical dependence on ritual" from which Benjamin suggested that motion pictures were freed. In other words, through the deliberate application of digital effects, Rodriguez and Tarantino fashion a self-reflective exercise in postmodern nostalgia that alludes to an always already illusory "authenticity." In the process, they ironically invest a carefully orchestrated and executed "state-of-the-art" multiplex event—like *Grindhouse's* creation, distribution, and exhibition—with a pretense toward a simulated "authenticity" that speaks volumes about the "state of the arts" in contemporary culture.

Furthermore, while Robert Rodriguez and Quentin Tarantino may imagine themselves as directors working within the "grindhouse tradition," such a stance is far from tenable. Rodriguez and Tarantino are, after all, A-list Hollywood directors with budgets that dwarf those granted to the directors of the very exploitation films from which they draw much of their inspiration. As Maximilian Le Cain remarks in his essay, "Tarantino and the Vengeful Ghosts of the Cinema":

> Tarantino might freely use such expressions as "grindhouse" in de-scribing his work, but he does so from within the safety of the mainstream, never expos-ing himself to the real dangers and messy pleasures of the B-film. His take on genre since *Pulp Fiction* is more like a theme park ride version of "grindhouse" than the real item, a place where actors can flirt with carefully packaged disreputability and come away looking and feeling hip while actually risking nothing. After all, how can a B-movie shoulder the responsibility of being a major pop-culture event, which is what is demanded of poor Tarantino every time out? (para. 9)

Despite the visual and auditory markers linking *Grindhouse*'s content with several popular exploitation film genres, the economics informing the *Grindhouse*'s production and distribution necessarily condition the way spectators receive and understand the film. While the affection Rodriguez and Tarantino feel for exploi-tation cinema is palpable in virtually every one of *Grindhouse*'s seemingly rickety frames, their film ultimately straddles the line between the aesthetics of the "small" yet "ferocious" works that it glosses and the ramifications of *Grindhouse*'s status as "a bloated self-important 'event'" (para. 9). What's more, their self-professed "film geek" posturing locates *Grindhouse* as, paradoxically, a big-budget exploitation film *about* low-budget exploitation films that deploys high-end digital technologies to (re)cre-ate a low-tech analogue experience to which only a fraction of their audience may be able to relate first-hand.[4]

This, however, is not to suggest that *Grindhouse* is incapable of impacting audi-ences in a visceral manner akin to that of the grittiest exploitation fare. Indeed, in its depictions of extreme graphic violence, *Death Proof*, Quentin Tarantino's contribu-tion to *Grindhouse*, functions as a particularly "magnificent and perilous weapon" (Buñuel 47) that may be wielded for the purposes of cultural critique. Thus, *Grindhouse* simultaneously challenges its viewers to consider the social and politi-cal ramifications of the very acts of corporeal trauma they so readily (and eagerly) consume.

"I'M AFRAID YOU'RE GOING TO HAVE TO START GETTING SCARED IMMEDIATELY": EXPLOITING/EXPLODING VIOLENCE IN *DEATH PROOF*

Death Proof, Quentin Tarantino's primary contribution to *Grindhouse*, is divided into two "parts," each focusing upon a group of beautiful women whose lives are permanently altered when they encounter, and are subsequently stalked by, a psychopathic daredevil named Stuntman Mike. In the first "part," an Austin, Texas, radio personality named Jungle Julia gathers her friends Shanna and Arlene for a night out at a local bar. While drinking with a group of randy men, they meet a "dirty hippy" named Pam, who, desperate for a lift home, agrees to ride in the make-shift passenger seat of the mysterious Stuntman Mike's allegedly indestructible/"death proof" racing car, a battered black vehicle with a menacing white skull painted on the hood. Pam's decision proves fatal, as Stuntman Mike sadistically careens his car down the dark Texas roadways before plowing head-on into the car carrying Jungle Julia, Shanna, and Arlene, killing them on contact. Only Stuntman Mike survives. Then, following a short but fruitless inquest by the town sheriff, the film's "second part" begins, set, as we learn from a title card, some fourteen months later in Lebanon, Tennessee. This time we follow the actions of a group of thrill-seeking actresses/stuntwomen—Lee, Abernathy, Kim, and Zoë, the latter of whom nearly meets her demise when, while fulfilling a personal fantasy by riding on the hood of a speeding 1970 Dodge Challenger, she is almost turned into human road kill by a marauding Stuntman Mike in a "death proof" 1969 Dodge Charger. The psychopathic daredevil soon learns that he has selected the wrong target for his bloodlust. The Charger's occupants prove to be every bit as violent as Stuntman Mike, ultimately destroying his "death proof" car and reducing him to a begging, bleeding pulp on the side of the road.

Graphic violence has been a staple of Quentin Tarantino's cinema since his debut feature, *Reservoir Dogs* (1992). Even the scripts Tarantino penned before establishing himself as a bankable commodity in Hollywood contain scenarios brimming with brutality; *True Romance* (1993), directed by Tony Scott, culminates with an epic shoot-out inspired by John Woo's spectacular Hong Kong "bullet ballets." Similarly, *Natural Born Killers* (1994), albeit substantially reimagined by writer David Veloz and director Oliver Stone, garnered notoriety for its profoundly violent premise. Like the pair of *Kill Bill* films he directed prior to his contribution to *Grindhouse*, *Death Proof* can be understood as an extensive homage to the numerous exploitation genres that have long informed his own cinematic output. However, to limit our comprehension of Tarantino's intentions to a simple exercise in imitation or rib-nudging pastiche would be to ignore that beneath the carnage and gore bracketed by his trademark logorrheic sparring exists a markedly, if only ultimately partially effective, critical intertextual dialogue. If the satirical trailers and abbreviated features that comprise the vast majority of *Grindhouse's* 190-minute running time offer audiences a veritable carnival of gore and mayhem, then might not the final roadside attraction that brings the film to a close offer, if not an outright corrective, then—at the very least—a frozen moment (via freeze frame no less) during which we might be asked to contemplate the ramifications of our own voyeuristic complicity.

To analyze more effectively the meta-cinematic critique Tarantino's narrative poses, it is first necessary to consider how violence is apportioned throughout *Death Proof's* diegesis. In *The Delights of Terror: An Aesthetics of the Tale of Terror*, Terry Heller claims the human perception of art differs according to how thoroughly one acknowledges the work of art as a representation of what we imagine to be a potentially "real" person, location, or object. In works of horror, Heller proposes, this distance is crucial. Building off of Edward Bullough's formulation of the principle of aesthetic distance, Heller notes that it "seems to be in the nature of the tale of terror to threaten aesthetic distance" (8). For a work of cinematic or literary horror to succeed in terrifying those who encounter it, the spectator must find herself vacillating between an acknowledgment of the action's literal plausibility and its implausibility, between the work's evocation of the "real" world and the spectator's acknowledgment of the text's artificiality. Successful horror films, in other words, threaten— if only momentarily—the buffer zones spectators erect between the possible and the impossible. Consequently, for Heller, the most effective tales of terror collapse aesthetic distance, causing the utmost decrease in aesthetic distance without its disappearance.

In *Death Proof*, Tarantino foregrounds this spectatorial process in several important ways. In its collision of two popular exploitation film genres—namely, the race-car and stalker film—*Death Proof* trumpets its grindhouse lineage while also tapping into contemporary "media-fashioned fad(s)" like "road rage" (Brottman xv). Moreover, in his occupation as a professional daredevil, Stuntman Mike provides a telling commentary on that "most symbolic construction of capitalism" (Brottman and Sharrett 207), the quasi-aristocratic formulation known as celebrity or, as Benjamin would articulate it, "the cult of the movie star" (231). By adopting his profession as a part of his name, Stuntman Mike obliterates the distinction between *who he is* and *what he does*. His identity *is* his social function within the late capitalist marketplace, thus rendering him as fully reified within a culture of consumption and exploitation. That no one he meets has ever heard of the stars, films, or television programs for whom he has provided his services as a stunt double further elucidates not only the creation of an artificial nostalgia upon which *Grindhouse* is predicated, but also evidences the collapse of human identity with use value. This phenomenon is further illustrated by the names that the film's characters use to mock Stuntman Mike's appearance (e.g., "BJ [sans 'The Bear'], "Stroker Ace," and, perhaps most appropriately, "Icy Hot"—the name of the muscle ointment advertised on the back of his jacket).

This deliberate construction of nostalgia in Quentin Tarantino's *Death Proof* is not just apparent through the digital manipulation of sound and image to (re)create a historically and geographically specific viewing experience, but also manifests itself during sequences in which Tarantino deploys strategic anachronisms to position the film's action within a temporally ambiguous "present." Whereas minuscule cell phones, references to contemporary alcoholic beverages, and a conspicuous litany of contemporary pop-culture references seemingly ground the narrative's action as transpiring during the late twentieth to early twenty-first century, jukeboxes filled with vinyl 45s and parking lots packed with thirty-year-old sports cars and sedans confound these temporal markers. Deliberate anachronisms have long been a hallmark of postmodern literature and film, and it is an aesthetic device Tarantino has frequently used. This collapse of space and time is likewise a cinematic maneuver about which much has been written in recent years. In her essay, "Cinema and the Postmodern Condition," for example, Anne Friedberg writes that "the disappearance of a sense of history, entrapment in a perpetual present," and the eradication of stable "temporal referents" (61) permeates the contemporary cinematic landscape. Thinking along similar lines, the cultural theorist David Harvey posits this aesthetic and narratological practice as indicative of larger paradigmatic shifts in a historical moment increasingly dominated by fluid economies: "The experience of time-space compression in recent years, under the pressures of the turn to more flexible modes of accumulation, has generated a crisis of representation in cultural forms, and [...] this is a subject of intense aesthetic concern, either *in toto* [...] or in part" (322).

While *Death Proof*'s temporal compression both reflects larger sociocultural logics *and* constitutes a nostalgic acknowledgment of Tarantino's stylistic forebears, its conflation of historical markers allows for the creation of "new ways of thinking and feeling" (322). This freedom from absolute temporal specificity permits Tarantino to explore the politics of filmic violence within the context of exploitation film genres and, more expansively, cinema itself. In this sense, the scenes of graphic violence that provide grisly climaxes to each of the film's "parts" emerge as indicative of Tarantino's complex critique of the aesthetics and implications of film violence.

The depiction of the spectacular head-on collision that brings the primary narrative drive of *Death Proof*'s first half to a crashing halt hinges upon a combination of sophisticated special effects and complex editing that paradoxically renders the events at once realistic, engaging the audience's sensibilities in a gut-wrenchingly visceral level, and blatantly artificial in that the entire episode is obviously rendered via access to technologies far in excess of anything available to exploitation filmmakers of the 1970s and 1980s. In addition, the entire event is telegraphed by Stuntman

Mike's direct address to the camera; his impish smile and knowing, conspiratorial wink not only leads the film's viewers to acknowledge their complicity *as willing spectators*, but also signals a crucial shift in form and tone. As if on Stuntman Mike's cue, *Death Proof* veers sharply from scenes of playful verbal sparring and clichéd innuendo to the gruesome genre-specific tropes the audience has been waiting to see since *Death Proof's* opening frames. To borrow the discourse of pornography, a body genre that, like horror cinema, builds steadily, and conspicuously, toward a predictable, and often overtly spectacular, "climax," Stuntman Mike's wink marks the moment in which *Death Proof's* initial foreplay shifts toward the violent collisions— the "big bang," so to speak—that viewers came to see in the first place. In this sense, Tarantino fetishizes the violent high-speed crash that forms the film's literal and figurative centerpiece, locating the catastrophic action to follow as blatant artifice orchestrated for our consumption.

As well as purposefully delaying this moment of visual gratification, Tarantino depicts this graphic high-speed vehicular homicide—a mass murder seemingly motivated, at least in part, by masculinist aggression evoked in response to emasculating discourse ("I'm not going to fuck him," Pam [the "dirty hippy"] informs Jungle Julia, Shanna, and Arlene. "He's old enough to be my father")—from five different angles and through the lenses of cameras located within and outside of the crashing cars. Consequently, the carnage gestures toward a kind of realism, in that spectators witness each girl's death in graphic slow motion (a leg, propped up on the passenger door's open window is brutally amputated; a spinning tire smashes through the windshield of the girls' car before rolling over a rear passenger's face), while maintaining the status of an obviously staged occurrence. By portraying this horrific event in an obviously "self-conscious and anti-illusionistic" manner, Tarantino "destroys the effect—via effects" and positions *Death Proof* as a "specifically filmic" work of art (Arnzen 180). Thus, the sequence dislocates its viewers from the spectacle's immediacy and veracity, providing a critical distance that forces the spectator to reevaluate her reaction to the events transpiring on the screen.

Likewise, the violent encounter that brings *Death Proof* to an abrupt close further complicates this critical relationship between the spectator and the action she views. In keeping with horror film conventions, in which the homicidal stalker is finally vanquished (barring a sequel, of course) by the film's resourceful—usually female—lead, Stuntman Mike meets his match in the form of a trio of daring stuntwomen. Here, too, the encounter is charged with language that pits Stuntman Mike's conspicuous misogyny against the female daredevils' stereotypically masculine and emasculating patois. For example, Kim, while ramming Stuntman Mike's battered, slowly disintegrating "death proof" race car off of the road, refers to her aggressive driving as "bust[ing] a nut up in this bitch" and "tapping [Stuntman Mike's] ass." Similarly, as the psychopathic-stunt-driver-suddenly-turned-defenseless-pedestrian begs for mercy on the side of the road, Kim savagely wrenches his obviously broken arm, exacerbating an injury that operates as a visual signifier of the stuntman's metaphorical impotence. As connoisseurs of exploitation films conforming to the slasher and rape-revenge genres well know, such reversals of power are well-worn conventions. Furthermore, as revenge is a recurring trope in Tarantino's oeuvre, from *Reservoir Dogs*' double-crossed thieves to *Kill Bill*'s vengeful bride, it is not surprising that his tribute to grindhouse cinema conforms to this formula. By depicting the stuntwomen's violence as every bit as sadistic and gratuitous as the assault advanced by their stalker turned prey, Tarantino ultimately lends *Death Proof* a more expansive critical and meta-cinematic dimension.

After the stuntwomen drag Stuntman Mike from his car, battering him into submission beneath a relentless barrage of vicious kicks and blows, *Death Proof*'s credits roll, accompanied by a series of photos intended to represent some of the women that Stuntman Mike has killed. Here, too, the audience is led to contemplate the implications of the violence they have witnessed and, quite possibly, relished. Tarantino's decision to juxtapose the women's attack upon Stuntman Mike's now helpless form with the photos of his victims begs viewers to understand Stuntman Mike as both predator and prey. The once- malevolent aggressor is now, like the women in the photos, *a victim* of violence. Thus, although the snapshots of Stuntman Mike's victims may at first suggest that a kind of "justice" has "been served," one cannot discount the extent to which the stills conflate the representations of violence transpiring throughout *Death Proof*'s parallel narratives. In this sense, unlike the phony trailers that open *Grindhouse*, Quentin Tarantino's *Death Proof* is far more than simple self-reflexive parody. Nor is it a big-budget imitation of a small-budget mode of filmmaking predicated upon "clearly defined oppositions" that "often can be reduced to some version of white hat versus black hat" (Grant 15), as is the case with Robert Rodriguez's by-the-numbers zombie film, *Planet Terror*. Rather, it is a fusion of homage and critique, a violent spectacle that ultimately interrogates the cultural logics behind its spectacular brutality.

CONCLUSION: LOOKING FORWARD, GAZING BACK

In a work populated by monsters both human and fantastical, the otherworldly entity *Grindhouse* most readily—though by no means explicitly—evokes is Janus, the dual-faced Roman god of transition, of endings begetting new beginnings. Because Tarantino's and Rodriguez's application of cutting-edge digital technologies emulates not only a mode of low-budget genre filmmaking, but also the inevitable degradation of celluloid prints spooled repeatedly through the mechanical entrails of countless projectors, *Grindhouse* engages one of the most-important and least-theorized nexus points in cinema history: the emergence of digital technologies within a motion picture industry long predicated upon analogue-based systems of production and post-production/exhibition. At the very least, it provides one of the finest examples of what Laura Mulvey recognizes as a vital paradox in cinema at the dawn of the art form's second century: specifically, that "new [digital] technologies are able to reveal the beauty of the cinema through a displacement that breaks the bonds of specificity so important to [. . .] filmmakers and theorists of previous generations" (135). Transformations within aesthetic traditions require serious and thoughtful reengagements with theories of spectatorship and economies of signification—what Mulvey refers to as the "significance" of "the indexical sign" (134). As a meta-filmic experiment with such concerns at its core, *Grindhouse* provides scholars with a fertile terrain from which to launch future explorations of the ways in which digital technology's burgeoning potential intersects with celluloid's waning aesthetic and material possibilities.

NOTES

1. See Rob Zombie's *The Devil's Rejects* (2005) and *Halloween* (2007), as well as Alexandre Aja's *The Hills Have Eyes* (2006) and *The Hills Have Eyes II* (2007). In each of these films, digital technologies are used to emulate the "look" and "feel" of worn celluloid.

2. Walter Benjamin's contention that film's reproducibility necessarily leads to the dissipation of the "aura" associated with painting, sculpture, and theater has by no means gone uncontested in cinema studies; see Walter Benjamin, *Illuminations: Essays and Reflections*, ed. Hannah Arendt (New York: Schocken Books, 1988). In *Film in the Aura of Art* (Princeton, N.J.: Princeton University Press, 1986), for instance, Dudley Andrew suggests that the mechanically reproduced aura remains when/because the spectator invests it with a meaning and value. Thus, Andrew posits, films, "readings of them, and theories about both are historical events in culture" (xiii). Moreover, Andrew claims, Benjamin's aura endures in the so-called art film because spectators who are drawn to such works attend them "with certain ambitious expectations . . . reinforcing values" (195).

3. According to Daly, Quentin Tarantino's original inclination during the *Grindhouse*'s planning stages was to "shoot on aged film." It was the "more technically savvy Rodriguez" who convinced Tarantino to shoot on the best film stock and then create the "well-loved grindhouse" look during post-production. In other words, the "well-loved" scratches and missing frames "could be recreated digitally without the need for love. Love as plug in"; Kristen Daly, "The Dissipating Aura of Cinema," *Transformations* 15 (November 2007), para. 5.

4. In *The 2nd Century of Cinema: The Past and Future of the Moving Image* (Albany: State University of New York Press, 2000), Wheeler Winston Dixon recognizes "topicality" as a vital component of exploitation cinema. In order for low-budget genre cinema to lure audience's, Dixon argues, they had to "cater to fads" and "deliver what an audience want[ed] to see *right now*, in order to take advantage of the public's interest" (79). Thus, according to Dixon, exploitation films "perpetually ride the crest of the wave of public taste" (79). In this sense, despite its large budget and blockbuster pretensions, *Grindhouse*'s production of nostalgia for the sake of financial

gain can be understood as the ideal cinematic work for the postmodern age in which, as Fredric Jameson notes in his *Postmodernism, or, the Cultural Logic of Late Capitalism* (Raleigh, N.C.: Duke University Press, 1991), popular notions of history are "flattened" and a people reminisce over the present.

WORKS CITED

Andrew, Dudley. *Film in the Aura of Art*. Princeton, N.J.: Princeton University Press, 1986.

Arnzen, Michael A. "Who's Laughing Now? . . . the Postmodern Splatter Film." *Journal of Popular Film and Television* 21.4 (Winter 1994): 176–88.

Benjamin, Walter. *Illuminations: Essays and Reflections*. Ed. Hannah Arendt. New York: Schocken Books, 1988.

Brottman, Mikita. "Introduction." *Car Crash Culture*. Ed. Mikita Brottman. New York: Palgrave, 2001. xi–xliii.

———, and Christopher Sharrett. "The End of the Road: David Cronenberg's *Crash* and the Fading of the West." *Car Crash Culture*. Ed. Mikita Brottman. New York: Palgrave, 2001. 199–214.

Buñuel, Luis. "Cinema, Instrument of Poetry." *The European Cinema Reader*. Ed. Catherine Fowler. New York: Routledge, 2002. 45–48.

Daly, Kristen. "The Dissipating Aura of Cinema." *Transformations* 15 (November 2007). http://transformationsjournal.org/journal/issue_15/article_09.shtml (accessed May 20, 2008).

Dixon, Wheeler Winston. *The 2nd Century of Cinema: The Past and Future of the Moving Image*. Albany: State University of New York Press, 2000.

Friedberg, Anne. "Cinema and the Postmodern Condition." *Viewing Positions: Ways of Seeing Film*. Ed. Linda Williams. New Brunswick, N.J.: Rutgers University Press, 1995. 59–61.

Grant, Barry Keith. "Second Thoughts on Double Features: Revisiting the Cult Film." *Unruly Pleasures: The Cult Film and Its Critics*. Eds. Xavier Mendik and Graeme Harper. London: FAB Press, 2000. 13–28.

Harvey, David. *The Condition of Postmodernity: An Enquiry into the Origins of Social Change*. Cambridge: Blackwell Publishers, 1990.

Heller, Terry. *The Delights of Terror: An Aesthetics of the Tale of Terror*. Champaign: University of Illinois Press, 1987.

Jameson, Fredric. *Postmodernism, or, The Cultural Logic of Late Capitalism*. Raleigh, N.C.: Duke University Press, 1991.

Katz, Ephraim. "Exploitation Film." *The Film Encyclopedia, 3rd Edition*. Ed. Ephraim Katz. New York: HarperCollins, 1998. 446.

Le Cain, Maximilian. "Tarantino and the Vengeful Ghosts of the Cinema." *Senses of Cinema* 32 (July–September 2004). http://www.sensesofcinema.com/contents/04/32/tarantino.html (accessed October 10, 2007).

Mills, Jane. "Catch Me If You Can: The Tarantino Legacy." *Bright Lights Film Journal* 36 (April 2002). http://www.brightlightsfilm.com/36/tarantino1.html (accessed October 10, 2007).

Mulvey, Laura. "Stillness in the Moving Image: Ways of Visualizing Time and Its Passing." *The Cinematic*. Ed. David Campany. Cambridge: MIT Press, 2007.

AFTERWORD

Memory, Genre, and Self-Narrativization; Or, Why I Should Be a More Content Horror Fan

—David Church

As a child inexplicably drawn to the morbid and macabre, I recall a time when the Universal horror classics were just no longer enough, but I was forbidden from watching R-rated films—thus banning the "bad" horror that intrigued me all the more through its prohibition. For sleepovers at a friend's house, my comrades and I routinely trekked down to "Family Video," the local small-town video store, and perused the "Horror" section located just adjacent to the flimsy wooden screen hiding the store's porn offerings from common view. Being a semi-dutiful child, I followed my parents' strictures and intentionally opted for renting those horror flicks that were technically "unrated," shielding myself from self-incrimination with a convenient half-truth that often exposed me to far more violent films than the R-rated alternatives.

From my own skeptical position toward American horror today, however, even this small memory seems quaint when viewed through a more mature awareness of studios' current marketing tactics; the word "unrated" no longer appears in the small print on the back of video boxes, but is typically splayed across DVD covers in dripping red letters, suggesting that this viewing experience will offer something markedly different from the theatrical release. And the films that I surreptitiously viewed as a child—*Maniac* (1980), *The Evil Dead* (1982), *Silent Night, Deadly Night* (1984)—those early artifacts of the VHS age are now the stuff of seemingly endless remakes, rip-offs, sequels, and throwbacks as the genre lumbers on indefinitely like a zombie with an intact brainstem . . . or so goes the lament.

Of course, as a genre very much driven by profit margins, modern horror has always been prone to such incestuous tendencies, so much so that it can be difficult to distinguish innovations from repetitions—a rhizomatic map would better fit the genre than a straightforward model of evolution. But isn't that precisely part of the genre's charm (and frustration) for those of us with more than a purely academic interest in its intricacies? Although our own engagement with horror films may develop in a linear fashion across our lifetimes, the genre itself seldom follows any such teleology, often to the consternation of fans. One might, for example, deride *Cloverfield* (2008) as a big-budget descendent of *Gojira* (1954), and of *Cannibal Holocaust* (1980), by way of *The Blair Witch Project* (1999), yoking together the mockumentary format with the spectacle of a giant monster undertaking urban destruction, but such sentiment does a disservice to the relative value and historical specificity of each film. Because cinematic horror (especially that produced since the mid-twentieth century) is primarily directed toward a youth market, we may spend time gaining (sub-)cultural capital surrounding the genre, only to eventually find ourselves distanced in age and (sub-)cultural competence from the audience currently being catered to—hence the tendency to distrust current trends and seek refuge in nostalgia.

Even if they are separated by only a few years, there is often a cultural divide between "seasoned" fans (and scholar-fans aiming for legitimacy in the academy) who will happily recite the virtues (and the scholarly appraisals) of canonical works like *The Texas Chainsaw Massacre* (1974) and *Dawn of the Dead* (1978), and teen viewers whose limited experience with those films comes through their contemporary iterations. But we can hardly blame audiences themselves; much as 1930s horror failed to frighten me after a certain age, so do 1970s and 1980s horror films apparently fail to unnerve today's teen viewers accustomed to the quicker editing, higher production values, slicker special effects, and more attractive casts endemic to Hollywood cinema in general. Meanwhile, horror aficionados often struggle for a sense of cultural distinction by retreating into genre currents—independent horror, foreign horror cinemas, historically marginalized horror trends—seemingly less penetrated by "mainstream" consumerism, disavowing the fact that most of these "other" films were likewise made to maximize potential profits.[1]

These comments about the genre and its various audiences are broad strokes, to be sure, but their broadness points to the dilemma addressed in the introduction to this book: how does one interpret recent generic threads without the requisite historical distance for narrativizing them (and, in so doing, ignoring some of their complexity)? How can we speculate about whichever trends will bubble up next without the larger perspective in which to locate current ones? In our attempts to understand the present, we often seem compelled to draw upon the rosiest of personal and cultural memories (as in the brief personal recollection I opened with)— anything to insert artificial chunks of distance between our contemporary selves and some romanticized past when we were perhaps more easily frightened, when the genre still seemed (to us, at least) fresh and new. In conjunction with these autobiographical narratives, we traditionally try to historicize the genre as a linear continuity between individual or clustered texts—much like classical Hollywood narrative continuity attempts to conceal the unavoidable seams and potentially estranging moments that would otherwise threaten any sense of monolithic unity. And yet we should increasingly resist that discursive urge. Magnifying the many fractures and slippages between disparate historical moments, which are productive of unexpected generic tangents and hybrids, is a way of destabilizing notions of generic continuity and interpreting films on their own terms, becoming a task less intimately entangled with the (sub-)cultural valuations of "authenticity" and "originality" that often infect horror fans (and arguably, scholars too) with nostalgia for perhaps a less complex, cynical time in their own lives.

It is too easy, for instance, to reject much of recent American horror (and, by extension, its audiences) by stacking it up against fans' and scholars' longtime investments in the genre's "progressive" thread of the 1970s—a thread that only really lingers within a few seminal films—and conveniently neglecting the larger share of "undistinguished" horror films produced during that same period. Meanwhile, some of those neglected films have been reanimated in recent years as "paracinema" and the recent trend in neo-exploitation or "grindhouse chic," providing a refuge for disgruntled horror fans with subcultural capital to burn. In the same vein, the mediocre horror of today may become ironically celebrated as the camp of tomorrow, serving the specific interests of genre devotees. Likewise, in any period, there will be a handful of films pushing the envelope of "good taste" in terms of violence; the controversy surrounding the current trend in "torture porn" is little different from that surrounding Herschell Gordon Lewis's films during the mid-1960s, for example.[2] And peering from another angle, the optimist in us may overreach, prematurely reading historical significance into certain texts against our better judgment; one might, for example, strategically ignore the blatant homophobia and xenophobia of Eli Roth's *Hostel* (2005) in the interest of reading it as a symptomatic post-9/11 horror film—only to have one's worst suspicions confirmed by its sequel.

In any case, it would be difficult to speculate with any degree of confidence about future directions for American horror cinema without falling back upon all-too-familiar discourses about the sameness between texts—at the expense of those smaller, potentially transformative differences that are often subsumed by a historicizing sense of generic continuity. For genre observers, the "return of the repressed" may not just involve the eruption of specific cultural fears at any given historical moment, but also the uncanny reappearance of once-passé horror trends themselves, threatening the tidy chronological categorizations we have previously made for them. Recent years have seen the apparent wax and wane of Asian horror remakes, "torture porn," 1970s and 1980s horror remakes, supernatural horror, zombie films, horror mockumentaries, neo-exploitation, and so on—though these may reappear sooner than expected, not as mere atavisms of continuing historical anxieties, but as temporal ruptures opening toward a multiplicity of diverse generic possibilities. At the time of this writing, for example, the residual effects upon American horror of a national trauma like 9/11 have yet to be adequately explained, but its aftershocks may reverberate within the genre for years to come. It is impossible to tell exactly what this will look like, though I strongly suspect that it will not occur in directly causal ways suggesting a linear generic evolution, but rather by chaotically sowing the seeds that may spawn or revive generic tangents or anomalies which today might seem largely irrelevant to our current cultural unconscious. Unlike the monstrously exaggerated sense of trauma constructed by more culturally "acceptable" media sources through endless video loops of collapsing buildings and barely veiled expressions of jingoism, the horror genre seems only capable of passively registering the pain. In recent horror films, the very absence of more telling clues about the American mentality in the post-9/11 period is itself perhaps indicative of the extent of the trauma.[3]

Yet, we might also question whether it is even historically valid to claim a select few films as symptomatic of the supposed zeitgeist in any given period—especially when such selections are often based more upon retrospective and highly personal assessments of "quality" than actual audience response to said films. Case in point: if I—unable to fully extricate myself from "within" the discourses of generic continuity structuring my performed self-identity as a fan—attempt to predict anything about the array of tendrils sent out by the American horror film in coming years, I often find myself chasing my own tail, narrativizing the genre in linear ways despite my best efforts to the contrary. As an extended example, I might posit that our conception of the genre in this post-*Scream* (1996) era will remain chiefly haunted by the specter of irony, which has survived more or less unscathed the hasty declarations of its demise in the immediate aftermath of 9/11. Irony is certainly nothing new in the horror film—a genre in which viewers may already seek distance (ironic or otherwise) from particularly shocking or ludicrous images—but the locus of irony has increasingly shifted in recent years from audience reception to the texts themselves. When horrified (adult) critics of early-1980s slasher films wrote about teen audiences laughing and cheering at the dismemberment of their on-screen surrogates, they apparently overlooked the possibility of teens' ironic responses to the very excessiveness of those films' conservative ideologies. Viewed at an age when their parents often attempt to instill the mantras of discipline, young audiences already familiar with the so-called subgeneric "rules" of slasher films (drugs, sex, bad behavior = gory death)—"rules" which may actually exist in far fewer films than prevalent stereotype of the subgenre suggests—can mock the ridiculousness of these "fatal," parental-revenge fantasies, making the thrill of horror spectatorship *seem* all the more "transgressive." Later films like *Scream*, however, seem to prepackage that irony as a preferred reading, wresting it away from the avid horror viewers who grew up during the heyday of slasher films (and who might assume themselves older and wiser than most teen audiences today)—effectively transplanting irony from the films' external reception to a central position within the text itself, hence the backlash from many horror fans threatened by their subcultural competences being spread thinly across the wider viewing public.

Though slasher films often originated as mainstream Hollywood products (despite their wide disrepute, which has frequently rendered them niche objects today),[4] *Scream's* self-reflexive parody allegedly mainstreamed the subgenre in a way that many horror fans forgave of neo-exploitation pastiches like *The Devil's Rejects* (2005) and *Grindhouse* (2007). Where *Scream* and its sequels disparage the conventions of 1980s slasher films (even as they ironically play by those same rules), the recent wave of "grindhouse chic" blatantly celebrates the pleasures of 1970s sleaze, often through aggressively ironic appeals to political incorrectness aimed primarily at male horror buffs. Though their respective tones and intended audiences may somewhat differ, we might see the prepackaged textual uses of irony in both cycles as roughly comparable, each alternating between tongue-in-cheek intertextuality and straight-faced brutality. With these films intentionally playing to viewers' (sub-)cultural competences, horror audiences may increasingly negotiate their own distanced responses in highly contingent ways, depending on how they wish to perform a sense of subcultural "authenticity" through accepting or rejecting certain elements of the films' ironic modes of address. For example, in conversation with avid horror devotees about *House of 1000 Corpses* (2003), one might play "spot the semi-obscure intertextual references" for subcultural one-upmanship, or privilege the film's hallucinatory, down-the-rabbit-hole tone through comparisons to the disjointedness of low-budget exploitation films; however, when talking with supposedly less "seasoned" viewers, one might declare the film a "sell out" for "exploiting" exploitation (if such a thing can be said without, dare I say, a trace of irony), or criticize as too "mainstream" the same music-video-style editing and garish *mise-en-scène* that help create the film's disorienting effects.

My point here is that such situational contortions—which should also be growing readily visible in the tortured logic of this pseudo-fannish scribble—can be as much inspired by our personal self-histories as the misleadingly linear conceptions of generic history we are inclined to interpret. As younger generations of horror viewers grow older and move into increased positions of sociocultural capital (e.g., as tastemakers or even as fans-turned-filmmakers, such as Kevin Williamson or Quentin Tarantino), they may look back toward horror's cherished place within a pop-culture wasteland tenuously associated with romanticized memories of youth. These ironic-cum-nostalgic celebrations of horror's past may partially account for the cyclical trends in recent American horror—from revisionist takes on the 1980s slasher cycle (which was never as formulaic as films like *Scream* would like us to recall) to slumming through fetishized cultural memories of a thriving

1970s grindhouse scene (with which few contemporary viewers had actual contact). But however appropriate I find it to cite *Scream* and *Grindhouse* as bookends for recent American horror, that choice also unduly narrativizes the genre, stressing broad similarities between rather disparate texts according to qualitative criteria springing from my own taste for certain horror varieties. My broad interpretation assumes (correctly or not) that the slasher film, and the exploitation aesthetic in general, still casts a long shadow over our current conception of American horror—a shadow that temporally overlaps with my personal history as a twenty-something horror fan—so that I tend to neglect other subgenres less inflected with ironic or exploitative connotations, to say nothing of anomalous films that belie any stable sense of generic continuity.

Because the horror genre fuels the (sub-)cultural competences that we acquire over time to legitimize our interests in it, we may interpret its history as a linear narrative so that it conforms to our own linear conceptions of identity; in other words, feeling our remembered personal histories structured by the genre, we can justify those histories by projecting them back onto the genre. As a discursive entity, the genre is partially constructed by our subjectivities, just as the genre itself partially constructs our subjectivities—hence our ever-threatened desire to make chronological sense of the genre based on concepts like "authenticity" and "originality" that we would like to see ourselves performing as individuals or fans or scholars. Challenging generic continuity by treating horror texts as historically specific fragments can likewise threaten to fragment the sense of self constructed through our academic knowledge of genre history or our techniques of subcultural belonging. Of course, we cannot step outside discourse, but perhaps we can work to modify it by resorting less to habitual experiences of pastness, and instead increasingly amplify those moments of difference within and between texts: those oft-fleeting cracks in historical or narratological coherence, which we may only instinctively perceive, but which radiate potentiality in non-linear directions across (and against) time.[5] In focusing on how horror is always in a process of becoming other than its current incarnation—with repetition understood less as stagnation than as the eternal return of difference—we can examine how its texts work uniquely in each historical moment, without fetishizing generic continuity as a primary source of symptomatic readings or standards of value.

More than one director has called horror a forgiving genre: give audiences some guts and scares, and they'll forgive some rough edges along the way. Though we, as scholars and fans, may hope to demand a bit more than that from the films we love, just as we demand much of ourselves, we might as well learn to be similarly forgiving of the genre and its seeming discontents—especially the ones that stare back at us as we stare into the cracked mirror of horror. Recognizing our own embeddedness in self-narratives need not erase our compulsive desire to construct them; rather, in gaining a critical awareness of the "generic" patterns that we re-present to (and about) ourselves, we might pleasurably mutate our self-conceptions in creative ways by embracing the fluidity of those numerous historical moments through which our identities are constantly re-formed. If we expect the horror genre to keep revitalizing itself with fresh pulses of creativity, even when current demands for "authenticity" and "originality" remain dubious at best, we should not neglect a corresponding aesthetic in our ongoing projects of piecing together those multiplicitous fragments that, for better or worse, make us who we are.

Another small memory now: in those first few months after the Twin Towers fell, I found myself an incoming college freshman, moving away from the comforts of home and out into what seemed a rapidly changing world. During that time, I first saw *Donnie Darko* (2001), a horror/sci-fi/teen-romance hybrid that has since become inseparable from my personal recollections of those strange days. Although filmed at least a year before 9/11 and set in 1988, the time-bending story of a young man's impending personal apocalypse felt especially prescient at the time. Re-watching the film today is itself an exercise in time travel for me. Its evocation of free-floating teenage angst is tempered by an equally ironic and nostalgic sincerity linked to its many intertextual references to 1980s music and cinema. It is this overarching sense of tension that always reminds me of the emotional numbness I forced upon myself as a defense against the ceaseless post-9/11 media barrage. In a particularly memorable scene in a near-deserted movie theater, a temporal portal opens in a screen showing *The Evil Dead*—one of the beloved horror films from my childhood—while Donnie receives an ominous premonition, his love interest sleeping peacefully beside him all the while. In contrast to much 1980s revivalism of recent years, the *Evil Dead* reference here seems neither cloyingly ironic nor mocking in spirit; instead, it resonates with my own fond memories of the genre. By using the horror film as a potential site of wistful emotion, not just a source of fear or humor, *Donnie Darko* momentarily pierced the strong cynicism that partially comprised my self-identity in the immediate post-9/11 moment. In fragmenting and rearranging horror's generic conventions, collapsing the temporal and generic distance between these two very different films, a relative anomaly like *Donnie Darko* has come to movingly embody the liminal space I experienced during that brief but violent rupturing of national and personal narratives. Recent American horror films may mean many things to many people, but perhaps these films might hold overlooked potential for personal and cultural memory to encourage productive transformations, if only as a way of reconciling within ourselves our fraught relationship with the genre we love.

NOTES

1. See Mark Jancovich, "Cult Fictions: Cult Movies, Subcultural Capital, and the Production of Cultural Distinctions," *Cultural Studies* 16.2 (2002): 306–22.

2. Perhaps it is little coincidence that several of Lewis's films have also been remade in recent years, including *2001 Maniacs* (2005) and *The Wizard of Gore* (2007).

3. The frequent conflation of absence and loss in trauma is examined at length in Dominick LaCapra, *Writing History, Writing Trauma* (Baltimore: Johns Hopkins University Press, 2001), 43–85.

4. See Matt Hills, "Para-Paracinema: The *Friday the 13th* Film Series as Other to Trash and Legitimate Film Cultures," in *Sleaze Artists: Cinema at the Margins of Taste, Style, and Politics*, ed. Jeffrey Sconce (Durham, N.C.: Duke University Press, 2007), 219–39.

5. In the spirit of speculation, my cues here are vaguely inspired by Gilles Deleuze's *Difference and Repetition*, trans. Paul Patton (New York: Columbia University Press, 1994); and by Robert B. Ray's use of the Surrealist strategy of "irrational enlargement" upon those strange and unexplained details in Hollywood films that inadvertently inspire reflection upon the multiplicity of creative possibilities that are commonly subsumed by traditional narrative choices and generic constraints. See Robert B. Ray, *The Avant-Garde Finds Andy Hardy* (Cambridge, Mass.: Harvard University Press, 1995), 64–68.

WORKS CITED

Deleuze, Gilles. *Difference and Repetition*. Trans. Paul Patton. New York: Columbia University Press, 1994.

Hills, Matt. "Para-Paracinema: The *Friday the 13th* Film Series as Other to Trash and Legitimate Film Cultures." *Sleaze Artists: Cinema at the Margins of Taste, Style, and Politics*. Ed. Jeffrey Sconce. Durham, N.C.: Duke University Press, 2007. 219–39.

———. *The Pleasures of Horror*. London: Continuum, 2005.

Foucault, Michel. *The Foucault Reader*. Ed. Paul Rabinow. New York: Pantheon Books, 1984.

Jancovich, Mark. "Cult Fictions: Cult Movies, Subcultural Capital, and the Production of Cultural Distinctions." *Cultural Studies* 16.2 (2002): 306–22.

LaCapra, Dominick. *Writing History, Writing Trauma*. Baltimore: Johns Hopkins University Press, 2001.

Ray, Robert B. *The Avant-Garde Finds Andy Hardy*. Cambridge, Mass.: Harvard University Press, 1995.

CONTRIBUTORS

Craig Bernardini is assistant professor of English at Hostos Community College, City University of New York, holding a B.A. in the Writing Seminars from The Johns Hopkins University and a Ph.D. in Creative Writing (Fiction) from the University of Utah. In the summer of 1990 he interned at *Fangoria* magazine, and has continued to study, write about, and write stories in the horror genre ever since. In addition to horror cinema, his research interests include popular music and American literature. His most recent work, "Heavy Melville," analyzes how issues of gender and aesthetics affected the reception of *Leviathan*, a heavy-metal album inspired by *Moby-Dick*. He is also researching and writing about the image of the frontier in Hector St. John de Crevecoeur's *Letters from an American Farmer* and Cormac McCarthy's *Blood Meridian*.

David Church is a Ph.D. student in Communication and Culture at Indiana University. He is currently editing *Playing with Memories: Essays on Guy Maddin*. He has contributed to *Disability Studies Quarterly*, *Film Quarterly*, *The Encyclopedia of American Disability History*, *Offscreen*, and *Senses of Cinema*.

Pamela Craig is a research candidate in the Institute of Film and Television Studies at the University of Nottingham, UK. Her current research project focuses on cinematic representations of Christmas and Halloween in the United States and their relationship to the Gothic mode.

Blair Davis holds a Ph.D. from the Department of Communication Studies at McGill University in Montreal. He has been an instructor in film studies at the School for the Contemporary Arts at Simon Fraser University since 2003. His essays are featured in *Caligari's Heirs: The German Cinema of Fear after 1945*, *Horror Film: Creating and Marketing Fear*, and *Reel Food: Essays on Film and Food*, as well as in the *Canadian Journal of Film Studies* and the *Historical Journal of Film, Radio and Television*.

Martin Fradley teaches American Studies at the University of Manchester, UK. His published work has appeared in Yvonne Tasker's edited collections *Fifty*

Contemporary Filmmakers and *Action and Adventure Cinema*, edited by Ginette Vincendeau and Alastair Philips; *Journeys of Desire: European Actors in Hollywood*; and *Falling in Love Again: The Contemporary Romantic Comedy*, edited by Stacey Abbot and Deborah Jeremyn.

Steffen Hantke has published essays and reviews on contemporary literature, film, and culture in *Paradoxa, College Literature, The Journal of Popular Culture, Post Script, Kinema, Scope, Foundation, Science Fiction Studies, Studies in Twentieth and Twenty-First Century Literature*, and other journals, as well as in anthologies in Germany and the United States. He is author of *Conspiracy and Paranoia in Contemporary Literature*, as well as editor of *Horror*, a special topics issue of *Paradoxa* (2002), *Horror: Creating and Marketing Fear, Caligari's Heirs: The German Cinema of Fear after 1945*, and, together with Rudolphus Teeuwen, *Gypsy Scholars, Migrant Teachers, and the Global Academic Proletariat: Adjunct Labor in Higher Education*. He serves on the editorial boards of *Paradoxa* and *The Journal of Adaptation in Film and Performance*. Since 1999, he has also been chair of the "Horror" area at the Southwest/ Texas Popular Culture and American Culture Association. He currently teaches at Sogang University in Seoul, South Korea, as Associate Professor in the American Culture Program.

Reynold Humphries has published *Fritz Lang: Genre and Representation in His American Films, The American Horror Film: An Introduction*, and *The Hollywood Horror Film, 1931–1941: Madness in a Social Landscape*. He has written on European horror (Argento, Bava, and Franju) for the Web site *Kinoeye*, on early Mario Bava for both *Monstrous Adaptations* and *100 European Horror Films*, and has contributed to the special horror issue of *Paradoxa*, the issue of *Post Script* devoted to serial killers, *101 Horror Movies, 101 Sci-Fi Movies*, and *The Cinema of Tod Browning: Essays of the Macabre and Grotesque*. A study (in French) of Tobe Hooper's *The Texas Chainsaw Massacre* and its sequel appeared in *Cauchemars Américains: Fantastique et horreur dans le cinéma moderne*, and a forthcoming French anthology devoted to George A. Romero includes chapters by him on *The Crazies* and *Dawn of the Dead*. His work in other fields includes contributions to *Film Noir Reader 4, Gangster Film Reader, Docufictions, Stanley Kubrick: Essays on His Films and Legacy, 501 Movie Directors*, and *Edgar G. Ulmer: Detour on Poverty Row*. His latest book is *Hollywood's Blacklists: A Political and Cultural History*.

James Kendrick holds a Ph.D. from Indiana University in Communication and Culture. He is an assistant professor in the Film and Digital Media division of the Department of Communication Studies at Baylor University, where he teaches classes on film theory/aesthetics, the history of motion pictures, the history of radio and television, and media and society. He has published several book chapters, as well as articles and reviews in such publications as *The Velvet Light Trap*, *The Journal of Film and Video*, *The Journal of Popular Film and Television*, *Film-Philosophy*, *Kino-eye*, and *The Moving Image*. In addition to his academic work, he is also the film and DVD critic for the Web site Qnetwork.com, where he has written more than 1,500 film reviews. He is currently working on two books about film violence.

Christina Klein is an associate professor of English and American Studies at Boston College and author of *Cold War Orientalism: Asia in the Middlebrow Imagination, 1945–1961*. She is currently writing a book about the effects of globalization on U.S. and Asian film industries. Her articles on contemporary Asian cinema have been published in *Cinema Journal*, *Journal of Chinese Cinemas*, *Comparative American Studies*, *American Quarterly*, the *Los Angeles Times*, and the *International Herald Tribune*.

Ben Kooyman is a doctoral candidate and part-time teacher at Flinders University, Australia. His Ph.D. thesis explores how filmmakers attempt to genealogize themselves within Shakespeare's legacy through adapting the Bard's plays to film, and how these self-fashioning gestures are built upon ideological contradictions and repressions which can be elucidated through applying theoretical concepts from the work of Julia Kristeva, Gilles Deleuze, and Felix Guattari. Textual analyses run the gamut from Kurosawa's *Throne of Blood* to Lloyd Kaufman's *Tromeo and Juliet*. Kooyman is also a longtime horror-movie and comic-book aficionado. He is the creator, writer, and illustrator of the underground comic-book series *Hamlet VS. Faustus*. His most recent scholarly publication was "'Back in the Bloody Smoke'—Dark Fantasy, Dark Reality: London in the Comic Books *V for Vendetta* and *Hellblazer*" in *London Was Full of Rooms*, edited by Barnett et al.

Jay McRoy is associate professor of English and Cinema Studies at the University of Wisconsin at Parkside. He is the editor of *Japanese Horror Cinema* and coeditor (with Richard Hand) of *Monstrous Adaptations: Generic and Thematic Mutations in Horror Film*. His monograph *Nightmare Japan: Contemporary Japanese Horror Film* is forthcoming.

Kial Natale is an award-winning filmmaker currently enrolled in Simon Fraser University's film production program. A past film teacher at the Flagstaff Arts and Leadership Academy and member of the Dean's Honour List for Northern Arizona University and Simon Fraser University, his academic and critical focus is grounded in the study of the horror genre. He is currently working on the scripts for two feature-length horror films.

Andrew Patrick Nelson is a Ph.D. candidate in the School of Arts, Languages and Literatures at the University of Exeter, where he is completing a dissertation on the Western. His broader research interests are film genres, Hollywood cinema, and American history.

Tony Perrello was born in Monroe, New York, and was educated at St. Bonaventure University, SUNY at Albany, and the University of South Carolina, where he received a Ph.D. in 1998. He specialized in Renaissance literature and Shakespeare and wrote a dissertation on the rise of the grotesque in Renaissance drama. He is currently an assistant professor of English at California State University, Stanislaus, where he teaches courses in British Renaissance and medieval literature and special topics courses such as Horror in Literature and Film. He has published several essays on British literature in books and in academic journals such as *English Language Notes* and *Postscript*. These include a translation and explication of a previously undiscovered medieval riddle, an argument for an Anglo-Saxon source for the Gloucester subplot in *King Lear*, and an analysis of the most recent film versions of *Othello* and their racial implications in the classroom. A die-hard horror fan since he was a child, Tony has recently taken a scholarly interest in the genre, and he regularly chairs sessions in horror film at conferences such as the Rocky Mountain MLA.

Philip L. Simpson received his bachelor's and master's degrees in English from Eastern Illinois University in 1986 and 1989, respectively, and his doctorate in American Literature from Southern Illinois University in 1996. He serves as North Region Vice Provost and Academic Dean of Humanities/Fine Arts and Behavioral/Social Sciences at Brevard Community College in Florida. Before that, he was a professor of Communications and Humanities at the Palm Bay campus of Brevard Community College for eight years and Department Chair of Liberal Arts for five years. He also serves as President of the Popular Culture Association and Area Chair of Horror for the Association. He received the Association's Felicia Campbell Area Chair Award in 2006. He sits on the editorial board of the *Journal of Popular Culture*. His book, *Psycho Paths: Tracking the Serial Killer Through Contemporary American Film and Fiction*, was published in 2000, and he is the author of numerous other essays on film, literature, popular culture, and horror.

INDEX